OXFORD HISTORICAL MONOGRAPHS

NOTE

Oxford Historical Monographs will consist of books which would formerly have been published in the Oxford Historical Series. As with the previous series, they will be carefully selected studies which have been submitted, or are based upon theses submitted, for higher degrees in this University. The works listed below are those still in print in the Oxford Historical Series.

The Estates of the Percy Family, 1416–1537. By J. M. W. BEAN. 1958.

The Radical Duke. Career and Correspondence of Charles Lennox, third Duke of Richmond. By ALISON GILBERT OLSON. 1961.

The Norman Monasteries and their English Possessions. By DONALD MATTHEW. 1962.

Edward III and the Scots. The Formative Years of a Military Career, 1327–1335. By RANALD NICHOLSON. 1965.

A Medieval Oxfordshire Village: Cuxham: 1240 to 1400. By P. D. A. HARVEY. 1965.

Cardinal Bainbridge in the Court of Rome 1509–14. By D. S. CHAMBERS. 1965.

The Later Lollards 1414–1520. By JOHN A. F. THOMSON. 1965.

The Impeachment of Warren Hastings. By P. J. MARSHALL. 1965.

The Passing of the Irish Act of Union. By G. C. BOLTON. 1966.

The Miners and British Politics 1906–1914. By ROY GREGORY. 1968.

The Pauper Press. By PATRICIA HOLLIS. 1970.

Victorian Quakers. By ELIZABETH ISICHEI. 1970.

English Gascony. By M. G. A. VALE. 1970.

Thomas of Lancaster 1307–22. By J. R. MADDICOTT. 1970.

Ducal Brittany. By N. C. E. JONES. 1970.

Papal Judges Delegate. By J. E. SAYERS. 1970.

CHARLES JAMES FOX and the DISINTEGRATION OF THE WHIG PARTY 1782–1794

BY

L. G. MITCHELL

OXFORD UNIVERSITY PRESS

1971

Oxford University Press, Ely House, London W.1

GLASGOW NEW YORK TORONTO MELBOURNE WELLINGTON
CAPE TOWN SALISBURY IBADAN NAIROBI DAR ES SALAAM LUSAKA ADDIS ABABA
BOMBAY CALCUTTA MADRAS KARACHI LAHORE DACCA
KUALA LUMPUR SINGAPORE HONG KONG TOKYO

PRINTED IN GREAT BRITAIN
BY WILLIAM CLOWES & SONS LIMITED, LONDON, COLCHESTER AND BECCLES

TO MY PARENTS

PREFACE

In writing a book of this kind, the author inevitably incurs debts of gratitude to a very large number of people. I would particularly like to acknowledge the kindness and efficiency of the staffs at the following institutions and libraries: the British Museum and the Public Record Office in London; the Bodleian Library; the Durham Public Record Office; Durham University Library; the Hampshire Public Record Office; the Northamptonshire Public Record Office; Nottingham University Library; Sheffield Central Library and the West Suffolk Public Record Office. Certain individuals have also been kind enough to allow me to see the collections of manuscripts in their possession, and their assistance has been invaluable: His Grace the Duke of Devonshire; His Grace the Duke of Marlborough; the Marquess of Lansdowne; the Earl Fitzwilliam; the Earl of Halifax; the Earl Spencer; and Capt. C. K. Adam of Blair Adam, Fife.

Finally, I have many friends in Oxford, to whom I am also indebted: Dr. J. B. Owen of Lincoln College, who supervised this study, for his unfailing help and good-humoured attention; the Warden and Fellows of Wadham College and the Master and Fellows of University College for allowing me the time and facilities to finish the work; and many others, for bearing with me and my preoccupation over the last four years.

University College, Oxford LESLIE MITCHELL
1968

CONTENTS

ABBREVIATIONS

In the references to works quoted in the text, the following abbreviations have been used:

Add. MS(S).	British Museum Additional Manuscripts
A.H.R.	*American Historical Review*
C.H.J.	*Cambridge Historical Journal*
E.H.R.	*English Historical Review*
Fortescue	*The Correspondence of George III 1760–1783*, ed. Sir J. Fortescue; London, 1928
Fox Speeches	*The Speeches of the Rt. Hon. C. J. Fox in the House of Commons*, ed. J. Wright, London, 1815
H.J.	*Historical Journal*
H.M.C.	Historical Manuscripts Commission
I.H.S.	*Irish Historical Studies*
L.Q.R.	*Law Quarterly Review*
Parl. Hist.	*The Parliamentary History*
S.H.R.	*Scottish Historical Review*
T.R.H.S.	*Transactions of the Royal Historical Society*

INTRODUCTION

At the moment of George III's accession to the throne in 1760, English Whiggery was a confident and a comfortable creed. By then, the idea that the Glorious Revolution of 1688 had guaranteed political liberties from the attempted incursions of James II was a commonplace assumption, to which the vast majority of the political world subscribed. For the Whigs, however, this event represented personal achievement. While Toryism was racked by doubt about the propriety of dismissing an anointed king, the Whigs of 1688 had seen what had to be done, and had acted accordingly. Calling on the memory of Hampden, Russell, Sidney, and other victims of despotic kings, the Whigs claimed the victory of 1688 as their own. As the Toryism of the seventeenth century disintegrated in self-doubt, the constitutional presuppositions of the Whigs had been confirmed, and they were therefore the best equipped to deal with the not inconsiderable problem of making the post-1688 system work, and of settling in the Hanoverians without disturbance.

Between 1688 and 1760, party war-cries were tempered into constitutional truisms. No one at the latter date thought of defending James II, or of attacking the 1688 settlement. To that extent, everyone in politics was Whig. Under the careful management of Walpole and the Pelhams, Whiggery was transformed into a comfortable, governing party, with undemanding terms of admission, which all the well-intentioned and peaceable were invited to join. The erection, at both the national and local levels, of a vast system of patronage overcame all but the most rigid consciences. All this fitted well into Whig theory. As long as the direction of politics was committed to the hands of Whig grandees like Newcastle, Rockingham and Devonshire, events could not run into extremes. As the natural leaders of landed wealth, the necessity of defending property rights precluded despotic or democratic leanings. By implication therefore, the Whig leaders, in representing their own property interests, guaranteed everyone else's. In 1688 and 1715, they had given evidence of their conscientiousness. The relatively peaceful years of the Walpole and Pelham ascendancy was explained by Whigs as the natural outcome of kings agreeing to work through the natural representatives of property. Such complacency, fostered by the willingness of the first two Georges to act in this manner, made no intellectual allowance for the possibility that a king might appear, who chose to do otherwise.

In the wealth of opposition propaganda sponsored by the hard core of the old Whig party after their resignation from office in 1762, one point stands out clearly. By 1782, there was, in Whig retrospect, the overwhelming impression that something had gone badly wrong in constitutional life. The most superficial comparison between the years 1722–62 and 1762–82 proved the fact. In the first period, domestic politics had been characterized by stability, trade had flourished, and France had been decisively and profitably defeated. In the second, the American empire had been lost, the trading community had suffered badly, and domestic politics had become the prey, until the advent of North, of insubstantial ministries. The contrast between the two periods could not have been clearer. Junius, writing in 1769, takes his comparison as his starting point;

'Perhaps there never was an instance of a change in the circumstances and temper of a whole nation so sudden and extraordinary as that which the misconduct of ministers has, within these very few years, produced in Great Britain. When our gracious Sovereign ascended the throne, we were a flourishing and a contented people. If the personal virtues of a king could have insured the happiness of his subjects, the scene could not have altered so entirely as it has done. . . . Unfortunately for us, the event has not been answerable to the design. After a rapid succession of changes, we are reduced to that state which hardly any change can mend.'[1]

Faced with this situation, the Whigs had again to think seriously about politics.

Their explanation for this sad turn of events was based on chronological coincidence. As example after example between 1762 and 1782 seemed to justify the Whig's case, they believed by the latter date that their ideas were irrefutable. According to them, the change in atmosphere had begun to become apparent in the early years of the 1760s. The resignation of the elder Pitt, in 1761, followed by that of the Duke of Newcastle a year later, had introduced a period of domestic instability, which had persisted for the rest of the decade. Not only had both the principal Whig groups been systematically affronted, but some permanent damage seemed to have been inflicted on the machinery of government. At very roughly the same time, the first protests against English actions arrived from America. In the Whig view, the only factor common to all these incidents was the policy of a new king. George III had succeeded his grandfather in 1760, and immediately gave strong evidence that he intended to take a more personal line in politics. Initially, the Whigs could not accuse him of illegality. The constitutional truism of the king being

[1] Junius to the printer of the *Public Advertiser*, 21 Jan. 1769; *The Letters of Junius* (London, 1915), i. 104.

able to choose his own ministers had never yet been contested, although severe inroads had already been made into it in practical terms. By 1782, however, they argued that by choosing Bute in preference to the accredited representatives of landed property, who for the past forty years had shown that they knew how to make the governmental system work, George III was inviting all manner of inconvenience. These inconveniences duly manifested themselves almost immediately.

Between 1760 and 1782, America was the indispensable backcloth to English politics. It was the example to which the Whigs continually referred, in order to demonstrate the point that George III was potentially dangerous. According to the finished myth, instead of governing America, as the Whigs had done, with that mixture of flexibility and broadmindedness which Burke praised as 'salutary neglect', George had dogmatically begun to insist on principle and the rigid application of the concept of a unitary empire. To do this, he had dismissed the Whigs, and had chosen instead to work through social and political nonentities. It was even possible that the King privately wished to terminate England's abnormal status as a constitutional power, and to erect instead some kind of fashionable despotism. In Whig eyes, it was not surprising that such a policy led to war with half Europe, appalling interruptions to English trade and the final loss of thirteen colonies. They claimed to understand the cause of the malaise and they predicted the effect. The problem remained, however, of how this royal initiative was to be held without contravening at least some of the constitutional shibboleths, which their Whig grandfathers had themselves written into the system in 1688. Only very slowly and very painfully did Burke and Fox evolve answers.

While Whig intellectuals pondered, however, allies were already appearing. When the feeling of unease in the 1760s was played on by the numerous calamities of the 1770s, the sheer pressure of events forced into life those parts of the eighteenth-century political system, which were responsive to movements in opinion. This build-up of votes gradually allowed the Whigs to hope that they might be able eventually to tie the King down in the House of Commons. Chronologically, the first group to declare themselves were the radicals of the metropolis. The large electorates of London, Westminster, Middlesex and Southwark had always singled this area out as a good barometer of opinion. Now the livelihood of its large trading communities was being jeopardized by the American question, and, in the early 1760s, 'Wilkes and Liberty' was already meeting with a large response. In London, the struggle against the domestic despotism associated with General Warrants and the plight of the Americans were linked issues. Under the guidance of Thomas Cartwright and John Jebb, the solution advocated was the radical reform of the House of Commons. The details of individual schemes varied greatly, but demands for the abolition of corrupt boroughs, a significant extension of the franchise, and annual Parliaments, were common to most.

As the American tragedy moved, after 1777, from political miscalculation to outright military disaster, the power of county opinion began to be mobilized. Normally, the independent knights of the shire were a politically apathetic group, many of whom thought it right in most circumstances to support the King's Government. The fact that Christopher Wyvill was able to organize standing County Associations to make permanent the protest against the American war in itself testifies to the sense of urgency in the situation. Between 1777 and 1782, the authority of independent opinion, usually disparate and unorganized, was given a degree of cohesion unprecedented in the eighteenth century. Wyvill and his friends shared the basic premise of the London radicals that the House of Commons was no longer capable of controlling the actions of the executive. They believed, however, that the remedy for this lay in a substantial increase in the number of county M.P.s as the only people, who could be relied on to resist becoming enmeshed in the patronage nets of the Crown.

Both these pressure groups were from the start in loose association with the two branches of the official Whig Opposition, the followers of Chatham and the adherents of Portland and Rockingham. It was a joint effort of all these groups that secured the passage, in 1780, of Dunning's famous resolution 'That the Influence of the Crown has increased, is increasing, and ought to be diminished.' The defeat of North's administration two years later was also a corporate undertaking. Unfortunately, the measure of agreement among these several factions had severe limitations. They could agree only that English politics had gone badly awry, and that the reason for this lay in the growth and misuse of royal power. Beyond that, they could agree on very little. The Rockingham Whigs, whom Fox was ultimately to join, were universally suspected of wishing to substitute a Venetian-type oligarchy for the monarchy they affected to fear. They were accused of wishing not to diminish executive power, but simply to lodge it in different hands. Similarly, the London radicals were seen by their allies as irresponsible and over-theoretical in their approach, and possibly anxious to tilt the whole system in a democratic direction. Finally, Wyvill was seen as the leader of rather uncertain forces, who insisted on making claims to leadership, which neither his social position nor the number of his adherents qualified him. The unanimity, which brought down North in 1782, was therefore very suspect. Once the American issue was removed from politics, there disappeared the only point to which a united opposition could refer to prove immediately the delinquency of the Crown. There was still great scope for any king with the skill and tenacity to exploit it.

Under the same pressure of events, the official Whig Opposition too had to make some more specific response. The older generation, as represented by the Duke of Newcastle, could not bring themselves to make any adjustments. Until his death in 1768, Newcastle continued to believe that the King's favour was a necessary condition of assuming office. Increasingly, however, the problem was more complex. The theorists had to decide what could be done if the King refused to behave reasonably, which implied not only denying power to the Whigs themselves, but also involved the national disasters of the 1770's. The Whigs could no longer afford to coast quietly along on the comfortable platitudes stemming from 1688. The unthought-of phenomenon of a king who refused to work through the accredited leaders of landed wealth, forced the Whigs to think again. Hesitantly and tentatively, they began to feel their way towards alternative justifications for holding office. Ultimately, they would discover the value of organized party structure in the House of Commons as a viable alternative to royal authority, but this process was to be a long one.

In this rather confusing situation, the political theorist, as the man who could impose intellectual order on events, came into prominence. Edmund Burke became the oracle and interpreter of Whiggery. Fortunately, he could argue on two levels. For the more conservatively-minded, he could restate with authority the standard Whig assumptions about politics. In *Thoughts on the Causes of the Present Discontents*, Burke maintained that, 'he who has no sway among any part of the landed or commercial interest, but whose whole importance has begun with his office and is sure to end with it, is a person who ought never to be suffered by a controuling Parliament to continue in any of those situations which confer the lead and direction of all our public affairs; because such a man has no connection with the interest of the people.' In the same work, however, Burke goes on to claim that the Whigs must undertake the disagreeable task of forming a cohesive party in the Commons, in order to hold the executive at that level. Such a step was taken with the greatest reluctance. The maxim of the king being free to choose his own ministers, carrying all the authority of prescription, could not be lightly overthrown, and, right up to 1782, the idea was treated with extreme caution. Clearly, however, with the evidence of the calculated destruction of Whig ministries in 1762 and 1765–6.

Whiggery would have to go forward intellectually or simply admit defeat.

It was therefore a highly fluid type of Whiggery to which Charles Fox gradually became accustomed during the 1770s. The fact that he should have even considered taking such a step was a matter for speculation. His father, Henry Fox, had never been burdened unduly with any political faith. Instead, he had developed immense managerial skill, which was normally placed at the disposal of the Crown. As Paymaster of the Forces, he had carved a vast personal fortune out of public funds, on which to support the dignity of an earldom and his spendthrift sons. Such a man could not afford ideals, and he, more than anyone else, had been responsible for the practical arrangements during the King's destruction of Newcastle in 1762. He was remembered in Whig circles as the unprincipled slaughterer of 'the Pelhamite innocents'. Fox's mother reinforced the family's recently acquired Tory traditions. Through her, Fox and his brothers could claim direct descent from Charles II and Louise de Kérouaille. It would be difficult to produce a more unpromising background for a future champion of English Whiggery. Indeed, for much of his early life, Charles Fox was marked down as the white hope of all ministerialists.

Having entered Parliament, in 1768, for the rotten borough of Midhurst, Fox gave every indication of faithfully following his father's general line in politics. As a supporter of Lord North's administration, Fox and his brother took a leading part in the anti-Wilkesite campaign, claiming that writer of the *North Briton* had been 'chosen by the scum of the earth'. Twice Fox held minor government offices, and twice he was forced out of them, but never for reasons of deep political principle. In 1772, he felt bound to oppose the Royal Marriages Bill, and to propose the repeal of Hardwicke's Clandestine Marriages Act, in that these measures reflected on the marriage of his own parents. Two years later, he was removed from office for demanding even stiffer penalties for a publisher of Wilkesite literature than even Lord North thought politic. Between 1768 and 1774 therefore, Fox's political career had been characterized by intense family loyalty and totally unbridled personal wilfulness. So far, he had done nothing to modify any of the predictions which had been made about him.

A devotion to family politics inevitably involved the contraction of family enmities. Henry Fox and the elder Pitt had been rivals throughout their political careers. The managerial cynicism of the one was thrown against the idealistic oratory of the other, and overlaying all other considerations was a deep personal antipathy. Pitt and his Chathamite heirs had always been intensely suspicious of the Rockingham Whigs, because their aristocratic exclusiveness bore heavily on the men of ability, but low birth, who followed the elder Pitt. When Fox eventually joined the Rockingham wing of the Whigs, the Pittite distaste for his family fused with their wider disgust at the pretensions of dukes with little mind. In the persons of the younger Pitt and Shelburne, Chatham's political heir, the rivalries of the 1740s and 1750s continued to poison politics for the next half century. Needless to say, Charles Fox dutifully shared all his father's reservations about the Pitt family as one in which megalomania was mixed uneasily with competing ability. The net effect of this rivalry was that the forces of English Whiggery were split. In 1765–7 and again in 1782, George III was able to play so effectively on this antipathy, that Whig ministries foundered under the pressure. Until his second loss of office, in 1774, however, Charles Fox had never stepped outside the family tradition. His political prejudices and his personal antipathies were those of his father.

Fox's conversion to Whiggery was, therefore, by a slow and halting process. The death of his father and his second loss of office both occurred in 1774, and effectively severed his emotional and formal ties with ministerial politics. He was at last free to think about politics independently. For him, as for so many others, the events in America provided the basic premises, on which political systems should be erected. As early as 1775, North's ex-junior minister wrote to Rockingham as follows:

I hope that it will be a point of honour among us all to support the American pretensions in adversity as much as we did in their prosperity, and that we shall never desert those who have acted unsuccessfully upon Whig principles. . . . I am also clear that firmness in Whig principles is become more necessary than ever, that I cannot help conjuring you, over and over again, to consider the importance of this crisis. . . . I am resolved . . . to adhere still more . . . to those principles of government which we have always recommended with respect to America.[1]

Such a declaration of faith must be treated with scepticism. Fox remained an independent agent in loose association with the Rockinghams for at least another three years. Yet, given this view of American events, his eventual absorption within the Rockingham ranks was always likely.

The major influence working towards this conversion was Edmund Burke. Almost immediately after Fox's loss of office, the unemployed minister was sought out by Burke, and bombarded with a stream of intellectual justifications for Whig principles:

Do not be in haste. Lay your foundations deep in public opinion. Though I have never given you the least bit of advice about joining yourself in a

[1] Fox to Rockingham, 13 Oct. 1775; L. Reid, *Charles James Fox*, p. 62.

declared connexion with our party, nor do I now—yet as I love that party very well, and am clear that you are better able to serve them than any man I know, I wish that things should be so kept, as to leave you mutually very open to one another in all changes and contingencies. . . . I . . . wish you a firm ground in the Country; and I do not know so firm and sound a bottom to build on as our party.[1]

Slowly and cautiously, Burke was instrumental in introducing Fox into the mysteries of English Whiggery. It was a debt which Fox was always ready to acknowledge. When therefore, in 1791, a formal separation between the two was made necessary by the issue of the French Revolution, the distress experienced by Fox was both personal and intellectual. Inevitably, Fox would one day challenge Burke for the intellectual leadership of the Whig party, but it would only be done at great personal cost.

Even so, the task of securing Fox's soul was only achieved by degrees. As late as 1778, offers from North to rejoin his administration were mingled with pleas from Burke that a formal declaration of faith in Whig principle should now be made. Gradually, however, as the tragedy in America deepened, it compressed all groups in opposition together, and identified Fox increasingly with the Rockingham point of view. In the late 1770's, Fox had also established contact with Jebb and the reformers of Westminster, and when it was announced that he had become Member of Parliament for that populous and radical borough, in 1780, this fact conveniently dates the end of all hopes that Fox might return to the ministerialist fold and the beginning of his career as the champion of English Whiggery. Six years had, however, been necessary to complete this startling transformation.

As Fox stood out therefore, in March 1782, as the man who had finally brought down North and his system, three things should be borne in mind. First, that Fox was a Whig of very recent date, and that there was always the danger that the enthusiasm of the neophyte might lead orthodox Whiggery into perilous waters. Secondly, that the magnificent achievement of removing North was likely to breed over-confidence and an unwillingness to face the realities of royal authority. Finally, that the coalition of opposition groups, over which Fox presided, in 1782, was not a homogeneous body, but rather a fissured and mutually suspicious collection of interest groups. The total effect of these factors was that, in March 1782, the struggle was not ended but merely adjourned. The American issue was finally decided, but battle was about to be joined in domestic politics, which was to involve even wider and broader considerations.

[1] Burke to Fox, 8 Oct. 1776; L. Reid, *Charles James Fox*, p. 70.

I

THE COLLAPSE OF THE SECOND ROCKINGHAM ADMINISTRATION AND THE FORMATION OF THE FOX–NORTH COALITION, MARCH 1782–FEBRUARY 1783

CHARLES Fox entered into the second Rockingham Administration in the full confidence that the fall of North had effectively ended eight years of opposition. The fact that this reversal of fortune had only been accomplished with the assistance of the Shelburne Whigs in no way diminished his hopes. The reformers of York, who, under Wyvill's[1] direction, were always anxious to test the sincerity of pretended reformers among the leading politicians, had themselves sent a resolution up to London, embracing both wings of the Whig party as 'Patriots, active to correct abuses themselves, and friendly to promote every wise and just measure of reformation.'[2] There seemed good ground for Fox's confidence. The fall of North appeared to inaugurate a new system in politics, which, if properly managed, could underpin a period of great Whig prosperity. In encouraging the Irish Whigs to be active and vigilant, Fox poured out his sanguine expectations:

> Why should not the complete change of system that has happened in this country have the same effect there [ie. Ireland] that it has here? . . . In short why should not the whigs, (I mean in principles, not in name) unite in every part of the empire, to establish their principles so firmly, that no future faction shall be able to destroy them.[3]

After an eight-year campaign, it merely remained for the Whigs to divide the spoils. Fox sat in Brooks's Club, dispensing promises of patronage to his large, and ever growing, circle of personal friends. In his euphoria, he was, according to one clerical observer, already

[1] Christopher Wyvill (1740–1822); large Yorks. landowner; Sec. and Chairman of the Yorks. Assoc. for Parliamentary Reform; broke with Fox over Coalition and supported Pitt in 1784; strongly disapproved of the war against France and rejoined Fox in 1793; highly influential pamphleteer.

[2] C. Wyvill, *Political Papers and Tracts*, i. 402.

[3] Fox to Lord Charlemont, 4 Apr. 1782; F. Hardy, *Memoirs of Charlemont*, ii. 13.

holding forth in 'the language of a Premier'.[1] Equally, George Selwyn,[2] admittedly a hostile witness, found him equating George III with Lucifer, and using words, which an absolute confidence in his own position had made unguarded; 'It is the bon vainqueur et despotique; he has adopted all the supremacy he pretended to dread in his Majesty.'[3] Fox was not alone in surrendering to this overweening self-confidence, but he was its most important victim.

Selwyn was convinced that Fox was greatly overestimating the strength of his position, and reported his doubts to Lord Carlisle;[4] 'It is much easier to throw things into confusion than to settle them to one's own liking. Troubled waters are good to fish in, it is true, but sometimes in searching for a fish you draw up a serpent. I have much more admiration of Charles's talents than opinion of his judgment and conduct.'[5] This point went home. Only two years before, there had been a rehearsal for the political situation of March 1782, when a faltering in North's administration led Rockingham and Shelburne to probe the possibility of a formal alliance. These negotiations had foundered on differing attitudes taken on such issues as reform and the Gordon Riots, some of which were still very relevant in politics two years later. Horace Walpole had concluded, in July 1780, that Shelburne and Rockingham were 'bitter enemies'.[6] Not even the destruction of North could entirely obliterate the memory of these proceedings, and Fox was certainly unwise to underestimate their significance. The points, on which the two halves of the Rockingham—Shelburne ministry were eventually to clash, were already written into the situation in March.

If Fox's trust in Shelburne was misplaced, his evaluation of the King's will to resist was even more tragically wide of the mark. George III, building on the experience, which Fox chose to ignore, was already preparing for the removal of his new Ministers. To his old servants, he never made any secret of his views. To North, he

[1] Add. MS. 34418 (Auckland Papers), f. 426; Bishop of Bangor to William Eden, 20 Apr. 1782.

[2] George Selwyn (1719–91), of Matson, Glos: M.P. Ludgershall (1747–54), Gloucester (1754–80), Ludgershall, (1780–91); nominated to both seats at Ludgershall; support sold to a succession of ministers in exchange for sinecures; reputed wit.

[3] George Selwyn to Lord Carlisle, 19 Mar. 1782; H.M.C. xv. 5. 6. *Carlisle MSS.* p. 599.

[4] Carlisle, Frederick Howard, 5th Earl (1748–1825); schoolfriend of Fox at Eton; supported American War; Ld.-Lt. of Ireland 1780–2; joined Fox 1783, and remained with him until the outbreak of the French Revolution; succeeded father as 5th Earl of Carlisle, 1758.

[5] George Selwyn to Carlisle, 19 Mar. 1782; H.M.C. xv. 5. 6; *Carlisle MSS.* p. 599.

[6] I. R. Christie, 'The Marquess of Rockingham and Lord North's Offer of a Coalition, June/July 1780', *E.H.R.* lxiv (1954), 390.

bewailed 'the fatal day . . . which the misfortunes of the times and the sudden change of sentiments of the H. of C. have driven me to of changing my Ministers'.[1] Almost immediately, he set out to recruit Shelburne as the instrument for destroying the new Ministry. A memorandum at Bowood[2] lists the topics touched on during an interview between the King and Shelburne on 21 March. The final entries included

His bad opinion of Ld. Rockingham's understg.
His horror of C. Fox.
His preference for me compared to the rest of the opposition.[3]

By the beginning of April, Shelburne was firmly settled in his role as the King's agent in the new Ministry. Reports of Rockingham's views were being regularly relayed to the King, who then had ample time to prepare an answer, before being confronted by the Marquis himself.[4] To use the bitterness existing between the Rockinghamite and Shelburnite Whigs, so clearly hinted at in 1780, was the King's main hope for breaking the back of the new ministry. There is no indication that Fox, in March 1782, had any idea that such a move was afoot. The defeat of one enemy after eight years in the political wilderness fostered an unwillingness immediately to face another.

The euphoria of March rapidly evaporated as the King's tactics became more obvious. Patronage wrangles, which punctuated the whole life of the Ministry, were the most damaging to its effectiveness, because, by setting Shelburne up as an alternative channel for obtaining preferment and places, George successfully undermined the very credibility of the administration. Influential peers, like the Duke of Grafton,[5] looking for some concession for a political client, turned to Shelburne before approaching Rockingham.[6] Doubts began to arise as to which of these men really had the ear of the King, and these were quickly resolved in Shelburne's favour. The evidence was unmistakable. Dunning's[7] elevation to the peerage had not been communicated to the Rockinghams, who, in a highly

[1] Add. MS. 47585 (Fox Papers), f. 113; George III to North, 27 Mar. 1782.

[2] The Home of the Shelburne Family in Wiltshire.

[3] Lord Shelburne's Memorandum, 21 Mar. 1782; Bowood MSS.

[4] George III to Shelburne, Mar. 1782 and 3 Apr. 1782; Bowood MSS.

[5] Grafton, Augustus Fitzroy, 3rd Duke (1735–1811); M.P. (Bury St. Edmunds) 1756–7; 1st Ld. of the Treas. 1766–70; Ld. Privy Seal 1771–5 and Mar. 1782–3; highly erratic political career; opposed American War; supported Shelburne in 1782, but took Fox's view of the French Revolution.

[6] Shelburne to Grafton, 12 June 1782; Grafton MSS. f. 682. Grafton to Shelburne, 4 July 1782; ibid. f. 680.

[7] John Dunning (1731–83); M.P. (Calne), 1768–82; eminent barrister, closely allied in politics with Shelburne; Sol.-Gen., 1768–70; Chanc. of the Duchy of Lancaster, 1782–3; cr. Baron Ashburton, 1782.

defensive manner, had to demand an equal honour for one of their own friends.[1] Burgoyne's[2] appointment to the command of the army in Ireland was pushed through with a similar sense of urgency.[3] By May, Fox was demanding that the Rockinghams become more aggressive. In urging the appointment of Lord Robert Spencer[4] to the position of Vice-Treasurer of Ireland, Fox explained to Rockingham how compromised their situation was becoming; 'Besides Ld. Robert's own claims, which are surely very strong upon us, it is surely reasonable and perhaps politic that it should appear to the world that I have some weight in the disposition of employments'.[5]

In this context, a vacancy in the Lord Steward's office brought on a determined trial of strength. Rockingham recommended Carlisle, and Shelburne, writing independently to the King, suggested that the Duke of Marlborough[6] should be sounded. To this latter idea the King agreed.[7] Fox, now deeply suspicious of Shelburne's intentions, wrote to Rockingham and demanded that Carlisle's appointment be vigorously pressed: 'I learned to night at Cumberland House that Carlisle certainly will accept the white stick if it [is] offered to him. However I am pretty sure Fitz[8] has been with him that you may have an exact account of the temper he is in. At all events I hope you will not suffer Shelburne to give it away for that must not be.' A post-script underlined the gravity of the situation: 'Pray my dear Lord fight stout with Shelburne about this Stewardship, or you & all of us shall be laughed at by the whole town.'[9]

At least a month before Rockingham's death, Fox was not alone in demanding a clarification of where exactly in the ministry authority

[1] H. B. Wheatley, *The Hist. and Posth. Memoirs of Sir Nathaniel Wraxall*, ii. 259.

[2] John Burgoyne (1723–92); M.P. (Midhurst) 1761–8; (Preston) 1768–92; playwright and Army officer; fought in American War of Independence; after defeat at Saratoga, changed allegiance and joined the Rockinghams (1779); remained loyal to Fox until his death.

[3] Fox to Shelburne, 2 Apr. 1782; Bowood MSS.

[4] Lord Robert Spencer (1747–1831); 3rd son of the 3rd Duke of Marlborough; M.P. 1768–99, 1802–7, 1817–20; close friend of Fox; partner in Fox's Faro bank at Brooks's; joined Rockinghams 1781, and remained loyal to the Whigs until his death; minor officeholder 1770–81, 1782, 1806–7.

[5] Fox to Rockingham, ? May 1782; Wentworth Woodhouse Muniments R.1 q.

[6] Marlborough, George Spencer, 4th Duke (1739–1817); politically erratic, but could generally be relied on to support the Court; succeeded father as 4th Duke of Marlborough, Oct. 1758.

[7] Shelburne to George III, 1 May 1782; Fortescue, vi. 3.

[8] Fitzwilliam, William Wentworth-Fitzwilliam, 4th Earl (1748–1833); nephew of the Marquess of Rockingham; schoolfriend of Fox at Eton; broke with him over the French Revolution; Ld.-Lt. of Ireland 1795; one of the most influential Whig peers; succeeded father as 4th Earl Fitzwilliam, 1756.

[9] Fox to Rockingham, ? May 1782; Wentworth Woodhouse Muniments, R i.

lay. Lord Upper Ossory[1] wanted 'a thorough explanation of which is to have the disposal of places'.[2] Fox himself wanted something more. If the Rockingham ministry was not to collapse amid derision, it had to be firmly demonstrated to the King and Shelburne that patronage recommendations lay exclusively within the province of the holder of the Treasury. Unfortunately, this point was not established before Rockingham's death. On 1 June, there was a violent disagreement in the Cabinet about whether Francis[3] or Cornwallis[4] should head the Council in India,[5] and, later in the month, Rockingham had to complain that he had not been notified of the peerage intended for Admiral Rodney. Throughout the life of the ministry, the King's device of setting up Shelburne as an alternative source of influence to Rockingham proved remarkably successful. At each stage, Shelburne was supported by the King and urged on to greater efforts.[5] Rockingham's death therefore created no new political situation, but merely made necessary a more explicit response to problems, which already existed.

Even where common ground was thought to exist, Shelburne's behaviour began to create difficulties. On 12 April, there was a Cabinet meeting to discuss the introduction of Edmund Burke's bill for economical reform, and when Shelburne began to second the doubts of Lord Chancellor Thurlow,[6] whom all knew to be the King's personal agent, the discussion became heated. Fox reported to Shelburne's brother-in-law, Richard Fitzpatrick,[7] that 'Nothing was concluded but in Ld. Chanc^r^. There was so marked an Opposition, and in your Brother-in-law so much inclination to help the Chancellor that we got into some thing very like a warm debate. I told them I

[1] Upper Ossory; John Fitzpatrick, 2nd Earl (1745–1818); M.P. (Beds.) 1767–94; voted steadily with Fox until the outbreak of the French Revolution; leading member of Brooks's Club; cr. Baron Upper Ossory in the English peerage, 1794.

[2] Add. MS. 47579 (Fox Papers), f. 85; Upper Ossory to Fox, 3 May 1782.

[3] Sir Philip Francis (1740–1818); M.P. (Yarmouth I.o.W.) 1784–90, (Bletchingley) 1790–6 (Appleby) 1802–7; protégé of Henry Fox; led opposition to Warren Hastings in Bengal, 1774–81, and leading promoter of his impeachment; caustic commentator on politics.

[4] Cornwallis, Charles, 1st Marquess (1738–1805); M.P. (Eye) 1760–2; most of his career spent on active service; fought in America and forced to surrender at Yorktown, 1781; Gov.-Gen. of Bengal, 1786–93; Ld.-Lt. of Ireland, 1798–1801; generally supported Pitt; given marquisate, Oct. 1792.

[5] Shelburne to George III, 1 June 1782; Fortescue, vi. 51–2.

[6] Thurlow, Edward, 1st Baron (1731–1806); M.P. (Tamworth) 1765–78; eminent lawyer and vigorous supporter of the American War; served under both Rockingham and Shelburne as royal agent; Ld. Chanc. 1778–83, Dec. 1783–92; cr. Baron Thurlow, 1778.

[7] Richard Fitzpatrick (1748–1813); M.P. in the Bedford interest (1770–1813); although Shelburne's br.-in-law, he joined Opposition in 1775, and never wavered in loyalty to Fox; minor officeholder in Whig ministries of 1782, 1783 and 1806–7; notorious gambler.

was determined to bring the matter to a crisis. As I am, and I think a few days will convince them that they must yield entirely. If they do not, we must go to war again, that is all, I am sure I am ready.'[1] It took, however, 'a very teizing & wrangling Cabinet',[2] three days later, which lasted for five hours, before Fox could report to Fitzpatrick that he thought the matter finally settled.

Of course, there is some substance in the claim that the attitudes of the two Whig groups towards economical reform had always varied a little. The Bowood circle had seen reform as the means to a complete remodelling of administrative procedures, whereas the Rockinghams were immediately concerned to delimit royal authority,[3] but this difference in emphasis cannot explain the quarrels of these months. Shelburne's open support for the Chancellor's wrecking tactics in Cabinet was a clear indication that his loyalties were at least evenly divided between the Court and his colleagues. Suspicions aroused in April were confirmed in May, when a bill for excluding government contractors from sitting in the House of Commons came up for consideration. According to Upper Ossory, 'The Chancellor made a more hostile speech upon the contractor's bill to the ministers than ever he did to them when they were in opposition. however Ld. Sh. thought it right to compliment him upon it.'[4] Shelburne's attitude was made doubly unfortunate by the fact that his dilatoriness on reform issues had been expressed in Cabinet or on a personal level only, and had not been made public. Indeed Wyvill, who obtained interviews with both Shelburne and Rockingham in June, expressed more satisfaction with the answers of the former, and read a paper to that effect to the reformers at York.[5] Fox's standing with the reformers was therefore being compromised by the very man whose support for Thurlow was endangering reform measures in Cabinet. The King's encouragement of Shelburne appeared capable of dividing the ministry, not only on matters where differences were known to exist, but also on points where all Whigs should have found common ground.

Pressure on the Ministry was kept up and intensified. In April, Lord Temple[6] approached the Duke of Leeds[7] at a masque at the

[1] Add. MS. 47580 (Fox Papers), f. 71; Fox to Fitzpatrick, 12 Apr. 1782.

[2] Add. MS. 47580 (Fox Papers), f. 77; Fox to Fitzpatrick, 15 Apr. 1782.

[3] D. L. Keir, 'Economical Reform 1779–1787', *L.Q.R.* l (1934).

[4] Add. MS. 47579 (Fox Papers), f. 85; Upper Ossory to Fitzpatrick, 3 May 1782.

[5] 'Short Account of the Interviews Between Lord Shelburne and Lord Rockingham, Seperately with Mr. Wyvill in June 1782.' Bowood MSS.

[6] Temple, George Grenville-Nugent-Temple, 3rd Earl (1753–1813); although born into a strongly Whig family, transferred allegiance to Court, helped to defeat the East India Bill; Ld.-Lt. of Ireland in 1782 and 1787; cr. Marquis of Buckingham, Dec. 1784.

[7] Leeds, Francis Osborne, 5th Duke (1751–99); M.P. (Eye) Mar.–Sept. 1774, (Helston) 1774–5; supported the American War until 1780; loosely connected with

Pantheon, and warned him that Shelburne was about to desert Rockingham, and that the King already had a replacement in mind.[1] In an atmosphere of mistrust, such a rumour could easily win credence, and poison further heavily strained relationships. In the middle of May, it was Sheridan's turn to complain to the unfortunate Fitzpatrick about his brother-in-law's duplicity. The concessions to Ireland were being entirely ascribed to Shelburne's initiatives, and in no way related to the Duke of Portland's[2] recommendations from Dublin Castle: 'And now observe you, I have Charles's authority, independent of my own opinion, for believing that you are a Brother-in-Law void of irrational prejudices or I should not write so, but . . . I must say a great deal on this subject, which is the horrible part of the Business here, and which tho' things are pretty quiet now, will I doubt overturn all and in the worst way—and so of that hereafter.'[3] Divisions within the administration were now widely reported. The King himself told North that he simply had to hold his Parliamentary forces together and wait.[4] The Opposition press exploited the rumoured differences of opinion almost daily, and impartially distributed responsibility to both factions. The principal exponent of this line of argument was the *Morning Herald*, whose description of divisions sounded petulant in April, but gravely realistic in June: '. . . and thus are those men squabbling, who should be unanimous in their opinion. Unanimity brought them into office, and it is only this that can keep them there.'[5]

For Fox himself, Shelburne's behaviour was endangering the very purpose, for which the administration had been formed. He had no difficulty in explaining this to a meeting of Westminster electors, when he was returned unopposed for that constituency on 3 April. Huzzas and cries of 'Amen' interspersed the declaration:

If, however, the present Administration, which must be called the Administration of the people, should at any time fly from the principles, which they had

both Rockingham and Shelburne; broke with Fox on the resignation issue; Sec. of State for Foreign Affairs Dec. 1783–91; succeeded father as 5th Duke of Leeds, Mar. 1789.

[1] Add. MS. 27918 (Leeds MSS.), f. 70; memorandum of the Duke of Leeds, 18 Apr. 1783 (misdated).

[2] Portland, William Cavendish-Bentinck, 3rd Duke (1738–1809); one of the most influential Whig peers; Ld.-Lt. of Ireland Mar.–July 1782; succeeded Rockingham as titular leader of the Whigs, July 1782; 1st Ld. of the Treasury Apr.–Dec. 1783; broke with Fox finally over French Revolution 1794; 1st Ld. of the Treasury 1807–9.

[3] Sheridan to Fitzpatrick, 20 May 1782; C. Price, *The Letters of Richard Brinsley Sheridan*, i. 144.

[4] Sir S. Romilly to Rev. J. Roget, 12 Apr. 1782; Sir R. Romilly, *The Memoirs of Sir Samuel Romilly*, i. 216.

[5] *Morning Herald*, 17 June 1782.

adhered to, or declared them to adhere to when out of place, they ought to be branded as the worst of men. The influence of the Crown had been one of the great grounds, upon which the present Administration had opposed the last. If they, when they might be supposed to have the power of giving out and sharing that corrupt influence, should make use of it, they would deserve to be charged with having deceived their constituents and the public.[1]

In Fox's eyes, Shelburne had not only surrendered to that corrupt power, but had clearly become its agent. The magnificent opportunity of vindicating eight years in opposition by a concentrated assault on royal influence in politics was accordingly placed in jeopardy. After only three weeks in office, Fox's expectations had been cut down from a belief that the Whigs were about to enter upon a long period of office, to the simple, and almost despairing, hope that they might be able to pass one or two measures before they were turned out. As he told Fitzpatrick, Shelburne 'affects the Minister more and more every day and is I believe perfectly confidant that the K. intends to make him so. Provided we can stay in long enough to have given a good stout blow to the Crown, I do not think it much signifies how soon we go out after.'[2] Many matters therefore took on an urgency which was made more pressing by the threat of impending dismissal.

No one at the centre of politics doubted that Shelburne's ambition was to acquire the Treasury for himself. Burke constantly warned Rockingham about Shelburne's canvassing activities among the Whigs, and about the uncertain state of the House of Commons, which made the formation of a large and threatening Shelburnite party politically feasible.[3] In April, Henry Dundas[4] was thought to be Shelburne's latest, and most valuable, acquisition, and if any doubt remained on the matter, it was speedily removed when the Lord Advocate joined Pitt in blocking Fox's suggestion that a full inquiry should be undertaken into the conduct of North's administration. It would, they contended, waste time and 'revive Animosity'.[5] Such arguments in defence of a régime, which had been vilified by the Opposition for eight years, were too flimsy to hide the connection between Shelburne, the King and North, whose interests were rapidly becoming interdependent on this point. Reporting Fox's

[1] *Morning Chronicle*, 4 Apr. 1782.

[2] Add. MS. 47580 (Fox Papers), f. 96; Fox to R. Fitzpatrick, 25 Apr. 1782.

[3] E. Burke to Rockingham, 27 Apr. 1782; J. Norris, *Shelburne and Reform*, p. 153.

[4] *Henry Dundas* (1742–1811); M.P. 1774–1802; eminent Scots advocate; holder of a number of imp. offices under North, Shelburne and Pitt; one of the latter's closest advisers; exercised enormous electoral influence in Scotland; cr. Visc. Melville, 1802; impeached 1805.

[5] Add. MS. 47582 (Fox Papers), f. 83; J. Hare to J. Burgoyne, 10 May 1782.

views on this incident to Burgoyne, James Hare[1] concluded that 'The Circumstance very much increased our Suspicion that the Advocate's Hostility was systematical, and concerted not a hundred miles from Berkeley Square.'[2]

In the face of this concerted obstruction in so many fields, and Shelburne's blatant attempts to prepare an alternative administration under his own leadership, Fox was increasingly torn between resignation and the desire to push through measures, while he still had the opportunity. The claim made by him after his resignation that he had seriously considered taking this step before Rockingham's death, a point which he found particularly difficult to put across, cannot be refuted. Three days before Rockingham died, Fox called on Grafton, 'complaining of the decided opposition of everything proposed by him; and added that it would be impossible to go [on] in such a way'.[3] He also announced his firm conviction, which Grafton in retrospect had to admit was probably true, that Shelburne was more completely committed to the Court than North had ever been. Grafton tried to calm Fox's suspicions, but noted later that 'Mr. Fox's advice previously to Ld. Rockingham's death, prevailed less often that would be expected from talents so superior.'[4] The experience of three short months in office had convinced Fox that the existing arrangement was unworkable. The King's presence in government was still formidable, and acted as an obstacle of fearful proportions when expressed in terms of Shelburne's ambition. Some resolution of this problem was essential. The difficulty lay in trying to communicate this knowledge of obstructionist tactics and royal interference to the Whig party as a whole. The protégé and the son of Chatham held excellent Whig credentials, which could not be easily impugned. With Rockingham's death, however, the attempt had to be made.

The American problem was the one, which Fox singled out as the basis of his justification for breaking up the Ministry. This was not surprising. However irritating Shelburne's behaviour had been on other issues, the American and French peace negotiations brought the two men into a direct confrontation. The *Morning Herald* had quickly recognized that this was the area, in which to assess their personal standing:

> Whenever any real negotiation shall come on the tapis with the revolted colonies of America, something curious must be manifested. Mr. Fox has

[1] James Hare (1747–1804); M.P. (Stockbridge) 1772–4, (Knaresborough) 1781–1804; renowned and penniless wit and scholar; formed friendship with Fox at Eton, and fully participated in all his social and political activities.

[2] Lord Shelburne's London house stood in Berkeley Square.

[3] W. Anson, *Memoirs of Augustus Henry, 3rd Duke of Grafton*, p. 322.

[4] Anson, *Memoirs of the Duke of Grafton*, pp. 318–9.

pledged himself that they have received overtures of accommodation from America. Lord Rockingham urges strongly to grant them independence. Lord Shelburne has repeatedly declared, in the Upper House, that he never would assent to such independence: the question then arising from these notorious facts is simply this. How is a peace to be made with America, and the above ministers keep their words, or their places [1]

Initially, the old Chathamite view seems to have prevailed. A Cabinet minute of 23 April 1782[2] specifically made the granting of independence conditional upon a return to the territorial arrangements of the Treaty of Paris, and commissioned Fox to make this clear to Vergennes.[3] In Fox's instructions to Thomas Grenville,[4] his agent in Paris, the conditional nature of the granting of independence was recognized, but this was overlaid by heavy ambiguity as to the authority for such a decision. Grenville was effectively left with considerable latitude. He was to quote his own authority, that of Fox personally, or that of the Cabinet as a whole, according to his assessment of the situation in Paris.[5] This was hardly the sense of the original minute, and represents a completely unwarranted attempt to remodel the Ministry's intentions.

Fox's action was, however, almost vindicated in practical terms, when Grenville reported, on 14 May, that the Spanish and French terms were too high because these powers counted on the American alliance, and that therefore America should be detached from her friends by the unconditional granting of independence.[6] This view came close to Fox's own, and Grenville was authorized to make this point to the Americans, even though official policy was still contained in the minute of 23 April. The Rockingham party justified this action by pointing to the tension existing between the two halves of the administration, and by almost insisting that dual policies had to be run in harness. The atmosphere of competition and rivalry between Grenville and Oswald,[7] Shelburne's agent in Paris, was merely a

[1] *Morning Herald*, 20 Apr. 1782.

[2] Add. MS. 47559 (Fox Papers), f. 9; Cabinet Minute, 23 Apr. 1782.

[3] Vergennes, Charles Gravier, Comte de (1717–87); stemming from a provincial, judicial family; protégé of Choiseul; succeeded him as Foreign Minister, 1770; succeeded Necker as First Minister, 1781.

[4] Thomas Grenville (1755–1846); M.P. 1779–84, 1790–1809, 1813–18; joined Fox in 1780; Rockingham envoy at Paris peace negotiations 1782; continued to support Whigs until his death; bibliophile and trustee of the British Museum.

[5] P.R.O. Foreign Office Papers, Series 27, vol. 2, f. 85; Fox to T. Grenville, 30 Apr. 1782.

[6] P.R.O. F.O.27/2, f. 144; T. Grenville to Fox, 14 May 1782.

[7] Richard Oswald (1705–84); govt. contractor, merchant and owner of considerable W. Indian and American property; early associate of Shelburne in the Bowood circle; Shelburne's nominee to treat with the Americans 1782; signed peace preliminaries, Nov. 1782.

reflection of the situation in London. As Sheridan explained to Grenville; 'If the business of an American treaty seemed likely to prosper in your hands, I should not think it improbable that Lord Shelburne would try to thwart it. Oswald has not yet seen Lord Shelburne; and by his cajoling manner to our secretary [Fox] and eagerness to come to him, I do not feel much prejudiced in his favour.'[1] On both sides, official decisions taken in Cabinet seem to have had only the most marginal effect on the actual conduct of Ministers. Effectively, two distinct administrations were already in being.

If Fox acted independently after 23 April, Shelburne acted in precisely the same manner after the Cabinet meeting of 23 May. He himself, together with Ashburton, Fox and Rockingham, was present, and it was decided, largely on the strength of Grenville's insistence on the necessity of detaching America from her allies, to offer unconditional independence.[2] In Shelburne's briefing to Oswald, no mention of a change in official policy was made. The naval victory at the Saintes had merely strengthened Shelburne's Chathamite prejudices against unconditional independence.[3] Fox, however, joyfully informed Grenville that his views had been accepted, which was an indirect compliment to the line Fox had unofficially been taking since April.[4] This official change of front in Cabinet thinking therefore failed to bring the two policies into harmony. The Fox line simply became official, and Shelburne's unofficial. As a result, Oswald and Grenville returned to the Paris negotiations with very different terms of reference.

Inevitably friction occurred. Grenville complained in a long letter to Fox that Oswald's arrival had effectively stopped Benjamin Franklin's[5] tongue, just as he was about to agree to treat separately on the basis of unconditional independence. Further, Oswald was offering to cede Canada without any obvious authority to do so. Grenville therefore asked to be released from what he regarded as a hopeless situation, and insisted that the negotiations should be placed in a single pair of competent hands.[6] In a most revealing reply on 10 June, Fox expressed his indignation at the Canadian proposal, of which he had not been informed, and insisted that the action of Shelburne and Oswald came near to treachery; 'When the object is attained—that is, when the duplicity is proved—to what consequences

1 Sheridan to T. Grenville, 21 May 1782; C. Price, *The Letters of R. B. Sheridan*, i. 147.

2 Add. MS. 47559 (Fox Papers), f. 21; Cabinet Minute, 23 May 1782.

3 J. Norris, *Shelburne and Reform*, p. 168.

4 P.R.O. F.O.27/2, f. 108; Fox to T. Grenville, 26 May 1782.

5 Leader of the American negotiating team in Paris.

6 T. Grenville to Fox, 4 June 1782; Duke of Buckingham and Chandos, *Memoirs of the Court and Cabinets of George III*, i. 33.

we ought to drive; whether to an absolute rupture, or merely to the recal of Oswald & the simplification of this negotiation, is a point that may be afterwards considered. I own I incline to the more decisive measure, and so I think do those with whom I act in concert.'[1] Even though this anger ended in a reasoned plea for two hundred bottles of champagne to be sent over, America was the principal field, in which Fox had experienced Shelburne's tactics at first hand, and this must have influenced his thinking at the time of his resignation.

The difficulty throughout these months was, however, in pinning Shelburne down. Fox and his friends may have persuaded themselves that the heir of Chatham was living up to his reputation, but this fact had to be demonstrated and proved. In this respect, the American issue was not perhaps the most opportune. Whatever Oswald may have been told in despatches, Shelburne's public pronouncements were impeccably orthodox, the most impressive being his letter to the military commander in New York, asking him to ensure that all the colonists knew of the offer of unconditional independence.[2] In these rather difficult circumstances, Fox decided to force a decision upon the Cabinet at a meeting on 30 June, the day before Rockingham died. No full report of this meeting exists. Grafton simply states that Fox demanded that the explicit and incontrovertible offer of unconditional independence be reaffirmed, and, when outvoted on this point, announced his intention of resigning.[3] It would seem that Fox encountered among the uncommitted in the Cabinet, like Camden,[4] Grafton, and Conway,[5] the conviction that the case against Shelburne was non-proven, an attitude which was very similar to that he was later to meet in his own party and in the political world at large.

Certainly, after this meeting, no one expected the Ministry to continue in its present form. Shelburne, in reporting the meeting to the King, was in fact also presenting an alternative administration led by himself;

The second [point] respects the weight which Your Majesty would think it proper to give Mr. Fox in case of any new arrangement. I have since Fryday

[1] Fox to T. Grenville, 10 June 1782; Buckingham and Chandos, i. 39.

[2] B.M. Microfilm 307 (Northumberland MSS.), f. 35; Shelburne to Sir G. Carleton, 5 June 1782.

[3] Anson, *Memoirs of the Duke of Grafton*, pp. 322 seq.

[4] Camden, Charles Pratt, 1st Earl (1714–94); M.P. (Downton) 1757–62; eminent lawyer associated in politics with Chatham and Shelburne; opposed American War and followed the younger Pitt; Ld. Chanc, 1766–70; Ld. Pres. Mar. 1782–Mar. 1783 and Dec. 1784–94; cr. Earl Camden 1786.

[5] H. S. Conway (1719–95); M.P. 1741–74, 1775–84; Army officer; originally of the Walpole–Pelham connection, loyalties becoming increasingly erratic; independent critic of the American War, C.-in-C. Army, Mar. 1782–Dec. 1783; supported Shelburne in July 1782, but resigned with the Coalition in Dec. 1783.

seen the most material Persons. I have had I think a satisfactory conversation with Mr. Pitt, and a confidential one with the Speaker, among other things upon the subject of Mr. Jenkinson,[1] whose assistance I wish for sooner or later in my Government.[2]

Some time before Rockingham's death therefore, Shelburne had been arranging his own administration, which, to use his own language, was already in existence on 30 June. For Fox and his immediate friends, this seemed the logical outcome of Shelburne's behaviour throughout the whole life of the ministry. If Shelburne was not to emerge as a new North, he had to be fought, but the timing of the contest and the choosing of the ground was forestalled by Rockingham's death.

Whatever the legitimacy of Fox's complaints against Shelburne, the element of personal ambition in the events leading up to Fox's resignation, by which his enemies were to set such great store, cannot be entirely discounted. Rockingham's health was known to be precarious, and the press continually printed details of meetings to arrange alternative Cabinets in the event of the Marquess's death. In May, even Shelburne was reported to have agreed that Fox should have the Treasury.[3] By July, Shelburne had emerged as the nominee of one group, while 'The Duke of Richmond,[4] Mr. Fox, and the House of Cavendish, have had several private meetings, to guard, if possible against an event so fatal to their several hopes and interests.'[5] Such journalistic rumours must be treated with caution, but the general pattern of Shelburne emerging as the rival of Fox during this three-month ministry would fit in well with the repeated complaints about Shelburne's attempt to build up a personal following in the Cabinet and among the Whigs as a whole.

There can be no doubt, however, that Fox, on 1 July, the day of Rockingham's death, considered that he had an excellent chance of the succession. In a letter to Dr. Jebb,[6] Fox particularly asked that his name should not be used in connection with the calling together

[1] Charles Jenkinson (1729–1808); M.P. 1761–6, 1767–72, 1772–86; career civil servant, voting with the Court party; office-holder in all anti-Whig administrations after 1761; close friend and adviser of Pitt; cr. Baron Hawkesbury 1786, Earl of Liverpool 1796.

[2] Shelburne to George III, 30 June 1782; Fortescue, vi. 69.

[3] *Morning Herald*, 18 May 1782.

[4] Richmond, Charles Lennox, 3rd Duke (1735–1806); Fox's uncle; opposed American War and supported advanced reform programmes in the 1770s; disappointed at not being offered the leadership in July 1782, he refused to resign with Fox, and took office under Pitt.

[5] *Morning Herald*, 1 July 1782.

[6] Dr. John Jebb (1736–86); theologian, doctor and politician; resigned Camb. Chair as a protest against compulsory subscription to the 39 articles; leading member of Westminster Assoc.; canvassed for Fox in 1780, but never forgave him for resigning in July 1782 and for forming the Coalition.

of the Westminster Committee; 'I have indeed a particular reason why I should not wish to have my name used just now, which I cannot explain, but notwithstanding this I would not decline if I did not know that there are other regular ways of calling the Comm: together'.[1] Advertising his close association with the London reformers at a moment when delicate negotiations might have to be undertaken in the Closet, would clearly be inadvisable. Even Thurlow was privately prepared to admit that, 'Upon the death of Ld. Rockingham, the principal pretender to the succession was Charles Fox.'[2] The distaste which Fox felt for Shelburne centred on a belief that the Whigs had been betrayed, and that their effective leader had been denied his inheritance.

America and the question of its independence synthesized these personal and constitutional reservations about Shelburne. In his dealings with his fellow Secretary of State, Fox saw the revivification of North's system. Part of the trouble can certainly be attributed to the imprecise terms on which the Rockinghams had come in,[3] but the trafficking with the issue of American independence had convinced Fox that the appointment of Shelburne would be 'a departure from those principles upon which they had come into office, and that it would tend to promote that disunion, which he had ever considered the misfortune of his Majesty's reign, by creating distrust and dissatisfaction amongst that description of men, whom he believed to be the best friends of his Majesty's family and to the interests of the public.'[4] America was therefore to be the chosen ground for battle, and it certainly became the accepted Whig explanation for the events of July.[5] The difficulty was to demonstrate the heavy constitutional overtones surrounding the issue, and to play down the equally real element of personal rivalry. The Shelburne case was naturally to emphasize precisely the opposite points.

Fox's conduct at this point was considerably more subtle than the later story, that the Whig position had been lost by a rash and precipitate resignation, would allow. In the Commons, on the day after Rockingham's death, Fox used a motion requesting placeholders in America to reside there to send up an ingenious *ballon d'essai*. He deliberately set out to link the issue of independence with an avowal of Cabinet unity:

[1] Add. MS. 47568 (Fox Papers), f. 101; Fox to Dr. J. Jebb, 30 June 1782.

[2] Thurlow to Duke of Sutherland, 6 July 1782; H.M.C. Vth Report, *Sutherland MSS.*, p. 210.

[3] J. Norris, *Shelburne and Reform*, p. 149.

[4] Journal of R. Fitzpatrick; Ld. J. Russell, ed. *Memorials and Correspondence of C. J. Fox*, ii. 435 sq.

[5] Add. MS. 27918 (Leeds Papers), f. 81; Memorandum of the Duke of Leeds, 8 July 1782.

He would speak for himself, that it was firmly his intention to grant unequivocal, unconditional independence to America; he would not speak peremptorily for others, but he believed he could say with confidence, that it was the opinion of all the members of the Cabinet. At any rate, he declared that he would not remain in the Cabinet one minute after he should discover an intention there, of bringing America to obedience either by force or negotiation: in this resolution he would say the Cabinet were unanimous: and he trusted, that so convinced were all his Majesty's Ministers of the necessity of giving to America everything she could ask, that no change of affairs, no stroke of Providence itself, and a severe one had yesterday been given in the death of the noble marquess, could separate or disunite them.[1]

After the decision taken in Cabinet on 30 June, this speech can only be taken as an attempt to pin Shelburne down. Either Shelburne, and by implication the King, would be bound to the idea of independence, or, if they denied it, would be seen to apostasize, whereupon Fox could resign as the undisputed guardian of the Whig conscience. When, however, Shelburne refused to be drawn on the issue, the plan backfired, for, as William Adam[2] noted, this speech of 2 July, with its emphasis on Cabinet unity, read oddly beside later protestations that Fox had intended to resign even before Rockingham's death.[3] The failure to trap Shelburne merely made Fox's position more difficult. This was indicated by the meeting at Fox's house, which it is impossible to date later than 2 July,[4] consisting of the Cavendishes, Keppel,[5] Burke, Richmond and Townshend,[6] which put forward the Duke of Portland as the official Whig candidate for the Treasury, and authorized Fox to wait on the King with this proposal next day.[7] The failure of Fox's speech had made it essential that his personal interest in this reorganization be covered by the promotion of a less controversial figure.

The personal retreat from pretensions to the Treasury was, however, the only concession Fox was prepared to make. Armed with

[1] *Parl. Hist.*, xxiii. 138; 2 July 1782.

[2] *William Adam* (1751–1839); M.P. 1774–94, 1806–12; supporter of the American War; fought a duel with Fox on this issue, 1779; strongly advocated the formation of the Coalition, however, and became manager of the finances of the opposition to Pitt; loyal to Whigs thereafter.

[3] *Mems and Corres. of C. J. Fox*, i. 438.

[4] Fox's interview with the King was held on 3 July.

[5] Admiral Keppel (1725–86); M.P. 1755–82; career seaman, sailed with Anson round the world, 1738; cr. admiral 1778; brought actively into politics by violent opposition to the American War; 1st Ld. of Adm. Mar.–July 1782, Apr.–Dec. 1783; remained loyal to Coalition.

[6] Thomas Townshend (1733–1800); M.P. (Whitchurch) 1754–83; initially a supporter of Newcastle, transferred loyalty to Shelburne, 1768; violent critic of American War; stayed with Shelburne in July 1782; cr. Baron Sydney 1783, Visc. Sydney 1789.

[7] *Morning Herald*, 8 July 1782.

the compromise candidature of Portland, Fox bluntly told the King, in his interview on 3 July, that 'the only means of securing the Support of those whom he believed to be the firmest friends to H.M.'s Government was to appoint some person to succeed Lord Rockingham, in whom that Description of Persons could place the most confidence.'[1] There followed an express veto on Shelburne. The King, in confirming his appointment to the Treasury, reported the conversation to Shelburne in almost identical terms.[2] Fox's demands amounted to the circumscription of the King's hitherto unchallenged prerogative of choosing his own ministers. This in no way stemmed from abstract thinking, but from the harsh experience of the three-month ministry. Even with Rockingham at the Treasury, the Whig programme had been systemmatically obstructed and undermined. Consequently, if Shelburne were to be elevated even further, any hope of securing measures, which the Court found distasteful, would be lost. By making these demands, Fox was effectively drawing up the lines of battle and setting the standards of Whig orthodoxy.

The political world as a whole accepted this fact. With regard to the Portland candidature, Lord Palmerston[3] observed that the Whigs 'are labouring to carry this point, on which it is not probable they will succeed, and if they do not, it is generally understood they will resign immediately.'[4] Whig terms were high, and should argue that Fox overestimated the cohesiveness of the Whigs. This is not necessarily the case. The Cabinet of 30 June had already demonstrated divisions. The pitching of Whig terms so high would almost certainly trouble other consciences. But for Fox and his immediate friends, the experience of Shelburne's conduct left them little choice. The American issue could be brought in to cover the baldness of their demands, but the underlying reality remained. Fox himself was far from sanguine, and, on the morning of 4 July, he faltered. Richmond's attempts at peacemaking were gravely weakening the Foxite position, particularly on the American issue:

Last night I thought everything finally and rightly settled. This morning I am again afraid. The D. of R^{d} has been with me and says he says Ld. S. willing (as I thought he would be) to give up the point of America. . . . One of the many mischiefs of all this negotiation is that when it breaks it will

[1] Add. MS. 47582 (Fox Papers), f. 162; Memorandum of R. Fitzpatrick, 3 July 1782.

[2] George III to Shelburne, 3 July 1782. Bowood MSS.

[3] Palmerston, Henry Temple, 2nd Visc. (1739–1802); M.P. 1762–1802; supported Court party until 1782; Ld. of the Treas. 1777–82; continued to support North in the Coalition, and voted with Fox until the outbreak of the French Revolution.

[4] Lord Palmerston's Diary, 3 July 1782; B. Connell, *Portrait of a Whig Peer*, p. 132.

prevent such of our friends as differ in opinion from us . . . from acting heartily with us hereafter. . . . I did not think it had been in the power of Politics to make me so miserable as this cursed anxiety and suspense does.[1]

Later the same morning, Fox put an end to his doubts by going into the Closet to resign the seals of office, in the full knowledge that Richmond and Conway at least would not follow him.[2] He paused only to have with Shelburne 'an angry Conversation as far as People co[d] judge who only saw it'.[2] The struggle for Whig minds and Whig votes began.

Shelburne's campaign had been launched at least two days before his appointment to the Treasury had been officially confirmed, and it was clearly built on the efforts, which he had made to strengthen his position while still a member of the Rockingham government. He knew from the start that the King was ready for war. George had notified Shelburne that 'it may not be necessary to remove him [Fox] at once, but if Ld. Shelburne accept the Head of the Treasury, and is succeeded by Mr. Pitt as Secretary for the Home Department and British Settlements, that it will be seen how far he will submit to it.'[3] While Fox was trying to establish the point about America on 2 July, Shelburne was already negotiating for the formation of a new ministry.[4] The Shelburne case was very much directed against Fox personally, concentrating on two particular charges. Initially, his action was described as incomprehensible, and due entirely to rashness born of pique. To the Duke of Leeds, Shelburne protested disingenuously that he knew of no public grounds, on which he differed from Fox, and that trouble had only arisen because the latter 'spoke to the King in a strong way and seemed surprised to find His M. dare have any opinion of his own.'[5] Grafton was informed of the situation in similar terms, with the added emphasis on Fox's unwillingness to negotiate.[6]

This initial point of Fox's essential unreasonableness was easily established among the more staid members of the political world, who found his whole way of life irresponsible. Grafton took comfort from Shelburne's letter, and hoped 'that this Rupture will end to the Disgrace & Disadvantage of those who Sought it'.[7] From here the

[1] Add. MS. 47580 (Fox Papers), f. 122; Fox to R. Fitzpatrick, 4 July 1782.

[2] Add. MS. 34418 (Auckland Papers), f. 477; Lord Loughborough to W. Eden, 4 July 1782.

[3] George III to Shelburne, 1 July 1782; Fortescue, vi. 70.

[4] *Morning Herald*, 2 July 1782.

[5] Add. MS. 27918 (Leeds Papers), f. 79; Memorandum of the Duke of Leeds, 4 July 1782.

[6] Shelburne to Grafton, 3 July 1782; Grafton MSS. f. 759.

[7] Grafton to Shelburne, 8 July 1782; ibid. f. 762.

attack could be broadened to include the main constitutional point at issue. A week after the crisis began, Shelburne described Fox's resignation to a friend as 'solely upon the ground of the King's not choosing a first commissioner from amongst the late Lord Rockingham's friends, which in fact brings the point to issue, whether the executive is to be taken altogether out of the King's hands and lodged, as Mr. Fox says, in the hands of a party, or, to speak more truly, in his own.'[1] The Duke of Marlborough's assistance was sought on similar grounds.[2] Beginning with criticism of Fox's impulsiveness, Shelburne quickly transformed himself into the guardian of the constitution against new and dangerous doctrines.

The Foxite case was less understood and less easy to put across. It was the penalty paid by all innovators in eighteenth-century politics. Whig reaction varied enormously. Temple, sympathizing with the Shelburne version, saw only personalities, and warned Fox 'that the people would not stand by him in his attempts to resign upon private grounds, which from their nature would appear to be a quarrel for offices, and not a public measure'.[3] General Conway was unhappy and confused, but tended to attribute the difficulties to 'Caballing about Posts and Power'.[4] Only a few of the party seem to have grasped immediately the issue in hand. One Suffolk Whig for example accepted the constitutional necessity of what Fox was doing, but insisted that America was not the right issue, on which to make a stand,[5] particularly after the speech of 2 July, which had again and again emphasized Cabinet unity on this point. This speech had merely brought confusion, and made Shelburne's insistance on personalities all the more plausible.

Each of the above views confirms the basic point that, before the decision to resign, the close connection between the American issue and the important constitutional point, which it clothed, had not been successfully put across to the Whig party as a whole, and had merely been obscured by Fox's initiative in the Commons on 2 July. It was to this lack of preparation and forethought that Palmerston drew attention. The King could only have been defeated by a unanimous withdrawal from office, and the circumstances in which this might have taken place had not been prepared. Palmerston believed that 'This resignation is a measure of Mr. Fox, disapproved of by part of his friends and not very cordially embraced by those that have

[1] Shelburne to W. Pery, 9 July 1782; H.M.C. xiv. R. 9; *Emly MSS*. p. 169.

[2] Add. MS. 34418 (Auckland Papers), f. 484; Shelburne to Marlborough, 8 July 1782.

[3] Temple to T. Grenville, 4 July 1782; Buckingham and Chandos, i. 50.

[4] Conway to Grafton, 5 July 1782. Grafton MSS. f. 137.

[5] W. Knox to Lord Sackville, 6 July 1782; H.M.C., xv; *Sackville*, I. 1904.

followed him. It has completely divided the Rockingham Party, as the Duke of Richmond, General Conway and Tommy Townshend do not resign. On which account they are in disgrace with C. Fox'.[1] Fox's only consolation was that his taking up of the American issue had succeeded in embarrassing the King with respect to the granting of independence.[2]

Fox was deeply conscious of the strain which his action had put on Whig loyalties. He insisted to Leeds that the unity of the Whig party was his first consideration, and that no efforts would be spared to secure this. Even his standing down in favour of Portland was not seen as a self-sacrificing move, but as a realistic response to 'the impossibility of the great Families who formed the Whig party submitting to become the creatures of Mr. Fox, however highly they might think of his abilities'.[3] Appeals to friends were an obvious means of rallying support. The letters sent out to Fitzwilliam and Coke of Norfolk,[4] asking for their immediate presence in Town, made no reference to the American issue, but dealt entirely with the constitutional points the significance of which Fox knew his close friends to be well aware.[5] The nearer any politician was to the centre of Whig politics, the more open he would be to the Foxite explanation of events. Those who were socially or geographically more distant might have to have the pill sugared with references to America, in order to demonstrate the point at issue. The mere assertion of long-standing suspicions was in these cases, not enough. To his closest friends, Fox talked constitutional principle, and to the remainder of the party he talked of America and hoped that the connection between the two would become apparent. Unfortunately all had not shared Grenville's experiences in Paris, and would not therefore easily see that, 'those who go are right; for there is really no other question but whether, having lost their power, they ought to stay and lose their characters. And so begins a new opposition: but woefully thinned and disconcerted I fear.'[6] Even Fox's letter to Portland, which included a formal offer of Rockingham's mantle, was couched in highly cautious terms,

[1] Diary of Lord Palmerston, 4 July 1782; B. Connell, *Portrait of a Whig Peer*, pp. 132–3.

[2] George III to Shelburne, 12 Aug. 1782; Bowood MSS.

[3] Add. MS. 27918 (Leeds Papers), f. 75; Memorandum by the Duke of Leeds, 2 July 1782.

[4] Thomas Coke (1745–1842); M.P. (Norfolk), 1776–84, 1790–1807, 1807–32; opposed American War; leading agricultural improver and supporter of Wyvill's petitioning movement; remained loyal to Whigs until his death; cr. Earl of Leicester 1837.

[5] Fox to T. Coke, 2 July 1782; A. M. W. Stirling, *Coke of Norfolk and His Friends*, p. 127.

[6] Sheridan to T. Grenville, 4 July 1782; C. Price, *The Letters of R. B. Sheridan*, i. 152.

underlining the real difficulty of Fox's position.[1] To talk constitutional principles was to countenance innovation, but without it, Fox's case was far from strong.

It was precisely on this difficulty that Shelburne counted. As long as the debate was carried on in personal rather than constitutional terms, he could affect bewildered innocence,[2] and wait until the jealousies within the Whig party worked themselves out.[3] Portland's candidature was a testimony to the strength of the latter consideration. The onus of proof rested squarely with Fox. As Grafton informed Shelburne, Fox's 'Consequence in his Retreat depends on the Number and weight of that Party which he can be able to draw with him, to prevent which will be your Lordship's Effort, & I trust will be Effected by your Attaching the greatest Part of them to the present System: the Rest will soon follow.'[4] On 6 July, Fox made his first attempt at self-vindication to the Whig party as a whole. Between thirty and forty of its more influential members met at Fitzwilliam's house to hear the resignation issue debated. No detailed report of this meeting exists, but it seems to have ended in a largely Foxite victory. Shelburne only knew that 'the Duke of Richmond, Lord Temple, and Mr. Pelham[5] of Lincolnshire withstood a great scene of violence upon the part of Mr. Fox and his particular Friends,'[6] and that 'Mr. Fox declar'd at this meeting that he intended taking all advantages and to have no managements in his Language. He has given proof by summoning every person possible to Town, with a view to bring on a question on American Independence tomorrow in the House of Commons.'[7]

Even though Lord Frederick Cavendish[8] thought that 'the independent part of our late Party'[9] had been satisfied with Fox's explanation, this apparent concentration on the American issue must be counted a mistake. Unless it could be linked to, and made to justify, constitutional demands, Fox's point would essentially be missed. George III was himself delighted that Fox continued to press this issue, because he rightly believed that uncertainty would allow

[1] Add. MS. 47561 (Fox Papers), f. 41; Fox to Portland, 5 July 1782.

[2] Add. MS. 47579 (Fox Papers), f. 141; Shelburne to Upper Ossory, 4 July 1782.

[3] Memoranda of the Duke of Leeds, 3 July 1782; O. Browning, *Political Memoranda of the Fifth Duke of Leeds*, pp. 69–70.

[4] Grafton to Shelburne, 5 July 1782; Grafton MSS. f. 760.

[5] Charles Pelham (1749–1823); M.P. (Beverley) 1768–74, (Lincs.) 1774–94; large landowner, who opposed American War, and consistently voted with Fox until the outbreak of the French Revolution; cr. Baron Yarborough 1794.

[6] Shelburne to Grafton, 7 July 1782; Grafton MSS. f. 761.

[7] Shelburne to George III, 9 July 1782; Fortescue, vi. 77.

[8] Lord Frederick Cavendish (1729–1803); M.P. (Derbyshire) 1751–4, (Derby) 1754–80; 3rd son of 3rd Duke of Devonshire; Army officer; voted steadily with his family against American War.

[9] Lord F. Cavendish to Lady Ponsonby, 8 July 1782; Grey MSS.

Shelburne to syphon off enough Whig votes to give his ministry a chance of survival. The loss of Richmond and Temple had already been heavy blows for Fox. The defectors were too numerous and too respectable for the blanket charge of treachery to be applied. After the failure of the Fitzwilliam meeting to restore unity in the party, even Fox was prepared to concede that Shelburne had won the first round. He admitted to Leeds a day later that 'it was impossible for any body to form a true opinion on the case who had not been in the Cabinet, he said he did not wonder people were displeased with him, but then he acted from conviction and would never hesitate to sacrifice popularity.'[1]

The range of pressures, under which Fox laboured at this time, was very wide indeed. Advice was plentiful, but not always of the most helpful kind. The Burkes, *père et fils*, inevitably offered well-argued and lengthy memoranda. Both accepted 'the impossibility of your acting for any length of time as a clerk in Lord Shelburne's administration',[2] but suggested that the battle should be fought from the strong ground of office rather than from the wastes of opposition. This carried the twin advantages of securing the Burke family finances for a little longer and of putting the burden of dismissal upon the King. After the experience of the Rockingham Ministry, however, this could hardly be called a practical suggestion. To accept Shelburne in July would have been to vindicate his activities over the previous three months. It must, however, have weakened Fox's position, when Burke's influence, which had always been strong on Fox himself,[3] was lost in sophistry.

Richmond's behaviour was even more galling. In March and April, his letters to Rockingham had advised strict caution in his dealings with both the Crown and Shelburne.[4] After the crisis, he was forced to write to Fitzwilliam, Rockingham's heir, to ask for the return of some letters advocating no accommodation with the Crown 'upon any other conditions than those of having possession of the Treasury'.[5] Unfortunately, it is not known whether these letters refer to the negotiations of March 1782 or to those of July, but in any case, they must, as the Duke of Portland pointed out, afford 'an ample field for speculation at least'.[5] And even if they only referred to the March

[1] Add. MS. 27918 (Leeds Papers), f. 79; Memorandum of the Duke of Leeds, 7 July 1782.

[2] Add. MS. 47568 (Fox Papers), f. 106; E. Burke to Fox, 3 July 1782. See also Add. MS. 47568 (Fox Papers), f. 104; R. Burke to Fox, 2 July 1782.

[3] J. Nicholls, *Recollections and Reflexions of Public Affairs During the Reign of George III*, i. 47.

[4] A. Gilbert, *Political Correspondence of the Third Duke of Richmond* (Oxford Univ. D.Phil. Thesis), 1956, p. 100.

[5] Portland to Lady Rockingham, 27 Dec. 1782; Portland MSS. PWF 9190.

negotiations, Richmond had undergone a very sudden change in his ideas about constitutional propriety by July. A century later, the story had become current that Richmond's behaviour was determined by the fact that Fox had been deputed to tell him that his pretensions to the leadership had to be discounted because of his close association with the more extreme reformers.[1] Whatever the truth of this, Richmond's distaste for Fox stemmed from a clash with the Holland family on the Wilkes issue in 1768, and obviously influenced his actions, when there was a chance that his nephew might succeed Rockingham. So strong was this antipathy that Richmond deserted Fox, even though he had been forced to admit, at the Fitzwilliam meeting, that not one of Shelburne's statements could be trusted.[2] Fox may be criticized in the immediate crisis period for failing to prepare his party for what was coming, but, as the cases of the Burkes and Richmond indicate, not all the hesitation and apostasy was prompted by political considerations alone. Fox's desire to make Richmond 'an outcast in all gentlemanlike society'[3] was readily comprehensible.

Fox's public justification took the form of a set-piece debate in the Commons, on 9 July, and in a speech to the electors of Westminster eight days later. Sir Samuel Romilly,[4] who was in the Visitor's Gallery for the debate, noted that the prospect of Fox's self-vindication had drawn the biggest audience for some years.[5] In his speech Fox abandoned the cover of the American issue, and attacked the main constitutional point. He had retired because a Northite system, against which he had fought for so long, was about to be re-established. It was less a speech to convince waverers than an attempt to confirm in their opinions those who had decided to follow him in last week. Regardless of the consequences, Fox expressed the determination 'to ring the alarum bell and tell this country that the principle on which they had, with due deliberation, formed an administration, was abandoned, and that the old system was to be revived, most probably with the old men, or indeed with any men that could be found'.[6] In the light of future events, the prediction that North would shortly re-enter government was unfortunate. Conway predictably took a

[1] *Edinburgh Review* (1854), xcix. 22.

[2] Add. MS. 27918 (Leeds Papers), f. 79; Memorandum of the Duke of Leeds, 7 July 1782.

[3] A. Olson, *The Radical Duke* (Oxford, 1961), p. 64.

[4] Sir Samuel Romilly (1757–1818); legal and political reformer; M.P. 1806–18; temporarily estranged from Fox over Coalition, but rejoined him to oppose the French War; defended members of the Constitutional Soc. 1797; Sol.-Gen. 1806–7; committed suicide.

[5] Sir S. Romilly to Rev. J. Roget, 16 July 1782; Romilly *Memoirs*, i. 232.

[6] *Fox Speeches*, ii. 71.

more prosaic line in reply, and insisted that none of the four great issues, to which the Whigs were pledged, economical reform, the Irish settlement, a reduction in royal influence and the granting of independence to America, were in any way threatened. Fox retorted, with some very sharp comments on Conway's naïvety, that the experience of the Rockingham administration had made such a statement absurd, particularly since it was Conway's vote, which had tipped the scales against unconditional independence in the Cabinet of 30 June.[1]

This uncovering of the central issue proved an excellent rallying cry. Gilbert Elliot[2] immediately wrote to his wife to say how delighted he was that he had decided to accept Fox's explanation earlier in the week. The speech of 9 July had removed all his doubts.[3] In view of the obvious success of this uncompromising speech, it was unfortunate that Fox had chosen to use the American issue earlier in the crisis. As it was, the powerful impression created on 9 July was somewhat reduced in scale by the knowledge that, only a week earlier, Fox had insisted that the Cabinet were united on this issue. The change of approach between these two dates inevitably entailed contradictions, which the Opposition press hastened to point out.[4] As a consolidating factor for Whig opinion, it was, however, a change for the better. The resurrection of North's system presented them with an enemy they recognized. The ground for political debate once again became familiar.

Having explained to his party and to Parliament, Fox turned to the political world at large. His Westminster constituency was his platform for this purpose, and he returned to it whenever a period of crisis demanded the wider publication of his views. Taking advantage of a reform meeting on 17 July, Fox addressed his constituents in terms they easily recognized. The cause of reform and the liberties of England were not safe in Shelburne's hands. The three-month Rockingham ministry had shown, notably on the American issue, how Shelburne was to be the new North. The hopes for reform and freedom for America, the two issues which had inspired the long opposition to North, were now turned against Shelburne. Jebb may have declared for Shelburne, but Fox told the reforming electors that 'no constitution upon paper or practice of any kind whatever, can

[1] *Fox Speeches*, ii. 78.

[2] Sir Gilbert Elliot (1751–1814); M.P. 1776–84, 1786–95; opposed American War and supported Coalition; deserted to Pitt after the outbreak of the French Revolution and undertook a number of diplomatic missions; Gov.-Gen. of India, 1806–13; cr. Earl of Minto, 1813.

[3] Sir G. Elliot to Lady Elliot, 10 July 1782; Lady Minto, *The Life and Letters of Sir Gilbert Elliot, First Lord Minto*, i. 81.

[4] *Morning Herald*, 13 July 1782.

preserve the just and natural consequence of this country, if the executive government is not lodged with able and honest hands'.[1] A return to the clear message of the old opposition seems to have counteracted Jebb's influence. Major Cartwright[2] mingled resolutions for parliamentary reform with the suggestion that the electors should allow Fox a pension.[3]

Personal *tours de force* on Fox's part could not obscure the fact, however, that grave damage had been done to the Whig party. Reaction to the resignation is interesting, not only with respect to Fox personally, but also because certain groups of Whigs tended to adopt similar attitudes. Hostile comment within the party followed two lines of thought. Some, like Horace Walpole, believed that Fox had simply become the tool of those great families, whose wealth and style of living separated them out as a great distinct circle within the party:

I never admired Lord Rockingham: shall his self-elected executors tell me that I am to take the oaths to Lord Fitzwilliam; I who was a nonjuror in the uncle's time! I see a very good reason why Mr. Fox should say that [the] imaginary King never dies; but, as I told him t'other night, my Whiggism is founded on the Constitution, not on two or three great families, who are forced to have Virtue for a claim to their dignity, and any able man they can find to execute the office for them. My Whiggism is not confined to the Peak of Derbyshire.[4]

Exposure to these people had ruined the bright prospect of Fox's career.[5] After his resignation, on 4 July, instead of beginning a campaign to educate his party, Fox dined with the Prince of Wales, gambled at Brooks's until 4 a.m., and then went on to White's.[6] Those outside the charmed circle of Devonshire House felt irritated that their advice had not been taken and that such outstanding abilities were being steadily misused. Lady Sarah Napier[7] echoed the last sentiment. Her nephew's career was in ruins because 'poor dear Charles is so surrounded by flatterers that tempt him to think he alone can overset

[1] Westminster Speech (1782).

[2] Major Cartwright (1740–1824); after service in both the Army and Navy, became a violent critic of the American War. Member of the Westminster Association and founder of the Soc. for Const. Information; tried for sedition 1820; loosely connected politically with the more radical Whigs.

[3] F. O. Cartwright, *The Life and Correspondence of Major Cartwright*, i. 145.

[4] H. Walpole to Lady Ossory, 7 July 1782; *Letters Addressed to the Countess of Ossory by Horace Walpole*, ii. 95.

[5] H. Walpole to Lady Ossory, 11 July 1782; ibid., ii. 99.

[6] H. Walpole to Rev. W. Mason, 8 July 1782; Mrs. P. Toynbee, *The Letters of Horace Walpole*, xii. 289.

[7] Lady Sarah Napier (1745–1827), dau. of the 2nd Duke of Richmond, and sister of Lady Caroline Lennox, Fox's mother; m. (i) Sir Thomas Bunbury, (ii) George Napier; generally followed her nephew in politics.

the whole fabric.'[1] Neither of these critics abandoned Whiggery as a result of what they took to be an aristocratic slight. The effect on others, however, whose affection for Fox was less pressing, was disastrous. Arrogance, impulsiveness and an unwillingness to take party leadership seriously were all charges that could easily be read into the situation.

As if to justify Walpole's strictures, most of the Whigs who came forward in Fox's defence were either from his personal coterie, centered on Brooks's and Newmarket, or came from the Devonshire House circle. Indeed, one of the Duchess's biographers specifically makes the point that it was Georgiana[2] herself, Sheridan, Prinny and Elizabeth Melbourne,[3] who were most insistent that Fox should resign.[4] For these people, Fox's action was entirely credible in terms of the political creed which had been theirs from the cradle. The events of July merely added another engagement to the long list of Cavendish battles with the King. Drawing on a long history of similar experiences, Lord Frederick Cavendish understood the situation immediately:

> It is pretty clear that the game in the year '66 is play'd over again. Ld. Shelburne may think as Ld. Chatham did, that he has got the King, but I fancy that he will find that the King has got him in his power, and he must submit or pretend to be mad as Lord Chatham then did.[5]

The analogy between Shelburne and Chatham was a good one, and fitted the incidents of July into a well-worn theme. Lady Louisa Connolly,[6] faced with an awkward decision between her brother Richmond and her nephew Fox, was ultimately only prepared to admit that Charles might have been a little 'hasty'.[7]

For this inner circle of Whiggery, the connection Fox was trying to establish between the American question and the constitutional

[1] Lady S. Napier to Lady S. O'Brien, 9 July 1782; Lady Ilchester and Lord Stavordale, *The Life and Letters of Lady Sarah Lennox*, ii. 19.

[2] Georgiana, Duchess of Devonshire (1757–1806); dau. of John, Earl Spencer and wife of William, 5th Duke of Devonshire; socially and politically, the Whigs' most imp. London hostess; led a team of canvassers into the Westminster Election of 1784; personal friend and admirer of Fox.

[3] Elizabeth, Lady Melbourne (1749–1818); dau. of Sir Ralph Milbanke, and wife of Penistone Lamb, 1st Visc. Melbourne; married 1769; habituée of the Devonshire House circle; mistress of the Prince of Wales; later a friend of Byron; mother of the future Prime Minister.

[4] I. Leveson Gower, *The Face Without a Frown*, p. 82.

[5] Lord F. Cavendish to Lady Ponsonby, 8 July 1782; Grey MSS.

[6] Lady Louisa Connolly (1743–1819); 3rd dau. of the 2nd Duke of Richmond, and sister of Lady Sarah Napier and Lady Caroline Fox; aunt of Charles Fox; m. Thomas Connolly of Castletown, Ireland.

[7] Lady L. Connolly to Lady S. Napier, 10 July 1782; Bunbury MSS. E.18/750/2, f. 57.

implications of July needed no elaboration. Burgoyne sent a sympathetic letter from Ireland,[1] and, more gratifyingly still, Portland had taken the point. Although the Duke's advice arrived after the event, his moral support was invaluable: 'Confidence I conceive to be wholly out of the Question. Power must be taken as its Substitute, and unless You can possess that & convince the Publick of your possessing it, Both Your Honour and Duty to the Country dictate your Retreat.'[2] Fox replied, in the most grateful terms, that the Duke had exactly stated his own view of the situation.[3] For those moving in the Devonshire House circle, and for those who had experienced Shelburne's tactics at first hand, it was easy to arrive at such decisions. For many members of the lower échelons of the Whig party, however, the issue was by no means so clear.

The predominant reaction among the Whigs and their enemies alike, however, was bewilderment. If the validity of the American issue was admitted at all, the connection with points of deep, constitutional importance was never perceived. Many people had therefore to fall back on Fox's personal impulsiveness for an explanation. Following this line of reasoning, Carlisle forecast fifty years in the wilderness for the Whigs,[4] and the Bishop of Peterborough[5] sadly predicted the return of North.[6] Even some of Fox's opponents were confused. Lord Sackville[7] admitted:

What still puzzles me is to account for the conduct of Mr. Fox; as he means granting independence to America, and to have the lead and direction in Government, why does he resign without waiting for some measure being proposed which might justify his leaving the King's service, and at the same time secure his popularity, for he cannot imagine to create a clamour against the King because he will not permit the shatter'd remains of the Rockingham party to nominate the first Lord of the Treasury.[8]

The truth was therefore not even credible. Contemporaries could not believe that Fox could be making such exaggerated claims, and, with Shelburne's position on America being roughly equated with Fox's,

[1] Add. MS. 47568 (Fox Papers), f. 104; J. Burgoyne to Fox, 5 July 1782.

[2] Add. MS. 47561 (Fox Papers), f. 42; Portland to Fox, 6 July 1782.

[3] Add. MS. 47561 (Fox Papers), f. 43; Fox to Portland, 12 July 1782.

[4] Carlisle to Gower, 8 July 1782; H.M.C. xv. 5. 6; *Carlisle MSS.* p. 632.

[5] Bishop of Peterborough, John Hinchcliffe (1731–94); tutor in both the Crewe and Devonshire families; cr. B. of Peterborough 1769; one of the only two bishops to oppose American War; supported religious toleration; broke with Fox on French Revolution.

[6] Bishop of Peterborough to Grafton, 8 July 1782; Grafton MSS. f. 757.

[7] Sackville, George, 1st Visc. (1716–85); M.P. (Dover) 1741–61, (Hythe) 1761–8, (East Grinstead) 1768–82; cashiered from the Army for cowardice at Minden; supported American War; Sec. of State for America, 1775–82; cr. Visc. Sackville, Feb. 1782.

[8] Sackville to W. Knox, 9 July 1782; H.M.C. *Var. Coll.* vi. 185.

the explanation of events in terms of personalities was the only one left. Fox made no attempt to clarify the situation to his party until 6 July. The political nation at large had to wait three days more. It was in these nine days of uncertainty that the Shelburne administration was constructed.

In retrospect, Fox's friends began to apportion responsibility for the heavy damage occasioned by the resignation. The most consistent and justified charge was that Fox, with long experience of Shelburne's activity, had not prepared his party for what might come. The astonishment at the resignation, expressed at all levels of the party, was a damning indictment of Fox's lethargy. An Irish Whig complained that 'Had they instantly formed a Plan of resigning in a body there would have been no need of trusting to Lord Shelburne's promises. He could not have formed an administration without them, unless he threw off the mask too soon, and took in some of the King's old & dear friends.'[1] This was a charge, which Fox himself was sadly prepared to admit.[2] Fox's defence must rest on the fundamental difficulty of how to make innovation in constitutional practice acceptable to the eighteenth-century political world. To demonstrate what he knew to be the wrecking tactics of Shelburne and the King, Fox would have required access to official documents, and would have been accused of the very serious charge of launching an unprincipled attack on the executive. It was therefore, as Portland reflected, 'not less unfortunate for the public than for his own character that he cannot be at liberty to state every circumstance which induced him to take that upright and manly decision'.[3]

In these circumstances, the distance separating an individual from an intimate knowledge of the course of affairs, was quite often the determining factor in deciding with what sympathy he would receive the news of Fox's resignation. In terms of actual votes lost, the resignation issue had a greater divisive effect on the ranks of the old opposition to North than any other single event between 1782 and 1784. According to a list drawn up by Burke, 84 members of the old Opposition were to be found voting with Pitt by March 1784.[4] Of these, 61[5] were already voting with Shelburne in March 1783, and

[1] Add. MS. 47582 (Fox Papers), f. 124; Lucius O'Beirne to Mrs. Crewe, 16 July 1782.

[2] Fox to T. Grenville, 13 July 1782; Buckingham and Chandos, i. 63.

[3] Portland to Burgoyne, N. D.; E. B. de Fonblanque. *Life and Correspondence of the Rt. Hon. John Burgoyne*, p. 413.

[4] E. Burke, 'An Authentic List of the Whole House of Commons', Milton MSS. axxxviii. f. 19.

[5] J. W. Adeane, F. Annesley, C. Archdeckene, Sir E. Astley, J. Aubrey, H. Banks, J. Baring, P. Bertie, Lord Bulkeley, C. Brett, J. S. Cocks, Sir R. Cotton, W. Drake (jnr.), H. Duncombe, E. J. Eliot, S. Estwick, M. Le Fleming, Sir J.

therefore the allegiance of these members had been lost, from a Foxite point of view, between February 1782 and March 1783. There can be little doubt that the crisis of July 1782 provided the major dividing line. Checking with votes actually recorded in the House of Commons, the turnover of votes in this period was far greater than in the crisis over the India Bill, by which time loyalties, formed on the basis of the July issue, seem to have hardened. In terms of votes actually lost therefore, the resignation issue was for Fox a major disaster. The Chathamite and Rockinghamite Whigs had been firmly prised apart.

After each of the major crises in his political life, Fox relapsed into that characteristic indolence, of which Walpole and his other critics so often complained. Hare's description of him during the summer recess shows him monopolizing the company of Perdita Robinson,[1] leading the social life of Brooks's, and taking no interest in public affairs at all.[2] When news reached Horace Walpole that Fox intended to go personally to the defence of Gibraltar, he unkindly commented that it would represent no loss to anyone.[3] Fox's apathy was only broken when his standing in Westminster itself was challenged. A group of dissident Whigs had repudiated Fox, and had set up a rival Whig circle centred on the Firm and Free Club. Fox, in a speech to his constituents, of whom only fourteen were present, attempted to defeat his opponents with ridicule:

> By FIRM was evidently meant a desertion of principle, and treachery to friends; and by FREE, the faculty or privilege of acting, without any regard to the claims of friendship, the influence of truth, or the dictates of honour.[4]

In spite of these words, however, Fox's standing in Westminster badly stood in need of repair. Even the prospect of a new session of Parliament failed to revive Fox's morale. His summer tour of Whig

Gardner, J. Garforth, G. Gipps, J. Grenville, W. Grenville, Sir R. Hill, A. Holdsworth, R. Hopkins, B. Keene, T. Kemp, L. Kenyon, Sir C. Leighton, Sir W. Lemon, Sir W. Lewes, Sir J. Lowther, J. Lowther, W. Lowther, Lord Mahon, J. Martin, Sir J. Mawbey, J. Montague, Lord Muncaster, R. Neville, Sir R. Palk, J. Parry, J. Parker, Sir J. Pennyman, J. Phipps, W. Pitt, W. Pochin, J. Pratt, C. Robinson, Sir J. Rous, R. Smith, W. S. Stanhope, T. Steele, G. Sutton, J. Sutton, J. Townshend, Lord Tyrconnel, W. Wilberforce, J. Wilkes, W. Williams, Sir G. Yonge.

[1] Perdita Robinson; a leading London courtesan, well known in Whig circles.

[2] Add. MS. 47582 (Fox Papers), f. 131; J. Hare to R. Fitzpatrick, 31 July, 1782.

[3] H. Walpole to Lady Ossory, 31 Aug. 1782; *Letters Addressed to the Countess of Ossory*, ii. 109.

[4] *Morning Post*, 14 Oct. 1782. See also Dr. F. Laurence, *History of the Political Life and Public Services as a Statesman of the Rt. Hon. C. J. Fox*, p. 506.

country houses was rather depressing. At Welbeck, he 'did not despond but . . . felt uncertain,'[1] and at Althorp he was unable to be 'sure of anything'.[2] At the start of the 1782–3 session therefore, the Opposition press tended to ignore the potential of Fox 'and those who are . . . like himself and Lucifer, past redemption'.[3]

Beneath this apparent inactivity during the recess, however, heads were already being counted. It was immediately obvious to professional politicians like William Eden[4] that, in spite of Shelburne's victory in July, his ministry was far from secure. The House of Commons was divided in its loyalties between Fox, North and Shelburne, any two of whom could command a majority, but none of whom could stand alone. On reviewing this situation, both Eden and Loughborough,[5] who relied very heavily on their friendship with George North,[6] agreed, within a fortnight of the resignation, that Fox's antagonism to North was purely political, and therefore subject to changing circumstances, whereas his hostility to Shelburne was personal, lately reinvigorated, and immensely durable. As Loughborough observed 'The first thing is to reconcile Ld. North & Fox. The first, you know, is irreconcilable to no man; the second will feel his ancient resentment totally absorbed in his more recent hostility, which I think he has no other probable means of gratifying.'[7] This was a conclusion, which Eden himself had reached a few days earlier.[8] The fact that Fox is known to have visited North as early as 14 July must underline the importance of Eden and Loughborough in the early initiatives. Without being unduly cast down by the disaster of Fox's resignation they had immediately begun to explore new possibilities. Managerial competitors were left behind in the race. The speed with which Fox

[1] Duchess of Portland to Lady Ponsonby, 19 Nov. 1782; Grey MSS.

[2] Althorp to Lady Spencer, 22 Nov. 1782; Spencer MSS.

[3] *Morning Post*, 23 Nov. 1782.

[4] William Eden (1744–1814); M.P. (New Woodstock) 1744–84, (Heytesbury) 1784–93; supported North throughout American War; early advocate of the Coalition; deserted to Pitt in 1786, and undertook a number of diplomatic commissions; negotiated Eden Treaty with France, 1786; cr. Baron Auckland, 1793.

[5] Loughborough, Alexander Wedderburn, 1st Baron (1733–1805); M.P. 1761–9, 1770–80; distinguished barrister; supported North during the American War and during the Coalition; continued to support Fox until the outbreak of the French Revolution; Ld. Chanc. 1793–1801; cr. Earl Rosslyn 1801.

[6] George North (1757–1802); M.P. 1778–92; eldest son of Lord North; one of the architects of the Coalition; continued to support Fox throughout the period of the French Revolution; succeeded father as 3rd Earl of Guilford, Aug. 1792.

[7] Loughborough to W. Eden, 14 July 1782; *Journal and Correspondence of William Eden, 1st Lord Auckland*, i. 9.

[8] W. Eden to J. Beresford, 10 July 1782; W. Beresford, *The Correspondence of the Rt. Hon. John Beresford*, i. 213.

was introduced to North as a possible partner in Government testifies to the foresight of Eden and Loughborough.

No great emphasis can, however, be placed on any of the negotiations before the opening of the new session. North, Shelburne and Fox were engaged in a diplomatic *pas de trois*, which never came anywhere near political commitment. Shelburne continued to lobby individual Rockinghamites, had wisely propelled the King into an assault on North's loyalties, and had opened up another channel of communication through Jenkinson and Robinson.[1] North, courted, advised and bullied on all sides, refused to be hurried. Carlisle, however, among others, thought that Fox's case was faring better, as 'Great wagers are depending, that the Man of the People, will be prime minister by the meeting of Parliament.'[2] In fact, Fox's overtures were receiving an equally cool response. In July, Fox suggested an alliance, but North showed no interest in the proposal. In August, Fox offered an important, though not 'superintending', post, which North treated 'with great derision',[3] and by early September, he had given up all hope of an accommodation. The essential point was that North simply wanted to hold his forces together and wait. The coming peace treaty with France and America, the quality of which would reflect very much on the reputation of his own administration, forced North to wait, in order to leave open as many options as possible. To attack the peace treaty with Fox would be to invite the criticism that he was attacking the results of his own policies. To defend them with Shelburne might provoke Fox to launch impeachment proceedings against him. North had to wait for the terms of the peace, before deciding on which way it was safest to jump.

Fox was also labouring under considerable difficulties. However ready he himself might be to adjust his policies, others, whose long opposition to North might have taken a more personal nature, had to be persuaded and cajoled. The Westminster reformers, who had been a great source of strength in July, would be an obvious embarassment in any negotiations with North.[4] Portland was reported to have doubts about entering into active opposition to Shelburne's peace, and Burgoyne was even more explicit: 'The taking North & his old set into employment seems to be a thing more to be wished by than to

[1] John Robinson (1727–1802); M.P. (Westmoreland) 1764–74, (Harwich) 1774–1802; one of the most expert managers of the late C18; supported the American War, and managed elections on North's behalf; after formation of the Coalition, Robinson transferred his services to Shelburne and Pitt.

[2] B.M. Egerton MS. 2136, f. 208; Carlisle to Lisburne, 14 Aug. 1782.

[3] W. Eden to Loughborough, 22 Aug. 1782; R. Lucas, *Lord North*, i. 205–6.

[4] Add. MS. 34419 (Auckland MSS.), f. 4; Loughborough to W. Eden, 2 Aug. 1782.

be believed. It would be a stain of insult that surely no party in the nation would bear.'[1] As in July therefore, Fox was faced with the problem of educating his party. The Coalition project was a radical measure, which might well give rise to further divisions in the Whig ranks, if it were not carefully handled. After the experience of July, this was a contingency Fox could ill afford.

Without a coalition of some kind, however, Fox faced the prospect of an unspecified number of years in the political wilderness. After July 1782, North was the only possible partner. Fox therefore needed an issue, which would demonstrate to his party that an association with North was unavoidable, and which would be equally effective in convincing North that the Foxite alliance was the best means of protecting his own interests. After the failure of the Coalition initiatives during the recess, Fox came to believe that only the issue of the coming peace could meet both these considerations. The Whigs could attack the peace as the outcome of a system, which they had systematically opposed, and which they now believed was resurrected in the person of Shelburne. North could hide his own vulnerability by pleading that it was the mismanagement of the negotiations, under Shelburne's direction, which had led to such dishonourable terms. Both could justify the making of an alliance between themselves as an attempt win the improved terms, which the true political and military situation demanded.

These twin considerations made an attack on the peace terms essential, even though privately Fox was prepared to allow Shelburne considerable credit.[2] The ground was prepared in Fox's reply to the King's Speech, which was nothing less than an attempt to synthesize a justification of his own resignation with an appeal to North to safeguard his own position by opposing the terms of a dishonourable peace. America must be independent, and the grudging tones of the King's Speech reinforced Fox's protestations. The peace must be 'equitable', with France and Spain, the traditional Bourbon enemies, kept strictly in their place. This point was underlined for the country gentlemen by a jingoistic parade of horror at any suggestion that Gibraltar should be ceded to Spain. And the two points were fused by the belief that, until America was effectively separated from the Bourbons, the true strength of the English bargaining position could not be felt. To admit that, in fact, the English position was relatively strong, was an open invitation to North to undertake the defence of his own ministry, the policy of which had produced the situation then

[1] J. Burgoyne to E. Burke, 22 Nov. 1782; Wentworth Woodhouse Muniments, Burke 1.

[2] Portland to J. Burgoyne, N. D.; de Fonblanque, *Life and Corres. of J. Burgoyne*, p. 415.

under debate.[1] Benjamin Vaughan[2] was not the only one to comment on the effect of this clever synthesis, which combined self-justification with a baited hook for North.[3]

Against this background, the demand by Fox to have details of the peace articles placed before the Commons, on 18 December, which was lost by the quite extraordinary figure of 219 votes to 46, must represent an open attempt to force North to commit himself. Ostensibly concerned with a desire to clarify the American issue once more, Fox's demand was clearly designed to intimate that the terms were so bad, that Shelburne dare not lay them before the House:

> I expect support on my motion, though I do not court it. I do not indeed know whether I may calculate on the aid of the noble lord in the blue ribbon [North] seated below me, as by a strange mode of reasoning, he brings himself to vote with ministers, though he totally disagrees with them in opinion.[4]

This attempt to bully North into decisive action had been prepared at least four days before, in the full knowledge that it might very well misfire.[5]

North refused to move in any direction, and insisted that he would wait until full details were ready. His position was, however, becoming increasingly difficult, and a decision could not be postponed indefinitely. Burke was, however, pleased that the step had been taken, because, 'if it were in my Lord North's power to command our conduct whenever he thought proper to come down, and that we could not move but at his pleasure, we could never consider ourselves as an independent party'.[6] He further insisted that the voting figures were misleading, estimating that the Ministry could command 70 votes and North 150, while the Foxite Whigs were 'the strongest of all'.[6] Their poor showing was entirely due to the reluctance of members to come to Town so early in the session. Further, the vote of 18 December had not changed the underlying reality of the situation. North's followers, peculiarly unaccustomed to the harsh conditions of opposition, were very open to offers from any ministry. If North wished to prevent his influence being whittled away by offers of this kind, he would have to act soon. The same options of Fox or Shelburne remained open.

[1] Fox Speeches, ii. 96.

[2] Benjamin Vaughan (1751–1835); M.P. (Calne) 1792–6; merchant and political economist; early member of Shelburne's Bowood circle; supported both the American Colonists and the French Revolutionists; attended Champ de Mars Fete, 1790; fled to France 1794, and retired to America four years later.

[3] Vaughan to Shelburne, 15 Dec. 1782; Bowood MSS.

[4] Wheatley, ed. *Hist. and Posth. Memoirs of Sir N. Wraxall*, ii. 408.

[5] Spencer to Althorp, 14 Dec. 1782; Spencer MSS.

[6] E. Burke to J. Burgoyne, 24 Dec. 1782; T. Copeland, ed. *The Correspondence of Edmund Burke*, v. 55.

After North's decision on 18 December, nothing further could be done until the full details of the peace treaty were published. For the remainder of December and the whole of January, each of the three parties took stock of the situation, and each leader found his position far from comfortable. As Wraxall[1] and other contemporaries realized, Shelburne, in the face of Fox's implacable hostility, could only have recourse to North, but the difficulty here was that Richmond and Pitt refused to countenance such a move, and were putting out feelers to Fox on their own authority. Jenkinson thought fit to complain that 'Ld. S. assures me that He never will have any connection with C. Fox & I confess I believe Him. Mr. Pitt is very much displeased with Ld. N's last speech & this disturbs Shelburne; I have done all I can to pacify him. . . . I wish that somebody of Weight would talk to Mr. Pitt.'[2] Even with the addition of North's numbers, the loss of Richmond and Pitt could not be faced with equanimity by a politician, who hoped to hold onto at least some Whig votes. As the debate on the peace treaty drew nearer, Pitt's insistence on an appeal to Fox became more pressing.[3] Fox was equally embarrassed by doubt in his own party about the prospect and value of an alliance with North. Portland was the most important member of this group and the most reluctant.[4] Finally, North's position was the most difficult of all. As the Duchess of Portland[5] pointed out, 'Ld. North did appear to be very strong in the House of Commons, but it hardly can be called actual Strength, his Support is made up of all the Shabby people, who will be just as ready to leave him as to go with him, which I daresay he well knows to be the case.'[6] The demand for some kind of clear decision was therefore great. Once the terms of the peace were published and were considered generally inadequate, North had no choice but to choose Fox. To join Shelburne, in defence of such a treaty, would by implication damn his own ministry. It would also conjure up the prospect of a Fox–Pitt opposition party, which might well embark on an impeachment. Both Wraxall and Loughborough had come to this conclusion about North's decision before the beginning of February.

[1] Sir Nathaniel Wraxall (1751–1831); M.P. (Hindon) 1780–84, (Ludgershall) 1784–90, (Wallingford) 1790–4; supported the Court party throughout his career; author of an important series of memoirs; created a baronet 1813.

[2] Jenkinson to W. Adam, 4 Jan. 1783; *Mems. and Corres. of C. J. Fox*, ii. 30.

[3] W. Pitt to Shelburne, 1 Feb. 1783; Bowood MSS.

[4] Portland to E. Burke, 11 Jan. 1783; Wentworth Woodhouse Muniments, Burke 1.

[5] Duchess of Portland (1750–94), Dorothy, dau. of William, 4th Duke of Devonshire; married 3rd Duke of Portland, 1766; actively shared all her husband's political prejudices.

[6] Duchess of Portland to Mrs. Ponsonby, 20 Jan. 1783; Grey MSS.

After the full terms of the peace treaty were presented to Parliament on 27 January, the round of negotiations began again. The points, made by contemporaries to justify their belief in the inevitability of a North–Fox understanding, injected a despairing urgency into Shelburne's activities. Negotiating with both Fox and North at the same time, he was forced to keep his contacts with the latter a secret from Pitt, and to work only through Jenkinson.[1] As the vote on the peace drew nearer, the terms offered to North became more and more liberal, ending in the promise of a dukedom and the Lord Presidency of the Council. Similarly, when North's concern for the fate of the Loyalists in America suggested that he was moving towards Fox and opposition, Shelburne at last obtained George III's grudging consent to open negotiations with the Whigs. On 10 February, Pitt, Fox, Portland and Thomas Townshend met in the Prince's Chamber of the House of Commons for a brief rehearsal of their views.[2] It was short and to the point. Fox insisted that no accommodation was possible while Shelburne remained at the Treasury, and Pitt refused to give his leader up. George III was delighted at this outcome: 'I am not in the least surprized at Mr. Pitt's interview with Mr. Fox having ended as abruptly as the hastiness and impoliteness of the latter would naturally lead one to expect.'[3] Such remarks were, however, of little assistance to a minister desperately trying to create a Parliamentary majority. Fox's truculence and North's continued hesitation seemed to indicate that the predictions of Wraxall and Loughborough were about to be fulfilled.

The final understanding between North and Fox, however, was not the outcome of long and detailed negotiations, but the hurried association of two men, who were frightened of finding themselves alone in opposition. Only a week before the final interview with North, Fox had confided to Grafton that 'he felt the greatest objections to joining Ld. North and his friends; & yet perhaps it was best [but] thought it could not last long'.[4] The makeshift origins of the Coalition are admirably set out in a long memorandum begun by William Adam on the day after the final Fox–North interview, 'while the facts are fresh in my Memory'.[5] On 12 February 1783, Adam had a long meeting with Dundas, whose aim was clearly to blackmail North into supporting the peace treaty by calling up all the possibilities, of which North was most afraid. Dundas insisted that, when the Address was brought forward, North had to offer his 'compleat

[1] W. Grenville to Temple, 6 Feb. 1783; Buckingham and Chandos, i. 142.
[2] *Morning Herald*, 12 Feb. 1783.
[3] George III to Shelburne, 11 Feb. 1783; Bowood MSS.
[4] Anson, *Memoirs of the Third Duke of Grafton*, p. 353.
[5] *Mems. and Corres. of C. J. Fox*, ii. 31–4.

support', in order 'to enable Ld. S. to overcome the prejudices of the others and that in that way he was sure that at the End of the Session of Parliament Ld. N. & his friends must be br^{gt} in in a respectable manner'.[1]

Vague promises for the future were underlined by growing threats. According to Dundas, Shelburne, after releasing both himself and Pitt from all personal loyalties, had begun to express a wish to retire. He [Shelburne] 'then said Fox & the D. of Portland must make up a Govt with Pit for I will not hear of Pit's high notions any more of forming no Govt but where I make a part'.[2] Dundas, well knowing North's weaknesses, underlined his point by saying that 'the Event will be a Government of Fox & Pit with the Rockinghams & all Lord S's party except himself. that they will dissolve Parlt. and there will be an end of Ld. North. That I see no means of preventing this but a support of the Address in which the difficulties will be got over.'[2] It was this highly melodramatic and frightening story, frequently repeated and liberally illustrated by parable, which Adam reported to North.

North had no immediate cause for alarm, however, because on the morning of the 13 February, Fox reported to North via Adam the breakdown of his negotiations with Pitt. The latter was determined to stand by Shelburne, thereby presenting an insuperable obstacle to any accommodation. As long as these two were prised apart, North still had room to manoeuvre. Later the same day, the situation changed dramatically. Lord Surrey[3] sent a message to North with the alarming news that Pitt's determination to stand by Shelburne was weakening: 'It was in consequence of this understood that Pitt wd. return to Fox with a proposal on this new footing.'[4] Whatever the truth of this report, its effect on North was decisive. He called Adam into the Speaker's Room in the House of Commons, and insisted that 'it would be necessary to prevent the threatened junction of Fox and Pit to avail himself of Mr Fox's communication'.[4]

Both North and Adam dined with Dundas that same evening. The Lord Advocate joyfully confirmed their worst fears, clearly in the belief that this would commit North to supporting Shelburne. In this, his plan badly misfired. So great was the panic engendered in North, that the Advocate's pessimism drove him straight into the arms of Fox. This decision was taken that evening at a meeting

[1] *Mems. and Corres. of C. J. Fox*, ii. 31–4.

[2] ibid.

[3] Norfolk, Charles Howard, 11th Duke (1746–1815); M.P. (Carlisle) 1780–6; opposed American War and remained with Shelburne in July 1782; transferred loyalty to Fox in Mar. 1783, and continued to support him until his death; succeeded father as 11th Duke of Norfolk, Oct. 1786.

[4] *Mems. and Corres. of C. J. Fox*, ii. 35.

attended by North, his son George, Adam, and Charles Townshend.[1] They were frightened and were compelled to act without delay. Fox was therefore not willingly accepted as a partner in government, but was seen as a political threat, which had to be neutralized by association.

Even on 14 February, however, the situation was still remarkably fluid. The Advocate went to North, in order to show him the terms of the Address before it was officially presented to Parliament. He clearly had every hope that North would support it. Only when met with the bland inquiry of whether the document had also been shown to Fox and Portland did Dundas realize that his blackmail attempt had miscarried, and he 'then observed that North's conduct had ruined everything that otherwise would have turned out well'.[2] At two o'clock, Fox and North met by appointment. Although both men later reported themselves satisfied with the encounter, the meeting was marked by postponed decisions and the need for a very liberal interpretation by both sides of what was actually said.

The most obvious example of this hesitancy concerned Parliamentary reform. According to North's version of the meeting, Fox agreed to support reform once more, but would then abstain from any further involvement in the campaign;[2] whereas Adam's version insists that Fox held himself 'pledged' on the issue, although prepared to admit that many of his friends were against the idea. In the most general terms, they agreed that the influence of the Crown had been curtailed enough, but also that any administration should govern independently of the king. In a Whig context, this was almost a contradiction in terms, and would therefore rely heavily, for its acceptability, on interpretation and the emphasizing of one part rather than another. No agreement was reached on the fate of Jenkinson, Stormont[3] and Thurlow, all of whom North wished to retain and Fox to reject. Nor was there any agreement on who should go to the Treasury. The important decision to oppose the Address jointly was taken, but the methods and tactics to be employed were not touched upon. This was quite clearly the conversation of two men driven into association through necessity rather than inclination. North won security and Fox the intellectual leadership

[1] Charles Townshend (1728–1810); M.P. (Gt. Yarmouth) 1756–84, 1790–96; friend and supporter of North and the American War; very strongly in favour of Coalition; lost control of Yarmouth in 1784, but regained it in the election of 1790; broke with Fox over the French Revolution; cr. Baron Bayning, 1797.

[2] Lord Guilford, Memorandum, N.D.; I. R. Christie, *Wilkes, Wyvill and Reform*, p. 177.

[3] Stormont, David Murray, 7th Viscount (1727–96); Scottish representative Peer 1754–93; supported American War; succeeded uncle as 2nd Earl of Mansfield, 1793.

of an administration without the irritating rivalry of Pitt. The details of Coalition had to be worked out under pressure from these two exigencies.

For two days, the details of the agreement, necessarily left vague in the interview between Fox and North, were thrashed out, but even so severe difficulties were experienced. It was not until 16 February that Portland's proposed appointment to the Treasury was accepted by North, and it was not until 4 a.m. the next day, on which the vital debate was due to start, that all outstanding issues were settled.[1] The Coalition had to be explained carefully to both the contracting parties. The fact that Shelburne was eventually only defeated by 16 votes suggests that the rank and file were just as unhappy about the arrangement as their leaders had been. On the day before the debate, for example, the Foxites refused to allow North to move the opposition amendments and insisted on Lord John Cavendish.[2] This dilemma was only resolved by Fox doing his utmost to bring about a compromise solution, acceptable to both sides.

In the actual debate, on 17 February, Fox roundly singled out the terms of the peace as the issue which might well throw himself and North together, although he consistently denied that any formal understanding had in fact been entered into. The Coalition was founded in an attack on Shelburne's treaty, and thereby unhappily committed itself to securing better terms. For the moment, however, Fox could indulge in broad protestations: 'You call for peace, says the noble person, you urge the necessity of peace, you insist on peace; then peace you shall have, but such a peace that you shall sicken at its very name.'[3] Next day, Shelburne duly went down to defeat, but by a surprisingly small margin, considering the theoretical strength of the Coalition forces. Far from being a Coalition of principle aimed only at bringing down Shelburne's system, the connection between North and Fox was a hastily arranged and loosely worded understanding, entered into reluctantly by men who saw no other way of safeguarding their political position.

Writing long after the event, Lord John Townshend[4] insisted that until the India Bill controversy came up, the point and value of the Coalition had been vindicated in the eyes of the political nation, and

[1] Wheatley, *Posth. and Hist. Memoirs of Sir N. Wraxall*, ii. 420.

[2] Lord John Cavendish (1732–96); M.P. 1754–84, 1794–6; the most able and influential member of the Cavendish family; firmly attached to the Rockinghams; Chanc. of the Excheq. Mar.–July 1782 and Apr.–Dec. 1783; broke with Fox on the issue of the French Revolution.

[3] Lord J. Russell, *The Life and Times of Charles James Fox*, i. 352.

[4] Lord John Townshend (1757–1833); M.P. (Camb. Univ.) 1780–4; (Westminster) 1788–90 (Knaresborough) 1793–1818; supported Fox throughout his career; enjoyed the reputation of being a playwright and poet of note.

pointed quite sensibly to the unopposed returns of Fox and Cavendish at Westminster and York, in April 1783, as proof of this.[1] For George III, 'the extraordinary and never-to-be forgot vote of February 1783'[2] was the origin of all iniquity. In fact, however, it was neither of these things. Principle was involved only to the extent that Fox now associated Shelburne with that system of government, which he had consistently opposed since 1774. North's qualms about the Loyalists were probably equally sincere. These points alone, however, would not explain their association. For North, Fox's friendship laid forever the ghost of impeachment proceedings, and also removed the fear that his followers, uncomfortably dependent upon Treasury and Admiralty Boroughs, would desert in the wastes of opposition. The prospect of opposition was hardly more attractive to Fox, but, joined to this very real consideration, was the knowledge that North's support, however incongruous, implied that he would once again be free to lead an assault on royal influence, in that there was never any doubt that Fox would be the driving force behind the new arrangement. When Shelburne fell, the Coalition was still a very loose association subject to great strain, but it was a workable relationship, because both men had much to gain from it. As Wraxall observed, 'The proscription of Ld. North by Pitt & Ld. Shelburne by Fox of necessity drove the two excluded ministers into each other's arms . . . & impelled them . . . only to look forward to the joint possession of power.'[3]

[1] Lord J. Townshend to Holland, 23 June 1830; *Mems. and Corres. of C. J. Fox*, ii. 24.

[2] Add. MS. 47559 (Fox Papers), f. 91; George III to Fox, 19 June 1783.

[3] Wheatley, *Hist. and Posth. Memoirs of Sir N. Wraxall*, ii. 420.

II

THE COALITION ADMINISTRATION, FEBRUARY 1783–MARCH 1784

THE Coalition government was essentially a foundling administration conceived out of necessity rather than affection. Neither parent was entirely happy with what had been created, and, even after the vote on 18 February, there was considerable doubt whether the Coalition would survive at all. A leading member of the Grenville family was not the only ministerialist to believe that this opposition onslaught would peter out in bickering and mutual abuse: 'The coalition bet'n Ld. North & Fox is very far from being formed: so far indeed, that I know they have differed, not only on loaves & fishes, but on the subject of high & responsible office, & particularly about the Treasury itself, which was not settled this morning.'[1] If Grenville could have seen contemporary Whig correspondence, he would have realized just how near the mark this judgement was. The long interregnum, which separated the fall of Shelburne and the entry of the Coalition into office, certainly gave the King the opportunity of looking round for a viable alternative, but it also suggests that George entertained the very real hope that, given time, the Coalition would founder under the pressure of its internal inconsistencies.

One of the major difficulties about what Grenville called 'this unnatural alliance'[2] was that North was proving more and more troublesome. Once the tension of early February had been relieved, North had coolly to reflect that he then found himself in opposition to the King's Ministers, and in alliance with a man whose antipathy to the Court was systematic and enduring. Adam specifically contrasted the delight of Loughborough, for whom the prospect of office was enough, with the gloom of North, who was not at all clear that the right course had been adopted. North had been hurried into the Coalition out of fear, and now had leisure to repent. The vote of 18 February was now a fact, but this in no way implied that he faced his new allies with pleasure or confidence. Throughout the remainder of February and for much of March, close political friends had to be

[1] W. Grenville to Temple, 19 Feb. 1783; Buckingham and Chandos, i. 157.

[2] R. Fitzpatrick to Upper Ossory, 22 Feb. 1783; *Mems. and Corres. of C. J. Fox*, ii. 19.

called in from time to time to remind him that the choice made had been the only one open to them in February, and that it was now essential to make the Coalition work, in order to avoid the possibility of political extinction.[1]

The other immediate problem facing Fox was that of filling the several offices of the new administration. This was always a delicate operation in the eighteenth century, but the fragile nature of the Coalition demanded unusual skill and tact in the dispensation of patronage. The imprecise nature of the Fox–North conversation on 14 February had not made things easier. Everything had been postponed and nothing decided. When final statements had to be made about such individuals as Thurlow and Stormont, the Coalition almost fell apart. Fox reported to Grafton that, when North on his own initiative offered the Presidency of the Council to Stormont, all his powers of persuasion had to be called in to pacify Portland.[2] According to Adam, the last two weeks in February were taken up in wrangles of this kind. Significantly, the leaders of the two wings of the Coalition never met formally. All business was conducted through the intermediaries of George North and Eden. In consequence, many points of detail remained a long time in a state of contention. This was simply the price to be paid for the conscious vagueness of intention, which had marked the formation of the Coalition, and which was a condition of taking united action on 17 February at all. Such reserve and hesitation, however, must have gone far to support the belief among supporters of the Court that the Coalition would never be able to transform itself into a viable administration.[3]

Similar obstacles were encountered when the lower offices of state came under review. In this case, the question was not centred on personalities but on numbers. Especially after the pruning of offices, which the Whigs themselves had undertaken in the previous year, there were simply too many applicants for the posts available. The Northite connection was known to contain an unusually high number of people, who, after thirteen years in support of the administration, were inclined to associate political involvement with the holding of office. Edmund Burke was well aware that this would cause considerable embarrassment:

> The party I act with, if they should be called into the King's service, will come to an establishment reduced by more than forty considerable employments; and the junction with a party the most numerous, and of some of the most weighty people in the kingdom, has made more claims than the old

[1] Add. MS. 34419, f. 113; W. Eden to North, 25 Feb. 1783.

[2] Anson, *Memoirs of the Duke of Grafton*, p. 375. 21 Feb. 1783.

[3] *Morning Herald*, 4 Mar. 1783.

establishment could satisfy. But then, without that junction, they could have no chance of coming in at all.[1]

This protracted wrangling over places inevitably meant that the Whigs themselves were very grateful for the breathing space afforded them by George III, for, while he looked for an alternative administration, they had time to transform themselves into a cohesive political connection. A summons to form a government at any time in February would have been gravely embarrassing.

This operation was not achieved painlessly, however, and, if Atkinson reported Lord Surrey's remarks correctly, Fox once again had to lead on his own terms, in the hope that the bulk of the Whig party would approve his actions later: 'Mr. Fox did not fully inform his own party of the true conditions entered into with Ld. North, and that the divided Cabinet was treated by them as an incroachment, and not as part of the bargain.'[2] Much of the indignation later expended on the Coalition was born of the secrecy in which these negotiations were carried on. Fox had to hold the Coalition together by whatever methods he could, and hope that his party would eventually understand. Much irritation was, however, also produced by the unavoidable fact that not all those with claims on the generosity of the partners in the Coalition could be accommodated. The Coalition was born of necessity, and had to run the risk of incurring the enmity of injured idealists and disappointed place-seekers.

The most critical period for the Coalition was that between the two divisions on Shelburne's peace proposals, on 18 and 21 February.[3] At the height of this crisis, the *Morning Herald* could, with plausibility, report that all ideas of coalition had been abandoned.[4] During these three days, Fox and Lord John Cavendish worked hard to find a formula, on which both wings of the Coalition could support a motion to reject the Peace out of hand.[5] On the morning of the Debate itself, Fox had to check an attempt by Jack Robinson to frighten North into supporting Shelburne. Robinson insisted that large numbers of North's friends were about to desert him, and that his political influence would be at an end, unless he supported the Peace. Eden was commissioned to take a canvass of the Northites, who were found to be largely firm. Only on the reiteration of these

[1] E. Burke to Jos. Bullock, 3 Mar. 1783; Earl Fitzwilliam, ed. *The Correspondence of Edmund Burke*, iii. 12–15.

[2] R. Atkinson to J. Robinson, 25 Mar. 1783; H.M.C. *Abergavenny MSS*. x. 6, p. 59.

[3] On 18 Feb. Shelburne was defeated by 224 to 208; 3 days later the margin was 207–190.

[4] *Morning Herald*, 20 Feb. 1783.

[5] J. Norris, *Shelburne and Reform*, p. 266, 21 Feb. 1783.

findings by three of his closest associates was North finally prepared to commit himself to the overthrow of Shelburne. The confidence, with which Fox enunciated his belief that a patriotic Coalition had been formed to save the country from being entirely despoiled by France and Spain, gave no indication of the heavy hours of cajoling and persuasion, which alone had made such a statement possible. Fox denied all interest in office in the fulfilment of a patriotic duty: 'If ever the situation of the country required a coalition of parties that could preserve the vigour of the state from debility, it is that of the present.'[1] Even so, the motion was only carried by 17. The Coalition was just vindicated, but the issue was close.

From 24 February to 2 April, the King did everything in his power to avoid recruiting Fox and North into his service. If the Coalition was unsure of itself, its reception in the Closet hardly strengthened its self-confidence. Every possible alternative was investigated,[2] in order, as Lord Palmerston understood, 'to make an administration without Charles Fox'.[3] The King's aversion to Fox, on both political and personal grounds, had been made very apparent in the coalition negotiations of 1780,[4] and the events of 1782–3 had done nothing to heal the breach. The long period of waiting imposed on the Whigs by George III was therefore prompted by a desire to frustrate the success of a man, whose career the King regarded as a political threat and a personal insult. On at least three occasions, North was subjected to personal appeals by the King, in an attempt to prise him away from his new associates. All the claims on loyalty, which had held North steady through the American War, were now reiterated and reinforced.[5] North, however, insisted that no arrangement could be made without Fox and the Whigs. This firmness argues less a sense of satisfaction with the Coalition, however, than a determination on North's part to take that role in politics which would guarantee that all his fears of proscription and impeachment would be allayed. The impregnable Coalition majority in the House of Commons seemed to secure this, and gave North the strength to stand up to the King.

George therefore had to hope that the partners in the Coalition would quarrel amongst themselves, and, as has been suggested above, there were good grounds for expecting this outcome. Patronage wrangles were continually providing causes of friction within the Coalition and also a steady stream of malcontents, who might be

[1] *Fox Speeches*, ii. 128 seq.

[2] Add. MS. 47582, f. 164; Fitzpatrick's Memorandum, Feb./Mar. 1783.

[3] B. Connell, *Portrait of a Whig Peer*, p. 134.

[4] I. R. Christie, 'The Marquis of Rockingham and Lord North's Offer of a Coalition', *E.H.R.* lxiv (1954), 399.

[5] George III to Thurlow, 3 Mar. 1783; Fortescue, vi. 258.

open to royal offers. By April, the Coalition was reduced to the rough expedient of providing for only one member of every family with claims upon them.[1] Between 18 and 21 March, the King's hopes were almost realised. Fox's demands that all the major offices of state should be distributed by Whig nomination, a very natural response after the experience of Thurlow's and Shelburne's activities in the second Rockingham administration, formed an obstacle at which North baulked. William Grenville[2] happily reported on 18 March that the Coalition had broken up on this issue.[3] Four days of persuasion were required to bring North to see that such demands were unavoidable, if the risks taken by the Rockingham administration were not to be run again. When both his hopes of detaching North from the Coalition and his expectations that the understanding would break up in mutual recrimination proved vain, George capitulated. Fox was, however, well aware that this withdrawal was tactical rather than absolute: 'The K. does it de la plus mauvaise grâce possible' he wrote to Fitzpatrick; 'and there are several unsatisfactory circumstances . . . I think this had better not be said, I mean the unsatisfactory part of it.'[4] Given the right issue on which to move, there could be no doubt that the King would counterattack.

George III was not the only person to have doubts about the Coalition. Once again, an action, which Fox took very much on his own initiative and without consultation, came under attack from certain sections of the Whig party. For the high-minded, Fox's standing as the disinterested champion of reform was severely undermined. Sir Samuel Romilly thought it 'a scandalous alliance'.[5] Sir George Savile[6] went further, and turned on Fox's belief that his relations with North should be governed by the maxim 'amicitiae sempiternae, inimicitiae breves':

What have we to do with friendships and enmities? It is indecent to talk of them. Charles Fox's own natural moral sense, would have made him not hazard such an expression, I am sure, but that all (even pretence of) *public feeling*, is laid aside; and it is so habitually understood and felt, that all save *private* feelings are a *sham;* that, neither C. Fox nor the public, are at all

[1] G. Martelli, *Life of John Montagu, 4th Earl of Sandwich*, p. 282.

[2] William Grenville (1759–1834); M.P. (Buckingham) 1782–4, (Bucks.) 1784–90; supported the younger Pitt until 1801; joined Fox on the issue of Catholic Emancipation and co-operated in the All Talents Ministry, 1806–7; cr. Baron Grenville 1790.

[3] W. Grenville to Temple, 21 Mar. 1783; Buckingham and Chandos, i. 202.

[4] Add. MS. 47580, f. 124; Fox to Fitzpatrick ? 1783.

[5] Sir S. Romilly to Rev. J. Roget, 21 Mar. 1783; Romilly, *Memoirs*, i. 269.

[6] Sir G. Savile (1726–84); 8th baronet; M.P. (Yorkshire) 1759–83; loosely associated with the Rockinghams, but deeply respected leader of the country gentlemen; joined Wyvill in pressing for economical and Parliamentary reform.

startled, at an expression, which, in private life, would make you kick that man downstairs, who gravely told you that *he* had settled to be *friends with*, and trust some of your concerns to, a man who had *cheated* you *as long as he could cheat you;* but, as that was utterly at an end (Viz. because he could cheat you no longer) he, for his part, bore no malice.[1]

Richard Price[2] was astonished that 'any parties could have been so proffligate',[3] and sadly recorded the end of any serious attempts at reform.

Fox's loss of stature among the reformers was serious enough, but it would be wrong to pre-date the moral indignation at the formation of the Coalition, which seems to be the creation of the propaganda campaign of the 1784 election. In February 1783, there is little sign of this. Fox and Lord John Cavendish were re-elected unopposed at Westminster and York, and Richard Atkinson[4] reported that the only threat to the Coalition was its internal difficulties.[5] Neither of these points would indicate that there was a deep fund of moral indignation, on which Fox's opponents could draw. Nor do the extant division lists support the thesis that the formation of the Coalition was greeted with moral outrage. Foxite losses were heaviest in July 1782, and North lost votes primarily between November 1783 and March 1784, implying that his supporters were prepared to desert the Coalition only when it was effectively challenged by the Crown, but were perfectly happy to follow it, while it seemed to have a reasonable chance of survival. In the pamphlet war of 1784, the moral turpitude of the Coalition was a recurrent theme, and one much emphasized by the Pittites, but it is difficult to demonstrate that indignation was an important factor in February 1783, except in the consciences of the idealists.

Only in the context of Westminster was the reforming interest of paramount importance to Fox, and here the quasi-moral implications of the Coalition might have a serious effect. On 6 March, a meeting of the Electors of Westminster[6] took place at the Shakespeare Tavern, at which the divisions appearing in the reforming ranks became

[1] Sir G. Savile to David Hartley, N.D.; R. Warner, *Literary Recollections*, ii. 242.

[2] Richard Price (1723–91); leading Nonconformist divine and moral philosopher; Member of the Bowood circle; opposed American War but broke with Fox over Coalition and attached himself even more firmly to Shelburne.

[3] R. Price to Shelburne, 24 Feb. 1783; Bowood MSS.

[4] Richard Atkinson (1738–85); M.P. (New Romney) 1784–5; W. India Merchantman and Govt. contractor during the American War; as a director of the East India Co., helped to defeat Fox's India Bill; assisted Robinson in management of the 1784 election.

[5] Add. MS. 37835 (Robinson MSS.), f. 202; R. Atkinson to J. Robinson, 21 Mar. 1783.

[6] *Morning Herald*, 8 Mar. 1783.

distressingly plain. Dr. Jebb 'intreated him [Fox], with much seriousness, not to form any coalition with such men, as it must be ruinous to his fair name, and destructive of the system, which, he sincerely believed, it was his intention to support'.[1] Fox in reply was forced to avoid the charge that his association with North had gravely injured the prospect of reform, by lamely pointing out that his opponents were just as much a coalition of groups and just as divided on the issue of reform.[2] Just as the resignation issue of July 1782 had led to the challenge of the Firm and Free Club in Westminster, so the Coalition engendered new divisions. On 7 April, Fox was re-elected for Westminster, but, as Romilly's report indicates, his passage was far from easy: 'The populace received him [Fox] with hisses, hooting, and every other mark of displeasure; he attempted to speak to them several times, but to no purpose'.[3] Fox himself was not unduly disturbed by this reception, being convinced that the clamour 'came not from the electors but from the lowest classes of society'.[4] There seems to have been good reason for this confidence. Fox was returned unopposed in spite of Romilly's wish that a worthy challenger could be found.[5] None could be found. If there had been a chance of giving Fox a hard fight, and thereby discrediting the infant administration at the outset, it would have been an opportunity, of which the opponents of Fox, led by the King, would certainly have taken advantage. As it was, Fox escaped with a few hisses and hoots. His standing in Westminster was shaken, but in no way undermined.

The importance of the Coalition lies not in cries of moral indignation, but in its function of underpinning the party divisions of the later 1780s and, when associated with the disruption caused by the India Bill, of giving a spur to the development of the concept of party in English politics. The more perceptive were aware that the old loyalties and divisions had somehow been thrown into the melting pot, and were no longer relevant. Not all, however, drew the right conclusions from this. For Lord Charlemont,[6] the new loyalties stemmed simply from yet another schism in the Whig ranks. He referred to the Coalition as 'the strange, and certainly unnatural coalition between Mr. Fox and Lord North, by which, though the Shelburne administration was overturned, a fatal wound was given

[1] J. Disney, *The Works of John Jebb*, i. 180.

[2] I. Christie, *Wilkes, Wyvill and Reform*, p. 178.

[3] Sir S. Romilly to Rev. J. Roget, 11 Apr. 1783; Romily, *Memoirs*, i. 273.

[4] *London Chronicle*, 5–8 Apr. 1783.

[5] Sir S. Romilly to Rev. J. Roget, 11 Apr. 1783; Romilly, *Memoirs*, i. 273.

[6] Charlemont, James Caulfield, 1st Earl (1728–99); Irish Whig leader; cr. Earl of Charlemont in 1763; closely connected with Irish nationalism; C.-in-C. Volunteer Army of Ireland, 1779.

to the Whig interest by dividing its principle members'.[1] Horace Walpole was prepared to take the matter further, and his letters of March 1783 refer again and again to the way old loyalties have been broken down: 'As to who are or shall be ministers, I care very little. All parties are confounded and intermixed, without being reconciled. My belief is, that new distinctions will arise, and, after some scene of anarchy, a new era.'[2] This is not, however, a thought, which gave Walpole pleasure. Fox was accused of removing the historical raison d'être of the Whig party by allying with North, who epitomized for many Whigs that system of royal influence, against which they had been fighting for so long. Walpole could not believe that a serious blow could be delivered against Court influence by the Coalition, when one of the partners had for so long been a close adviser of the King. Fox had shifted the ground of Whiggery from the vantage point of its old principles for the sake of a short-term and compromising victory. By way of conclusion, Walpole allowed himself the title of 'the last unadulterated Whig in England'.[2]

Walpole was right in seeing the events of 1783 as a watershed, but his conclusions were unduly pessimistic. In the wrangles of this and the succeeding year, Fox, in his demands on the King, was able to polarize loyalties between the Commons and the Crown, which gave a new impetus to the development of party structure and organization in the 1780s.[3] Fox, in his claims on behalf of the legislature and a prospective Whig cabinet, was redefining the aims of Whiggery in an entirely relevant sense, and, in so doing, created an opposition movement in the 1780s, the cohesion of which was only broken by the full weight of the French Revolution. Commentators writing much later and with the benefit of hindsight had no difficulty in seeing the issues presented by the Coalition and the India Bill as the bases of the political system as they knew it. Thomas Paine, although fully subscribing to the idea that the Coalition was from the start covered in moral opprobrium, a story which had become current by 1791 (when *The Rights of Man* was written), emphasizes the importance of these two years:

> The indignation at the Coalition so effectually superseded the indignation against the Court as to extinguish it, and without any change of principles on the part of the Court, the same people, who had reprobated its despotism united with it to revenge themselves on the Coalition Parliament.[4]

[1] Journal of Lord Charlemont, Feb. 1783; H.M.C. *Charlemont* I, 12 x, p. 100.

[2] H. Walpole to Sir H. Mann, 13 Mar. 1783; Mrs. P. Toynbee, ed. *The Letters of Horace Walpole*, xii. 418–22.

[3] D. Ginter, 'The Financing of the Whig Party Organization 1783–1793', *A.H.R.* lxxi (1966.)

[4] T. Paine, *The Rights of Man* (London, 1791), p. 116.

Croker, writing in 1824, went further, and saw the career of the Coalition as the starting point of the party system as he knew it:

> Newcastle, the elder Pitt, and Fox, [Henry] the Grenvilles, Lord Bute, and all their underlings . . . conducted their administration by a balance of factions, and the alternate purchase and dismissal of little political coteries. The fate of the Coalition was the deathblow of that system.[1]

Far from destroying the Whigs as Walpole imagined, the formation of the Coalition and its struggles with the Crown gave that party a cohesion, which it had never before enjoyed. It confirmed the experiences of 1765–6. The problem therefore arises of how far Fox, in the confusion and panic surrounding the formation of the Coalition, was in any way consciously redirecting the course of Whiggery.

On a superficial level, Fox simply gave himself up to the delight engendered by the defeat of Shelburne. After the trials and delays of the preceding year, the Whigs had finally succeeded in establishing themselves in what looked like an impregnable political position. Fox's court at Brooks's took on a new gaiety, which was sarcastically described by George Selwyn; 'I own that to see Charles closeted every instant at Brooks' by one or the other, so that he can neither punt nor deal for a quarter of an hour, but is obliged to give an audience . . . is a scene "la plus parfaitement comique qu'on puisse imaginer", and to nobody it seems more ruisible than to Charles himself.'[2] Invitation cards were sent round advertising a performance of *The Alchemist*, in which all the eminent opponents of the Whigs were given suitably unfortunate parts. Pitt led the cast as the Angry Boy, an epithet Sheridan was to use to considerable effect in the Commons, Lord Shelburne was to play Subtle and the Lord Advocate Doll Common.[3] The Court party seemed to have lost so badly, that its claims could be reduced to ridicule.

Beneath the lightheartedness, however, there are signs that Fox was aware that new claims for party had been made, which would have considerable constitutional importance. In the set-piece debates between Fox and Pitt between December 1783 and March 1784, this theme would be fully elaborated, but the outlines of Fox's case had been drawn much earlier. Fox is reported at the time to have come very near Burke's vindication of party as a legitimate instrument of politics, and to have said that 'Our party is formed on the principle of Confederacy; ought we not, then, to confederate with him who can give us the greatest strength? And who can give us greater strength

[1] J. Croker to Liverpool, 31 Oct. 1824; L. J. Jennings, *The Croker Papers*, i. 272.
[2] Lord E. Fitzmaurice, *Life of William, Earl of Shelburne*, ii. 231.
[3] Palmerston MSS. 1 Mar. 1783 (unfoliated).

than Lord North.'[1] Such an eminently practical approach to politics was reinforced by the evidence of Fitzpatrick, to whom Fox said, referring to the Coalition, 'that nothing but success can justify it'.[2] Fox was well aware that he had stepped outside the accepted canons of political life, in attempting, on the strength of a majority in the House of Commons, both to unseat a Minister and to claim to nominate his successors. It was possible to explain the Coalition away by reference to earlier combinations of political groups, but Lady Sarah Napier's sophistries do less than justice to the novelty of the situation; 'The Ministerial Party abuse Charles pis que prendre for joining with Lord North, and they won't admit that to follow or lead Lord North are two very different things. . . . Why should it be a crying sin in Charles to do what every other Politician does for ever?'[3] The answer was that Fox had joined together two groups, which the political world believed God had very firmly put asunder. This made defences of the Coalition based on an appeal to principle hard to sustain. The unprecedented demands made of the King with regard to Whig nomination of Cabinet offices confirmed this opinion. As Fox pointed out, the Coalition, being a new phenomenon in eighteenth-century politics, would justify itself only by being effective. The slightest faltering would call down on its head a torrent of anger and irritation. Fox gambled on a majority in the House of Commons and the cohesion of his party.

Fox's public defence of the Coalition began badly, in that he simply brought out the clichés, which were always available to those who wished to veil an assault on the executive. On 24 March, Fox, in seconding Coke's resolution asking for the formation of a new Ministry, insisted that this move represented criticism of the King's former ministers and not of George himself.[4] Even Fox was not satisfied with this, and a week later he changed his ground. On this occasion, Fox explained that 'The motives which had induced him to agree to the coalition . . . were, that nothing but a coalition of party could remove the political obstruction given to the business of the state.'[5] This again was not very credible, in that the Coalition, in challenging the executive with the authority of the legislature, was as much the cause of the hiatus in government as a response to it. Finally on 25 April, Fox was compelled by Pitt's probing to fall back directly on the authority of the House of Commons. This debate

[1] J. Nicholls, *Reflexions and Recollections . . . on the Reign of G III*, i. 172.

[2] R. Fitzpatrick to Upper Ossory, 18 Feb. 1783; *Mems. and Corres. of C. J. Fox*, ii. 16.

[3] Lady S. Napier to Mrs. Connolly, Mar. 1783; Bunbury MSS., E 18/750/2, f. 21.

[4] *Fox Speeches*, ii. 150; 24 Mar. 1783.

[5] *Parl. Hist.* xxiii. 707; 31 Mar. 1783.

was a dress rehearsal for the encounters of nine months later, when Fox would set out unequivocally his defence solely in terms of acting on the authority of the Lower House, from which there was no higher court of appeal. In April 1783, Fox had reached an interesting half-way stage in his progression to this final defence. In reply to Pitt, who argued that the only right enjoyed by the House of Commons with regard to Ministers was to institute punishment proceedings from time to time, Fox insisted that this very right of punishing implied also the right to take some part in the choosing of Ministers, if only to the extent that, by successfully impeaching individuals, the area of royal choice was circumscribed.[1] At this stage, Fox is only claiming for the Lower House a share in the nomination of Ministers, but the change of emphasis is important. If Fox more and more relies on the authority of the Commons for ministerial advancement, his belief in party is wholly credible. The two things were intimately linked, in that the one was the instrument for achieving the desired constitutional claims of the other. For Fox, party and a majority in the Lower House had become a net for ensnaring the King. As the press reported, 'The Foxites laugh at the present opposition to their aristocratic views: their wily leader says: "they have at last taken the GREAT FISH in their net, and let him get out if he can".'[2]

This reliance on the power of the Commons and the demands which Fox made on the strength of it, were not the result of a long period of thought, but rather a direct reaction to the experience of the second Rockingham administration. In Fox's view, this ministry had been deliberately undermined from within the Cabinet by Shelburne and Thurlow. Such a risk could not be run again. Not only would the Whigs be forced to nominate the man to lead the Ministry,[3] but they would also have no choice but to demand that all the minor offices be filled according to their wishes as well. Confident of their position, the Whigs took a very high tone indeed. They refused to negotiate with the King through North, but insisted that Portland be permitted to show the King a list of his proposed Cabinet in person. Nor was George allowed to see the names suggested for minor offices, until he had formally agreed to the main Cabinet proposals. As Atkinson noted: 'We understand that it is *King Fox* compleatly but I have not learnt any further particulars except that the Duke of Portland refuses to shew a List or send one by Lord North. to the King, deeming it *unfit* that he should *presume* to name a Ministry till he had had the Honour in person to receive His Majesty's Commands thereon.'[4] Part of the reason for the difficulties

[1] *Parl. Hist.* xxiii. 794; 25 Apr. 1783. [2] *Morning Herald*, 26 Mar. 1783.
[3] R. Lucas, *Lord North, Second Earl of Guilford*, p. 231.
[4] Add. MS. 37835, f. 199; R. Atkinson to J. Robinson, 18 Mar. 1783.

with North in mid-March stemmed from the fact that he was unhappy at pressing the King so hard.[1] These demands on the Crown and the increasingly daring language in the Commons were not produced by Fox in any lightheaded manner. His experience of Shelburne's activities in the preceding summer had convinced him that confidence between a Whig Ministry and the Crown was impossible, and where he could not trust, he had to control. The King had to be tied down with the strength of party and the authority of the House of Commons. When the Coalition took office in April 1783, Fox was sure he had secured this. His mistake lay not in misinterpreting the intentions of the King, but in undervaluing his strength, tenacity and resilience.

Not all contemporaries shared Fox's confidence. The known reluctance of the King to receive Fox into government was thought by many, very reasonably, to be a fatal flaw in the Ministry's structure. Horace Walpole, writing to Lady Ossory, allowed them strength, simply because there were no alternatives: 'I am a little of your ladyship's opinion, that the new administration is not founded upon a rock; however, if they fall, I see no reason for expecting any other to be more permanent. The cards have been so thoroughly shuffled, that it will require several deals before they get into suits again.'[2] By May, the bookmakers at Brooks's were, with a nice sense of timing, giving four to one that Pitt or Temple would be in charge of the Treasury by the end of the year.[3] The smallest acquaintance with the contents of George's letters of this period would have quickly convinced these gentlemen that their odds, if anything, were too generous. The King's letters to Temple and William Grenville become almost frenzied, as the attempts to find an alternative to the Coalition proved fruitless. His determination to resist their attacks and to show them no favour is absolute. As he told Temple, 'Judge, therefore, of the uneasiness of my mind, at having been thwarted in every attempt to keep the administration of public affairs out of the hands of the most unprincipled coalition the annals of this or any other nation can equal.'[4] So great was the King's agitation, that even a paternal plea for assistance to the Prince of Wales was not ruled out.[5] Pitt was called upon again and again to release the King from the necessity of accepting the Coalition into his service,[6] and every

[1] A. F. Stewart, *The Last Journals of Horace Walpole* (London, 1910), ii. 501.

[2] H. Walpole to Lady Ossory, 17 Apr. 1783, *Letters Addressed to the Countess of Upper Ossory*, ii. 151.

[3] *Morning Herald*, 24 May 1783.

[4] George III to Temple, 1 Apr. 1783; Buckingham and Chandos, i. 218. See also W. Grenville to Temple, 17 Mar. 1783; ibid. i. 187.

[5] George III to Prince of Wales, Mar. 1783; ed. A. Aspinall, *The Correspondence of George, Prince of Wales*, i. 104.

[6] P.R.O. Pitt Papers Series 30, vol. 8, f. 7; George III to Pitt, 24 Mar. 1783.

conceivable political arrangement was tried to this end, in the six-week period between the fall of Shelburne and the recognition of Portland as master of the Treasury. Once the awful necessity of admitting the immediate invincibility of the Coalition had been accepted, the desire to abdicate was replaced in the King's mind by the cool realization that, if patiently played, the game was by no means over. The patronage difficulties of the Coalition were great, and they were hopelessly divided on all reforming issues. By bringing Shelburne down, they had committed themselves to securing better peace terms, which would not be easy, while a refusal of the King to bestow any mark of royal favour would lead to a serious questioning of the Ministry's future.[1] The King determined to make it very obvious that the Coalition ministry was not of his choosing, and to wait, with as much self-control as possible, for the moment when he would be able to rid himself of a group of men, for whom he felt an almost physical revulsion.

The Whigs were painfully aware of the King's attitude. The Duchess of Portland complained, that, during the Ministerial negotiations, the King showed 'an inveterate obstinacy to resist every endeavour on the Part of the Whigs to break the System which it has been his Constant object to Establish since he came to the Throne'.[2] Fox, himself, although fundamentally sure of the Whig's position, nevertheless consoled himself with the idea that 'he, meaning the K. will dye soon and that will be best of all'.[3] There were, however, signs, during the first month of the new Ministry's life, that continued royal truculence could bear heavily on Whig nerves. The King's petulant remonstrations over the removal of the Duke of Dorset from the French embassy, which took the Whigs completely by surprise, having had no intimation that the King objected to the change, led Fox to confirm Burgoyne's appointment to the command of a regiment before the post actually became vacant: 'I thought it best that all this should be so, because in case of our being out of power, the circumstance of your being actually named will give you an irresistible claim afterwards.'[4] The Whigs' confidence was only restored after they had survived their first real crisis in the Commons on 19 May over the reinstating of Powell and Bembridge[5] in the Pay Office. Several votes were lost, but there was no sign of a royal attempt to

[1] George III's Memorandum, 28 Mar. 1783; Fortescue, vi. 316–17.

[2] Duchess of Portland to Mrs. Ponsonby, 23 Mar. 1783; Grey MSS.

[3] Add. MS. 27918, f. 67; Memorandum of the Duke of Leeds, 26 Mar. 1783.

[4] Fox to Burgoyne, May 1783; E. de. Fonblanque, *Life and Corres. of J. Burgoyne*, p. 429.

[5] Powell and Bembridge; two clerks in the Pay Office; protégés of Henry Fox; dismissed by Barré on suspicion of embezzlement; reinstated by Burke until the charges had been dealt with; subsequently found guilty.

exploit the situation, and the majority in the Commons was still demonstrably impregnable. After this division, all Fox's optimistic unconcern came flooding back; '... considering the great unpopularity of the question, what passed seems to me to be rather a proof of strength than of weakness. I may be sanguine but this is my real opinion.'[1] The important point for Fox was that the majority in the Commons had held, and, as long as this was the case, hostility in the Closet was an embarrassment and an irritation but not a threat.

This assured tone was only shaken by the King's offensive on the issue of the Prince of Wales's debts in the following month. The support of the Prince of Wales was, for the Whigs, as valuable in terms of places and prestige as it had ever been, but Prinny's conduct was increasingly associating his political allies in all manner of scandal and embarrassment. To ask the Commons for a very considerable sum of money to defray this young man's debts was an exceedingly distasteful duty for the Whigs, and there is no doubt that the King, remembering his resolution of March that he would counterattack as soon as a suitable measure presented itself, believed that the moment had come. A week before the crisis broke, Portland was demanding a meeting with Fox in order to concert policy.[2] The Whig and Court stories of what passed between 13 and 17 June vary enormously.[3] Both versions agree that on 13 June, the King accepted the figure of £100,000 as that to be paid to his son, but George insisted that he thought the money was to come entirely from Parliament, whereas the Whigs were equally confident that part at least would come from the Civil List. At this time, the Whigs had good reason to be pleased with themselves. The King had been made a party to the settlement, and the burden on Parliament had been reduced. When the King suddenly announced two days later, on 15 June, that he had been misled and that the figure offered was far too high, the Whigs were profoundly taken aback. Self-congratulation turned into apprehension. The King's claim that he had earlier been misled as to where the money was to come from was disingenuous in the extreme, in that he had been shown and had sanctioned the draft bill, which was to be presented to Parliament. The crucial point seems to be that Temple, returning from Ireland, saw the King on 14 June, was offered the Treasury, and accepted. Unlike the situation in March, there was now an issue at hand on which to counterattack. A full report was sent to Eden by an unknown correspondent:

[1] Add. MS. 47562, f. 115; Fox to Sir John Stepney, 20 May 1783.

[2] Add. MS. 47561, f. 35; Portland to Fox, 8 June 1783.

[3] George III to Portland and Fox, 16 June 1783; A. Aspinall, *Corres. of Prince of Wales*, i. 80–3; and A. Stewart, *Last Journals of Horace Walpole*, ii. 525, 16 June 1783.

The Duke of Portland carried the message to the King, on Friday last for his Signature, when the King appear'd in a very good Humour, & desir'd him to send it with some other Papers to be sign'd at Windsor. Lord Temple was afterwards with the K. between 2 & 3 Hours! & when the Duke of P. sent the Message according to the King's Order to Windsor, his Majesty return'd it unsign'd with a very angry letter.[1]

Fox himself was not aware of the gravity of the situation in 16 June, when he assured Prinny that 'there is not the least reason for apprehension'.[2] Next day, however, the news from Windsor had certainly reached him, and prompted him to write to Northington,[3] 'that there is great reason to think that our Administration will not outlive tomorrow or at least that it will be at an end in a very few days. Your Predecessor [Temple], it is supposed, will be the D. of P's Successor. The whole is quite sudden and was never dreamt of by me till yesterday.'[4] In fact, the King gave way on the day the above letter was written, presumably because both he and Temple had been forced to admit that the issue of the Prince's debts could weaken the Whigs but not overthrow them.[5] There can be no doubt, however, that the Whigs had been badly shaken. Although Fox could report on 19 June that the immediate danger had passed,[6] he was still presented with the dilemma of either pressing for the original figure of £100,000, which would certainly meet with heavy opposition in the Commons, or of accepting the lower sum offered by the King, which in turn would create difficulties at Carlton House. The fact that Fox and Portland chose the second of these two courses suggests that they were not so confident of their standing as to risk a major engagement with the King on this issue. Adam's plea for a clarification of their position by defiance was unheeded. Fox was, on the contrary, determined 'to keep everything quiet'.[7] If the King's coup had been mistimed, the Whigs themselves were so uncertain of their forces, that their advantage could not be pressed home.

Difficulties arose when Fox tried to persuade the Prince of Wales that the demands of party made it necessary for him to accept something below that which he had originally expected. It fell to Fox, as the

[1] Add. MS. 34419, f. 223; ? to Eden, June 1783.

[2] Fox to Prince of Wales, 16 June 1783; A Aspinall, *Corres. of Prince of Wales*, i. 120–1.

[3] Northington, Robert Henley, 2nd Earl (1747–86); M.P. (Hants.) 1768–72; initially supporting North and the Court; Clerk on the Hanaper 1771–86; joined Coalition as Ld.-Lt. of Ireland, June 1783–Feb. 1784; succeeded father as 2nd Earl of Northington, 1772.

[4] Add. MS. 47567, f. 1; Fox to Northington, 17 June 1783.

[5] Portland to Loughborough, 17 June 1783; Portland MSS. PWF 9212.

[6] Add. MS. 47567, f. 3; Fox to Northington, 19 June 1783.

[7] Add. MS. 47567, f. 3; Fox to Northington, 19 June 1783.

Prince's moral tutor, to ask his authority to settle for the lower figure: 'All I hear inclines me to the opinion that it is your Royal Highness's interest as much as ours to temporize in some degree.'[1] To this was joined an injunction 'to conduct yourself so as to put the world on your side'.[2] The necessary permission was grudgingly given at Carlton House on 18 June, and the Whig Cabinet took the decision to settle for the lower figure a day later. There is no doubt, however, that Prinny was deeply disenchanted with his political allies, and with Fox in particular as their spokesman. The authority of the Duchess of Devonshire had to be called in to support Fox, and, as late as 20 June, he was still trying to convince Prinny at Devonshire House of the circumstances, which had made moderation essential.[3] The Whigs had been shown to be vulnerable to pressure. The Prince's debts controversy had not met the King's purpose. The India Bill would be more successful.

A few weeks later, Fox, in a long letter to Northington, reflected sombrely on the probable fate of the Ministry, and he was well aware of the significance of the June crisis:

> As to the opinion of our having gained strength by it, the only rational foundation for such an opinion is that the event has proved that there subsists no such understanding between the King and Ld. Temple as to enable them to form an administration, because if there did, it is impossible but they must have seized an occasion in many respects so fortunate for them. They would have had on their side the various cries of paternal authority, oeconomy, moderate establishment, mischief making between father and son & many other plausible topics. As therefore they did not avail themselves of all these advantages it seems reasonable to suppose that there is as yet nothing settled and understood amongst them, and in this sense, and inasmuch as this is so felt & understood in the world, I think we may fairly flatter ourselves that we are something stronger than we were. In every other view, I own I think quite otherwise.[4]

Fox admits that the Whigs had been forced to temporize, because no unanimity could have been guaranteed, even in the Cabinet, for a full battle on behalf of Prinny. North and Lord John Cavendish in particular were very unhappy about defending the Prince's extravagances. In spite of this strain, however, Fox can still conclude optimistically. The two halves of the Coalition had stood up to considerable strain without flying apart, and their strength in the Commons had

[1] Fox to Prince of Wales, 18 June 1783; A. Aspinall, *Corres. of Prince of Wales*, i. 127.

[2] Fox to Prince of Wales, 20 June 1783; ibid. i. 127.

[3] Duchess of Devonshire to Lady Elizabeth Foster, 20 June 1783; Chatsworth MSS. f. 508.

[4] Add. MS. 47567, f. 9; Fox to Northington, July 1783.

not been diminished. It is to this latter authority that Fox once again turns for comfort and re-assurance:

Parliament is certainly our strong place, and if we can last during a recess I think People will have little doubt of our lasting during the Session. . . . I own when I look over our strength in the H. of Commons and see that all hopes of dissension between the two parts of the Coalition are given up by the Enemy . . . I cannot help thinking the fear of our being overturned in Parliament quite chimerical.[1]

In view of the severe jolt, which the Whigs had received, such a conclusion would have been absurd had not Fox placed absolute confidence in a majority of the House of Commons.

Throughout the summer recess, the King kept up a guerilla war of sniping at the prestige and cohesion of his Ministers. Peerages were either refused outright or subjected to long delays, which involved Fox in embarrassing explanations to potential political allies.[2] Objections were persistently raised to the manner in which Fox was conducting the negotiations for peace, and a demand was made for the removal of Fox's private secretary, although, as Fox himself admitted, the man was perfectly competent and reliable.[3] At the same time, Jenkinson's sharp political sense told him that the King was deliberately trying to isolate Fox by soliciting the friendship of Portland and the renewed obedience of North.[4] Against this background, Fitzpatrick's report on the condition of the Ministry was, if anything, overenthusiastic: 'The situation of the ministry is just what it was. They are supposed to be as well at Court as any other set of men, and that is nothing to boast of.'[5]

The result of this campaign was that, once again, royal intransigence sapped belief in the viability of the Ministry. By August, the press was predicting the early overthrow of the Coalition, and suggested that Shelburne was the man, who had been called upon to effect this.[6] In Paris, Vergennes was reported to be delaying the negotiations in the belief that the Ministry would soon change, and, instead of addressing himself solely to the Ministry's accredited representative in the French capital, had sent a close friend to Spa for secret talks with Shelburne.[7] In spite of these reports, which were confirmed by the

[1] Add. MS. 47567, f. 9; Fox to Northington, July 1783.

[2] Fox to Grafton, 12 July 1783; Grafton MSS. f. 668.

[3] Fox to Manchester, 3 July 1783, H.M.C. 8R, *Manchester MSS.* Appendix, p. 127a.

[4] C. Jenkinson to J. Robinson, 31 Oct. 1783; H.M.C. *Abergavenny MSS.* x. 6, pp. 60–1.

[5] R. Fitzpatrick to Upper Ossory, 26 July 1783; *Mems. and Corres. of C. J. Fox,* ii. 199.

[6] *Morning Herald*, 15 Aug. 1783.

[7] Manchester to Fox, 18 July 1783; H.M.C. 8R, *Manchester MSS.* Appendix, p. 128a.

opening of Shelburne's letters to the Continent, Fox refused to be shaken from his belief that as long as the strength of the party in the House of Commons held, their general position was impregnable: 'I have no notion of any change being intended before the meeting of Parliament; and when Parliament is met, what happens *there* must determine the situation.'[1] At no time would Fox admit that displeasure in the Closet, however embarrassing and awkward, could or should overturn an administration. To him, the idea of a change in the administration, in the face of so sound a majority in the Commons, was 'entirely and necessarily groundless'.[2] So firm was this belief, that attempts to strengthen the Ministry by offers to Thurlow or Pitt were never seriously considered.[3] The India Bill would put this faith in the Commons to the test.

From the moment the Coalition was formed, it became increasingly clear that one of the major problems facing them was the necessary reorganization of the government of India. Unfortunately, in March, Lord North failed to see the possible implications of the measure, and instructed his supporters at India House to vote as usual for those Directors with whom he had usually been associated.[4] Fox was much more aware of the advisability of having a more friendly directorate in charge at East India House, but his attempts at personal lobbying[5] were pre-empted by the friends of the old directors, who were consequently re-elected. As Fox feared, these men reacted violently against any attempt to remodel Indian government in a way, which would infringe, however slightly, their long-established monopoly. This great vested interest, so intimately connected with political life, was not going to be overthrown easily. Viscount Althorp,[6] reporting political affairs to his mother in May, noted that the Ministry were very reluctant to grasp this particular nettle: 'I am rather afraid from some reasons I have for the suspicion that upon that head the administration do not go on quite so glibly as on most others . . . especially as there seem people enough extremely ready & even impatient to take hold of any handle of opposition.'[7] Fox himself, after the experiences of June, was prepared to admit that the Indian undertaking

[1] Fox to Manchester, 29 July 1783; ibid. p. 129a.

[2] Add. MS. 34419, f. 253; Eden to Loughborough, 25 Aug. 1783.

[3] T. Orde to Shelburne, 17 July 1783; Bowood MSS. and Add. MS. 47568, f. 71; Loughborough to Fox, Aug. 1783.

[4] Lord North to E. Burke, 28 Mar. 1783; Copeland, *Burke Corres*. v. 83.

[5] L. S. Sutherland, *The East India Company in Eighteenth Century Politics*, p. 395.

[6] Visc. Althorp, George Spencer (1758–1834); M.P. (Northampton) 1780–2, (Surrey) 1782–3; firmly attached to the Rockingham Whigs; opposed American War and remained loyal to Fox until 1794; succeeded father as 2nd Earl Spencer, Oct. 1783.

[7] Althorp to Lady Spencer, 29 May 1783; Spencer MSS.

would be 'formidable', and that opposition would be unusually severe.[1] Once again, however, he insists that, since the Ministry's majority is firm in the Lower House, their survival was assured. The Indian question would be unpleasant, but it was an unpleasantness, which could be overcome.

Burke was undoubtedly the man, who persuaded the Whigs to take the matter up, and it was on his very considerable knowledge of Indian affairs that Fox and Portland leant. As Sir Gilbert Elliot observed, the drafting of the Bill was begun by Burke in August under Fox's supervision: 'I breakfasted to-day with Burke at Mr. Fox's. . . . Everything is very much afloat, except that a Commission of the sort I mentioned to you with very extensive powers is quite determined upon. Burke is to draw out on paper some sort of plan, which Fox is to consider as soon as possible.'[2] William Adam's commentary supports this evidence. In origin, the Bill was certainly a simple response to the demand for a reorganization of Indian government, which everyone in politics agreed was necessary. The lines of the Bill, involving the punishment of abuses, the observance of Indian rights and customs, and much stricter control from London, had been foreshadowed for at least two or three years in the correspondence of Burke, who, as a member of the select committee on India since 1782, had become deeply involved in these affairs. Inevitably, Burke also introduced heavy moral overtones into his work, but these were incidental to the basic necessity of doing something about India. Fox shared both the practical and moral platforms of Burke:

> If I had considered nothing but keeping my power, it was the safest way to leave things as they are or to propose some trifling alteration and I am not all ignorant of the political danger which I run by this bold measure; but whether I succeed or no, I shall always be glad that I attempted because I know I have done no more than I was bound to do in risquing my power and that of my friends when the happiness of so many millions is at stake.[3]

The reorganization of Indian patronage, which the Whig proposals would entail, necessarily involved considerations of party advantage, but it would be a mistake to underestimate the practical and moral motives of the framers of the India Bill.

The first signs of strained nerves among the Whigs came in November. Loughborough wrote to Fox to suggest that the holders of India stock should be mollified in advance by the guarantee of a return of between 6 and 8 per cent on their investments during the life

[1] Add. MS. 47567, f. 12; Fox to Northington, July 1783.
[2] P. J. Marshall, *The Impeachment of Warren Hastings* (Oxford Univ. D.Phil. Thesis, 1962), p. 36.
[3] Add. MS. 47570, f. 153; Fox to Mrs. Armistead, undated.

of the bill.[1] This idea was all the more relevant in November 1783, since the rumour of the introduction of a new Indian measure had sent the Company's stock spiralling downwards in the City.[2] In spite of William Eden's confident report that the division in the Commons was likely to end in a Whig victory by at least a hundred,[3] apprehension grew steadily through November. One of the most ominous signs was that by the third week of the month, there had been no comment on the proposed measure from the Closet. The King's attitude could only be guessed. Jenkinson had already attacked the plan as injurious to the interests of the Crown, and Fitzpatrick not unreasonably took these remarks as 'strong symptoms of the opinions of the Closet'.[4] The majority in the Lower House could always be referred to for consoling the hesitant, but the anxiety remained. None of the Whig grandees, for example, was anxious to become Chairman of the Commission, which would control Indian affairs from London. A post, which theoretically offered great prestige and influence, simply could not be filled. In September, the Duke of Manchester[5] was offered the post and promptly declined it.[6] Fox himself tried to change the Duke's decision without success, and was reduced to imploring his assistance in the Lords: 'I am very sorry that you have determined as you have about the E.I. business. It will be a troublesome affair here; and in the House of Lords in particular I am afraid the Duke of Portland will meet with much opposition, so that your Grace's presence and support may be peculiarly desirable.'[7] Manchester's second refusal left the Whigs only three weeks to find a Chairman, whose name they could offer to Parliament. Fitzwilliam was asked and replied immediately with a refusal and a long list of reservations about the Bill.[8] Two letters from Portland, couched in the most imploring terms, were necessary to effect a change in Fitzwilliam's decision: 'Fox's anxiety for Your undertaking the E.I. Administration increases daily, & he desires me to say . . . that the whole depends upon Your Acceptance, Ld. Spencer will not go down as First Commissioner, & it is vain to attempt it.'[9] Even so, Fitzwilliam only

[1] Add. MS. 47568, f. 222; Loughborough to Fox, 19 Nov. 1783.

[2] *Morning Herald*, 21 Nov. 1783.

[3] Add. MS. 33100 (Pelham Papers), f. 401; Eden to Northington, 25 Nov. 1783.

[4] R. Fitzpatrick to Upper Ossory, 21 Nov. 1783; *Mems. and Corres. of C. J. Fox*, ii. 212–3.

[5] Manchester, George Montagu, 4th Duke (1737–88); M.P. (Hunts.) 1761–2; joined the Rockinghams in 1765, and remained with them until his death; Ld. Chamb. Apr. 1782–Apr. 1783; Ambassador in Paris, Apr.–Dec. 1783.

[6] Portland to Manchester, 20 Sept. 1783; H.M.C. 8R, *Manchester MSS*. Appendix, p. 133.

[7] Fox to Manchester, 1 Nov. 1783; ibid. p. 137b.

[8] Fitzwilliam to Portland, 16 Nov. 1783; Portland MSS. PWF 3757.

[9] Portland to Fitzwilliam, 24 Nov. 1783; Milton MSS. Box 37.

accepted on 30 November, when the debate on the Bill had already begun in the Commons. Such a retiring disposition on the part of Whig leaders was not a good omen.

The anxiety of the Whigs manifested itself in precautions. Not only were friends to be secured, but enemies were, as far as possible, to be conciliated. The East India interest itself was brought into the negotiations. East India House was always riven by personal and political rivalries, which gave great scope to a government for ensuring that the full weight of the Company's interest was not thrown against it. According to Robinson's list, of the 31 nabobs or directors sitting in the Commons in November, 1783, 13 only were anti-Coalition. Five directors of the Company actually held office in the Coalition. Even in the heated general election of the next year, the East India interest was far from firm, and, in some constituencies, East India men fought each other.[1] It was therefore with Sir Henry Fletcher[2] and other Whigs in the Company that regular consultations were held throughout October.[3] Safety measures were taken further, however. Sheridan, with or without the knowledge of Fox and Burke, attempted to buy off the displeasure of the friends of Warren Hastings.[4] It seems likely that Fox would have approved of this initiative, in that he himself was trying to come to some arrangement with Pitt, a matter which Temple reported to the King:

> on Thursday last an opening was made to Mr. Pitt on the part of Mr. Fox, inviting him to discuss the measure of acceding to the present coalition, which without waiting for an explanation was immediately negatived by Mr. Pitt. As various circumstances seemed then to point out the possibility of this ineffectual attempt being followed by more distinct propositions, we have delayed till this moment troubling Your Majesty with the communication of it.[5]

If leading Whigs were reduced to asking for the support of Hastings and Pitt, men for whom they had nothing but distaste, this must be an eloquent testimony to the depths of their concern.

In consequence, Whig activity before the opening of Parliament, to secure their maximum vote in both Houses, was energetic and thorough. Two circulars were sent out, one to all Members advising

[1] C. H. Philips, 'The East India Co.: Interest and English Government', *T.R.H.S.* xx (1937), 92–3.

[2] Sir Henry Fletcher (*c.* 1727–1807); M.P. (Cumberland) 1768–1806; director of the East India Co. 1769, 1771–5, 1777–80, Chairman 1782–3; helped to frame East India Bill; voted with Fox until outbreak of the French Revolution.

[3] *London Chronicle*, 1 Nov. 1783.

[4] J. Scott to N. Halhead, 18 Nov. 1783; P. J. Marshall, *The Impeachment of Warren Hastings*, p. 37.

[5] Temple to George III, 15 Nov. 1783; Fortescue, vi. 466.

them of the early opening of the new Session, and one to known Whigs, which was 'more specific'.[1] Every vote was canvassed and provided for. A Whig victor in a by-election at Clitheroe was provided with relays of horses to bring him to London in twenty-four hours.[2] Fox, normally unconcerned with the details of organization, was now himself lobbying both peers and commoners. Begging the Duke of Manchester to send over his proxy and that of another Whig peer abroad, Fox demonstrated his wish to allow for all contingencies, because 'whenever we shall have got our India measure through the House of Commons, the House of Lords will become the scene of action, and a very distressing one possibly . . .'.[3] Every inducement was employed to bring the Whigs to Town early. A notoriously rural cousin of Fox's was brought up by the reminder that, 'Whether one lives in town or in the country, it is a great thing in this country to have some influence, and no influence is to be had but from consequence in Parliament.'[4] Doubts about the constitutional propriety of the proposed Bill, particularly among North's followers, were traced and put down before the measure actually came onto the floor of the House.[5] Adam was commissioned to draw up a list of the members of the Commons, showing relative strengths. In terms of organization therefore, the Whigs stood prepared, but there can be no doubt that their activity was prompted by nervous apprehension.

Fox, once again, however, was considerably more sanguine about the eventual outcome of the Bill than some of his colleagues. Lord North in particular tried to modify his optimism: 'Influence of the Crown & Influence of Party against Crown & People are two of the many Topicks which will be argued against your plan. The latter of the two objections will not be sounded so high and loudly in the Ho. of Commons but it may be one of the most fatal objections to your measure. It certainly ought to be obviated as much as possible.'[6] Fox, although admitting that the measure carried dangers, nevertheless believed that it would go through. His language to Burgoyne and Northington, asking for the attendance at Westminster of members of the Irish Administration, who held seats there, should be taken guardedly: 'We shall meet with very great embarrasments and difficulties. The variety of private interests that will militate against us can not fail of making it a most tempting opportunity to

[1] *London Chronicle*, 1 Nov. 1783

[2] T. Lister to John Lee, 24 Nov. 1783; Lee MSS. D/BO, f. 13.

[3] Fox to Manchester, 7 Nov. 1783; H.M.C. 8R, *Manchester MSS*. Appendix, p. 138a.

[4] Add. MS. 51467 (Holland House Papers), f. 24; Fox to Ilchester, 5 Sept. 1783.

[5] Sandwich to Fox, Nov. 1783; G. Martelli, *Life of 4th Earl of Sandwich*, pp. 282–3.

[6] Add. MS. 47561, f. 23; North to Fox, *c*. 21 Nov. 1783.

Opposition and therefore it is to be presumed they will lay hold of it. You will of course consider This as said to yourself only and not let it be known that I am holding croaking language: but the fact is that our measure though a very right will be a very strong one, and I can not help being a little alarmed.'[1] In these same letters, Fox goes on to deal with points of Irish patronage, which would only become relevant long after the India Bill could reasonably be expected to have passed into law.[2] The several precautions undertaken by the Whigs received Fox's full approval and co-operation, but he believed that, although the passage of the Bill might be stormy, its eventual success was assured. It at least carried the advantage of removing from the political scene several other issues, which were potentially troublesome for the Whigs, notably the necessity of securing better peace terms than those rejected in February. Pitt very properly attacked the Whigs' inability to do this. Fox's reply, weak in substance and logic, depended very largely on the argument that the country could not avoid in December what had been intolerable ten months earlier.[3] This issue was entirely eclipsed by the India Bill, on which the future of the Ministry was staked.

Fox was right in fearing the Opposition attack. The full arsenal of eighteenth-century fears was called out and directed against the India Bill. The most serious concerned what was described as the diversion of the patronage of the East Indies to party ends. As the argument was formulated, Whig Commissioners for India would wield influence enough to return a favourable House of Commons, which would then confirm them in office for a further five years, and thereby set up a vicious cycle of corruption, of which Indian patronage would be the linking mechanism.[4] The Coalition had forced itself on the King and the nation, and now sought to establish itself by the overt diversion of patronage opportunities to specifically party ends. This case was extremely plausible and calculated to play on some of the deepest fears of eighteenth-century M.P.s. It was all the more plausible in view of the fact that, only eighteen months before, Fox had stated, as Pittite pamphleteers hastened to point out, that he 'thought it more prudent to leave the appointment of its servants to the Company'.[5]

Just as plausible and equally disturbing was the reflection that, if the Coalition could deprive the East India Company of rights, which were guaranteed by Charter, what other rights of property might meet

[1] Add. MS. 47568, f. 205; Fox to J. Burgoyne, 17 Nov. 1783.

[2] Add. MS. 38716 (Northington Papers), f. 139; Fox to Northington, 7 Nov. 1783.

[3] *Fox Speeches*, ii. 185 seq.; 11 Nov. 1783.

[4] L. V. Harcourt, *The Diaries and Corres. of George Rose*, i. 43.

[5] Anon, *The Beauties & Deformities of Fox, North & Burke, selected from their Speeches from the year* 1770 *to the Present Time.*

the same fate. Fox and his friends, 'as yet as poor as Church rats',[1] invaded other peoples' property with unconcern, having none themselves. As an anti-Coalition pamphleteer pointed out: 'The East India Company have to their Charter, the faith of the legislature, and the same right which you have to your house and your fire-side, purchased with your money, the sweat of your brow.'[1] Finally, there was the point put forward by Wraxall and others, that many independents, who had faithfully followed Fox throughout the American War, now deserted him through the apprehension of the vast conglomeration of power, which would result from the patronage of India being directly in the gift of either the Crown or a specific political group. These men voted against Fox because 'the man of the people was converted into the champion of influence'.[2] These points would make up a formidable case against any administration in this century. The King, at the head of the anti-Coalition forces, could not fail to take advantage of the situation.

Fox's defence of the East India Bill was set out in four speeches in the Commons. In the first of these, on 18 November, Fox stressed necessity as the sole factor prompting the measure. The administration of India was in chaos as a result of 'the disobedience of the orders of the court of directors and the rapacity of the company's servants in India'.[3] and the commercial direction of the Company was so deficient that the whole enterprise was badly in debt. In this last statement, Fox was supported by the *Morning Herald*, which, in an elaborate article, demonstrated that the Company's books could only be balanced by a dexterity with figures, which almost amounted to fraud.[4] The treatment of Cheyt Singh and the Begums was already referred to by Fox to substantiate his description of rapacious disorder. In proposing a Commission of seven directors, appointed by Parliament, to deal with the government of India, and a further nine to manage commercial transactions, Fox went out of his way to deny that any considerations of party were involved. The India Bill in his eyes was a practical remedy for a pressing problem, which badly needed attention. Such a denial might have carried more weight if all the proposed Directors had not been staunch Coalitionists, but the argument from necessity had at least the merit of appearing to spring from the well-known facts that Indian government left much to be desired, Hastings recently having ignored a Directors' summons recalling him, and that the Company's finances were exceedingly precarious. These arguments were rehearsed again on 27 November

[1] Anon, *A Letter from a Liveryman . . . Their Charter.*
[2] Wheatley, *Hist. and Posth. memoirs of Sir N. Wraxall*, iii. 172; 1 Dec. 1783.
[3] *Fox Speeches*, ii. 196; 18 Nov. 1783.
[4] *Morning Herald*, 27 Nov. 1783.

for the second reading of the bill, and were made to override every objection.[1] In this debate, Fox was, as Burgoyne reported, lucky enough to receive an advance copy of an account, with which Pitt hoped to prove that his fears for the Company's solvency were unfounded: 'Some person had been so weak (if a friend to the Company) or so kind as a friend to Charles, to procure him a copy of this account early in the morning—He had had time to examine it & to discover its several fallacies—He therefore went through a dissection article by article of this complicated and artful statement in a manner that did wonderful service to the cause.'[2] As a result of Whig preparedness and Fox's defence, the Bill passed by 229 to 120. Fox immediately lapsed into euphoria. The margin was so comfortable that he told Eden that, 'the more I reflect upon last night, the more I consider it as decisive in every respect'.[3]

Fox was enormously strengthened by this vote. The speech on 1 December was more aggressive and less cautious than the earlier ones. For the first time, the moral implications of the Bill were brought out and elaborated;

> What is the end of government? Certainly the happiness of the governed. Others may hold other opinions, but this is mine and I will proclaim it. What are we to think of a government, whose good fortune is supposed to spring from the calamities of its subjects, whose aggrandisement grows out of the misery of mankind? This is the kind of government exercised under the East India company upon the natives of Indostan; and the subversion of that infamous government is the main object of the bill in question.[4]

For those still troubled by the violation of Chartered rights, Fox pointed out that the Revolution of 1688 involved precisely this in its unseating of James II. To those worried about a massive build-up of power in the Crown or its ministers, Fox insisted that no power could be threatening, which came under the direct supervision of Parliament. Finally, without in any way weakening the previous point, Fox admitted the value of party: 'I have always acknowledged myself to be a party man; I have always acted with a party, in whose principles I have confidence.'[4] As long as sources of patronage were ultimately under the control of the Commons, Fox refused to believe that party and its workings represented any threat to liberty, and two days later, he opposed an amendment asking Directors to give up their seats in Parliament on this ground.[5] Control had to be direct and firm. The impressive victories in the Commons on the India Bill

[1] *Fox Speeches*, ii. 220; 27 Nov. 1783.
[2] Add. MS. 33100, f. 423; J. Burgoyne to Northington, 28 Nov. 1782.
[3] Fox to Eden, 28 Nov. 1783; *Journal and Corres. of Ld. Auckland*, i. 63.
[4] *Fox Speeches*, ii. 237 seq.; 1 Dec. 1783.
[5] *Parl. Hist.* xxiv. 1; 3 Dec. 1783.

suggests that this point carried credibility. For a Whig party, which had been in the wilderness for almost twenty years, the opportunity of drawing on Indian patronage was too tempting to miss, but the constitutional point, which Fox was trying to put over with regard to the Commons holds, and was convincing. The outburst of indignation, which covered the Coalition and its India Bill with opprobrium, came later.

While the Whigs indulged in understandable self-congratulation for having won the battle in the Commons so convincingly, the counter-attack was already in preparation. According to the orthodox story, Temple had an interview with the King on 11 December, during which he explained how iniquitous the proposed measure was, whereupon George was 'excited in a very high degree'.[1] Such a story hardly does justice either to the facts or to the known political acumen of the King. The royal coup had been in preparation for at least a week. On 3 December, Atkinson informed Robinson that, 'Everything stands prepared for the blow, if a certain person has courage to strike it.'[2] Among the latter's papers, there is a canvass list of the Lords, giving 79 peers against the India Bill, 66 for, with 26 doubtful and 42 absent. Each doubtful vote is accompanied by the name of the man, who was to be responsible for its safe delivery. The accuracy of Robinson's forecast and the detail of the canvass suggests that the Lords had long been the Crown's chosen battlefield, and that the campaign was carefully planned.[3] On 8 December, three days before Temple's conversation with the King, Atkinson gave Robinson a progress report, which was in all senses favourable.[4] In view of this very extensive operation, it is surprising that the Whigs were not earlier apprehensive of what might happen in the Lords. Suspicion was allayed, because Robinson, now the manager of the King's votes, was still thought to be a loyal adherent of Lord North. As late as 16 December, George North wrote to Robinson asking for a strong turn-out of his father's friends, a request with which, in the circumstances, Robinson would have been unable to comply.[5] This betrayal of the North interest by Robinson allowed the King's campaign to go forward unnoticed. Certainly the Whigs showed no early knowledge of Robinson's operations, and the only check to their optimism was the failure of Sheridan to carry a toast of 'D—. to the Charter of the East India Company', at the Constitutional Society.[6]

[1] W. Belsham, *Memoirs of the Reign of George III*, iii. 344.

[2] R. Atkinson to J. Robinson, 3 Dec. 1783; H.M.C. *Abergavenny MSS*. x. 6, p. 61.

[3] Brit. Mus. Abergavenny MSS. facs. 340, p. 292; undated.

[4] R. Atkinson to J. Robinson, 8 Dec. 1783; ibid. p. 293.

[5] G. North to J. Robinson, 16 Dec. 1783; ibid. p. 299.

[6] *Morning Herald*, 10 Dec. 1783.

No hint of this royal offensive appears in Whig writings before 13 ecember. The decisive vote on 27 November had produced euphoria n the Whigs, and Fox's naturally sanguine temperament led him to ndulge in this fully: 'Their whole dependence is now in the House of ords, where the majority of debaters against us is, no doubt, formid-ble, though in point of numbers, I am told, there is no cause to fear'.[1] few days later the tone of Fox's remarks had become more cautious, ut the underlying optimism remained; 'Do not fancy from all this hat I am out of spirits or even that I am much alarmed for the success f our Scheme; on the contrary I am very sanguine, but the reflec-ion of how much depends at this moment upon me is enough to make ny Man who has any feeling serious.'[2] It would be unfair to single ox out, however, as the only promoter of optimistic forecasts. Eden, vith great experience of political management, thought the Bill vould clear the Lords by about thirty votes.[3] Admittedly, Fox was oping for something better in conversations with Burgoyne as the atter reported: 'In opinion & vote, our friend Charles, who is pretty ccurate in calculation, is clear that the bill will be carried two to ne, or over it.'[4] This confidence was shared by all sections of the Vhig connection. Fitzwilliam, who would be in charge of the new atronage arrangements, began to be inundated with recommenda-ons and requests by party stalwarts, in the expectation of the Bill assing in the near future.[5] In Whig thinking, the Commons was the nportant hurdle, and this had been overcome. The greatest danger ad been circumvented, and there was no hint of Robinson's activities blunt their rejoicing.

Fox's anxiety began on 13 December. He heard that two Lords of e King's Bedchamber, Lothian and Carmarthen, were spreading e rumour among their fellow peers, that anyone voting for the ndia Bill in the Upper House would be considered henceforth as the ing's personal enemy. Fox checked with both men, and both denied e rumour. Superficially therefore, Fox proclaimed himself satisfied at no harm was intended. Even when the Archbishop of Canterbury[6] as called into the Closet, Windham observed that Fox 'does not em to apprehend that any thing is to be inferred from this'.[7]

[1] Fox to Manchester, 2 Dec. 1783; H.M.C. 8R, *Manchester MSS.* p. 138b.

[2] Add. MS. 47570, f. 153; Fox to Mrs. Armistead, *c.* 10 Dec. 1783.

[3] Add. MS. 33100, f. 466; W. Eden to Northington, 6 Dec. 1784 (misdated year).

[4] Add. MS. 33100, f. 450; J. Burgoyne to Northington, 9 Dec. 1783.

[5] Various Correspondents to Fitzwilliam, Dec. 1783; Wentworth Woodhouse uniments, F. 123a.

[6] Archbishop of Canterbury, Dr. John Moore (1730–1805); initially Bishop of angor; raised to the See of Canterbury, Mar. 1783; brother-in-law of William den, 1st Baron Auckland.

[7] Add. MS. 33100, f. 522; W. Windham to Northington, 13 Dec. 1783.

Privately, however, Fox had been really shaken, and he lost no time in communicating his fears to Portland: 'I have heard of so many defections to night that the things appears to me more doubtful than I ever thought it before. I really think you should call a Cabinet tomorrow and some way of acting should be adopted in concert. . . Onslow, Essex and Brudenell will all be against us or at best absent I think you should see every doubtful Peer you can in the morning.'[1] Errors of grammar and syntax merely underline Fox's anxiety. On 15 December the day of the Lords' debate itself, press reports dramatically confirmed that the Ministry was about to fall.[2] The danger to the stability of the Coalition once again lay in the Northites. These men had followed the King throughout the American War had grown very accustomed to marks of royal favour, and were more than usually susceptible to royal commands and appeals.

On this crucial day, Fox was very aware of the grave constitutional implications of the Lords' debate, but was still confident that the Coalition would have a majority, and Burgoyne transmitted this optimism to his friends in Ireland: 'Great as the defection may be Charles is still confidant the bill will be carried, & that in that case there is not boldness enough to give the negative of the Crown.' On the morning of the debate itself, Fox was discussing points of patronage with Andrew St. John,[4] who reported that they both expected a majority of twenty-five.[5] It was almost inconceivabl that the King should intervene in the legislative process to such an extent that the success of the Bill would be in jeopardy. The transformation in Fox's position became a source of great amusement to his opponents, notably Thomas Orde:[6]

C. Fox was behind the throne during the whole time of the business yesterday and seemed to be in great agitation at every turn particularly on the admissio of Evidence. He however earnestly cryed out for a division on the questio of adjournment and expressed the fullest confidence of Victory. I am told, tha his countenance, gesture and expressions upon the event were in the highes degree ludicrous from the extremity of distortion and rage, going off with a exclamation of despair, lugging G. North along with him and calling out fc

[1] Fox to Portland, 13 Dec. 1783; Bodleian MSS. Eng. Lett. *c.* 144, f. 66.

[2] *Morning Herald*, 15 Dec. 1783.

[3] Add. MS. 33100, f. 464; J. Burgoyne to Northington, 15 Dec. 1783.

[4] St. Andrew St. John (1759–1817); M.P. (Beds.) 1780–4, 1785–1805; clos friend of Fox, supporting him throughout; manager of Hastings' impeachmen succeeded brother as 14th Baron St. John, Dec. 1805.

[5] Add. MS. 47579, f. 145; St. A. St. John to Upper Ossory, 15 Dec. 1783.

[6] Thomas Orde (1746–1807); M.P. (Aylesbury) 1780–4, (Harwich) 1784–96 supported North and the American War; transferred loyalties to Shelburne, 178 and became one of his principal agents in the House of Commons; cr. Baro Bolton 1797.

Sheridan.—So Caliban, Stephano and Trinculo reeled off upon the disappointment of their similar project. . . .[1]

After defeat on 15 December by eight votes in the Lords, Fox's reaction was angry denunciation of the King for attempting to re-establish his old system of governing by the most blatant and impertinent interference with the workings of the legislature. The constitutional implications of the December votes were Fox's immediate preoccupation. In calling up Coke from Norfolk, Fox explained that, '. . . we are beat in the House of Lords by the direct interference of the Court, and if some vigorous measures are not immediately taken the Parliament will be dissolved, and a system of influence be established by acquiescence, of the most dangerous of any yet attempted.'[2] This violence of language was, however, founded on something stronger than mere resentment. Fox believed the dismissal of the Coalition possible, but, still relying on their strength in the Commons, was also convinced that no alternative administration could be found, which would not be immediately brought down by Whig votes in the Lower House. He confidently assured Mrs. Armistead[3] 'that nobody else can undertake without madness, and if they do we shall destroy them almost as soon as they are formed.'[4] In point of fact, the House of Commons had become the final authority for the Whigs. The theory to support this position would soon follow. When the Ministry was finally dismissed, after the second defeat in the Lords, on 17 December, 'Mr. Fox, in particular, refused to credit it, for he said, it was impossible to believe that the King in his actual circumstances would hazard such a step.'[5] Both sides were now, however, too heavily committed to draw back. In terms of personal vindication and constitutional theory, victory or defeat could now only be absolute.

The Whigs rose to the challenge enthusiastically. Brooks's was a scene of feverish activity, and Fox, fully confident that the King had squarely placed himself at the mercy of the Whigs was 'in an ecstasy of spirits'.[6] At last the King had been forced to demonstrate openly his hostility to the Lower House, the full weight of which could now be directed against the Crown. The King's actions had given the custody of the rights of the Commons into Whig hands, and this was

[1] T. Orde to Shelburne, 16 Dec. 1783; Bowood MSS.

[2] Fox to T. Coke, 16 Dec. 1783; A. M. W. Stirling, *Coke of Norfolk and his Friends*, p. 135.

[3] Elizabeth Armistead (1750–1842); Fox's mistress from 1785; secretly married to Fox in 1795, but the marriage was not made public until 1802.

[4] Add. MS. 47570, f. 156; Fox to Mrs. Armistead, *c.* 17 Dec. 1783.

[5] J. Hutton, ed. *The Letters and Correspondence of Sir James Bland Burges Bt.*, p. 65.

[6] L. Benjamin ed. *The Windham Papers*, i. 54.

a powerful vantage point. On 17 December, Fox fired the first broadside. Prefacing his remarks with an apology for his candour, which was prompted only by his sense of the dangers threatening English liberty, Fox went on to lay the responsibility for the crisis squarely at the door of the Closet. The India Bill had been prepared and drawn up with the King's full knowledge and approval, and had then been killed by rumour and inference in the Lords. The moral to be drawn from this was clear. As the Whigs had always declared, the principal danger to English liberty lay in the unbridled licence of Kings and an encroaching executive:

> ... the Crown, kept within its legal boundaries, is essential to the practice of government; but woe to this country the moment its operations are not as public and notorious as they are sensible and effective! ... We shall certainly lose our liberty, when the deliberations of Parliament are decided—not by the legal and usual—but by the illegal and extraordinary exertions of prerogative.[1]

The episode was set in Whig context by reference to the same 'plodding and illiberal Cabal',[2] which had brought down Chatham, and Fox concluded by insisting that unless the India Bill passed, the constitutional fiction that the King can do no wrong would have to be drastically revised. This magnificent and self-confident speech called on the correct passages from the Whig testament as a rallying cry for the faithful. The challenge offered by the Crown was met in the full expectation of eventual success.

The Whigs had good reason to be optimistic. The King's intervention in the workings of the legislature was novel and potentially alarming. The *Morning Herald*, for example, which, on 13 December, had implored the King to use his veto on the India Bill, now swung round to defend the Whigs against this extension of royal influence, which seemed the more pressing danger.[3] The issue of royal influence gave pamphleteers and rhymsters something tangible, on which to deploy their skill:

> The King one day in his temple of late
> Took Council therein concerning the state
> He viewed his affairs in a desperate light
> And wish'd to God he cou'd set them right;
> This East India Bill it will lessen our power,
> So in office they shall not continue an hour,
> I'll use my prerogative bid them begone;
> Rogues and scoundrels every one.[4]

[1] *Fox Speeches*, ii. 266; 17 Dec. 1783.
[2] ibid.
[3] *Morning Herald*, 13 and 16 Dec. 1783.
[4] Anon, *The Fox and the Badger Dismissed. A New Song.*

Orde himself admitted that the India Bill was the only measure, which made the prospect of royal interference of this kind even remotely tolerable, and that even so several of the leading country gentlemen were dividing with Fox. Both sides were employing methods and making constitutional claims of a very unusual kind, which brought open violence to politics:

The language held in Parliament . . . is truly menacing both on the part of Mr. Fox and Ld. North, which latter indeed seems to talk more determinedly even than the other of the necessary exertions and daring of the great Faction, by which they are upheld. Allusions to the time of the Civil Wars were not merely made for the doctrine of not allowing the Royal Interference in the consideration of Bills.[1]

Fox was sure of his party and his position. The die had been irrevocably cast, and he could give free rein to his thoughts. The hesitations and suspicions of the preceding eighteen months had been synthesized into open conflict, which Fox believed he could win. A few days after his dismissal, he was taking bets that Pitt's stay at the Exchequer would not be longer than a week.[2]

Fox's immediate problem was to forestall a dissolution of the House of Commons, in which the Coalition enjoyed a majority. As Fox suspected, as soon as the drama of the India debates had passed, the correspondence of John Robinson was filled with the details of management necessary for the coming election.[3] Any delay in calling an election on the King's part was due principally to the realization that his Managers needed time for their work to be perfected, and in no way stemmed from a desire to observe constitutional form by allowing the Parliament to run its full life. Fox himself was not going to be taken unawares, and the days immediately following the India debates were taken up with the personal canvassing of the Whig grandees,[4] among them the Duke of Grafton: 'I lose no time in acquainting you that we have just received our dismission, and that a dissolution will undoubtedly take place immediately. I take it for granted, that you will like the earliest information of this event; & that you will permit me . . . just to suggest to you, that it is worth-while to enquire into the means by which our successors have come in; & the ground on which they stand, before any honest man gives them his countenance.[5]' With their strength deployed as it was, the Whigs never welcomed the prospect of a dissolution, but, in December, the revulsion against the King's action led some of them to expect,

[1] T. Orde to Shelburne, 18 Dec. 1783; Bowood MSS.
[2] T. Orde to Shelburne, 22 Dec. 1783; Bowood MSS.
[3] Robinson Correspondence, H.M.C. *Abergavenny MSS.* x. 6, pp. 58 seq.
[4] Brit. Mus. facs. 340, f. 327; R. Rigby to J. Robinson, 18 Dec. 1783.
[5] Fox to Grafton, 18 Dec. 1783; Anson, *Memoirs of the Duke of Grafton*, p. 385.

against all precedent, that the royal forces would be defeated should an election be called.[1]

Votes certainly moved towards the Coalition as the prospect of the life of this Parliament being prematurely curtailed for electoral advantage was added to the King's irregular use of the Lords in the India debate.[2] In two speeches on a motion asking the King not to dissolve Parliament, Fox attempted to set this latest threat to the Commons within the general context of the King's unconstitutional activity. If the King's actions went unheeded, the result could only be chronic instability, with the Court as the only arbiter of political rectitude: 'the very means, by which the power of the present advisers of the Crown had been obtained, might deprive them of stability: that secret influence, which made them ministers might in the end operate to their downfall.'[3] The rise and fall of Temple as Secretary of State between 18 and 22 December was merely illustrative of Fox's point. The King had deliberately set executive against legislature, and the predictable result was a stop to all government.

In the debates on the prospect of a dissolution, two points emerge which are to become immensely important in and characteristic of the set-piece debates between December 1783 and March 1784. In almost every encounter with Pitt, Fox begins with what he takes to be a misuse of royal authority, and, prompted by this, goes on to make claims for the Commons, which were just as new and controversial as those he imputed to the Crown. Thus, the royal threat to dissolve Parliament well before its constitutionally appointed life had run out was condemned, but Fox proceeds to claim that such an action could be checked by a resolution of the House of Commons, 'the Voice of the people of England'.[4] By implication, therefore, the undoubted prerogative of the Crown to dissolve Parliament at will has been circumscribed by a new authority resting in the Commons. For those attacking the prerogatives of the Crown, the alternative of placing responsibility in the Lower House was essential for reasons of constitutional respectability, but Fox, in these four months, took this line of argument much further than the crisis strictly demanded. Secondly, Fox's major problem, in these months, was already apparent. The Land Tax had to be passed without opposition, even though it was the measure of an administration, of which Fox disapproved. As Rigby[5] reported: 'Fox will not oppose the Land Tax passing, but He

[1] Add. MS. 47579, f. 127; R. Fitzpatrick to Ossory; Thursday [Dec. 19], 1783.

[2] *Morning Herald*, 22 Dec. 1783.

[3] *Fox Speeches*, ii. 39 seq.; 22 Dec. 1783.

[4] *Fox Speeches*, ii. 305 seq.; 19 Dec. 1783.

[5] Richard Rigby (1722–88); M.P. (Castle Rising) 1745–7, (Sudbury) 1747–54, (Tavistock) 1754–88; supported North throughout American War; held several minor govt. posts; consistently opposed all reform measures; joined Shelburne 1782.

will keep the House sitting as long as He possibly can without essential detriment to the Publick in stopping the Land Tax.'[1] Here was the dilemma. Fox could only bring pressure to bear on the Crown by using his power in the Commons to check essential measures, but if he did this too long, many Members, on whose votes he depended, would be lost to the argument that the smooth running of the King's government was the first end of politics. If Coalition strength in the Commons was to hold firm, Fox needed to win quickly, before the hiatus in government unduly troubled independent minds. Both these points, apparent at the very beginning of the struggle, would become more pronounced as the crisis grew worse.

In the last week of December, however, neither side could be absolutely sure of its position. The firmness, with which George had expelled the Coalition hid the fact that he believed himself 'on the Edge of a Precipice'.[2] The King's intervention in politics was seen by many as more reprehensible than either the Coalition or the India Bill, and opinion continued to move in Fox's favour.[3] In the face of a hostile Commons, Temple's brief ministry had collapsed, and its head, 'a d-d, dolterheaded Coward',[4] was now immobilized by the fear of impeachment. Pitt was himself so unsure of his position that he unequivocally opposed the calling of an election.[5] So insecure were the King's friends, that George had to countenance an open appeal to Fox through Lord Spencer.[6] After the events of the last eighteen months, and only four or five days after the dismissal of the Coalition, this offer of employment to Fox eloquently testifies to just how desperate a throw the King's action on the India Bill had been. Fox's faith in the Commons seemed to be well founded. Temple had fallen after three days. Pitt would not survive very much longer. Pitt's offer of employment was dismissed contemptuously by Fox with the remark 'Why don't they advise us to pick pockets at once.'[7]

In the period up to the Parliamentary recess, on 27 December, Fox believed himself, with some justification, to have won: 'What will follow, is not yet known, but I think there can be very little doubt but our Administration will again be established. . . . The Confusion of the Enemy is beyond all description, and the triumph of our friends proportionable.'[8] The King had badly overplayed his hand in challenging

[1] Brit. Mus. facs. 340, f. 327; R. Rigby to J. Robinson, 18 Dec. 1783.
[2] P.R.O. Pitt Papers, Series 30, vol. 8, f. 15; George III to Pitt, 23 Dec. 1783.
[3] *Parker's General Advertiser*, 26 Dec. 1783.
[4] T. Orde to Shelburne, 22 Dec. 1783; Bowood MSS.
[5] B. Connell, *Portrait of a Whig Peer*, 22 Dec. 1783.
[6] Pitt to Spencer, 21 Dec. 1783; Spencer MSS.
[7] Sir G. Elliot to Sir J. Harris, 1 Jan. 1784; Earl of Malmesbury ed. *Diaries and Correspondence of Lord Malmesbury*, ii. 59.
[8] Add. MSS. 47567, f. 73; Fox to Northington, 22 Dec. 1783.

the Commons, Temple had fallen, and Pitt had been reduced to begging for assistance. Fox seemed to be the arbiter of politics. As Lady Sarah Napier reported: 'Never was there a more triumphant power than Charles', nor mortification to the folly of those who attempted such rash measures.'[1] The Coalition majority in the Lower House seemed, as Fox had predicted, to be the strongest force in politics, against which the King was impotent. In the direct confrontation of these two forces, which had resulted from the dismissal of the Coalition, the King had been badly humiliated. Fox waited for the reassembling of Parliament, on 12 January 1784, with every confidence of even more decisive victories. He told Northington not to think of giving up: 'I am quite clear that you should take no step towards resignation . . . till you hear the event of the 12th of January. I have no doubt but that it will be the most decisive victory on our side that ever happened in Parliament.'[2] Sooner or later, Pitt, like Temple, would be broken by a self-confident majority in the Lower House.

Fox allowed Pitt to call a recess in the belief that, 'the present Ministers cannot stand long, indeed, to talk of the permanency of such an Administration would only be laughing at and insulting them.'[3] In fact, as Wraxall and others pointed out, an interval of nearly three weeks allowed the Crown to mobilize its political and emotional forces. George himself was indefatigable in the personal canvassing of every peer, whose assistance might be evoked by appeals to personal loyalty or political principle: 'The times are of the most serious nature, the political struggle is not as formerly between two factions for power, but it is now no less than whether a desperate faction shall not reduce the Sovereign to a mere tool in its hands.'[4] Press reports during the recess gave details of what inducements had been held out to various politicians, and with what success.[5] As the recess drew to a close, it became clear that the Crown's campaign was directed towards two objectives. Large numbers of country gentlemen could be expected to come up to Town after Christmas, and these were men to whom an appeal for loyalty might be addressed with some profit.[6] Secondly, there was the obvious gambit of attacking the cohesion of the North interest, most of whom had been King's men throughout the American war. Wraxall gives details of this onslaught, and the switch in votes between January and March

[1] Lady S. Napier to Lady S. O'Brien, 22 Dec. 1783; Lady Ilchester and Lord Stavordale eds. *Letters of Lady Sarah Lennox*, ii. 44.

[2] Add. MS. 47567, f. 75; Fox to Northington, 26 Dec. 1783.

[3] Wheatley *Memoirs of Sir N. Wraxall*, iii. 120; 24 Dec. 1783.

[4] George III to Duke of Marlborough, 29 Dec. 1783; Blenheim MSS. E.62.

[5] *Morning Herald*, 30 Dec. 1783 and 5 Jan. 1784.

[6] 'Palmerston's Diary', 31 Dec. 1783; Palmerston MSS.

784 was concentrated in this group.[1] Given determination and nergy, a great deal of damage could be done to the Coalition interest n the Commons, if the most vulnerable targets were attacked, and he King's long experience of politics made it likely that this would e the case.

By contrast, the Whigs allowed the recess to pass in self-congratula-ion. Fox was brimming over with confidence, believing not only hat his position was still secure, but that it was daily becoming tronger. The King's lobbying was either unknown to Fox or dis-ounted as a political weapon: 'You are certainly right in not wishing ne to join Pitt but as to the other Coalition even those who dis-pproved it formerly are now come over to it from the very honourable vay Ld. N. has conducted himself and from the heartiness with which is friends and ours have acted upon this occasion.'[2] Sir Gilbert Elliot vas equally sure that the King had lost all sympathy and that 'in a ew days all will have returned to its former course.'[3] The source of his euphoria was simply that their gamble on the authority of the Iouse of Commons seemed to be paying off. As the Duchess of Devonshire pointed out: 'we have the Majority still in the H. of C. vhich is suppos'd must rout them.'[4] The only sign of wavering on the art of the Whigs came from the Prince of Wales, who, according to nsubstantiated press reports, was attempting to bring Fox and Pitt nto Coalition.[5] A meeting took place at Carlton House on 7 January etween Richmond and Fox, 'but his Grace insisting upon Lord North's exclusion as the preliminary article of the negotiation, Mr. ox instantly got up, and retired, without uttering a syllable on the ccasion.'[6] As Fox realized, the crushing of the India Bill and the ismissal of the Coalition had raised the stakes of the political game too igh for settlement by negotiation. Victory or defeat would be absolute. The *Morning Chronicle* set out the issue beautifully:

> he contest which has been carrying on by the Whigs since the beginning f the present reign, against secret influence, opposed to the spirit of the onstitution, is now at public issue, and will be decided finally on Monday ext [January 12]. The late East India Bill has no more to do in the question han a turnpike road bill. The points to be decided are, whether the Crown, y privately issuing forth its mandates, can crush every measure it chooses o disapprove, and whether the sense of the House of Commons is to have any arther weight in the great scale of Government. . . .[7]

[1] Wheatley *Memoirs of Sir N. Wraxall*, iii. 236, Dec. 1783.

[2] Add. MS. 47570, f. 154; Fox to Mrs. Armistead, 30 Dec. [1783].

[3] Sir G. Elliot to Hugh Elliot; 30 Dec. 1783; Lady Minto, *Life and Letters of ord Minto*, i. 89.

[4] Duchess of Devonshire to Lady Spencer, 3 Jan. 1783; Chatsworth MSS.

[5] *Morning Chronicle*, 3 Jan. 1784.

[6] *Morning Herald*, 14 Jan. 1784.

[7] *Morning Chronicle*, 7 Jan. 1784.

Fox had succeeded in bringing what he took to be malign royal influence out into the open. The political world now had to judge between the pretensions and claims of Crown and Coalition.

The high drama of the debates between January and March 1784 stemmed from the fact that the game would be lost by the side, whose nerve broke first. The determining factor was that the Mutiny Bill expired on 25 March, and, unless this were renewed, government was at a stand. Debate tended to centre on where responsibility for this threat to the smooth running of government should be laid. The King could be accused of obstructing the known wishes of the Lower House thereby causing an impasse. Equally Fox could be charged with misusing the Commons to obstruct the King's government. At base this argument resolved itself into what each member of the political nation thought more valuable, the King's prerogative or the claim of the Commons. The figures[1] suggest that, as the crucial date drew nearer, most men preferred to support the known authority of the Crown. Fox's miscalculation lay not in underestimating the hostility of the Crown, but in not foreseeing Pitt's ability to hold out against a hostile majority in the Commons for three months, each day of which would increase the pressure on each member's conscience. A short, sharp victory had been envisaged on 12 January, which would have made a prolonged call on the loyalty of the Coalition's supporters unnecessary. Instead, Pitt's tenacity rendered everything once again uncertain.

The Mutiny Bill problem presented the Crown with only two alternatives. Either the King could dissolve Parliament, in the hope of a more amenable House being returned, or, as Pitt continually advocated, they should wait for Fox's majority to crumble before the necessity of passing a new Mutiny Bill. The trend of Foxite majorities which, with fluctuations, was generally downward throughout January and February, supported Pitt's thesis. It received additional assistance in mid January from the practical consideration that a new House could not then be assembled to push a new Mutiny Bill through by 25 March.[2] By force of necessity Pitt's hope for a war of attrition was the only feasible course. Dissolution only became useful again as a royal weapon, when Fox, under extreme pressure, allowed the Mutiny Bill through on 9 March. The decision to dissolve was taken twelve days later.[3] If Fox could have held out just a little

[1] G. Tomline, *Memoirs of the Life of the Rt. Hon. W. Pitt*, i. 464–5. Fox majorities were as follows: 12 Jan., 39 and 54; 16 Jan., 21; 23 Jan., 8; 2 Feb., 19 3 Feb., 24; 16 Feb., 29; 18 Feb., 12; 20 Feb., 20 and 21; 27 Feb., 7; 1 Mar., 1 5 Mar., 9; 8 Mar., 1

[2] O. Browning, *Political Memoranda of the Fifth Duke of Leeds*, 25 Jan. 1783, p. 9

[3] ibid. 21 Mar. 1783, p. 99.

longer, the choice would have been squarely presented to Pitt, with the option of a dissolution removed, of either capitulating or of facing the full consequence of a stop in government. As it was, his war of nerves against Fox was successful; but the issue was close.

The Crown campaign was therefore relatively straightforward. The lobbying, which had been begun during the recess, would go on,[1] linked with a persistent disavowal on Pitt's part of any intention to resign under pressure from resolutions of the House of Commons.[2] If maximum strain was to be imposed on the nerves of the Coalition, no concessions could be made to the authority of the House. Pitt stood his ground on the undoubted right of the King to choose his own ministers, and dared Fox to challenge this. Throwing the onus of introducing constitutional innovations on to Fox would not make it any easier for him to hold together the essentially heterogeneous component parts of the Coalition. The only break in this embattled situation was Pitt's suggestion in 13 February that he and Portland should confer on the possibility of coalescing. The extreme distaste displayed by the King for such a proposal, and the sharp denial by Portland that anything useful could be achieved at such a meeting only emphasized how far the situation had gone beyond the realm of negotiation. George agreed to the project with 'mortification'.[3] Portland quashed it by insisting that he was too committed to the Commons: 'Your Lordship is too well apprized of my unalterable opinion, that the confidence of the House of Commons is indispensably necessary for any arrangement which can promise quiet to the Country or energy to His Majesty's Government, not to perceive the impossibility of my conferring with Mr. Pitt. . . .[4] There were to be no short cuts to a more stable tenure of office for Pitt. His only hope was that the nerve of Fox and his supporters would break as the date for the renewal of the Mutiny Bill drew nearer.

Fox's problem was naturally the inverse of Pitt's. He had to keep his majority together in the Lower House by drawing the constitutional issue at hand in bright and uncompromising colours, which would give defection the character of apostasy. The difficulty was that, in deliberately polarizing loyalties in this manner, Fox was led to make claims on behalf of the Commons, which were highly disturbing to conservative minds, and which superficially made Pitt's statement that the responsibility for the impasse in government lay with the Whigs, more credible. This dilemma was a cruel one, but Fox had no choice

[1] George III to Duke of Marlborough, 17 Jan. 1783; Blenheim MSS., E 62.

[2] Pitt to Sir. J. Sinclair, 31 Jan. 1784; *The Correspondence of Sir John Sinclair*, i. 82.

[3] P.R.O. Pitt Papers 30/8.103, f. 54; George III to Pitt, 15 Feb. 1784.

[4] Add. MS. 47561, f. 68; Portland to Sydney, 15 Feb. 1784.

but to try to convince the political world that the dismissal of the Coalition was the last step in a concerted Crown campaign, set in motion after the fall of North, to overbalance the constitution in favour of the executive. Fox's speech on 12 January, when Parliament reassembled, was a brilliant synthesis of two years of political experience into a coherent pattern of the Crown systematically assaulting the position of the House of Commons. Fox's resignation in July 1782 had been the first warning of this attack. The India Bill had been the instrument for bringing the whole strategy into the open, a Bill whose only fault, in the King's eyes, was that 'it prevented a large and dangerous degree of influence from going into the hands of the Crown, and lodged it where it was safe, in that House.'[1]

Fox was already making of the years 1782–4 a political piece, the reaction against which would underpin the highly developed party organization of the 1780's. The royal attack made party the only alternative authority to sanction claims to political power, and Fox naturally went from an assault on the prerogative to a defence of party:

> If it was a trial of strength, it was whether this country was in future to be governed by a ministry supported by that House, or by the secret advisers of the Crown? This was the question at issue, and he trusted it would very soon be decided. Party was vulgarly said to be the madness of many for the advantage of few; but this was the advantage of it; that it gave stability to the system and therefore he had always been a party man.[2]

As these themes were elaborated over the next two months, Fox concentrated his attack on three fronts, each of which was designed to demonstrate how the Crown was diverting authority from the Commons. Pitt was the major target, because constitutional issues could be easily grasped in the bitter personal duel between the new agent of the Crown and Fox. Pitt throughout maintained an impeccable adherence to strict eighteenth-century theory:

> Though the situation of a minister maintaining his post, after the House of Commons had declared him undeserving of their confidence, was novel and extraordinary, yet it was in his opinion, by no means unconstitutional. He conceived that, by the constitution, neither the immediate appointment or removal of a minister rested with that House.[3]

Fox was therefore in the uncomfortable position of challenging doctrine and redefining theory. As representation after representation failed to remove Pitt, and as the strain on Coalition members grew, Fox's language became more and more unguarded. On 16 January, Fox agreed that the King could choose his own ministers with the

[1] *Parl. Hist.* xxiv, 315; 12 Jan. 1784.
[2] *Fox Speeches*, ii. 315; 12 Jan. 1784. [3] ibid., ii. 356; 26 Jan. 1784.

approval of the Commons.[1] Four days later, Fox stated that: 'no minister can stand, who had not the support and confidence of the House of Commons.'[2] By March, Fox was stating quite baldly that: 'The House of Commons consequently were possessed of the power of putting a negative on the choice of ministers. . . .'[3] Under extreme pressure from the dogged tenacity of Pitt, Fox was led to make more and more claims of an innovatory nature, which could not appeal to members worried principally about the stop in government. Pitt's words and arguments were more familiar to the eighteenth-century world.

Secondly, the resolutions passed in the Lords in early February in direct contradiction to those of Commons regarding the stability of the East India Company's finances, naturally led Fox to take the matter up. With a back reference to the use made of the Lords in the defeat of the India Bill, Fox objected to the way in which the Crown and its agents deliberately set the Lords up against the Commons.[4] The House of Commons was being denied the exercise of authority, and the Crown was willing to use any alternative instrument in order to belittle the Lower House. Thirdly, even appeals to opinion outside Parliament were not ruled out. Fox's protests against these appeals read oddly coming from someone endowed with the title of Man of the People, but once again the threatened authority of the House of Commons was uppermost in his mind. The Addresses from various parts of the country in support of Pitt, which began to flow into London during February and March, were seen by Fox to be a wholly unacceptable attempt to bring pressure on the House of Commons:

> There is an intention in ministers to establish themselves on a foundation unfriendly to the constitutional privileges of this House. They court the affection of the people, and on this foundation, they wish to support themselves in opposition to the repeated resolutions of this House. Is this not declaring themselves independent of Parliament?[5]

Pitt naturally made capital out of the paradoxical picture of Fox the reformer placing his whole faith in an unreformed House of Commons, and denying the value of outside opinion,[6] but Fox had no choice. His commitment in political terms to the authority of the Commons was absolute, and he had to defend it against what he took to be a systematic attempt to undermine its standing.

Fox's major embarrassment, however, lay not in constitutional inconsistency, but in difficulties of strategy. His only valuable weapon

[1] *Fox Speeches*, ii. 343; 16 Jan. 1784.
[2] ibid., ii. 348, 20 Jan. 1784.
[3] ibid., ii. 414; 1 Mar. 1784.
[4] *Parl. Hist.* xxiv. 529; 5 Feb. 1784.
[5] *Fox Speeches*, ii. 377; 2 Feb. 1784.
[6] *Parl. Hist.* xxiv. 574; 9 Feb. 1784.

against the Crown was his power to withold supplies in the Commons, but this increasingly placed on Fox the responsibility for government grinding to a halt. He was conscious of this danger at a very early date. On 12 January, Fox tried to maintain that the Crown's action in appointing Pitt was to blame for the stop in government.[1] The defeat of Pitt's India Bill two days later by only eight votes was a convincing demonstration of how quickly the seemingly impregnable position of the Coalition in the Commons could be whittled away under the incontrovertible necessity of keeping government running smoothly. Henceforth, Fox's attacks on the Crown are interspersed with appeals for solidarity to Coalition members.[2] When he successfully moved that the Ordnance Estimates be put back on the 10 and 18 February, until the King had replied to a Commons resolution asking for the removal of his ministers, Fox was at considerable pains to show how reluctant he was to hold up business in this manner, and how completely responsibility lay with Pitt, in thus defying the declared wishes of the Commons; 'Confusion could only be created by his [Pitt's] remaining in office; and the moment he should retire from it, all would be harmony again.'[3] The Mutiny Bill was still, however, the deciding factor. When Fox allowed it past the Commons on 9 March, he was effectively admitting defeat. Two considerations prompted his decision. On the day before, his majority in the Commons had held by only one vote. The Coalition's nerve had broken. Secondly, Pitt had communicated to Fox his intention of introducing the Mutiny Bill into the Lords rather than the Commons if necessary.[4] If Fox then chose to obstruct its passage in the Commons, the breakdown of government would literally be of his choosing, and further, with Coalition majorities steadily diminishing, it was not at all clear that Fox could carry the Commons in such a step. Fox's decision to let the Bill through justified Pitt's belief that the Coalition's nerve would break before the prospect of an absolute stop in government. The Crown's victory was less in constitutional terms than in the practical fears of independent M.P.s, who preferred to accept Pitt rather than the prospect of anarchy.

Although Northite votes were being lost by the Coalition throughout February and March, Fox had succeeded in imbuing the old Whig party with new energy and cohesiveness. When the crises of the years 1782–4 had been placed in the general context of the King's long history of unconstitutional behaviour, the Whigs understood where their political duty lay, and closed ranks. The Duchess of

[1] *Parl. Hist.* xxiv. 300; 12 Jan. 1784.
[2] *Fox Speeches*, ii. 358; 29 Jan. 1783.
[3] *Parl. Hist.* xxiv. 618; 18 Feb. 1783.
[4] Hutton, *Life and Correspondence of Sir James Bland Burges*, pp. 72–5.

Devonshire repeated her political lesson to her mother: 'If Mr. Pitt succeeds he will have brought about an event that he himself as well as ev'ry Englishman will repent ever after, for if the K. and H. of Lords conquer the H. of C. he will destroy the consequence of that house and make the government quite absolute.'[1] Within Fox's own family, Lady Louisa Connolly, originally siding with Richmond against his nephew, now changed sides: 'I am not sure, that I don't also find myself a Tory *originally*, tho' by no means one now, and I think that Charles's humane India Bill, would attach one to his party at any rate.'[2] Fox had succeeded in polarizing loyalties around the central issue of the Crown's rôle in politics and the alternative claims of the House of Commons. In February, a certain Captain Mostyn was killed in a duel by a fellow officer, and 'the quarrel originated in defence of a Jew who goes about diverting company by taking off Mr. Fox.'[3] A situation had been created in which the Whigs would be impelled to devote time and energy to politics.

As Coalition majorities began to falter in the Commons owing to the defection of Northite votes, Fox energetically called into service the traditional reserves of Whig support. On 5 February, Fox himself presided over a meeting of the electors of Westminster at the Shakespeare Tavern, where a resolution was passed to the effect that Fox's conduct had been 'consonant to the practice and principles as established at the glorious Revolution'.[4] The unanimity of this meeting suggests that it was merely a set-piece demonstration by known Whig sympathizers in preparation for a much larger meeting in Westminster Hall nine days later. This assembly was far from unanimous, and reports vary greatly in the ministerialist and opposition press as to which side emerged as victors. Certainly Mahon and Wray, the Pittite leaders, succeeded in forcing the Foxites to move into Palace Yard. Whatever the confidence of the Duchess of Portland, Westminster was riven by animosities in a quite unprecedented manner: 'Mr. Fox had a meeting Yesterday at Westminster, You will see in the Newspapers that he was defeated, but it really was as much the Contrary as possible; He had at least Three to One and we have no doubt if there should be a new Election that he will carry it.'[5] Two points stand out clearly, however. The heightening of the political temperature, in order to confirm Whigs in their creed, naturally carried the corollary of inflaming Pittite sympathizers. The Westminster meeting, at

[1] Duchess of Devonshire to Lady Spencer, 8 Feb. 1784; Earl of Bessborough, *Georgiana, Duchess of Devonshire*, pp. 74–5.

[2] Lady L. Connolly to Lady S. Napier, 22 Jan. 1784; Bunbury MSS. E18/750/2, f. 31.

[3] *Gentleman's Magazine*, 13 Feb. 1784.

[4] *Morning Chronicle*, 5 Feb. 1784.

[5] Duchess of Portland to Mrs. Ponsonby, 15 Feb. 1784; Grey MSS.

which noxious chemicals were thrown at Fox, demonstrated how far this antipathy had gone. *The Beauties and Deformities of Fox, North and Burke*, a highly skilful pamphlet which demonstrated the inconsistences embraced by the Coalition by printing extracts from past speeches in which the partners in coalition had systematically vilified each other, proved a best-seller and ran through four editions in a month.[1] Secondly, in spite of the disorder, Fox succeeded in using this meeting as a national platform, from which to describe the issue at hand and the Whig position on it:

The true simple question of the present dispute is, whether the House of Lords and Court Influence shall predominate over the House of Commons & annihilate its existence, or whether the House of Commons, whom you elected, shall have power to maintain the privileges of the people, to support its liberties . . . & regulate the prerogatives of the Crown, which was ever ready to seize upon the freedom of the Electors of this country.[2]

The platform of Westminster was disputed, but still enormously valuable as a sounding board for Foxite views, and as such was put to good use during the crisis.

Further, Whig cohesion during these months was greatly assisted by Fox's willingness, unlike his actions during the resignation dispute of July 1782, to call his party together from time and time, in order to explain and cajole. As Wraxall pointed out, such action was necessary if Fox was to lead a united party into the very radical demand that the King should remove his ministers at the behest of the Lower House.[3] On 26 February for example, a large number of Whig members, together with a few of the St. Alban's Tavern group of independents, gathered at Fox's house to hear him state the problem in clear terms. Among those present was Sir Gilbert Elliot: 'Fox in speaking to his company tonight, reminded us that it would be necessary for us to make up our minds fairly on the question of how far we could go in the contest; for, if the cause of the House of Commons was to be given up by a want of unanimity amongst ourselves, it would be proper to think of some means to surrender our claims in the manner the least disgraceful and the least fatal to the House; but if we thought it right, at all events, to resist the attack, we must determine on the necessary measures.'[4] Such cogent presentations of the dilemma facing the Whigs must have greatly contributed to the steadiness of Whig votes under this very heavy strain. As the battle in the Commons

[1] *The Beauties and Deformities of Fox, North and Burke.*

[2] W. T. Laprade, 'William Pitt and the Westminster Election' *A.H.R.* xxiii. (1912), 263.

[3] Wheatley, *Memoirs of Sir N. Wraxall*, iii. 277; 16 Jan. 1784.

[4] Sir G. Elliot to Sir J. Harris, 26 Feb. 1784; *Diaries and Corres. of Ld. Malmesbury*, ii. 60.

slipped away from him, Fox turned once again to Westminster. On 7 March, yet another meeting of Electors was held, at which Fox was carried in triumph around Devonshire House. The Duchess had to admit, however, that Wray's[1] meeting was better attended.[2] On the 12 March, Fox dined at the Shakespeare with a large company, and repeated the performance at Willis's on 19 March and at the Rose in Ludgate St. a day later. This last dinner campaign was clearly designed as the opening of an election canvass rather than a strategy related to the contest in the Commons, but it formed a fitting end to an energetic attempt by Fox to carry Westminster and the bulk of his party with him through very contentious debates, in which the Whig creed had to be restated.

So conscious was Fox of the high party nature of this three-month duel in the Commons, that the mediating efforts of the St. Alban's Tavern group were never likely to meet with any success. Fox's dealing with this group of about seventy M.P.s was uncompromising, and even high-handed. Whig grandees objected to their political actions being dictated by what Lord John Cavendish called 'a very absurd sett of people & yet every body is obliged to compliment them as the greatest men in the world.'[3] There was too the well-founded suspicion that the independence of this group was open to question, in that many of them were avowed ministerialists. Cornwallis honestly admitted this: 'Now I do not see how a number of Pitt's friends can make a fair and equal treaty between him and Mr. Fox.'[4] Essentially, however, it was not a situation in which compromise was possible. Pitt, under the stern observation of the King,[5] was just as unbending as the Whigs.[6] Both he and Fox knew quite well that politics had reached a stage, where victory and defeat would be absolute. During debates on motions proposed by members of the St. Alban's group, Fox always expressed his readiness to act in concert with Pitt, but his conditions for doing so amounted to a full capitulation on the part of the Crown.[7] To each of the three private initiatives set in motion by this group between January and March, Fox was firm and unbending. On 27 January, he told them that: 'the first point

[1] Sir Cecil Wray (1734–1805), 3rd Bt.; M.P. (East Retford) 1768–80, (Westminster) 1782–4; independent Lincs. landowner; opposed American War and supported Wyvill's reform movement; broke with Fox over Coalition, and defeated by him at Westminster in 1784.

[2] Duchess of Devonshire to Lady E. Foster, 8 Mar. 1784; Chatsworth MSS.

[3] Lord J. Cavendish to Spencer, 27 Jan. 1784; Spencer MSS.

[4] Cornwallis to Lt.-Col. Ross, 26 Jan. 1784; C. Ross, ed. *Correspondence of 1st Marquis Cornwallis*, i. 156–7.

[5] P.R.O. Pitt Papers, 30/8.103, f. 44; George III to Pitt, 30 Jan. 1784.

[6] Pitt to Portland, 1 Feb. 1784; Portland MSS.

[7] *Fox Speeches*, ii. 39; 20 Feb. 1784.

undoubtedly was the resignation of the Ministers, for nothing on earth could be attempted while they stood up in defiance of the House of Commons.'[1]

From the moment of the rejection of the India Bill and the dismissal of the Coalition, compromise had been out of the question. Pitt and George III had to be made to do constitutional penance before the Whigs would return to office. Every possible qualification of this very rigid position was rejected. As late as 24 February, Fox refused to allow the Duke of Portland to be tempted by the St. Alban's Tavern proposals: 'You and not Pitt must be the King's Agent as far as he is supposed to have one and to this I think you should adhere but I own I think that part of the difficulty which relates to the honour of the H. of C's will be in great measure got over whenever the King shall have sent to you to assist Him (not Pitt) in forming a new Administration, because nobody will suppose that *He* takes such a measure but from a sense of the impossibility of maintaining His Servants against the House of Commons.'[2] This three-month battle in the Commons had committed the Whig party as a whole to a clear reliance on the House of Commons, and an equally clear interpretation, provided by Fox, of the events of 1782–4. The King's actions in dishing the Whigs twice within eighteen months and the methods he had employed were catalogued and duly entered into Whig political lore. The cohesion, which the Foxite members of the Coalition demonstrated during these months, showed how effectively Fox had galvanized the Whigs into new activity. Only the unexpected resilience of Pitt and the desertion of some Northites frustrated the Whigs' campaign, but, although office had eluded them, their anger and irritation remained as a spur to political involvement.

Commentators looking back on the years 1782–4 were universally convinced that they represented nothing but continual defeat. Lord John Russell lamented this, because, in the bitter antagonism between Fox and Pitt, the cause of reform was split irrevocably.[3] Philip Francis, with less charity, blamed the whole thing on Fox's gambling instinct: 'From his cradle to his coffin he was a gamester . . . gaming was the master passion that ruled and ruined him.'[4] In fact, however, the voting figures suggest strongly that Foxite votes held under the most severe pressure, and that it was only the Northite wing of the Coalition which disintegrated. Burke, in March 1784, divided the House into those voting for and against Pitt, and also added what he

[1] *Morning Chronicle*, 29 Jan. 1784.

[2] Add. MS. 47561, f. 74; Fox to Portland, 24 Feb. 1784.

[3] *Mems. and Corres. of C. J. Fox*, ii. 242 seq.

[4] J. Parkes and H. Merivale, *Memoirs of Sir Philip Francis* (London, 1867), ii. 446.

took to be their former allegiances before loyalties polarized between Pitt and Fox.[1] By checking the voting records of those former Northites and those supporters of 'the old opposition' to North, who, by March 1784, were found to be voting with Pitt, it is possible to establish very approximately when these votes were lost to the Coalition. Fifty-four Northites, according to Burke's calculations, voted for the India Bill at some stage, but, within the next three months, had transferred their votes to Pitt.[2] Only three members of 'the old Opposition' to North had done so in the same period.[3] In fact, the Foxite interest enjoyed a net gain of four between December 1783 and March 1784, in that seven members joined Fox because, as Burke put it, 'Pitt was resisting the resolutions of the House of Commons.'[4] As these figures suggest, the Coalition fell, not through an upsurge of moral indignation at the enormity of the India Bill, on which issue Coalition votes held steady, but because, between December 1783 to March 1784, the Northite wing of the Coalition, firm supporters of the King throughout the American War, succumbed to royal offers, royal threats, and the awful fear that the Coalition might not only be a failure, but was also a potential threat to the smooth running of government. The steadiness of the Whig vote, under attack from a similar battery of arguments, demonstrates how convincingly Fox had brought energy and vigour to his party. The Whig trials of 1782–4 had been worked up by Fox into a coherent political whole, which would inflame and mould the political attitudes of a generation. The steadiness of the Whig party in the 1780s and the growth of the instruments of party organization in the same decade stem directly from the trauma of these years. The Whigs were angry and humiliated, and they were now prepared to give time and money to politics.

[1] Milton MSS. a xxxviii. f. 19.

[2] C. Ambler, A. Bayntun, Sir C. Bishop, H. Boscawen, J. Calvert (jnr.), Ld. Fred. Campbell, Ilay Campbell, T. Caswell, W. Chaytor, J. Cleveland, Sir Jo. Cockburn, Sir J. Coghill, L. Cox, N. Curzon, Sir E. Dering, Sir W. Dolben, A. Drummond, J. Dutton, Sir A. Edmonstone, J. W. Egerton, Sir C. Furnaby, Sir S. Gideon, Ld. A. Gordon, Ld. W. Gordon, Sir C. Gould, J. Halliday, A. Herbert, Hinchingbrooke, Sir H. Hoghton, J. P. Hungerford, Hyde, T. Johnes, H. Jones, Kensington, Sir R. Laurie, Lincoln, W. Masterman, G. Medley, S. L. Morris, J. Murray, Newhaven, Sir G. Osborn, Sir H. Palliser, J. Peachey, Ld. A. Percy, G. Pitt, J. Robinson, G. Rodney, J. Sinclair, A. Smith, P. Stephens, J. Stephenson, W. Ward, N. Wraxall.

[3] A. Goddard, H. W. Mortimer, B. Rouse.

[4] W. A'.Court, W. H. Bouverie, F. Honeywood are given in Burke's list. If Burke's assessment of voting in Mar. 1784 is correct, the following, who voted against the India Bill, must also have transferred their allegiance to Fox in this period: C. A. Marsham, T. Powys, R. Thistlethwaite, J. Tempest.

III

THE WHIG OPPOSITION 1784–1789 AND THE IMPEACHMENT OF WARREN HASTINGS

THE dismissal of the Coalition on the question of the East India Bill and the simplification of important constitutional points in the personal duel between Pitt and Fox determined the political allegiance of a whole generation. To follow one or other of these men was to be committed to a set interpretation of the events of 1782–4, and therefore to a fixed series of political values. The embryonic growth of party organization among the Whigs in the 1780s, which has recently come under close scrutiny, must be firmly related to these events. Fox interpreted them, and set them within a recognizable Whig tradition. His extravagant character and his loathing of Pitt placed the issue on such a broad canvas, that even the most simple-minded backbencher could easily associate himself with one of the contestants. Hyperbole was in fashion, and it gave cohesion to politics. To have voted on the India Bill was to commit oneself for the rest of the 1780s. The effect was the same on those new members entering Parliament in the 1784 election, in which the fate of this same Bill played so great a part. Only the full impact of the French Revolution could break the loyalties forged in these years. As late as 1793, Fox had only to remind Portland of Pitt's actions a decade earlier for that gentleman to reconsider any proposal coming from the King or his first minister. For Fox himself, these two years were decisive. In his opinion, radicalism, Tom Paine, and the French Revolution itself paled into insignificance beside the demonstrable threat coming from the Crown. It was on this danger that Fox fixed his eyes, and never again averted them.

All contemporaries and most historians have freely admitted that the election of 1784 was remarkable in the amount of time, energy and money devoted to it. Debate has centred on the extent to which political opinion, by the limited channels open to it in eighteenth-century electoral life, played a part in defeating the Whigs. The publication of John Robinson's papers seemed to show convincingly that it was simply good management and influence which defeated Fox, and that, in electoral terms, the debates with Pitt were largely an irrelevance.[1] Such a view would severely militate against all considerations of party in the 1780s, because, even if the will to form party institutions was present, their practical effect in electoral terms would have been illusory. This view was later challenged simply from the observation that in a number of seats, long-established and eminent Whig members were defeated, and that in constituencies with large electorates, Pittites again scored some very remarkable successes.[2] If this latter interpretation proves correct, the election of 1784, by upsetting strongly entrenched electoral interests, would support the view that so bitter was the battle between Fox and the Crown, that the expression of opinion upon this issue might temporarily overcome the normal workings of eighteenth-century electoral machinery. This is to argue that the view taken by both Fox and George III, that the country was faced with an extreme constitutional crisis, was shared and found expression throughout the political nation.

Contemporary evidence almost unanimously admits both the extraordinary character of this election and the part played by opinion in it. The *Morning Herald*, for example, explained the Whig defeat by insisting that Fox had failed to persuade people of the wider constitutional implications of the quarrel, which the Crown successfully insisted was a crisis generated by the selfish ambition of a few men to seize power. The crisis is admitted and views are taken of it. The Whigs are defeated because the Crown's interpretation wins general acceptance:

> The question shall be between Mr. Fox, with whom the people are displeased, and the Crown, and not between the Crown and the people. . . . Through this artifice of the Court the people have been completely blinded, and the more ardently Mr. Fox supported their rights, the more they reviled him.[3]

This is not to deny the obvious importance of Robinson's careful management of seats, which had been taken in hand as early as December 1783, but Crown management alone would not have unseated Thomas Coke in Norfolk or Lord John Cavenidish at York. Some new factor must be introduced into the situation to account for these defeats. Fox had deliberately brought the situation to the point of crisis only to discover that the King's case carried more general credence.

The strength and bitterness of the forces marshalled against the Whigs in this election testified to Fox's success in bringing politics

[1] W. T. Laprade, 'Public Opinion and the General Election of 1784', *E.H.R.* xxi (1916). C. E. Fryer, 'The General Election of 1784', *History*, ix. no. 35 (1924).

[2] Mrs. E. George, 'Fox's Martyrs: The General Election of 1784', *T.R.H.S.* xx. (1937).

[3] *Morning Herald*, 11 May 1784.

to life. Robinson's task in managing the Crown's electoral assets was made much easier by the realization on the part of many Ministerialists that the King's whole status in government had been called into question. All Dr. Johnson's royalist leanings were confirmed: 'Fox is a most extraordinary man; here is a man who has divided the Kingdom with Caesar; so that it was a doubt whether the nation should be ruled by the sceptre of George the Third or the tongue of Fox.'[1] Pittites, as well as Coalitionists, had been stung into action by Fox's claims. The opprobrium and vilification meted out to Fox in Court pamphlets were an indirect compliment to his capacity to shock. Equally serious for the Whigs, from an electoral point of view, was the challenge presented to the vested interests of the existing establishment in India House. All corporate bodies were circularized by the East India men, who ironically employed against Fox the old cry of charters in danger, which had once been so telling a point against the Stuarts. As ever, the Company's influence was divided, but there can be little doubt that the bulk of it was directed against the Coalitionist forces. Those who were economically threatened by Fox's campaigns threw their electoral weight behind the Crown. Finally, the India Bill and Coalition had effectively cut Fox off from that reforming interest in English politics, which had been growing steadily stronger since the late 1770s, and whose electoral strength found no mention in Robinson's carefully managed statistics. Philip Yorke[2] was informed by his agent in Cambridgeshire that the reforming gentlemen of that county would not vote for the Coalition candidates: 'One of the parties Mr. Fox has professed much in favour of a Reform in Parliament. The other had as honestly declared himself against it. And on the whole it is supposed my Lord North has not given up his original Idea of this business, but Mr. Fox had at least agreed to decline it. Such are the Ideas of many of the common freeholders in the Country.'[3] Fox's claims against the Crown were not believed, because the Coalition and India Bill had severely compromised him in the eyes of the reformers.

York provided an interesting test case for the value of opinion in this election, both because the unseating of Lord John Cavendish from an old Rockingham stronghold requires considerable explanation, and because this city was one of the main centres of the reforming interest. Early in January 1784, Wyvill's correspondents in York were

[1] J. Boswell, *The Life of Dr. Samuel Johnson*, p. 1292.

[2] Philip Yorke (1757–1834); M.P. (Cambs.) 1780–90; independent county member; unhappy about the American War, but fearful of seeing Fox in office, supported both Shelburne and Pitt; succeeded uncle as 3rd Earl of Hardwicke, May 1790.

[3] Add. MS. 35641 (Hardwicke Papers), f. 77; J. Bedlam to P. Yorke, 28 Feb. 1784.

informing him that they now feared aristocracy more than uncontrolled monarchy: 'For what good possible think you could occur to the nation, (was our point now actually carried) if Charles Fox had the Indies at our [his] disposal?'[1] Two months later, the whole issue presented by the India Bill and its constitutional implications was debated by the city's electors in the Yard of York Castle. Led by Wilberforce, elector after elector rose to condemn the whole of Fox's conduct since 1782.[2] Manoeuvres, like the formation of the Coalition, which had not necessarily been condemned a year earlier, were now synthesized into an aristocratic plot and universally condemned. Wyvill himself believed that Fox's success 'would have introduced Corruption to a degree of profligacy which this Country had never seen, and would, in fact, have changed our limited Monarchy into a mere Aristocratical Republic'.[3] The result of this pressure was that the Rockingham interest at York, although personally defended by Fitzwilliam, Carlisle, and Lord John Cavendish, collapsed. This transfer of allegiance was effected without the direction of Robinson, and the same kind of spontaneous rebellion, which took place at York, must account for at least some of the other Whig disappointments. The Whigs themselves were astonished by the reaction, which they had provoked. Lord John had to admit that; 'The turn that all our Elections have taken is very surprizing to me, & my own more than all, where I thought myself as safe as at a Burgage Tenure borough.'[4] The crisis, which gave cohesion to the Whigs, also gave determination to their opponents.

Difficulties arise when an attempt is made to estimate just how many Foxites suffered Lord John's fate in this election, and how far the heavy Whig losses of this year are simply due to the fact that large numbers of Lord North's supporters, who had been elected with royal backing in 1780, now suffered because this backing was withdrawn. A pamphlet[5] published in 1784 listed 89 Members of Parliament, who lost their seats as a direct consequence of following Fox. When this list is compared to the party division lists drawn up by Burke,[6] these 89 names break down into 43 Foxites, 38 Northites, 2 Independents and 6 pro-Coalition votes, for whom no more precise loyalty is given. When Dundas's[7] list of February 1783 is taken as the

[1] Rev. W. Mason to Rev. C. Wyvill, 22 Jan. 1784; Wyvill, *Political Tracts and Papers*, iv. 352.

[2] *Debate among Yorkshire Members on Recent Occurrences*, 25 Mar. 1784; C. Wyvill, *Political Tracts & Papers*, ii. 328.

[3] N. C. Philips, *Yorkshire and National Politics 1783–4*, p. 59.

[4] Lord John Cavendish to Mrs. Ponsonby, 6 May 1784; Grey MSS.

[5] Anon. *Fox's Martyrs or a New Book of the Sufferings of the Faithful.*

[6] Milton MSS. xxxviii, f. 19, Mar. 1784.

[7] J. Norris, *Shelburne and Reform*, pp. 290 seq.

yardstick, these same 89 names break down into 44 Foxites, 32 Northites, 7 Independents, 2 Shelburnites and 4 Coalition supporters with no more specific loyalty. Allowing for obvious discrepancies, these figures would seem to suggest that the Whig defeat in the 1784 election cannot be explained simply in terms of the unseating of Northite placeholders, but that Foxites suffered in at least equal numbers, and often in constituencies, where the Whig predominance had been long established. Robinson, even at his most assiduous, could not have hoped to win these seats without the added factor of the movement of opinion against Fox and his Coalition. Fox succeeded in polarizing politics, but unfortunately the majority of the political world decided against him.[1]

For Fox himself, the contest for Westminster was vital. This prestige constituency had operated as a national platform for the Whigs at each step of the crisis. If Fox's views were defeated in the Commons, he could always refer his ideas to the electors of Westminster, and their approbation allowed him to claim that the Whigs genuinely represented opinion in the country, and that they were only thwarted by an unreformed legislature. Pitt himself fully appreciated the value of Westminster to the Whigs, and determined to break their control.[2] The personal defeat of Fox was equally to be hoped for, in that much of the impact of the crisis stemmed from the confrontation of these two men. Westminster could not be won by management, however. During the campaign, appeals had to be made to issues and broad party attitudes. Pitt's main hope that the Whig control of Westminster might be broken, lay in the fact that each of Fox's major decisions since July 1782 had splintered his support in the constituency. The Firm and Free Club in 1782 and the defection of Jebb a year later indicated that opinion in Westminster was moving against Fox. Both sides fully realized what was at stake and their confrontation made this contest one of the most formidable of the eighteenth century. Dukes opened their purses, duchesses kissed tradesmen, and Fox canvassed from door to door, in an attempt to save Westminster, because, if this constituency were won, some shred of support was left to the claim that in making new demands on the King in the last two years, the Whigs were effectively giving voice to the true wishes of the country.

Although Fox subscribed liberally to the principal charities of Westminster,[3] there is no indication that the Whigs thought they could win before the end of April. Indeed, the Duke of Portland

[1] See Chapter 7, 244–5.

[2] W. T. Laprade, 'William Pitt and Westminster Elections', *A.H.R.* xviii. no. 2 (1913).

[3] Add. MS. 51466, f. 4; Receipt, 9 Apr. 1784.

reported that their greatest problem was in persuading Fox to continue the contest: 'Mr. Fox has gone too far at present to give up, & though there is no chance, I believe & wish, of success, he should not appear to desert His Friends.'[1] In almost daily reports to Mrs. Armistead, Fox talked only of defeat and a withdrawal from politics: 'I must not give up yet tho' I wish it. Indeed I feel that I ought not while there is a bare possibility . . . I have serious thoughts if I am beat here, of not coming in to Parliament at all.'[2] Fox's attempts to find another seat were proving equally futile. Impatience led him into blatant bribery at Bridgwater,[3] while even the refuge of a closed Scottish borough was not ruled out, although hardly suited to the Man of the People. Between 1782 and 1784, Fox faced the electors of Westminster three times, and on each occasion, his return was more and more difficult, providing a rough measure of the movement of opinion against him.

George III was, at this stage, equally prepared to interpret the election results in Norfolk and Yorkshire as 'the genuine Sense of the People',[4] and was very aware of the importance of defeating Fox personally: 'Though the advance made by Mr. Fox this day can only have been by bad Votes, yet similar measures must be adopted rather than let him get Returned for Westminster.'[4] Much of the pamphlet material on the Crown's side was aimed directly at Fox, as if in open recognition of the extent to which he had come to represent a given set of constitutional claims.[5] It seems likely, however, that the virulence and bitterness of the royal campaign in Westminster produced the opposite effect to that intended. When the mood of the Whigs becomes increasingly optimistic in the last week of April, Fox, in a letter to the electors published in the *Morning Chronicle*, attributed this turn of events entirely to a reaction against royal pressure:

> The unprecedented exertions which the servants of the Crown have thought themselves at liberty to make against me . . . have produced the effects naturally to the expected from such proceedings, by raising the spirit and awakening the indignation of every honest and independent elector.[6]

Both sides were therefore ready to allow that opinion was a factor of some importance in certain constituencies at this election, and the extraordinary nature of the Westminster contest was due entirely to

[1] Portland to Lady Rockingham, 8 Apr. 1784; Portland MSS. PWF 9193.

[2] Add. MS. 47570, f. 159; Fox to Mrs. Armistead, 8 Apr. 1784.

[3] Sir J. Harris to Mrs. Robinson, 29 Mar. 1784; Malmesbury MSS. Box 1.

[4] P.R.O. Pitt Papers, 30/8.103, f. 93; George III to Pitt, 13 Apr. 1784.

[5] e.g. Anon. *The Dying Words of Reynard the Fox*, Apr. 1784.

[6] *Morning Chronicle*, 1 May 1784. Fox only overtook Sir Cecil Wray on 27 Apr. 1784, when he went into the lead by 27 votes. By 7 May, his majority was up to 176 votes.

the bitterness, which Fox's polarization of politics had introduced into the constituencies. Both the King and Fox knew that real issues were at stake. The fact that Fox lost in the short term is unimportant beside the realization that politics had been given a new definition, which would make the institutional development of party in the later 1780s possible.

So uncompromising were the politics of these months, that the Crown was not prepared to allow Fox his majority at the polls without recourse to a scrutiny. Fox, well aware of the climate in which the contest was taking place, had foreseen this manoeuvre, 'which will be troublesome beyond measure'.[1] The Westminster Scrutiny, which dragged on until March 1785, was motivated purely by vindictiveness against Fox, and led Pitt uncharacteristically to give opposition the opportunity of humiliating his Ministry.[2] Fox was quick to point out that, if scrutinies could be prolonged indefinitely, members opposed to the Ministry could be kept out of the Commons as long as the Crown desired.[3] By June, the notorious attempt to annul the Whig's victory in the Commons by an indefinite scrutiny had been placed in context. It merely represented yet another device of the Crown for thwarting the wishes of the people and the authority of the Lower House.[4] Fox's anger and bitterness were uncompromisingly expressed: 'The shuffling mean tricks of the present administration excite no sensations in my mind but contempt for the cause, and pity for the effects of it. To be present at the daily or rather hourly equivocations of a young hypocrite is at once so disgusting to observe and so infamous for men to tolerate, that the person who listens to them with forbearance, becomes almost an accomplice in them.'[5]

Pitt's distaste for Fox quite gratuitiously allowed the opposition to taste victory. On 3 March 1785, the House voted by 162–121 to allow the returns for Westminster to be made without any further scrutiny. Although Fox had been preoccupied with the scrutiny while Pitt's India Bill was safely engineered through the Commons, the Minister's majority was such that concern for the passing of this measure could not have prompted his action. The Scrutiny was undertaken out of pure malice, and it brought Pitt's first defeat in the

[1] Add. MS. 47570, f. 162; Fox to Mrs. Armistead, 27 Apr. 1784.

[2] Part of the trouble lay in the fact that in many eighteenth-century constituencies, there was genuine doubt about electors' qualifications, which would make a scrutiny in so large a constituency as Westminster necessarily troublesome. Pitt must however, have been aware of this fact in deliberately challenging Fox's return. *See* S. Heywood. *A Digest of So Much of the Law Respecting Borough Elections as Concerns Cities and Boroughs in General* (London, 1797), pp. 188 seq.

[3] *Fox Speeches*, ii. 439; 24 May 1784.

[4] *Fox Speeches*, ii. 481 seq.; 8 June 1784.

[5] *Morning Herald*, 30 July 1784.

Commons. Pitt, as Thomas Orde reported, was vulnerable, and the scrutiny gave Fox the opportunity to attack: 'I think, I perceived some Symptoms of Jealously in Pitt, when any mention was made of persons as having claims on government, because of attachment to the *Crown*, and a word ab^{t} the *royal recommendation* seemed to call up more blood than usual into his cheeks.'[1] After the Commons' vote, Whig houses were illuminated for three nights in succession, and Fox was drawn in triumph to the House of Commons.[2] To make the point quite certain, Fox successfully sued the Bailiff of Westminster for not returning him in due form, and, with politic generosity, distributed the damages of £2,000 among the charities of Westminster.[3]

Superficially, the humiliating defeat in the 1784 election left the Whigs broken and dispirited. Burke was soon complaining that all attempts at organized opposition had disappeared: 'As to any plan of Conduct in our Leaders, there are not the faintest Traces of it—nor does [it] seem to occur to them that any such thing is necessary. Accordingly every thing is left to accidents; I thought Fox had great Faith in the Chapter of that Scripture.'[4] With the exception of the Scrutiny business, no attempt was made for the remainder of the 1784 Session to keep up the opposition to Pitt. Through a lack of co-ordination, division lists were often derisory, as Pittite commentators were quick to point out: 'I hear Fox's friends are quite disgusted with him for having tried a division, and, except Mr. Burke and Mr. Sheridan, and one or two more who were very grave, the rest seemed to join in the laugh at their ridiculous situation . . . so little pains had Steel taken about members that I suppose 100 of his friends were absent & did not know of any debate.'[5] The same kind of comment on the laxity of the Whigs was made throughout the 1785 session of Parliament as well.[6] It appeared to the political world that the trauma of their experiences between 1782 and 1784 had broken the Whigs. For two years, Pitt's victory went almost undisputed.

In spite of the tactical withdrawals Pitt had to make, over the Irish Commercial Bill, the fortification plan for Portsmouth and Plymouth, and the Reform Bill of 1785, Fox fully shared this general desire for a relaxation of effort. For much of the 1784–5 sessions, bills had to be sent down to St. Anne's Hill, because the principal

[1] T. Orde to Shelburne, 17 June 1784; Bowood MSS.

[2] J. Baynes to Sir S. Romilly, 7 May 1785; Romilly, *Memoirs*, i. 318.

[3] *Gentleman's Magazine*, Dec. 1786.

[4] Add. MS. 37843 (Windham Papers), f. 5; E. Burke to W. Windham, 14 Oct. 1784.

[5] D. Pulteney to Duke of Rutland, 27 May 1784; H.M.C. *Rutland MSS*. iii. 14.1. pp. 97–8.

[6] Camden to Grafton, 27 Jan. 1785; Grafton MSS. f. 100.

spokesman of the Whigs saw little point in coming up to Town. His profligate and irresponsible behaviour at Brighton in the autumn of that year gave new offence to the high-minded, reforming interest,[1] and George III was convinced by his enemy's disinclination to attend at Westminster, that he was determined to retire from politics completely.[2] Fox substituted for concentrated opposition a series of schoolboy tricks, designed to irritate rather than threaten, which were reported by the Duchess of Devonshire: 'On Wednesday Morning C. Fox, Fitzpatrick & Ld. Robert [Spencer] happened to meet by Ld. Shelburne's gate, Sheridan and Hare come up & the Prince of Wales rode by when they saw they were watch'd from Lord Chatham's & they directly made Fitzpatrick go & enquire after his nephews etc: at Shelburne House to make them believe there was a treaty . . .[3]

Fox's inactivity aroused anger and irritation throughout all sections of the party. Even Pitt's India Bill could not tempt Fox up from the country. When Burke moved that a committee be appointed to investigate the veracity of the reports from India, 'Fox and several others would not stay even for that',[4] and none of the Whigs could be quite sure whether he would appear for the third reading of the Bill or not.[5] For those, who were professionally interested in politics, like Burke and Francis, Fox's complaisance was inexcusable. The reaction of the Duke of Portland, viewing politics with more detachment, was mere confusion: 'The Egregious misconduct of Administration seems to me to justify the recess Fox has given this Session to those exertions which have been heretofore necessary for bringing forward questionable matter, but at the same time I must entirely agree with you that it has furnished matter worthy of his utmost powers, & of his most active co-operation with you & other real friends of the Publick.'[6] Dissatisfaction was easily carried over from Fox's political life to his personal affairs. It was even suggested that he should legitimize his relations with Mrs. Armistead for the good of the party. At all levels of the Whig connection, Fox's laxity and self-indulgence seemed reprehensible in the extreme.

The two years following the 1784 election therefore convinced a large number of contemporaries that, very far from giving a new emphasis to party cohesion and organization, the defeat of that year had shattered the Whigs forever. The pattern of the future seemed

[1] R. Price to Shelburne, 24 Nov. 1784; Bowood MSS.

[2] Pitt Papers, 30/8.103, f. 119; George III to Pitt, 29 July 1784.

[3] Duchess of Devonshire to Lady Spencer, 26 June 1784; Chatsworth MSS. ff. 624–5.

[4] E. Burke to Sir G. Elliot, 3 Aug. 1784; Copeland, *Burke Corres.* v. 166.

[5] D. Long to E. Burke, Tuesday 1784; Wentworth Woodhouse Muniments, Burke 1.

[6] Portland to W. Eden, 24 Apr. 1784; Portland MSS. PWF 3971.

to be an endless and incoherent period in the wilderness, with Pitt picking off individual members of the party, who were susceptible to the call of ambition or duty. Camden, on joining the Administration in 1786 offered the following apologia:

The Coalition has destroy'd the Whig party forever & we the forlorns of that description have been forced to unite in some sort with our old Enemys. I am not fond of their Company but must co-operate with them. I lament this necessity the more as it has separated me from Mr. Fox whom I wish'd of all men to see among the first in the Admin^{n} of this Country, but that's past & I will say no more upon this subject.[1]

Wraxall, writing a review of English politics early in 1786, agreed very largely with this assessment. After emphasizing the extent to which politics had become a personal duel between Pitt and Fox,[2] Wraxall insisted that the latter's major defect was that no one was now sure on what principles he stood: 'He is capable by turns, of aggrandizing, or of diminishing the power of the Crown; and of justifying by reasons and arguments the most plausible, the measure of whatever nature which he shall have seen fit to adopt.'[3] The two-year hiatus in serious opposition gave an impression of disintegration, and it is presumably this period in particular, which has led one authority to the very severe judgement that 'Fox did not yet fully appreciate the role of party in the political arena; even if he had understood it, he lacked the conviction that might have translated theory into action.'[4] This claim demands close examination.

Too much should not be made of this relaxing of opposition after the defeat of 1784. It was a tactical withdrawal from political engagements rather than a total admission of defeat. Fox was convinced that Pitt's strength owed more to the opprobrium, which surrounded the Coalitionists, than to any positive movement of opinion in the Ministry's favour: 'It is impossible not to see that the majority is much more *against* us than *for* the Ministry, and their behaviour on the India Bill which had begun to excite much discontent till I opposed it is a very sufficient lesson in my mind. . . . I know that, both on my own account and in consideration of the present state of the House, I can serve it better by lying by for a little while.'[5] Facing a House of Commons, many of whose Members were elected on a specifically anti-Fox platform, this policy was by no means unwise. Time was needed for tempers to cool and memories to grow dim.

[1] Camden to Grafton, 6 Jan. 1786; Grafton MSS. f. 97.

[2] Sir N. Wraxall, *A Short Review of the Political State of Great Britain . . . 1787*, pp. 28–9.

[3] ibid. pp. 40–41.

[4] F. O'Gorman, *The Whig Party and the French Revolution*, p. 6.

[5] Add. MS. 47561, f. 81; Fox to Portland, 27 July 1784.

Opposition during these two years therefore took the pattern of sharp, concentrated attacks at points of extreme Pittite vulnerability, separated by long periods of quiescence. This policy was by no means unsuccessful, for Pitt was beaten on the issues of the Westminster scrutiny, the Irish Commercial Bill, and the proposal to fortify Portsmouth and Plymouth. Three victories in two years was no mean achievement for an opposition party in the emphatically Pittite Parliament of 1784–90. On each occasion, independent votes were decisive, and this sort of support was not won by factious opposition. In what was admittedly a highly defensive letter to William Eden, Fox pointed out that Pitt's India Bill would have to pass, because 'the House will upon this Subject give them credit to save themselves the trouble of attending and to avoid giving any countenance to the exploded India Bill.'[1] The experiences of 1782–4 had committed Pittite as well as Foxite votes for the future. If Pitt was to be defeated, it would be on general issues, which were not immediately related to the politics of the previous two years.

The more perceptive political observers realized that this hiatus in opposition represented less a sign of disintegration than a truce. Thomas Orde, Lord Lansdowne's very experienced informant, insisted, at the beginning of 1786, that matters were still very much in the balance: 'I agree at all events with you, that this will be a Session of Tryal for Mr. Pitt, and that He will now be shaken, or his Stability confirmed.'[2] Such comments, far from supporting the view that Whig disintegration had been the result of the recent election, suggests that Fox was holding his party in reserve for an issue on which to resume the attack, and refused to commit his forces on issues which stood no chance of being defeated in the Parliament of 1784.

The dangerous corollary of this period of waiting was that the cohesion of the Whigs would break up into petty squabbling, and be be weakened by inactivity. As the criticisms reported above indicate, dissatisfaction was very real among those politicians, like Burke and Francis, whose only political manoeuvre was the frontal assault. In fact, however, the polarization of politics, during the 1782–4 period, had been so pronounced, that Fox was proved successful in his intention of uniting the Whigs around the constitutional claims he voiced at that period. Between 1784 and 1788, when, during the Regency crisis, it is again possible to measure voting behaviour along fairly clear party lines, the cohesion of Whig votes is astonishing. Certainly, prominent individuals like Eden and Camden joined Pitt, but these men were very much the exception. Most of the Coalitionists clung firmly and uncompromisingly to the interpretation of the events of

[1] Add. MS. 34419, f. 357; Fox to W. Eden, undated.
[2] T. Orde to Lansdowne, 24 Jan. 1786; Bowood MSS.

1782–4, which Fox had given them. Of the 90 Foxites, who had supported the Coalition and who were still in Parliament in 1788, only 5[1] had transferred their votes to Pitt, while 2[2] others were ambivalent in their attitudes. The Northite wing of the Coalition, as set out by Burke in 1784, showed an even more astonishing loyalty to Fox, in that the past history of these men would make them peculiarly susceptible to Ministerial bribes and blandishments. Of the 57 members of this group still in the Commons in 1788, only 6[3] were found to be voting with Pitt, while a further 3[4] have no recorded votes during the Regency crisis at all. The steadiness of Coalition voting under the wearing pressure of unrelieved opposition is a remarkable indication of how firmly Fox, in his duel with Pitt, had redefined the terms of the political battle.

The extraordinarily impressive development of embryonic party institutions is obviously a related phenomenon.[5] During the period 1783–8, general funds were established for the contesting of elections, agents were placed on regular salaries, newspapers were bought up and pamphleteers subsidized. Under the supervision of William Adam, this detailed development of party structure among politicians in opposition is a new and important phenomenon in English politics. Far from disintegrating as a result of being defeated in 1784, the Whigs were busy giving their beliefs institutional form. Men were now prepared to devote large amounts of time and money to politics, and it was on this commitment that Adam capitalized. Fox was not involved with the details of organization, but this is not necessarily a function of leadership. Peel was equally separated from such administrative concerns. Fox's relations with Adam were, however, increasingly cordial, and his name was enrolled among the first hundred members of the Whig Club,[6] which was founded in May 1784. Fox very quickly turned that assembly into a forum for party views and a platform for the exposition of party doctrine. Much of the difficulty in communication between Fox and his supporters, which had made the decisions of 1782–4 so troublesome to put across, would in future be obviated. The Club remained loyal to Fox throughout the period of the Revolutionary Wars, and was to prove an invaluable asset in the propagation of the Foxite creed.

[1] J. F. Cawthorne, H. Minchin, Sir R. Lawley, Sir J. Rushout, R. Thistlethwaite.

[2] W. H. Bouverie, C. Marsham.

[3] M. Brickdale, R. P. Carew, B. Lethieullier, T. Onslow, R. Shaftoe, Westcote.

[4] Wm. Eden, E. Lewis, Sir T. Rumbold.

[5] D. Ginter, 'The Financing of the Whig Party Organization, 1783–93', *A.H.R.* lxxi. no. 2 (1966).

[6] *The Whig Club Rule Book*, 13 May 1784.

Those who question Fox's grasp of the possibilities of party in English politics quote Burke's remark that he became disillusioned with the opposition in the 1780's, because they 'proceeded upon the separate measures as they separately arose, without any vindictive retrospect to Mr. Pitt's conduct in 1784'.[1] This comment was made in 1793, at a time when the first aim of Burke's writings was to discredit Fox in the eyes of certain leading Whigs, and should not therefore be given undue weight. In fact, the developments of the later 1780s suggest that Fox had good reason to be pleased. Fox had presented the Crown, in the debates with Pitt, with an alternative scheme of government. This flirtation with new ideas sprang directly from necessity and Fox's experience of dealings with the Crown, but it was coherent and valid. Although defeated in the 1784 election, Fox had nevertheless divided English politics. 'Pittite' and 'Foxite' divided London society along different interpretations of the events of 1782–4. Fox's definition was sufficiently attractive to engage the sympathies of young men like Charles Grey[2] and Michaelangelo Taylor,[3] who entered Parliament in 1786, and, though ambitious, joined opposition rather than the Ministry. The solidity of Whig voting in the later 1780s suggests that party was a fact. William Adam gave it institutional form. Fox gave it an intellectual basis. The two were interdependent.

Fox's grasp of the possibilities of party organization can be most clearly demonstrated by the part he played in the prosecution of Warren Hastings. Before the defeat of the India Bill, Fox's interest in the bringing down of Hastings was virtually non-existent. On 28 May 1782, he had voted for the recall of Hastings, but ruled out the possibility of prosecution, and joined Dundas in speaking of the Governor's 'unimpeachable integrity'.[4] In the negotiations with the Hastings group before the publication of the India Bill, Fox played no part, and was, according to one observer, entirely ignorant of the proceedings: 'Fox, who knew nothing of the matter, had nothing to say in reply, . . . it appeared that the negotiation had been set on foot without the knowledge of Fox and that Sheridan was the chief agent in it.'[5] Whig contacts with India before December 1783 were limited

[1] Quoted in F. O'Gorman, *The Whig Party and the French Revolution*, p. 11.

[2] Charles Grey (1764–1845); M.P. (Northumberland) 1786–1807 (Appleby) May–July 1807, (Tavistock) July–Nov. 1807; almost immediately aligned himself with Fox on entering Parliament, and remained a leading Whig thereafter; Sec. of State for Foreign Affairs, Sept. 1806–Mar. 1807; Prime Minister, 1830–4.

[3] Michaelangelo Taylor (?1757–1834); M.P. 1784–1802, 1806–31, 1832–4; representing seven boroughs; entered Parliament as a Pittite, but gradually moved closer to Fox; manager of the Hastings impeachment; thereafter a firm Foxite.

[4] Marshall, *The Impeachment of Warren Hastings*, p. 19.

[5] T. Moore to Dr. Parr, Nov. 1783; W. Sichel, *Sheridan*, ii. 44.

to the emotional aggressiveness of Burke and Francis and the diplomacy of Sheridan. Fox was not obviously impressed with the moral pleadings of Burke against Hastings and knew nothing of the diplomacy.

Once the India Bill had been defeated, however, Fox's interest in the fate of Hastings quickened. This Bill came to be the issue, on which the reputation of the Coalition rested. To prove it necessary, Fox had to show that India had been misruled and oppressed. To convict Hastings of despotic behaviour was therefore to establish the innocence of the India Bill and its parents, the Coalitionists. Hastings therefore became inextricably caught up in the constitutional wrangling of the 1782–4 period. In supporting Francis' motion for papers relating to the Hastings administration of India, Fox succinctly set this issue in context, on 16 February 1784;

> It was for this reason he wished an investigation into the whole affairs of the East India Company; that every proceeding of the court of directors might be examined into, and that every measure adopted by the new board of commissioners might be laid before the public, because he was convinced the more the real state of the Company's affairs became known, the less unpopular would be his Bill.[1]

The Hastings interest was itself aware of how dangerous the defeat of the Coalition on an Indian issue could be. The close understanding between Pitt and the Hastings interest, though largely founded on the fear of the latter, was a fact at the dissolution of 1784. The press reported this more as a political commonplace.

> The moment that Mr. Fox attempted a measure which was not only calculated to abridge the authority of Mr. Hastings, but to make him responsible for his former conduct, the agents and dependents, the mercenaries of the *Asiatic Prince* took the alarm; they flew to the pen; they fastened upon the Minister . . .[2]

Hastings and his administration had become an issue of party and as such Fox took the matter up.

In spite of Burke's complaints about Fox's carelessness and indifference during the passing of Pitt's India Bill, this opportunity was taken of sketching a case in outline against Hastings, and of implicating the new Ministry in the opprobrium. Fox insisted that the alarming state of the Company's finances was entirely due to the disobedience and corruption of their servants in India:

> It was well known that they were the masters, and not the servants of the Company: this must have been the case, or a governor-general would never have dared to disobey the orders of the court of directors, and give the audacious reason for his disobedience, that it was because it was their order.[3]

[1] *Parl. Hist.* xxiv. 150; 16 Feb. 1784.

[2] *Morning Herald*, 2 Aug. 1784.

[3] *Parl. Hist.* xxiv. 1080; 2 July 1784.

In the light of this bankruptcy and insubordination, Fox joyfully pointed out how oddly Pitt's Bill read, the two major provisions of which were the delegation of even greater authority to the Governor-General of India and the meeting of its debts out of general taxation.[1] The very plausible conclusion to be drawn from this was that Pitt had entered into an understanding with the Company for the mutual enjoyment of the wealth of India and a joint control over the disposal of patronage: 'When, we connect the present Act with the bill now pending in the Upper House for the regulation of that Company, may we not justly assert that, instead of establishing an English government over India, as the bill which I presented in the late Parliament professed and attempted to do, the inevitable tendency of the measures now in agitation is the establishment of an Indian government in England.'[2]

Given careful preparation, here was an issue, which could not only compromise Pitt very badly, but which could also vindicate the Coalition and the measure on which it was brought down. Pitt was aware of the danger. His concern, at the beginning of the impeachment that, overtly, it should not become the straight party issue Fox wished to make it, was an attempt to parry the blow.[3] For the Whigs, Hastings' impeachment offered great opportunities. If he were convicted, the Coalition would in some measure be vindicated. There was a possibility that Pitt himself might be forced to share the opprobrium. At the very least, the Pittites would be severely embarrassed, in that Dundas, after his work on India in the early 1780s, was virtually committed to a position of hostility to Hastings. Pitt would therefore be caught between the claims of Dundas and those of East India House, and would at the same time have to hold the support of the Company, while avoiding any personal involvement in the legality or illegality of the Hastings administration.

After the debates on Pitt's India Bill, Fox clearly warmed to the idea of impeaching Hastings. On 8 August 1784, he met Francis 'to request conference, connexion, and intimacy—opened his thoughts about moving for the recall of Hastings, and then impeaching him'.[4] No evidence exists of any practical steps in this direction for the remainder of 1784, but it is almost certain that the eagerness of Burke and Francis to begin an investigation about the possibilities of impeachment would hardly require more prompting. Throughout the session of 1785, India was kept before the attention of Parliament. On 28 February for example, Fox moved for papers on the issue of the Nabob

[1] *Fox Speeches*, iii. 2 seq.; 16 July 1784.
[2] Wheatley, *The Memoirs of Sir N. Wraxall*. iv. 8; 4 Aug. 1784.
[3] ibid. p. 6.
[4] Marshall, *The Impeachment of Warren Hastings*, p. 34.

of Arcot's debts, hinting that secrecy was veiling a system of corruption and peculation.[1] The King failed to understand why the opposition continued to refer to Indian affairs during this period. For him, Fox's conduct resembled 'that Dictatorial Spirit which I should have thought the framers of the famous East India Bill might now have thought it wise to draw a veil over, not by continual unsuccessful attempts to keep the remembrance of it in full face.'[2] In fact, however, during this period, when Fox believed it wise to relax the pressure of opposition, India had to be kept before the public mind, in preparation for the moment when it could be taken up again in an attack on the person of Hastings.

Even at this early stage, Burke's motives differed considerably from those of Fox. In Burke's view, the defeat of 1784 had so effectively thrown the Whigs into the wilderness, that considerations of party could no longer have any practical effect:

> I consider the House of Commons as something worse than extinguished. We have been labouring for near twenty years to make it independent; and as soon as we had accomplished what he had in View, we found that its independence led to its destruction. . . . This has left us (in the most favourable point of view for our affairs) just where we were at the End of the reign of Charles the Second.[3]

The practical possibilities of the Hastings case therefore made little impression on Burke. For him, the making of a moral point was all important. Even if the Whigs were defeated in the Courts, their protest would be on record and their consciences would be clear. Unfortunately, 'The Tyrrany, robbery, and destruction of mankind practised by the Company and their servants in the East, is popular and pleasing in this Country; and . . . the Court and Ministry who evidently abet the iniquitous System, are somewhat the better liked on that account.'[3] With this premise, neither the timing of the attack nor the numbers, who might support it, were of any importance. During December 1785, when a serious debate was in progress in the Whig party as to whether the impeachment of Hastings should be undertaken, Fox was still uncertain whether the time was yet ripe. He was very afraid that, if the matter was taken up without care, the Whig's showing in division lists would be derisory. Burke, while admitting that 'it might not become a man, situated like Mr. Fox to move without a retinue',[4] wanted a moral gesture at once. Their opinion on the practical relevance of party considerations after the defeat of 1784 led the two men to take a very different view of the

[1] *Fox Speeches*, iii. 45 seq.; 28 Feb. 1785.
[2] P.R.O. Pitt Papers, 30/8.103, f. 165; George III to Pitt, 6 May 1785.
[3] E. Burke to W. Baker, 22 July 1784; Copeland, *Burke Corres*. v. 154.
[4] E. Burke to P. Francis, 10 Dec. 1785; Fitzwilliam, *Burke Corrs*. iii. 38–44.

purpose of Hastings' trial, and this disagreement became more acute as the impeachment proceeded.

Early in 1786, Fox tested the ground. On 17 February, Fox supported Burke's motion for the production of all the letters passing between Hastings and the Company since 1782. Most of the speech was, however, devoted to reminding Pitt and Dundas of how closely associated they had been with attempts to investigate Indian affairs in 1782.[1] A month later the plausible notion of collusion between the Ministry and East India House, which prompted Pitt to allow the Company complete autonomy in the patronage of the sub-continent, was rehearsed and elaborated.[2] Pitt was therefore caught in a pincer movement. To support the prospect of impeachment would be to involve Pitt in severe difficulties with both the King and the East India interest. To oppose them, however, would make credible the charge that he had turned his back on his reforming ideas in return for some kind of understanding with the Nabobs.[3] Attendances at these debates were not heavy, but the fact that Pitt felt compelled to allow Burke's motion for papers through encouraged Fox to press forward.

When the actual charges came to be presented, no one doubted that Fox was prompted entirely by ideas of party advantage. Wraxall was most explicit: 'Fox himself had been wrecked by the East India Bill & Pitt might commit a similar error. These motives, as I have always conceived, more than any thorough conviction of Hastings' criminality, propelled Fox to support the impeachment.'[4] Thomas Erskine,[5] in agreement with Wraxall, disassociated himself from the impeachment for this reason: 'But when Error in Judgment is made the subject of criminal charges, it is very different; there prejudice and misconception, & to sum up every possible evil in one word, party in Parliament takes the lead; & the wickedest man would be acquitted, or the most innocent man would be convicted according to the strength of the party prosecuting or defending.'[6] Fox, unlike Burke, had not been led by the defeat of 1784 to take refuge in moral diatribes alone. Under his tutelage, the prosecution of Warren Hastings was squarely undertaken for party advantage.

Gilbert Elliot, after the presentation of the main charges against Hastings, in the summer of 1786, believed that 'It will not lead to anything in a party view, & may perhaps lead to a little good in

[1] *Fox Speeches*, iii. 179; 17 Feb. 1786.

[2] Wheatley, *The Memoirs of Sir N. Wraxall*. iv. 283–4; 23 Mar. 1786.

[3] ibid. iv, 147–8.

[4] ibid. iv. 300–3.

[5] Thomas Erskine (1750–1823); M.P. (Portsmouth) 1783–4; brilliant barrister brought into the Commons by the Foxites; Att.-Gen. to Prince of Wales, 1783–92; Ld. Chanc. Feb. 1806–Mar. 1807; cr. Baron Erskine, Feb. 1806.

[6] Add. MS. 29196 (Hastings papers), f. 6; Erskine to ?(undated).

India. This particular vote [on the Benares charge] is forced by the power of truth & will probably not carry such unwilling converts much further.'[1] Few of his contemporaries would have agreed with him. Fox, in his speeches on the several charges, again and again broadens the issue to include the necessity of control from London, which had been the central theme of his measure two years earlier. After giving details of the background to the Rohilla War, Fox went on to insist that disasters of that kind proved that 'The whole government of India rests upon responsibility. If, in every instance & at every point of time, you have not the means of enforcing this principle, it is not possible that the government of this country can be preserved in its purity in the east.'[2] On the Benares charge, Fox was even more explicit. In the face of such barbarism, every M.P., including Pitt, 'must appear either as the avengers of the oppressed or the accomplices of their oppressor'.[3] At each stage, disasters in India are brought back to relate to decisions taken in England over the preceding three years. Burke concentrated on moral lectures, while Fox had thrown out a challenge to Pitt in purely political terms. As Fox's cousin observed, 'The Trial . . . is likely to be a party business, and, of course, no justice done.'[4]

After the defeat of the Rohilla War charge early in June 1786, it was generally believed that Pitt had committed himself to the Hastings interest. All the evidence seemed to point to that conclusion. The Ministers' volte face on the Benares charge was unexpected and disturbing. In this division Pitt and 50 supporters voted with opposition against 79 of their colleagues. The position Pitt took up in this debate is itself illustrative of the extremely difficult position, in which he found himself. His vote was determined, not by the mere fining of Cheyt Singh, which he believed to be perfectly permissible under Indian law, but by the size of the sum demanded.[5] Pitt thereby reduced Hastings' crime from one of principle to a simple problem of mathematics. Even so, sufficient damage had been done. Both the Court and East India House were displeased. Pitt, however, had to take the issue out of a party context, and the only way in which this could be done was to associate himself with the prosecution. As one of Fox's correspondents pointed out later, Pitt 'voted for him [Hastings] on the first article that of the Rohilla War & justified him in every thing but the Magnitude of the punishment in Benares business. But Mr.

[1] Sir G. Elliot to Lady Elliot, 15 June 1786; Lady Minto, *Life & Letters of Lord Minto*, i. 104.

[2] *Fox Speeches*, iii. 220 seq.; 1 June 1786. [3] *Fox Speeches*, iii. 224; 13 June 1786.

[4] Journal of Lady Sophia Fitzgerald, Feb. 1788; B. Fitzgerald, ed. *Emily, Duchess of Leinster*, p. 183.

[5] Wheatley, *The Memoirs of Sir N. Wraxall*, iv. 337–8; 13 June 1786.

Pitt was soon compelled to change his conduct & lest the Opposition should run away with all the popularity of bringing to punishment Indian Delinquents to join the prosecution.'[1]

Pitt's embarrassment seemed to suggest that Fox's hopes of this issue were to be fulfilled. In fact, however, Pitt extricated himself from this awkward position with the minimum of damage to his authority. His position on the Benares charge had set the pattern for his future conduct. He would associate himself with the prosecution in just sufficient measure to make it impossible for Fox to convert the impeachment into a party issue, out of which the Whigs could have made great capital. At the same time, no Pittite was so intimately involved that he could not withdraw with honour. If the impeachment succeeded, the triumph would be shared. If it failed, Pitt would disengage himself and allow the Whigs a monopoly of the opprobrium. One of his backbenchers noted, as early as 1787, that 'if Pitt is at last obliged to a junction with opposition on the subject, will it be for any other purpose than to frighten the East Indians, and to employ Burke, Sheridan, and their friends as the scarecrows for that purpose?'[2] By this manoeuvre, Pitt weakened much of the party advantage, which Fox had hoped for from this issue. Further, the onus of proof was now with Fox. Unless the impeachment of Hastings were successful, the possibility of a change in Pitt's attitude might very well leave the Whigs in an exceedingly uncomfortable position. There was a real danger that Fox's ideas on the impeachment would miscarry.

Pitt's ambivalence was practically expressed by official support for the impeachment coupled with a systematic undermining of its effectiveness. At the very outset, none of the leading Pittites actually committed himself so far as to join the board of Managers, entrusted with the prosecution, and this point was noted by the press:

> Mr. Pitt, Mr. Dundas, and Mr. Grenville were invited to become members of the Committee appointed to prepare the articles of Impeachment against Warren Hastings Esq, by Mr. Burke, previous to his moving for the appointment of the Committee, but severally declined it as likely to take up more of their time than they could conveniently spare from their publick and official duties.[3]

Even more sinister was the exclusion of Philip Francis from the board of Managers, in December 1786. Francis was possibly the most informed man on Indian affairs in the Commons at that time, and, although his hostility to Hastings was well known, there could not be any objection, as Fox insisted, to his acting as a prosecutor.[4] By

[1] Add. MS. 47589, f. 53; Sir G. Colebrook's Reminiscences.

[2] D. Pulteney to Rutland, 8 Feb. 1787; H.M.C. *Rutland MSS*. iii. 14.1, 369.

[3] *Morning Chronicle*, 5 Apr. 1787.

[4] *Fox Speeches*, iii. 347; 11 Dec. 1787.

excluding Francis, Pitt deprived the Managers of an immensely valuable asset, for which there was no substitute. All the Managers wrote to Francis expressing full confidence in his ability and integrity, but no one doubted that the prosecution case had been severely impaired.[1] All eighteen Managers were therefore political associates of Fox. In theory they enjoyed the backing of Pitt, but it was already becoming clear that, if they failed, the opprobrium would be theirs alone. Pitt had now the choice of transforming the Hastings case into an issue of party, if he thought it advantageous.

Official attitudes towards press comment was also another early indication of Pitt's attitude. In 1788, Pitt addressed the Crown for the prosecution of certain newspapers for alleged libels on Sir Elijah Impey,[2] whose possible impeachment was then under consideration. Fox objected violently to the methods employed, and, with a telling reference back to 1784, commented that, 'Considering how addresses of that House had been treated on former occasions, how could they flatter themselves that the rt. hon. gentleman would counsel his majesty to comply with their requests.'[3] This decision became more poignant two years later, when Major Scott,[4] the principal agent of Hastings in the Commons, published a series of letters and articles, which the Managers took to be libels on themselves, and yet was afforded the protection of the Pittite majority in the Lower House. Fox called unavailingly for the expulsion of Scott from the Commons and the imposition of heavy penalties:

> He believed the managers of the prosecution initiated by that House against Mr. Hastings, were the first men who had ever been appointed by that House to carry on so important a proceeding, and were afterwards suffered to be libelled in the public newspapers and in that House as often as an opportunity offerred, by one of their own members, with impunity.[5]

By 1790, however, the political potential of the impeachment had been lost in apathy and indecision, and Pitt could in consequence show his hand more plainly.

This sniping at the Managers' authority was kept up throughout the course of the impeachment. Details of expenses were demanded of the Managers, even though Fox insisted that this was the responsibility

[1] Managers to P. Francis, 18 Dec. 1787; *Parl. Hist.* xxvi. 1324.

[2] Sir Elijah Impey (1732–1809); trained as a lawyer; appointed Chief Justice of Bengal, 1773; loyal ally of Warren Hastings; narrowly escaped impeachment, 1787; retured to live the life of a country gentleman.

[3] *Fox Speeches*, iii. 357; 8 Feb. 1788.

[4] Major John Scott (1747–1819); M.P. (West Looe) 1784–90; (Stockbridge) 1790–3; Bengal army; A.D.C. to Warren Hastings 1778; became the accredited agent of Hastings in the Commons, his seat costing Hastings £4,000.

[5] *Parl. Hist.* xxviii. 545; 10 Mar. 1790.

of the House of Commons as a whole.[1] When Hastings petitioned the Commons against Burke's use of the word 'murder' in connection with the death of a certain Indian prince, and against his veiled reference to more charges being brought, which were not contained in the original indictment, the Pittites supported him unanimously. Burke was in fact censured on both counts. Fox was convinced that the whole episode was simply an excuse to disqualify Burke also from taking any effective part against Hastings. He reminded the House that, 'No procedure could tend more to disgrace the character and honour of the House, which the rt. hon. gentleman had stated to be deeply interested in the prosecution, than to weaken the hands of the managers, by doing anything which would reflect on their conduct.'[2] So severe was this blow that the Managers were forced to call a meeting, in order to decide whether they could continue at all.[3] Every point and issue, which could be turned to the disadvantage or embarrassment of the Managers, was voted by the Pittite Lower House.

Only one exception was made to this general rule. In 1790, the friends of Hastings attempted to have the impeachment quashed on the grounds that the indictment expired with the natural life of the Parliament, which had framed it. Fox fought this idea on the grounds that the value of the Crown's power to dissolve at will would be immeasurably increased by such a doctrine,[4] and Pitt supported him. He did so less from a concern with constitutional issues, however, than from the realization that, by 1790, the impeachment was no longer a danger to the Ministry, but rather had become a tedious and embarrassing inconvenience for the opposition. Three years later, Lord Bessborough[5] reported a similar situation to his wife: 'Hasting's Trial I am afraid will not end this year. Pitt has a mind to keep it on to employ the Opposition.'[6] Pitt's turning of the tables on Fox could not be more succinctly described. As the trial dragged on, its political possibilities were eroded by indifference and the genuine doubt created by the evidence. As soon as these moods set in, Pitt could quietly disengage himself from the matter, and indulge in indiscriminate sniping at the unfortunate Managers. Hastings became an

[1] *Parl. Hist.* xxvii. 539; 20 May 1788.

[2] *Fox Speeches*, iii. 465; 27 Apr. 1789.

[3] *Fox Speeches*, iii. p. 484 seq.; 4 May 1789.

[4] *Fox Speeches*, iv. 126; 23 Dec. 1790.

[5] Bessborough, Frederick Ponsonby, 3rd Baron (1758–1844); M.P. (Knaresborough) 1780–93; entered the Commons in the Cavendish interest, and always adhered firmly to the Rockingham–Fox group; succeeded father as 3rd Baron Bessborough, Mar. 1793.

[6] Lord Bessborough to Lady Bessborough, 31 May 1793; Earl of Bessborough, *Lady Bessborough and her Family Circle*, p. 89.

albatross tied to the neck of the Whig party, which yearly became more and more heavy.

Very occasionally, an issue arose which restored some life and interest to the impeachment, but these were few and relatively short-lived. In 1788, a crisis in India forced Pitt to push through a Declaratory Bill, giving him the authority to send four regiments to the subcontinent at the Company's expense and without reference to the directors. In theory claiming a superintending military authority in India, Pitt approached that system of control from London, which, as Fox was quick to point out, had been the object of his bill four years earlier.[1] Similarly, the war with Tippoo Sultan was plausibily ascribed by Fox to the fact that the amount of power left to a governor-general in India would corrupt even a man of the standing of Cornwallis.[2] Such topics naturally gave new relevance to the trial of Hastings, but they did little to redeem the Whigs. Fox very quickly appreciated that, from a party point of view, Hastings was little more than an irritation, and turned his thoughts towards extricating himself from a most unpleasant situation.

Inevitably, however, any thought of disengagement would involve Fox in quarrels with Burke, for whom the moral basis of the impeachment remained valid, whether political advantage could be drawn from it or not. Throughout 1786, Burke was pushing the other Whigs in this direction. As he informed an Irish friend: 'Some of our army more to their conviction than their original good Liking have found that they have not come off the worse for Listening a little to the Counsels of an old friend.'[3] At the beginning of 1787, he could report to Francis that Fox and other leading Whigs 'feel . . . about India, nearly as I could wish, and as we do ourselves'.[4] Fox, as has been shown above, had always borne in mind the political possibilities of such an impeachment, and he was now persuaded to commit himself by Burke's belief that the whole proceedings would not last for more than a year,[5] and by the fact that Burke himself seemed to view the matter in a party context stretching back to 1784: '. . . This House of Commons, chosen for the express purpose of discrediting the last, has acquitted its predecessor with honour—and has justified by something much stronger than resolutions, the ground upon which the late Parliament stood and fell; and it has prostrated the very delinquent which it was (very near expressly) chosen to protect and exalt.'[6]

[1] *Fox Speeches*, iii. 373; 5 Mar. 1788.
[2] *Fox Speeches*, iv. 372; 28 Mar. 1788.
[3] E. Burke to L. O'Beirne, 29 Sept. 1786; Copeland, *Burke Corres.* v. 280.
[4] E. Burke to Francis, *c.* 2 Jan. 1787; ibid. v. 304.
[5] E. Burke to Adam Smith, 7 Dec. 1786; Copeland, *Burke Corres.* v. 296.
[6] E. Burke to T. Burgh, 1 July 1787; ibid. v. 340.

Once, however, the party value of the issue began to diminish, the conflict between the two men became increasingly sharp.

In spite of the theatrical success, with which Fox opened the Benares charge in Westminster Hall,[1] there is no evidence that he evinced any interest in the details of the case and was not expected to speak again.[2] His attendances at meetings of the Managers were few and irregular.[3] As soon as it became clear that Pitt had not only maintained command of the situation, but would also be in a position to turn the impeachment against the Whigs, Fox was convinced that the matter should be dropped. The first crisis of confidence came in May 1788, after the Commons decision to prosecute Impeys libellers indicated how precarious the Managers' position was. Burke, canvassing support from Burgoyne, reported that Grey was for an immediate ending of the prosecution as too costly and too troublesome. Burke insisted on continuing in case his convictions should be brought into question.[4] Fox was so uninterested in this debate, that throughout its course he was at Newmarket, also missing Sheridan's opening of the Begums charge[5] as a result. There was a real fear, however, that Fox, out of purely party considerations, would give full support to Grey.

Francis finally tracked Fox down at Bath and, with evident relief, reported to Burke that Fox's reaction had not been too unfavourable: 'I have had an opportunity which probably I should not have met with anywhere else, of conversing at full length with Mr. Fox about the actual state and future conduct of the Impeachment, I think I found him, and I am sure I left him, in a better temper on the subject, than former appearances, or perhaps my own apprehensions had led me to expect.'[6] Even though both men agreed that Hastings' acquittal was daily becoming more likely, it was determined 'to proceed with vigour, and at least secure an honourable retreat. So says Mr. Fox, as firmly and heartily as I do.'[3] The emphasis must, however, be placed

[1] *Morning Chronicle*, 23 Feb. 1788.

[2] Journal of Lady Sophia Fitzgerald, Feb. 1788; Fitzgerald, *Emily, Duchess of Leinster*, p. 184.

[3] Add. MS. 24266 (Managers' Minutes) 1787–91; excluding those meetings, for which no attendance list given:

Year	*Fox Present*	*Fox Absent*
1787	2	8
1788	6	40
1789	2	24
1790	3	14
1791	8	6

[4] E. Burke to J. Burgoyne, 4 May 1788; de Fonblanque, *Life and Corres. of J. Burgoyne*, p. 448.

[5] *Morning Chronicle*, 7 May 1788.

[6] P. Francis to E. Burke, 2 Jan. 1789; Wentworth Woodhouse Muniments, Burke 1 (Letter misdated 1790).

on the desire to retreat, because the same letter deals extensively with Fox's reluctance to embark on the bribery and contracts charges against Hastings. As Francis was forced to conclude: 'He dreads, as I do, the effect of any operation on our part, of which the limitation is not seen.'[1]

When the vote of censure on Burke was carried on 4 May 1789, the Managers once again had to reconsider their position, and it was clear that the reports of Francis had been far too sanguine. Burke's case won largely because Fox was late for the meeting, but he later complained that the decision to continue the impeachment could only be taken 'as a great slight of him',[2] and Burke had to apologize. From this moment, Fox's interest in Hastings waned perceptibly. Burke attempted to keep the matter open by briefing the Managers personally: 'By sending the brief, syllabus and heads of evidence to Fox and Sheridan, we endeavour to awaken them to some sort of attention.'[3] These efforts were, however, unavailing. Fox's appearances in Westminster Hall were less and less effective because of his unfamiliarity with the evidence. James Hare succinctly described this falling off in performance: 'Charles Fox is to sum up the present Charge against Mr. Hastings, & for want of training will, I fear, be terribly short of wind.'[4] By 1790, any party advantage to be drawn from the impeachment was unequivocally Pittite. The proceedings in Westminster Hall came more and more to resemble an elaborate folly, inhabited only by Burke.

One of the leading elements in Burke's hostility to Fox, after the outbreak of the French Revolution, was the belief that he had been abandoned by the other Managers, with the result that what he believed to be a moral crusade against injustice was brought into ridicule. Although superficially the Managers acted as one body, all cordiality had long since disappeared between Fox and Burke.[5] They had never entertained the same interpretation of Hastings' impeachment, and the passage of time brought their views into conflict. At the end of the trial, Burke accepted a vote of the thanks on behalf Managers as a whole, but refused to deny Windham's[6] remark that

[1] P. Francis to E. Burke, 2 Jan. 1789; Wentworth Woodhouse Muniments, Burke 1 (Letter misdated 1790).

[2] E. Burke to Fox, 11 May 1789; Copeland, *Burke Corres.* v. 472.

[3] E. Burke to P. Francis, Dec. 1789; Parkes and Merivale, *The Memoirs of Sir P. Francis*, ii. 263–5.

[4] J. Hare to Duchess of Devonshire, 9 Feb. 1790; Chatsworth MSS. 1036.

[5] E. Burke to R. Burke, 20 Feb. 1792; Wentworth Woodhouse Muniments, Burke 1.

[6] William Windham (1750–1810); M.P. for four boroughs 1784–1810; scholar and mathematician; broke with Fox on the issue of the French Revolution; Chief Sec. to Ld.-Lt. of Ireland, Apr.–Aug. 1783; Sec. for War, July 1794–Feb. 1801; Sec. for War and Colonies, Feb. 1806–Mar. 1807.

he had separated himself from his colleagues.[1] Fox had seen the impeachment of Hastings only in terms of party. When these considerations lost their relevance, Hastings and India itself were of no further importance to him.

By 1794, virtually all the Whigs were prepared to admit that the impeachment had been a terrible blunder. The scene in Westminster Hall had merely become a macabre farce.[2] As Lord John Cavendish pointed out; 'Hastings trial seems to me most amazingly foolish on the part of our Governors: they should not have brought him to his tryal unless they were sure they had evidence enough to convict him, & nothing can be so absurd or mischievous as to let a man in his circumstances he made a Hero of the populace.'[3] Fox was in full agreement with this assessment. By 1794, the Managers' Box was for him 'this cursed Place'.[4] No pamphlet was required to inform Fox of the magnitude of the disaster.[5] For seven years, some of the most talented members of the Whig party had been embroiled in the details of the British administration in India. After 1789, the Hastings issue contributed materially to the breach between Fox and Burke. And worst of all, the hope that the quick conviction of Hastings would vindicate the Coalition and its India Bill had been dashed. The longer the trial went on, the more the balance of party advantage swung in Pitt's favour. Instead of a short, tactical party victory, Fox was faced, after seven years of embarrassment, with wearied defeat.

The evidence of the 1780s therefore suggests that the feeling for party, which made Adam's organizational innovations possible, and which gave cohesion to Whig votes, was fully shared by Fox. The events of 1782–4 had stimulated this feeling, and no one was more bitterly affected by these same events than Fox himself. His sense of frustration and personal loss was itself a contributory factor in the sharpening of the lines of party division. The exclusion of his undoubted talents from office by reason of personal vindictiveness on the part of the Crown was a standing grievance among the Whigs. The Whig party under Fox in the later 1780s was founded on the experiences of 1782–4, which, in a very real sense, could be reduced to Fox's duel with George III. The handling of the impeachment of Warren Hastings demonstrates how conscientiously Fox followed the sole aim of party advantage. The quarrels with Burke sprang directly from this. Fox can very reasonably be criticized for indolence, rashness

[1] *Parl. Hist.* xxi. 946 seq.; 20 June 1794.
[2] J. Greig, *The Farington Diary*, i. 51.
[3] Lord John Cavendish to Miss Ponsonby, 'Sunday'; Grey MSS.
[4] Add. MS. 47571, f. 122; Fox to Holland, 29 Apr. 1794.
[5] J. Owen, *Letter to Mr. Fox on the Duration of the Trial of Mr. Hastings.*

and a refusal to attend to detail. These points may have weakened the effectiveness of Fox as a party leader, but they in no way detract from his conscious recognition of his function.

IV

THE REGENCY CRISIS, NOVEMBER 1788–MARCH 1789

In theory, the onset of George III's illness should have presented the Whigs with a magnificent opportunity for ousting Pitt. The coherence and organizational capacity shown by the Whigs after their defeat in 1784 indicated that a viable, alternative administration was at hand, which required only a change of attitude in the executive, in order to be able to realize its ambitions. In the event, such a prophecy proved unduly optimistic. Long before the King's recovery finally dashed Whig hopes of a return to power, Pitt had successfully outmanoeuvred his opponents. As in the Warren Hastings affair, Fox was very ready to place the problem within a broad party context, but was incapable of that attention to detail, which was necessary on an almost daily basis as the crisis developed. More serious still was his unwillingness or inability to control the extravagant personalities of the leading Whigs. Repeated references to the paucity of talent in the Pittite ranks fail to make the point that Pitt at least would not be faced with the problems of co-ordinating the tempers of Sheridan, Grey, Burke, and Prinny himself. In fact, the Regency Crisis inflicted wounds on the Whig party, which were later to bleed more strongly under the impact of the French Revolution.

As soon as the Prince of Wales had come of age, the Whigs, like most oppositions in the eighteenth century, benefited from the bitter hostility always existing between Hanoverian fathers and sons. From 1783 onwards, the reversionary interest was again a factor in politics, but never perhaps had its advantages for opposition been hedged about with quite so many qualifications. The new Prince of Wales was a profligate and a lecher, and, even in the late eighteenth century, these attributes did not go unnoticed. For the Duke of Portland and the other leading Whigs, who were not immediately connected with Fox's gambling and drinking circle at Brooks's, Prinny was at best an unattractive asset, and Fox later came to regret the association.[1] The King, as in June 1783,[2] had already used the Prince's profligacy as a powerful weapon against the Whigs. Between 1783–7, the

[1] Duke of Leinster to ?, 1806; Fitzgerald, *Emily Duchess of Leinster*, p. 276.
[2] See Chapter II, pp. 60–3.

Prince's dependence on Charles Fox was almost absolute. Fox was his political and moral tutor. At the height of the crisis over the Prince's debts in 1783, George made Fox his political proxy: 'After what has already passed I did not require this additional proof of yr friendship & attachment, & you will see by a Letter I have this instant written to the D of P—how ready I am to take yr advice, & yt I leave it entirely to the Cabinet.'[1] The Prince became the most important of Fox's political dependents.

This relationship was by no means an unmixed blessing for Fox. The slightest problem would bring an agonized appeal for assistance from Carlton House: 'I am waiting for you . . . pray come directly if you can as I wish very much to speak to you . . . If you have not got yr own Carriage, you had better take anybody else's.'[2] When in 1785, Prinny threatened to leave England forever, Fox was called in to dissuade him.[3] This alarming escapade centred on rumours, in December 1785, that Prinny was about to marry Mrs. Fitzherbert,[4] and it was again Fox who was compelled to offer paternal advice, asking him 'not to think of marriage until you can legally marry. A mock marriage, for it can be no other, is neither honourable for any of the parties, nor with respect to your Royal Highness even safe.'[5] The Prince immediately assured Fox that there was no substance in the rumours, and proceeded to marry Mrs. Fitzherbert four days later.[6] Such conduct hardly made Prinny the ideal political associate, and his connection with the Whigs was the source of much criticism within the party itself, but the simple fact of his rank made him invaluable. As long as Fox could control his more exuberant flights of fancy, the accession of Prinny to the throne would still mean employment and office to the Whigs.

The strains which Prinny imposed on the Whig party were most clearly demonstrated in 1787, when the problem of the Prince's renewed insolvency, linked with continued speculation about the Fitzherbert marriage, was presented to Fox. Lord Spencer was informed in April that Fox had, by letter and interview, secured from the Prince further assurances about his bachelor status, before agreeing to ask Parliament to relieve his debts. Even so, the matter

[1] Add. MS. 47560, f. 13; Prince of Wales to Fox, 8 June 1783.

[2] Add. MS. 47560, f. 7; Prince of Wales to Fox, undated.

[3] A. Aspinall, *The Later Correspondence of George III*, i. 149–51.

[4] Maria Fitzherbert (1756–1837); Roman Catholic; dau. of W. Smythe of Hampstead; secretly married to the Prince of Wales, Dec. 1785; patron of Sheridan; separated from Prince of Wales, 1803; retired into private life with annuity of £6,000 p.a.

[5] Fox to Prince of Wales, 10 Dec. 1785; G. M. Trevelyan, *Lord Grey of the Reform Bill*, p. 18.

[6] Prince of Wales to Fox, 11 Dec. 1783; ibid.

was potentially explosive. A back-bench Whig reported to Spencer as follows: 'My D. Lord we have great Plenty of wit & Raillery & Eloquence on our side of the House but we have been accused of Want of Judgment & we are going to prove the Accusation true.'[1] Having checked his facts, Fox supported a motion to relieve the Prince of Wales of his debts, but associated his remarks with a specific denial of any formal alliance between Prinny and Mrs. Fitzherbert.[2] This statement had been authorized by the Prince himself,[3] but it nevertheless produced such a degrading controversy that the King himself was forced to meet the debts rather than allow this matter to go any further.[4]

Many years later, George IV's disingenuous explanation of these events was that the argument centred not on the marriage itself, but on certain comments which Fox saw fit to make about Mrs. Fitzherbert's character:

> On the subject of my supposed marriage with Mrs. Fitzherbert, and the debate upon Mr. Rolle's observations, some false statements have been made. When Fox mentioned it to me, I contradicted the supposition at once, with 'pooh', 'nonsense', 'ridiculous' etc., upon which Fox in the heat of the debate . . . was induced, not merely to contradict the report, which was right enough, but to go a little further and to use some slighting expressions, which, when Mrs. Fitzherbert read them in the paper next morning, deeply affected her, and made her furious against Fox.[5]

In this same conversation, Prinny also denied that he had asked Sheridan, after Grey had refused, to go down to the House to make a statement at least sufficiently ambiguous to leave Mrs. Fitzherbert her pride. In fact, as Lord Holland[6] later insisted, Fox had been deliberately misled. Acting on Prinny's express authority, Fox had made a statement to the House of Commons, only to see it contradicted by Sheridan a few days later. The Whigs then had the humiliating experience of being extricated from this situation by the King, not because the Prince's claims carried any conviction, but because the scandal was becoming too great and too public.

Some eighteen months before the question of a regency arose therefore, the Prince of Wales had been responsible for creating real

[1] H. Minchin to Spencer, 29 Apr. 1787; Spencer MSS.

[2] *Fox Speeches*, iii. 321 seq.; 30 Apr. 1787.

[3] Ld. J. Russell, *Memoirs, Journal and Correspondence of Thomas Moore*, iv. 227

[4] Portland to Loughborough, 3 May 1787; PWF 9217, Portland MSS.

[5] L. Jennings, ed. *The Croker Papers*, i. 292.

[6] Holland, Henry Fox, 3rd Baron (1773–1840); Fox's nephew and principal disciple; patron of the Holland House circle; supported all his uncle's views of the French Revolution and reform; one of the most impt. leaders of Whiggery 1806–40 Chanc. of D. of Lancaster under Grey and Melbourne.

tension in the party, which would normally be expected to support his claims. Experienced politicians, like William Eden, were aware of this:

In the whole of this Transaction, the Pr. seems to have acted more from his own Counsels than from Those of the D. of Portland, Mr. Fox, Ld Loughb'gh etc: It is not easy at this distance nor perhaps upon the spot to conjecture what Impression the Result will make as to the Various Connections to which He has long been attached; but we have all seen in Life that Differences of Opinion as to public Circumstances & Conduct generally affect personal Friendships & Partialities & sometimes in a great Degree.[1]

New hostilities were created and old ones confirmed. The Duke of Portland, whose wife had always refused to receive Mrs. Fitzherbert, had had a long argument with the Prince, and was no longer on speaking terms with him.[2] The Duke had always entertained doubts about the Whigs' connection with the Prince, and had recently had to intervene personally when he heard that the heir apparent was about to accept a personal loan from the Duc d'Orléans.[3] The conduct of the Prince was also proving to be a matter of contention between Fox and Portland, and Sir Gilbert Elliot was hourly expecting the disintegration of the party on this issue: 'This is the only party existing in the country, & the only strength that can ever be opposed to the perpetual & indissoluble weight of Court influence, so that I should consider it as a misfortune to see this faggot split into separate twigs, which may be easily broken singly.'[4] Further, Sheridan's willingness to run even the most unpleasant errands for Carlton House led Fox to ponder on Burke's accusation, that his fellow Irishman was trying to establish himself as an equal influence with the Prince of Wales. The dishonesty and profligacy of this prince continually involved the Whigs in opprobrious undertakings, leading to considerable bitterness within their own ranks.

If Portland could afford to take a high-minded attitude about the escapades at Carlton House, Fox could not. For him, the connection with the Prince of Wales was essential, not only for the hope of future office but also for the availability of immediate credit. The Prince's difficulties mirrored Fox's own problems, and highlighted the contrast between the wealth of the Whig dukes and the insolvency of the Brooks's circle, of which Fox was the leader. Fox himself was in desperate trouble in 1787. Early in the 1780s, he and Fitzpatrick had accepted large loans in return for the promise to repay their

[1] Brit. Mus. Egerton 3260; W. Eden to Hertford, 17 May 1787.

[2] H. Minchin to Spencer, 29 Apr. 1787; Spencer MSS.

[3] Portland to Sheridan, 13 Dec. 1787; T. Moore, *Memoirs of R. B. Sheridan*, i. 470.

[4] Sir G. Elliot to Lady Elliot, 5 May 1787; *Life and Letters of Lord Minto*, i. 159.

creditors by annuities, and these commitments they were no longer able to meet. Thomas Coutts,[1] one of London's leading bankers immediately offered his services: 'Perhaps you will laugh at my letter but I feel an impulse to write it, & to make you an offer, in case you have Annuities or Debts, to lend you money to pay them.'[2] He naturally disclaimed all intention of gambling on Fox's future prospects, but as he told the Duchess of Devonshire, another of his clients: 'If the King dies I lose a good friend; but I am in hopes I may still be employed by his successor. For I was his *first* banker, and he has always approved my conduct . . . Mr. Fox, I believe, your Grace will find much my friend.'[3] Over the next twelve months, Fox cheerfully enumerated his outstanding debts, and Coutts disbursed some £10,000 in discharging them.[4] Fox could not therefore be severe with Prinny, because his shortcomings were very similar to his own, and because much had been invested in his political future, for which the favour of Carlton House was the most hopeful guarantee.

After the Westminster election of 1788, the pressure to keep all possible avenues to office open became irresistible. According to Lord Robert Spencer, the return of the Whig candidate had cost £30,000.[5] Although a welcome victory, Burke doubted the wisdom of the exercise: 'You will imagine perhaps, or you will hear, that this struggle was set on foot by Fox: No such thing: He was rather against it: so Was the Duke of Portland. So was I . . . To this hour I do not know whose measure it was. Some unknown impulse began it and all of us were obliged to follow.'[6] With party and personal credit so seriously overdrawn, the Whigs could not afford to turn their backs on the Prince of Wales. In 1788, George III at fifty had already experienced one bout of mental instability and the prospects of his heir looked good. The confidence, with which the Whigs approached the crisis, stemmed from the realization that such a situation had been expected in the very near future, and from the knowledge that a great deal depended on a successful outcome.

The onset of the crisis found Fox in Italy. Long before he could return, Sheridan, profiting greatly from the reputation he had acquired

[1] Thomas Coutts (1735–1822); founder with his brother James of the banking house of Coutts & Co.; numbered George III and leading members of the aristocracy among his clients; married one dau. to George North and another to Sir F. Burdett; left a personal fortune of £900,000.

[2] Add. MS. 51466, f. 17; T. Coutts to Fox, 30 July 1787.

[3] T. Coutts to Duchess of Devonshire (undated); J. Carswell, *The Old Cause*, p. 291.

[4] Fox to T. Coutts, 1 Aug. 1787 and 15 June 1788; E. Coleridge, *Life of Thomas Coutts*, i. 214–17, 243–6.

[5] Ld. R. Spencer to Fitzwilliam, Sept. 1788; Milton MSS. Box 39.

[6] E. Burke to Sir G. Elliot, 3 Sept. 1788; Copeland, *Burke Corres.* v. 413.

at Carlton House by salvaging a little of Mrs. Fitzherbert's reputation a year earlier, had already drawn up a plan of action for the Whigs to follow. On the evidence of Dr. Warren,[1] he believed with Loughborough that George III had been effectively eliminated from politics: 'An entire and speedy recovery seems to me beyond the reach of any reasonable hope.'[2] Even so, Sheridan was determined that the Whigs should not prejudice their chances of office by any high-handed or arrogant behaviour, but should secure their positions before capitalizing on them. Thurlow, whose personal distaste for Pitt was well known, was chosen rightly as the weak link in the Ministry, who might be prepared to enter into negotiations. To make this idea more palatable, Sheridan assured the Prince of Wales mendaciously that Loughborough, who would normally have been expected to supersede Thurlow as Lord Chancellor in any future Whig administration, had given his assent to the plan. The first meeting with Thurlow took place on 8 November, and Sheridan reported that it had been extremely encouraging.[3] Two weeks before Fox's arrival in England, the Carlton House circle, of which Sheridan was increasingly the spokesman, had adopted a distinct programme. The King's political demise would allow the Whigs to step quietly into office, and Thurlow's assistance would make for the minimum of difficulty and contention. This policy implied the sacrifice of Loughborough, the playing down of constitutional pretensions, and the confirmation of Sheridan's assumption of the position once held by Fox at Carlton House.

Each of these three conditions could very properly be expected to be highly contentious, and, until a slight improvement in the King's condition on 13 November raised the possibility that prevarication alone might carry them through,[4] the Pittites pinned all their hopes on the likelihood of Whig divisions. In the early days of the crisis, the Grenvilles, Pitt's very political cousins, eagerly reported all rumours about splits within the ranks of their opponents. One of the Prince's aides was quoted to the effect that 'He was persuaded that the Prince was afraid of Fox . . . and that this coolness to Fox was much increased by Mrs. Fitz Herbert, who never would forgive his public declaration on her subject in the House of Commons, and had taken

[1] Richard Warren (1731–97); physician; appointed physician-in-ordinary to George III, 1763; strongly Whig in politics; appointed personal physician to the P. of Wales, 1787; enormously successful practice; enjoying income of £9,000 p.a. at his death.

[2] Loughborough to J. W. Payne, *c.* 8 Nov. 1788; A. Aspinall *Corres. of George, Prince of Wales*, i. 367.

[3] Sheridan to Prince of Wales, 8 Nov. 1788; A. Aspinall, *Corres. of George, Prince of Wales*, i. 290–2

[4] W. W. Grenville to Marquis of Buckingham, 13 Nov. 1788; Buckingham and Chandos, i. 448.

every opportunity of alienating the Prince's mind from him.'[1] In fact, in two weeks, the Grenvilles built up a fairly accurate picture of the basic antipathy between Carlton House, to which Sheridan had joined his personal ambitions, and the more established figures of English Whiggery around Portland: 'Fitzgibbon confirms most strongly the account of the steps which Sheridan has taken to secure his personal ground, and the jealousy which this has given to the rest of the party, of two of whom, the Duke of Portland and Burke, the Prince has spoken unfavourably within the last ten day's.'[2] Age was pitted against experience, insolvency against established social and political credit. In the absence of Fox, the linking mechanism between these two very important elements in the Whig party had been temporarily removed. Because, when a crisis arrived, the Prince of Wales chose to work through Sheridan, rather than the accredited head of the party, the Duke of Portland, Pittite hopes of schism within the Whig ranks were, at this stage, well founded. Lamenting the absence of Fox, a back-bench Whig gave warning of danger: 'The P. of Wales sends all his expresses to Sheridan & not to the Duke of Portland, tho' he knows that he is in town, so that I think the opposition need not look as smiling as they do.'[3]

The project hingeing on the co-operation of Thurlow was exclusively the concern of Carlton House. Whatever Sheridan may have told Prinny about Loughborough's views, it is likely that both he and Portland were ignorant of these negotiations. As William Adam later insisted: 'Upon my own unassisted recollection I should say that Loughborough never acquiesced in any arrangement which would have prevented the Seals being offered to him.'[4] In fact, Loughborough was himself plying Carlton House with memoranda in his capacity as the leading Whig lawyer. Far from subscribing to any theory about coming into office by negotiation, Loughborough set out the Whigs' claim in broad constitutional terms: 'It is the result of my most deliberate judgment that the administration of the Government is as directly cast upon the Heir Apparent as the right to the Crown is in the last case [i.e. in the event of the King's death]; all are alike the act of God, & the law of England knows no interval in which there can be an interregnum.'[5] The Prince's staff gave a formal acknowledgement to Loughborough's ideas,[6] and continued

[1] Buckingham to W. Grenville, 11 Nov. 1788; H.M.C. *Fortescue MSS*. i. p. 362.

[2] Buckingham to W. Grenville, 23 Nov. 1788; ibid. p. 374.

[3] R. Bingham to Spencer, 12 Nov. 1788; Spencer MSS.

[4] Add. MS. 47591, f. 85; W. Adam to Holland, 1839.

[5] Loughborough to J. W. Payne, 8 Nov. 1788; Aspinall, *The Corres. of George, Prince of Wales*, i. 367.

[6] J. W. Payne to Loughborough, 10 Nov. 1788; Lord J. L. Campbell, *Lives of the Lord Chancellors*, viii. 86.

to negotiate with Thurlow without his knowledge. Sheridan, without officially denying Loughborough's views, was indefatigable in reducing his precise constitutional claims to harmless generalities: 'I own I think the wording of this stiff, and not in the style which would answer what may be expected from the Feelings which will be in the Prince's mind. At the same time it cannot be too general and safe.'[1]

Even before Fox set foot in England therefore, two rival Whig programmes were already in existence. Loughborough's ideas on proclaiming loudly the details of constitutional law were not openly disavowed, even if Sheridan privately ignored them. His plan for entering quietly into government with the assistance of Thurlow seemed to be becoming generally accepted. On 23 November, at a meeting at Lord North's house, the Whigs, instead of offering immediate battle to Pitt on points of constitutional principle, followed Sheridan's call for moderation and agreed to the Minister's suggestion that Parliament be adjourned for two weeks.[2] The next day, Sheridan, after incidentally mentioning Fox's return to England, informed a friend that his strategy had been accepted by the Whigs and would prove successful: 'I have not myself a Doubt of anything being done or even attempted against the Prince in the House of Commons. I assure you, if they were rash enough to try their utmost our Strength there would be beyond what you could conceive.'[3] Sheridan's apparent victory bred much ill-feeling among the Whigs, but even Burke's intellectual stature and personal vindictiveness against his fellow Irishman could not check his progress, as long as he had the Prince's ear. When Burke complained that Hastings' trial was being neglected, the reaction of Sheridan was, according to the Duchess of Devonshire, abrupt: 'Sheridan, who is heartily tired of the Hastings trial, and fearful of Burke's impetuosity says that he wishes Hastings would run away and Burke after him.'[4] Significantly therefore, Fox's return was eagerly awaited by the moderate elements within the Whig party as the principal hope of averting a serious clash of personalities. Two lines of policy had been drawn up, separating two broad types of Whig attitudes. Lady Palmerston hoped that Fox would be able to reconcile them; 'I hope Charles Fox will Return before the Call of the House. Should the Poor Thing be released by that Time from his present melancoly situation. I think things would then go on well, which I fear can not be the Case if he should continue with this

[1] Sheridan to J. W. Payne, 9 Nov. 1788; C. Price, *The Letters of R. B. Sheridan*, i. 191.

[2] Add. MS. 41579 (Journal of Lady Elizabeth Foster), f. 4; 23 Nov. 1788.

[3] Sheridan to J. W. Payne, 24 Nov. 1788; Price *The Letters of R. B. Sheridan*, i. 199.

[4] Diary of Duchess of Devonshire, 20 Nov. 1788; Sichel *Sheridan*, ii. 404.

unhappy Malady.'[1] When Fox returned to England therefore, on 24 November 1788, he entered upon that office of peacemaker within the party which he was to fill for the next five years.

Although very ill, Fox immediately had to set about co-ordinating the efforts of the extremely able, if very egocentric, leaders of the Whig party. The prospect of an early dispersal of offices, as the Duchess of Devonshire recorded, gave new impetus to the recurrent clashes of personality: 'Grey says he will give way to Ld. John, Charles Fox or Sheridan—but not to those Norfolks, Wyndhams and Pelhams.'[2] Fox's house at St. Anne's Hill became the centre of peace-making operations. Sheridan and Prinny came down on 26 November, where the latter was induced to offer the Duke of Portland the opportunity for a reconciliation: 'The P. said he certainly had been angry with the D. of Portland for his conduct about the payment of his debts, but having said that he had vented his resentment & now commissioned Mr. Fox to shake hands with him in his name; & that he would come to B.H. Saturday.'[3] As a token of his goodwill, Prinny asked Fox to reconvene Portland's Cabinet of 1783, in order that he should be given counsel in due form.[4] In the presence of North, Fox, and Loughborough, Portland and the Prince of Wales shook hands formally three days later, which was their first meeting since the unfortunate Fitzherbert scandal of the previous year.[5] Five days had been spent in smoothing the ruffled plumage of the Whigs, but, although formal unity had been re-established, no decision had yet been taken by Fox between the ideas of Sheridan and Loughborough. Two contradictory policies were still being run in harness.

In the mind of Fox, however, considerations of policy were of less importance than the reconciling of personalities. It was universally believed at this stage that the King's condition was beyond all assistance, and that therefore a Whig administration was inevitable, whether they chose Sheridan's methods or Loughborough's. The only possible check to their progress was division within their own ranks, and this Fox had avoided. Windham insisted that 'Whatever fever his Majesty had had, has been only symptomatik, and not at all the cause of his disorder, which is pure & original insanity. The symptoms of this have been increasing by slow degrees, & for a considerable period.'[6] Lord Charlemont was reliably informed that the only

[1] Lady Palmerston to Palmerston, 18 Nov. 1788; Palmerston MSS. f. 133.

[2] Diary of Duchess of Devonshire, 26 Nov. 1788; Sichel, *Sheridan*, ii. 406–7.

[3] Add. MS. 41579, f. 5, 26 Nov. 1788; Journal of Lady Elizabeth Foster.

[4] Sir G. Elliot to Lady Elliot, 26 Nov. 1788; Lady Minto, *Life and Letters of Lord Minto*, i. 239.

[5] Sir G. Elliot to Lord Palmerston, 29 Nov. 1788; Connell, *Portrait of a Whig Peer*, p. 185.

[6] Add. MS. 37873, f. 159; Windham to ?, 26 Nov. 1788.

question outstanding was the disposal of Cabinet offices,[1] while the Duchess of Marlborough's servant asked leave to discontinue regular reports on the King's condition, because, after dining with one of the royal doctors, he had been assured that no change was expected for a very long time.[2] All shades of Whig thinking were united by a feeling of euphoria. It seemed that not even Pitt's great tactical ability would release him from the prospect of a long period in opposition.

Precise information on the King's condition only became available on 3 December, when the royal doctors were examined before the Privy Council. Very different conclusions, however, were drawn by Whig and Tory from the evidence presented. Pitt, who had abruptly silenced the Whig Dr. Warren, as soon as he mentioned the word insanity, was convinced that recovery was likely, and that therefore a skilful programme of procrastination might yet defeat the Whigs: 'The King's situation continues for the present much the same; But the Opinion of the Physicians is very favourable as to the Prospect of Recovery, tho' they cannot venture to ascertain any particular Period.'[3] William Grenville was equally pleased. At least the evidence had been sufficiently ambivalent to give potential Pittite defectors pause: 'I hear of no rats yet, but I suppose a few days will bring some to light: tho' I cannot help thinking that the examinations of yesterday *donneront à penser à Messieurs les Rats*.'[4] Thurlow, ever the most cautious of politicians, was certainly less pleased with his flirtation with the Whigs after the physicians had given evidence.[5]

Fox was convinced that the examination of the physicians and the abrupt treatment of Warren were merely Pittite devices to hide the real state of the King's health. Illness had forced him to miss the examination himself, and this undoubtedly contributed to his misreading of the situation.[6] Fox was therefore intent on having the physicians re-examined at the Bar of the House, where a Pittite direction of affairs would be more difficult to effect. A second factor determining Fox's attitude towards the King's condition was that he tended to rely on the evidence of Dr. Warren, whose Whig sympathies seem to have overborne his medical knowledge, and of Thurlow himself, who was in regular attendance on the King at Kew. According to the Duke of Leeds, Fox was still having meetings with Thurlow as late as 8 December, where details about the King's condition were

[1] E. Malone to Charlemont, 2 Dec. 1788; H.M.C. *Charlemont MSS.* ii. 13.8, p. 81.

[2] J. Bryant to Duchess of Marlborough, 1788; Blenheim MSS. E.61.

[3] Pitt to Grafton, 4 Dec. 1788; Grafton MSS. f. 155.

[4] W. Grenville to Buckingham, 4 Dec. 1788; Buckingham and Chandos, ii. 32.

[5] W. Grenville to Buckingham, 7 Dec. 1788; Buckingham and Chandos, ii. 35.

[6] Wheatley, *The Hist. and Post. Memoirs of Sir N. Wraxall*, v. 207; 8 Dec. 1788.

given.[1] It is possible that Thurlow may have deliberately encouraged Fox's optimism in the hope of pleasing his new masters, or, if events should turn out differently, of having some claim on the gratitude of Pitt. At least until 10 December therefore, when Fox made his celebrated speech in defence of the Prince's claims, he had no reason to change his opinion that, whatever line was taken by the Whigs, the proclamation of a Regency was inevitable.

From 24 November until the end of the month, Fox made no obvious commitment about policy, but seemed inclined to accept Sheridan's ideas. His contacts in this week were almost entirely with the Carlton House circle. According to Lady Elizabeth Foster, both Prinny and Sheridan saw Fox on the day he returned to England: 'The P saw him secretly at first on account of Mrs. F's dislike to him. Sheridan was obliged to go away early, as C. Fox was not well enough to come out, and he wanted to see him.'[2] Fox had the same company for dinner on 25 November, and, on the following day, received them at St. Anne's Hill. At very approximately the same period, he too had an interview with Thurlow, of which he sent a favourable report to the Prince;

> From all I have heard as well from Lord Chancellor as others I am convinced . . . that the only possible alternative besides the right measure is a temporary Regency limited in powers, but not by Councillors. Whether your Royal Highness would accept of such an offer is a mere question of Dignity because either by accepting it or rejecting it your Royal Highness would be equally sure of enjoying the situation that belongs to you . . . in a few weeks.[3]

Though confident of eventual success, therefore, Fox's dealings with Carlton House and the interview with Thurlow led to the view that Sheridan's ideas had prevailed.

Between the end of November and 10 December, when Fox's speech in the Commons proved that he had opted for Loughborough's opinion, a marked movement away from Sheridan and his ideas took place. A number of influence had come to bear on Fox's mind, and one of the most important was not immediately related to politics. George Selwyn's keen nose for scandal quickly scented the crucial point that, if Fox fell in with Sheridan's ideas, he would merely be confirming the authority which the Irishman had acquired at Carlton House since 1787, and would in consequence diminish his own: "Charles you know is come. . . . I want to know, how he has relished Sheridan's beginning a negotiation without him. I have figured him,

[1] Browning, *Memoirs of the Fifth Duke of Leeds*, pp. 132–3; 8 Dec. 1788.

[2] Add. MS. 41579, f. 5; Journal of Lady Elizabeth Foster, 24 Nov. 1788.

[3] Fox to Prince of Wales, *c.* 26 Nov. 1788; Aspinall, *Corres. of George, Prince of Wales*, i. 383.

f it be true, saying to him, at his arrival, as Hecate does to the Witches n Macbeth, 'Saucey and bold, how did you dare to trade and traffic etc:, and I, the mistress of your charms, the close contriver of all harms, was never called to hear my part etc:—I will not go on with he rest of the passage for fear of offending.'[1] The same wit, cleverness, and egocentric display which made the Whigs formidable in debate, also made them a prey to jealousies and personal vindictiveness. Fox had effectively taken over from Burke as the intellectual eader of the party, and, after his experiences in the Fitzherbert affair, was afraid that Sheridan might prove a serious threat to his position.

Burke, too, threw his still considerable weight against Sheridan's deas. Writing to Fox late in November 1788, Burke relied on the elling point that the Regency crisis offered an opportunity, not only of coming into office, but also of demonstrably breaking the Pittite system. The growth of Whig strength and organization in the 1780s was directed solely to this end, and it was a consideration that Fox could certainly not ignore. Burke therefore insisted that the Prince of Wales should take the initiative and put his full claims before the Commons, because 'the great point is in my opinion not to let the Ministers take the lead in the Settlement. They are men undoubtedly n legal situations of Trust, to perform such functions as can be performed in Office, without resort to the Crown. But the King's confidential servants they are not. . . .'[2] Any call to use the Regency crisis to humiliate Pitt and break that system, which had defeated he Whigs in 1784, could be sure of a warm response in Foxite circles.

Finally, Sheridan's scheme involved the sacrifice of Loughborough and the retention of Thurlow, and it is some measure of Fox's egard for the claims of party allegiance, that he found this manoeuvre exceedingly distasteful. To compromise with Thurlow, as Fox told Sheridan, was to compromise the purity of their opposition to the events of 1782–4: 'I have swallowed the pill—a most bitter one it was . . . but I am convinced . . . that the negotiation will fail.'[3] Matters were not made easier for Fox by the fact that he was responsible for informing Loughborough that his career would not be advanced. So great was Fox's embarrassment at this point, that he had recourse to the disingenouus argument that he believed the etention of Thurlow was the general wish of the party. Even so he

[1] G. Selwyn to Lady Carlisle, 26 Nov. 1788; Roscoe and Clergue, eds. *George elwyn, His Life and Letters*, p. 242.

[2] E. Burke to Fox, late Nov. 1788; Copeland, *Burke Corres.* v. 427.

[3] Fox to Sheridan (undated); J. W. Derry, *The Regency Crisis and the Whigs 788–9*, p. 210.

had to admit that 'You know enough of the nature of our party to know how rapidly notions are sometimes propagated among them, and how difficult it often is for us, who ought to lead, not to be led by them. . . . I feel the part I am acting to be contrary to every principle of conduct I ever laid down for myself.'[1] Excuses of this kind were less than satisfactory, in that reports of Fox's conversations with Thurlow on 26 and 30 November were known to the Ministry,[2] and had reached Paris by 4 December.[3] When the negotiations with Thurlow began to show signs of flagging, Fox reported this outcome to Sheridan with unconcealed relief: 'I am convinced, after all, the negotiation will not succeed, and am not sure that I am sorry for it. I do not remember ever feeling so uneasy about any political thing I ever did in my life.'[4]

In Fox's mind, the lines of party conflict had been so clearly defined, that the normal kind of trafficking in offices and personnel, which preceded the formation of most eighteenth-century ministries, was no longer possible. To negotiate with Thurlow was acutely embarrassing. Once Fox's party spirit had been rekindled by appeals from Burke and the distasteful attempt to sacrifice Loughborough, Sheridan went unheard when he recommended 'great moderation, disclaiming all Party views, and avowing the utmost readiness to acquiesce in every reasonable Delay'.[5] Loughborough's opinion was still highly valued, and among Fox's papers, there is a memorandum, unfortunately undated but in Loughborough's handwriting, setting out the full case for the Prince claiming the Regency by hereditary right, together with possible objections and their solutions.[6] If, as seems likely, this memorandum was written before 10 December, Fox's speech, far from being a sudden outburst, was based on a considered opinion by a leading English lawyer.

As these several influences were brought to bear, the meeting at Burlington House on 29 November, at which Portland and the Prince were formally reconciled, takes on a new significance. A meeting composed of Portland, Fox, North and Loughborough looks very much like an anti-Sheridan pressure group, and the absence of the Prince's principal adviser hitherto is significant. So too is the statement by Sir Gilbert Elliot that, at this meeting, Prinny was

[1] Fox to Loughborough, Dec. 1788; Campbell, *Lives of the Lord Chancellors*, viii. 93.

[2] W. Grenville to Buckingham, 30 Nov. 1788; Buckingham and Chandos, ii. 22.

[3] Brit. Mus. Egerton 3262, f. 154; Beauchamp to Hertford, 4 Dec. 1788.

[4] Fox to Sheridan (undated); Moore, *Sheridan*, ii. 31.

[5] R. Sheridan to Prince of Wales, 2 Dec. 1788; Price, *The Corres. of R. B. Sheridan*, i. 203.

[6] Add. MS. 47560, ff. 86–94; Memorandum (undated).

induced to declare that he would not accept a limited Regency.[1] The same group dined at Burlington House two days later.[1] If Elliot's statement is true, the Prince and Fox had taken a decisive step against Sheridan's idea of attaining office at virtually any price. The authority which Sheridan had built up in Fox's absence, was demolished. Confident that the King's recovery was out of the question, Fox responded to the promptings of party and the Prince followed suit.

Three days after the Burlington House meeting, Fox suffered a relapse, and, 'lowered by a Flux & other Complaints',[2] was unable to attend the examination of the King's physicians on 3 December. Even so, Fox had clearly fallen out with certain sections of the party, as Lord Frederick Cavendish ruefully noticed: 'It was said at St James this morning that C. Fox was dead but we hear he is pretty well. he certainly did harm tho' I believe there would have been enough without it.'[3] George Selwyn, echoing Lord Frederick's words, went on to suggest that Fox's illness was of the diplomatic variety, induced to avoid further party embarrassments: 'The Party . . . is very angry with Mr. Fox, and will not believe the indisposition, which confines him to his bed, not to be a feigned one.'[4] Both men make no reference to the exact nature of Fox's offence, but, since it must have taken place before his relapse on 2 December, they were probably referring to the Burlington House meeting of 29 November, and the annoyance which Prinny's declaration about the Regency must have given Sheridan and his friends. This would underline the importance of this meeting, as marking Fox's overt conversion to Loughborough's ideas.

Between 29 November and 10 December, the debate in the Whig party between these two sets of ideas went on. On 5 December, Fox was 'rather agst'[5] any further parliamentary discussion of what should be done, suggesting that he favoured an outright declaration of the Prince's claims without further loss of time. Significantly, Loughborough was 'quite agst'[5] any such proposal. On the next day, there was a further meeting at Fox's house, the personnel of which strongly resembled those attending on 29 November.[5] Two such meetings of Sheridan's opponents within seven days can hardly be coincidental. Nor is it surprising that, according to Lady Elizabeth Foster, in

[1] Sir G. Elliot to Palmerston, 29 Nov. 1788; Connell, *Portrait of a Whig Peer*, p. 185.

[2] Palmerston to Lady Palmerston, 4 Nov. 1788 (incorrectly dated); Palmerston MSS.

[3] Lord F. Cavendish to Mrs. Ponsonby, 4 Dec. 1788; Grey MSS.

[4] G. Selwyn to Lady Carlisle, 4 Dec. 1788; Roscoe and Clergue, *George Selwyn, His Life and Letters*, p. 245.

[5] Diary of Duchess of Devonshire, 5 Dec. 1788; Sichel, *Sheridan*, ii. 412.

summing up,[1] 'Lord Loughborough said he did not know why the P. should not go as D. of Cornwall to the H. of Lords, get a few Westminster people to Huzza him & make a speech about his claims to the sole Regency.'[2] On the same day, and possibly as a result of this second meeting, Fox approved a suggestion by Sir Gilbert Elliot that the House of Commons should be induced to send the Prince a memorandum inviting him to accept the Regency without delay.[3] Much of the drama of the 10 December speech, with its unequivocal assertion of the Prince's rights, is diminished when these preliminary meetings and manoeuvres are taken as a preface. Neither his temperament nor his consciousness of political issues would allow Fox to follow Sheridan's policy of compromise and negotiation. The enmities born of 1784 were too strong. It is even doubtful whether, in a practical sense, Fox could have derived advantages from such a policy. His hatred of the King was so well known that a diarist in North Wales heard rumours of murder: 'The Common people have an idea that Mr. Fox administered Poison to the King and went abroad to await the effects of it. The report has gained credit with those who ought to know better.'[4] Fox stood on party ground, and this fact was known.

The speech of 10 December occasioned surprise in some sections of the party because, although Fox was clearly moving towards Loughborough's position, there was still some room for doubt. Only two days before the debate, Sheridan was still confident that his views would prevail.[5] Fox's movements and contacts in the crucial forty-eight hours before the debate are not easily pinned down. According to the Duke of Leeds, he was closeted with Thurlow at Windsor,[6] while Lady Rockingham[7] believed that he was with Burke at Beaconsfield.[8] This is clearly a problem of some importance. The Beaconsfield visit is the more likely, because Fox's views about Thurlow would make a further visit to Windsor unlikely, and because Lady Rockingham's letter was a contemporary one, and therefore owed

[1] Lady Elizabeth Foster (1759–1824); dau. of 4th Earl of Bristol; in the 1780s, became the close friend of Georgina, Duchess of Devonshire, and the mistress of her husband; became the Duke's second wife, 1809; important diarist.

[2] Add. MS. 41579, f. 8; Lady Elizabeth Foster's Journal, 6 Dec. 1788.

[3] Sir G. Elliot to Lady Elliot, 6 Dec. 1788; Lady Minto, *Life and Letters of Ld. Minto*, i. 242.

[4] Diary of Lady E. Butler, 8 Dec. 1788; Mrs. G. H. Bell, ed. *The Hamwood Papers*, p. 156.

[5] Add. MS. 41579, f. 9; Lady Elizabeth Foster's Journal, 8 Dec. 1788.

[6] Browning, *Memoirs of the Fifth Duke of Leeds*, 8 Dec. 1788, pp. 132–3.

[7] Lady Rockingham, née Maria Bright (?–1804); dau. of Thomas Bright of Badsworth, Yorks; never shared her husband's political prominence.

[8] Lady Rockingham to E. Burke, 8 Dec. 1788; Wentworth Woodhouse Muniments, Burke 1.

nothing to a diarist's memory. Further, a visit to Burke, whom Fox later acknowledged as his political tutor, would greatly strengthen Fox's confidence to enunciate the doctrine of hereditary regency two days later, and would be fully consistent with his conduct since 29 November. Fox later insisted to Lady Elizabeth Foster that he had never wavered from this firm line. As she noted, 'I told Mr. Fox that I had heard the D. of Richmond say that Mr. Fox been said to be of opinion at first that the P. sd. not change his father's Ministers under a certain time—Mr. Fox said "no I never said that", & repeated it twice, but said no more.'[1] Such unswerving allegiance to the Loughborough view of the situation was hardly manifested, but it would be equally misleading to see the speech of 10 December as an entirely unpremeditated move. From 29 November onwards, Fox had been moving quite consistently in this direction. A belief in the King's incurability and an eagerness to draw party advantage from the situation would lead him naturally towards Loughborough and away from Sheridan.

Fox's speech in the Commons on 10 December set the terms for the Regency Crisis as a whole. Both Pittites and Whigs adapted their policies to meet its challenge. When Pitt, by way of procrastination, suggested a committee to look into precedents, Fox opposed such a measure in uncompromising terms:

> There was then a person in the kingdom different from any other person that existing precedents could refer to—an heir apparent of full age and capacity to exercise the royal power. It behoved them, therefore, to waste not a moment unnecessarily, but to proceed with all becoming speed and all becoming diligence to restore the sovereign power and the exercise of royal authority.[2]

Since the monarchy was not elective, the vacancy occasioned by the King's insanity had to be filled by the hereditary principle. Standing by this belief, Fox refused to serve on the committee looking for precedents, on the ground that its researches were superfluous.[3] Much later, this speech was regarded as a tragic mistake, and was imprinted in the minds of Whig diarists as an example of how 'Mr. Pitt conceives his sentences before he utters them. Mr. Fox throws himself into the middle of his, and leaves it to God Almighty to get him out again.'[4] Such a judgement, as a recent writer on the subject suggests,[5] is not really fair. Fox had taken a point of view which Loughborough, one of the most eminent constitutional lawyers in England, echoed the next day in the Lords. Fox's arguments were constitutionally

[1] Journal of Lady Elizabeth Foster, 5 Mar. 1789; Chatsworth MSS.
[2] *Fox Speeches*, iii. 400; 10 Dec. 1788.
[3] *Morning Chronicle*, 13 Dec. 1788.
[4] Add. MS. 47590, f. 40; Commonplace Book of Samuel Rogers.
[5] Derry, *The Regency Crisis and the Whigs*, pp. 78–9.

plausible, and, far from being devised on the spur of the moment, were almost certainly thought out in the meetings held between 29 November and 8 December. The speech was of course not entirely prompted by constitutional concerns. If successful, it would confirm Fox's standing in the party over Sheridan and would involve no compromise with any Pittites. But even so, the points brought forward were clear and cogent.

Whatever the academic coherence of Fox's remarks, they were none the less jarring. For a leading Whig to plead for the uninterrupted and undiluted exercise of royal authority was an extraordinary spectacle, which Pitt quickly turned to his own advantage. Prefacing his remarks with the well-known hope that, after his opponent's speech, he would 'un-Whig' Fox for life, Pitt went on to defend the Commons' rights in the matter. Claiming that Fox's interpretation would destroy the avowed prerogatives of the Lower House, Pitt insisted that the Prince had no more right to exercise a Regency than other subject, although his claim to do so required special attention.[1] In this, Pitt could usefully refer to the opinion of Blackstone, who declared that:

> If the Throne be at any time vacant, which may happen by other means besides that of abdication; if, I say, a vacancy by any means whatsoever should happen, the right of disposing of this vacancy seems naturally to result to the Lords and Commons, the Trustees and Representatives of the Nation.[2]

It was not the academic accuracy of the rival claims, which really mattered, however, for Pitt had primarily to convince the House that Fox's motives were almost entirely prompted by the interests of party and the desire for office. In this he succeeded, as individuals not unreasonably recognized how closely Fox's actions were determined by considerations of this kind.

Leading supporters of Pitt were delighted with what they took to be Fox's error. Leeds insisted that, 'in mentioning the question of right, C. Fox had let the cat out of the bag—he said so much the better for the rats are growing very troublesome'.[3] William Grenville was even more astonished: 'Only think of Fox's want of judgment, to bring himself & them into such a scrape as he has done, by maintaining a doctrine of higher Tory principle than could have been found anywhere, since Sir Robt. Sawyer's speeches.'[4] Jenkinson, with the benefit of hindsight, concurred.[5] Even among more neutral

[1] *Fox Speeches*, iii. 402; 10 Dec. 1788.

[2] Sir W. Blackstone, *Commentaries on the Laws of England*, i. 214.

[3] Add. MS. 41579, f. 20; Lady Elizabeth Foster's Journal, *c* 4 Jan. 1789.

[4] W. Grenville to Buckingham, 11 Dec. 1788; Buckingham and Chandos, ii. 53.

[5] Journal of Lady Elizabeth Foster, 28 Jan. 1794; Chatsworth MSS.

olíticians, there was bewilderment about Fox's motives. Ignorant f the pressures Fox was acting under, this provocative speech appeared uriously redundant. The Duke of Grafton for example was bomarded with reports of this kind. One friend asserted that he 'never new more warmth upon any Subject; . . . Surely Mr. Fox will not all his Doctrine a Whig one;—I think the Country will not regard t as such.'[1] The Bishop of Peterborough was even more explicit; I am wholly unable to conceive the necessity of this assertion as it eemed to be a point universally admitted.'[2] Few men understood ox's position. They could accept Pitt's simple description of the o December speech as an undignified bid for power, but could not ee that it might also be an attempt to win power without compronising with the Ministers. If the King was believed incurable, a Whig dministration was inevitable, and therefore Fox had nothing to lose y refusing to compromise. The Whigs would come in without the ontaminating assistance of the men of 1784. Internal pressures within he Whig party led Fox in the same direction. Little of this was nderstood by contemporaries, who saw only a scramble for office.

The speech naturally increased tension among the Whigs themselves, nd this was faithfully recorded by the diarists of Devonshire House. ccording to the Duchess, Sheridan, whose earlier work had been ompletely undone by Fox's initiative, 'seems out of spirits and I fear nuch some little Bickerings between Fox and him and perhaps misepresentations of what Sheridan previously did'.[3] Even in the innernost circles of Whiggery, where Fox normally received an immediately ympathetic audience, there were doubts. Lady Devonshire's brother admires Mr. Fox, for thus taking the Bull by the horns and thinks t a fine trait in his Character, but fears it was an unfortunate measure, oth as to its effect in the houses and in the Country—and especially s it seems now as if we were imbibing Tory principles'.[3] Yet after ataloguing disappointment and irritation, the ladies of Devonshire Iouse always return to questions of who was bidding for which office, uggesting that the Whigs were not aware that their chances of office ad been seriously impaired. Warren again told the Prince not to ccept anything less than a full Regency on 15 December.[4] As long s the King was believed to be incurably insane, the Whigs in general vere not of the opinion that Fox's speech had greatly damaged their opes. The quarrels within the party in mid-December were conerned with the disposal of offices and not with the details of constituional law. When a breach threatened between Fox and the Prince

[1] R. Hopkins to Grafton, 11 Dec. 1788; Grafton MSS. f. 746.

[2] Bishop of Peterborough to Grafton, 11 Dec. 1788; Grafton MSS. f. 958.

[3] Diary of Duchess of Devonshire, 11 Dec. 1788; Sichel, *Sheridan*, ii. 414.

[4] Add. MS. 41579, f. 11; Lady Elizabeth Foster's Journal, 12 Dec. 1788.

of Wales, its origin lay entirely in the fact that Prinny had offered Lord Sandwich the Admiralty without consulting his chief advisers.[1] Sheridan was naturally angry, but Burke was prepared to humour him: 'My idea was, that on Fox's declaring that the precedents, neither individually nor collectively, do at all apply, our attendance ought to have been merely formal. But as you think otherwise, I shall certainly be at the Committee soon after one.'[2] Fox's speech had launched the Whigs on an ambitious course, but the coherence in Whig voting in the crisis[3] testified to their belief that, as long as the King's condition showed no improvement, Fox's toying with constitutional law was not immediately relevant.

The speech was, however, eagerly seized on by the pamphleteers Re-employing a method, which had proved highly successful four years earlier, Fox's remarks from past speeches were damagingly exhumed. On 4 January 1784, for example, Fox had declared that 'the Prince of Wales, though the first subject in the kingdom, was but a subject. He was highest in the ladder of the peerage.'[4] Inconsistency could easily be shown, but the curious and important point is that, whereas a Foxite change of front was almost always paralleled by a Pittite tergiversation, Pitt escaped the charges which were readily levelled at Fox. Pitt's Ministry in 1784 was hardly less of a coalition than Fox's opposition. Similarly, Pitt's defence of the rights of the House of Commons in 1788 was in marked contrast to his defiance of majorities in that House four years earlier. On each occasion, however, Fox becomes the target of the pamphleteers, who lean heavily on the charge of inconsistency. The explanation for this lies in the fact that Fox is always the attacker, to whom the attention of the political world is drawn. Pitt was able to work in shadow Similarly the private life of Fox bred distrust of his political views. A correspondent of the Grenvilles, unable to decide whether Fox was more weak than profligate, concluded that 'Fox, having on a former occasion sought to trespass on the royal just prerogative, had now completed his attack on the Constitution, in denying the rights of Lords & Commons . . .'[5] Similarly, a spectator of the debate on 10 December lost the constitutional arguments, but referred to 'Pitt's Dignity' and 'Fox's meaness'.[6] Fox was therefore not alone in his inconsistency, but his reputation and his attacking policy made his theoretical lapses the more glaring.

[1] Add. Ms. 41579, f. 11; Lady Elizabeth Foster's Journal, 12 Dec. 1788.

[2] E. Burke to Sheridan, 11 Dec. 1788; Copeland, *Burke Corres.* v. 432.

[3] See Chapter III, pp. 102–3.

[4] Anon, *Fox Against Fox.*

[5] Sir W. Young to Buckingham, 11 Dec. 1788; Buckingham and Chandos, iii. 4

[6] Lady A. Wesley to Lady E. Butler, 12 Dec. 1788; Bell, *The Hamwood Papers* p. 159.

Fox's second excursion into the field of constitutional theory came two days later on 12 December 1788. Lord Palmerston saw this speech as directed at clarification only: 'The declaration Fox made on Wednesday about the Prince's right seems to have been rather unfortunate, as it has been misunderstood by some of our friends not remarkable for clear comprehension and misrepresented by all the opposite party. It became necessary for Fox therefore to bring it up again in order to explain clearly what he had said, which he did ably.'[1] This is not entirely accurate. Although Fox again demanded a full and unrestricted Regency for the Prince of Wales, the language employed was more cautious, and there was some attempt to set the claim in a more recognizably Whig context:

> The regency was a trust, on behalf of the people, for which the Prince was responsible, in like manner as his majesty and every monarch that ever sat upon the throne were responsible for the due execution of their high office. Sovereignty therefore is a trust depending on the natural liberties of mankind.[2]

No part of the Prince's claims was given up, but the superintending authority of the legislature was admitted. This was not simply a clarification of an earlier position, in that it involved a toning down of demands and language. But equally this speech was not a surrender or concession to opinion. Much had been modified, but the hereditary claim of the Prince of Wales to an unrestricted regency was reiterated and confirmed.

The speech of 12 December created considerable confusion as to what value Fox now attached to the hereditary claim. The Bishop of Peterborough was of the opinion that Fox 'seems to have abandon'd the idea of an indefeasible right in the Prince to the Regency'.[3] The Eden family agreed, and thought that Fox was simply attempting to correct a bad tactical error.[4] The more perceptive politicians realized, however, that, although Fox's language had become more moderate, his claims remained unchanged, and that Pitt would base his plan for a restricted Regency on the opposition generated by Fox's speeches.[5] Once, again, however, the predominant feeling among the Whigs was that, as long as the King had been permanently removed from office, the question of the Prince's rights was at best an interesting side issue. With regard to this problem, Lord Spencer concluded

[1] Palmerston to Lady Palmerston, 12 Dec. 1788; Connell, *Portrait of a Whig Peer*, p. 188.

[2] *Fox Speeches*, iii. 405; 12 Dec. 1788.

[3] Bishop of Peterborough to Grafton, 13 Dec. 1788; Grafton MSS. f. 957.

[4] Sir J. Eden to W. Eden, 12 Dec. 1788; *Journal and Corres. of Ld. Auckland*, ii. 253.

[5] Palmerston to Lady Palmerston, 12 Dec. 1788; Palmerston MSS. W. W. Grenville to Buckingham, 13 Dec. 1788; Buckingham and Chandos, ii. 56.

that 'Every moderate man must wish [it] had never been stirred, but which to be sure it must be owned was first stirred by Mr. Fox, however all the rest of the Party & Mr. Fox himself in the debate today have shewn their averseness to deciding such a Question one way or the other.'[1] Even if Pitt succeeded in imposing limitations on the Prince as a result of Fox's outburst, these could not be kept in force indefinitely. Mrs. Sheridan,[2] in spite of her husband's humiliation, took a highly practical view of the situation. In the long run, Fox's speeches were an exciting irrelevance:

Pitt fights hard, and clings with all his might to the Treasury bench; but it is all in vain; . . . An unlucky word about right, made use of by C. Fox in the House, has made some little confusion in the heads of a few old Parlementaries, who did not understand him; Pitt has taken advantage of this, and means to move a question about it on Tuesday. . . . It is supposed there will be a great battle; there are five hundred and fifteen members in town, and great interest is making on both sides. We hope to have a majority; but, if we have not, it will not be of any great consequence.[3]

Fox was fully in agreement with this opinion, and showed no sign of repenting his actions. Between 12 December and 18 December, when he suffered another relapse into fever,[4] his public and private statements in no way deviated from the line he had taken up in his early speeches. On 16 December, he rejected all suggestions in the Commons that precedents might be instructive, claiming that any constitutional practice before 1688 was not relevant.[5] He further insisted that, if the House of Commons committed the Regency to any hands but the Prince's, this would represent an unpardonable invasion of the executive, and would seriously unbalance the constitution.[5] Unaware of the news from Kew, where the King was showing signs of recovery, allowing Grenville to hope that the reign of 'Charles III' would be short,[6] Fox's confidence was unshaken. Convinced that the King 'is certainly worse & perfectly mad',[7] Fox's conduct was governed by the inevitability of Whig success: 'We shall have several hard fights in the H. of C. this week and next, in some of which I fear we shall be beat, but whether we are or not I think it

[1] Spencer to Countess Spencer, 12 Dec. 1788; Spencer MSS.

[2] Mrs. Sheridan (1754–92); dau. of Thos. Linley; renowned for both beauty and a fine soprano voice; assisted husband by keeping the accounts at Drury Lane, canvassing political supporters and acting as a secretary during the impeachment of Hastings.

[3] Mrs. Sheridan to Dr. Parr, 13 Dec. 1788; J. Johnstone, ed. *The Works of Dr. Samuel Parr*, i. 467.

[4] Palmerston to Mrs. Palmerston, 20 Dec. 1788; Palmerston MSS.

[5] *Fox Speeches*, iii. 414; 16 Dec. 1788.

[6] W. Grenville to Buckingham, 17 Dec. 1788; Buckingham and Chandos, ii. 61

[7] Add. MS. 47570, f. 178; Fox to Mrs. Armistead, 15 Dec. 1788.

certain that in about a fortnight we shall come in. If we carry our questions we shall come in in a more creditable & triumphant way, but at any rate the Prince must be Regent and of consequence the Ministry must be changed.'[1] This being the case, Fox felt it incumbent upon him not to advise Prinny 'to claim any thing else as Regent, but the full power of a King, to which he is certainly entitled'.[1] A direct approach by the Prince of Wales to the House of Commons was not ruled out.[2] The King's insanity was the Whigs' guarantee of office, and Fox believed that there was little reason for further concern.

Until at least 25 December, there is no hint of compromise in Whig speeches. Precautions were taken against possible Pittite manoeuvres, and it was even agreed that a limited Regency should be accepted, if the Queen looked like setting herself up as a rival to her son,[3] but essentially such moves were thought unnecessary. As Palmerston observed, Pitt may have derived advantages from the question of the Prince's rights, but he still had to convince the Commons that the Regency should carry limitations: 'I think things look better than I thought they did when I wrote last. The Question of right being out of the way there are certainly many who would not hear of such a Claim who yet are for putting the Government into the Prince's hands without Limitations.'[4] Overconfidence led Fox to bungle the issue of the value of precedents, which came up for debate again on 22 December. As a recent writer on this subject has pointed out, Fox's thinking on this subject was muddled and highly confused.[5] Having originally denied the value of all precedents before 1688, Fox was faced with the problem of what English law as a whole was based on, which plainly had a much longer history. The speech of 22 December therefore saw Fox going back on his original position, and offering interpretations of the reign of Henry VI.[6] Pitt easily pointed to the deplorable inconsistency of Fox's remarks, and justifiably carried the division by 251–178:

> In the first instance they had been pronounced to be wholly irrelevant; and now they had been admitted as authorities, not merely in point against the mode of proceeding, which he [Fox] had submitted to the House as the most constitutional and most eligible, but as clearly establishing the direct contrary.[6]

Not even admitted errors of this kind shook the Whigs' confidence. Speeches, pamphlets and motions were irrelevant beside the central

[1] Add. MS. 47570, f. 178; Fox to Mrs. Armistead, 15 Dec. 1788.
[2] Prince of Wales to Lonsdale, 14 Dec. 1789; H.M.C. *Lonsdale MSS*. xiii. 6–7, p. 142.
[3] Add. MS. 41579, f. 14; Journal of Lady Elizabeth Foster, 17 Dec. 1788.
[4] Palmerston to Lady Palmerston, 20 Dec. 1788; Palmerston MSS.
[5] Derry, *The Regency Crisis and the Whigs*, p. 111.
[6] *Fox Speeches*, iii. 429; 22 Dec. 1788.

fact that the only person, who could possibly be regent, was Whig. By 25 December, no trace could be found of Sheridan's ideas. The Whigs would enter office as a party and without compromise. Reports from Kew that the King might be recovering were dismissed as Pittite devices to create uncertainty.[1] Burke, completely undismayed, reported a long conversation with Fox to Windham, in which he had fortified Fox's intentions to hold out for total victory: 'Now is the time to push; & I am sure if we looked to the publick, instead of individuals, these individuals would be forced to submit to the publick, when we cannot gain from any efforts of our own.'[2] When Thurlow's speech in the Lords, announcing his intention to stand by the King, closed a very plausible path to office, Fox's reaction was not disappointment but relief. He immediately informed Loughborough that he could resume his position as the party's candidate for the Chancellorship: 'It was much the pleasantest conversation I have had with him [Thurlow] for many years . . . If I were to tell you how the advantage my health and spirits have received from our conversation yesterday morning, you would perhaps think either that I exaggerated, or that I am weaker than a man ought to be.'[3] At the end of December, the political situation had become uncomplicated for the Whig leaders. Embarrassing negotiations with traitorous Pittites had been broken off, the lines of a policy of no compromise had, not always without damage, been worked out, and Fox had the comforting task of assuring all his friends that their claims on the party would be met.

The simplification of Whig ends and policies, however, involved criticisms of Fox's leadership. Many Whigs, while still confident that the King's continued incapacity would bring them into office, were sharply critical of Fox's tactics. Too much ground had been surrendered to Pitt for no obvious reason. Lord George Cavendish[4] complained that 'On our side there was some misfortunes & perhaps some mismanagement. We despise Parliamentary Craft too much & are sadly deficient in it.'[5] Palmerston was of the same opinion: 'I have often thought we have more wit and Ingenuity on our side than sound judgment in managing Parliamentary matters.'[6] Dissatisfaction with the Whig campaign was even turned by Sir Gilbert Elliot into a personal attack on Fox's shortcomings: 'Fox . . . has

[1] W. Lefanu, ed. *Betsy Sheridan's Journal*, p. 139.

[2] Add. MS. 37843, f. 13; E. Burke to W. Windham, 25 Dec. 1788.

[3] Fox to Loughborough, 26 Dec. 1788; Campbell, *Lives of the Lord Chancellors*, viii. 98.

[4] Lord George Cavendish (?1727–94); M.P. (Weymouth) 1751–54; (Derbyshire) 1754–80, 1781–94; invariably voted with the other members of his family in the Rockingham connection; broke with Fox over the French Revolution.

[5] Lord George Cavendish to Mrs. Ponsonby, 25 Dec. 1788; Grey MSS.

[6] Palmerston to Lady Palmerston, 26 Dec. 1788; Palmerston MSS.

great difficulty or backwardness in resolving as if he had no interest or no judgment in the affairs that are depending, and . . . he lets anybody else decide for him; so measures are often the production of chance instead of wisdom.'[1] The wilfulness, with which Fox had launched into the discussion of constitutional points, fully justified such complaints, particularly when it became clear that, on the question of precedents and limitations, the Whig position had not been thought out coherently. The only factor keeping such criticisms in check was the certainty of eventual success. Tactically, Fox had been at fault, but his swaggering forays into the field of constitutional law were only possible because he felt his general position to be impregnable.

Of more importance was the poisoning of Fox's relations with Sheridan. Between 24 November and the end of the year, Fox had not only reasserted his influence at Carlton House, but had also convinced the Prince and the party that they should follow Loughborough's uncompromising ideas. The meticulously prepared plans of Sheridan were ignored. The wound given to their friendship went deep. The Fitzherbert marriage debate and the early stages of the Regency crisis had convinced Fox that Sheridan's ambition had to be controlled. According to Philip Francis, Fox only hated two people in his whole career, and Sheridan was one; 'Of Sheridan he said little, but that little was enough: "*Cui altius irascebatur, silentio transmisit.*"'[2] The whole course of the crisis is littered with disagreements between these two men. Sheridan, although losing the struggle to have his ideas adopted by the party officially, continued to promote negotiations on his own account. Devonshire House was the arena, in which their rival claims were debated. As the Duchess of Devonshire recorded, the egocentric jealousies of these two highly talented men often led them into embarrassingly juvenile quarrels: 'Fox was angry yesterday with Sheridan for letting some of our friends go out of town upon the idea of there being no debate afterwards; Charles made him excuses for having snubb'd him and Sheridan s[d] quite as to a child—pooh pooh be as cross as you will.'[3]

Rancour in Whig circles always found political expression, and usually of a debilitating kind. While Fox's speeches were basing Whig claims on constitutional imperatives, Sheridan continued to initiate private negotiations without any reference to the other Whig leaders. In December, he was suspected by the diarists of Devonshire House of inviting the co-operation of certain independent groups 'by talking other sentiments y[n] Foxes'.[4] Two weeks later, Fox had to insist that

[1] Sir G. Elliot to Lady Elliot, 6 Jan. 1789; *Life and Letters of Ld. Minto*, i. 257.
[2] Parkes and Merivale, *Memoirs of Sir P. Francis*, ii. 451.
[3] Diary of Duchess of Devonshire, 20 Dec. 1788; Sichel, *Sheridan*, ii. 418.
[4] ibid.

Sheridan's clandestine talks with John Robinson should cease.[1] Fox could not afford, either politically or personally, to allow Sheridan to deviate from the party view of the crisis, which, at great price, he had outlined to the Commons. The abuse and denigration was mutual. Sheridan was convinced that Fox was responsible for the attacks on him, which were appearing in the Whig press, and spread the story that he was the innocent victim of malicious slander.[2] The Foxites were equally sure that Sheridan was once again trying to establish a private interest, using the Prince of Wales as a figurehead. The Duchess of Devonshire recorded 'Great private treachery . . . this is the old attack of Sheridan courting the Prince and encouraging the Praise of him in the world and papers where Fox is abused.'[3] The Sheridans, recently evicted and temporarily homeless, had in fact taken refuge with Mrs. Fitzherbert. For Fox, this crisis underlined the danger of allowing Sheridan to form a personal connection within the party under the patronage of the Prince of Wales, which would jeopardize the cohesion won since 1784.

Again and again, Fox's command of a situation was undermined by Sheridan's contrived or accidental negligence. In January, Lady Elizabeth Foster noted that 'Sheridan came—said he had made it up with C. Fox but that he hated any personal abuse, & that if he had left the room in the anger he had been in, he never should have spoke to him again—he said Charles abus'd him, for his irregularity & want of punctuality . . . but Charles was in the right I think, for the letter Sheridan neglected was of consequence.'[4] More serious still was the fact that, owing to Sheridan's dilatoriness, Fox had no time to read the Prince's answer to Pitt's proposed list of limitations before he was called on to offer Prinny formal advice on the matter. Lady Elizabeth Foster noted that this behaviour generated another quarrel, even more violent than the last: 'It was Sheridan's delaying to send this answer to Fox who wish'd to see it & consider it before the P came to see him, wch caus'd the quarrel between them. Sheridan had promis'd it by nine, but he only carried it at two—& found his note wch promised an earlier hour pinn'd up against the glass—& the P. of W. there.'[5] This last breach in a series of debilitating squabbles was more final. Disgust with Sheridan was freely given by many contemporaries as the reason for Fox leaving London for Bath: 'Mr. Fox seems to me to be offended at Sheridan's violent passion;

[1] Add. MS. 41579, f. 20; Journal of Lady Elizabeth Foster, 4 Jan. 1789.

[2] Journal of Lady Elizabeth Foster, 11 Jan. 1789; Chatsworth MSS.

[3] Diary of Duchess of Devonshire, 12 Jan. 1789; Derry, *Regency Crisis and the Whigs*, p. 127.

[4] Add. MS. 41579, f. 20; Journal of Lady Elizabeth Foster, 4 Jan. 1789.

[5] Journal of Lady Elizabeth Foster, 20 Jan. 1789; Chatsworth MSS.

his journey to Bath is not for health alone.'[1] Fox was therefore presented with the problem of controlling not only his own temper, but also those of highly gifted men, whose brilliance made the Whigs overpowering in debate, but whose selfishness and egocentricity infused weakness and disunion into all the party's efforts. During the French Revolution, these personal vendettas would become more marked, and Fox never found a satisfactory way of dealing them.

Not until the limitations which Pitt proposed to make to the Regency were made known, was there any hesitancy on the part of the Whigs, however.[2] Fox's immediate reaction was to bluff his way out of a very awkward situation by attacking the evidence of the physicians, on which Pitt's case rested.[3] The Minister was accused of suppressing accurate reports about the King's health in an undignified attempt to hang on to power at any price. These reports, Fox claimed, would have demonstrated the futility of a restricted regency for a term of years by confirming that there was no chance of the King's recovery. The speech was less a reasoned reply to Pitt's case than a trading on past confidence in the King's incurability, coupled with threats and blandishments that a future Whig ministry would remember its friends and punish its enemies.[4] The divisions of this period convincingly showed that Fox's belief in the King's hopeless insanity was no substitute for a reasoned answer to the Minister's case. When Fox next touched on the issue of limitations to the Regency therefore, it was a much subdued performance, which kept strictly to constitutional arguments. Pitt was at last to be answered in kind. Fox then opposed the limited Regency idea not from theory but on strictly practical grounds. A King or Regent without the full range of executive powers would be unable to administer the country effectively. Proposals to leave the Queen in charge of the King's Household was making the executive weak for the undisguised advantage of party: 'To prevent that party from enjoying office, whom he thought ineligible, he [Pitt] attacked and violated the constitution.'[5] Between 6 January and 19 January, when these two speeches were delivered, blustering self-confidence had given way to a reasoned answer to Pitt on his own terms. It was now too late. The Whig's position still depended absolutely on the King's remaining indisposed, but in January, the reports from Kew daily grew more optimistic.

[1] J. Huber to W. Eden, 3 Feb. 1789; *Journal and Corres. of Ld. Auckland*, ii. 266.

[2] Lord G. Cavendish to Mrs. Ponsonby, 31 Dec. 1788; Grey MSS.

[3] *Fox Speeches*, iii. 442; 6 Jan. 1789.

[4] Wheatley, *Memoirs of Sir N. Wraxall*, v. 250; 6 Jan. 1789.

[5] *Fox Speeches*, iii. 447; 19 Jan. 1789.

The questions surrounding the limitation issue and their solution brought a new dimension into the jealousies dividing the Whigs. Burke now became an active combatant. Theoretically, the wounds had healed by early January. Prinny, 'Henry the Fifth . . . beyond our warmest wishes',[1] was living with Fox at Mrs. Armistead's, and showed no more signs of taking an independent line. When Pitt's statement on the proposed limitations was presented to the Whigs, Fox was with Burke at Beaconsfield, suggesting that the policy of no compromise would be carried through and that Sheridan would remain an isolated figure within the party. Indeed, William Adam believed that the first draft of the Whig reply to Pitt was the joint product of Burke and Fox. It was therefore extremely galling for Burke to discover later that Sheridan had taken it upon himself to tone down the language of Burke's draft in the direction of compromise, and that Fox had agreed to it. George IV later laid great emphasis on this volte face on the part of Fox: 'I know not how Burke knew that Sheridan had thus revised this work of which he was proud, and very justly; but he never forgave him. I believe that Burke guessed it from the warmth with which at a meeting at the Duke of Portland's, Sheridan supported my amendments to the original draft . . . which was rendered more offensive to Burke by Fox's agreeing with Sheridan.'[2] At some point in early January therefore Fox abandoned the uncompromising stance he had taken up on 10 December, and was now primarily concerned to see Prinny installed as Regent, with or without limitations. Either his belief in the King's incurability was weakening, or, more probably, he entertained a real fear that the Queen would take the Regency over herself. This change of course was no doubt politic, but it involved a quarrel with Burke, which was just as bitter as his earlier encounters with Sheridan. It was no coincidence that three different interpretations of the French Revolution should later be represented by these egocentric and ambitious men.

For much of January therefore, the Whig party was caught in a highly paradoxical situation. The same uneasiness, which led Fox to think of compromise, prompted the Whigs, belatedly, to become active in mobilising their full strength. Fox personally invoked the services of William Adam, calling for addresses, meetings and pamphlets: 'Upon the Whole, I think it was right to drop the Westminster Meeting, but I am very much afraid of the same Timid disposition, which was the Occasion of our perhaps doing right in this instance, causing such mischief in the future.'[3] Usually dependable

[1] Bell, *The Hamwood Papers*, pp. 174–5; 21 Jan. 1789.
[2] George IV to J. W. Croker, 25 Nov. 1825; Jennings, *The Croker Papers*, i. 289.
[3] Add. MS. 47568, f. 244; Fox to Adam, 2 Jan. 1789.

Whig areas like Norfolk were called upon to petition. Fox's willingness to accept a limited Regency, and his new enthusiasm to organize Whig opinion in the country in early January, are clearly related phenomena. As he explained to Portland, the struggle in the House of Commons had not gone well, and it was therefore time to choose other ground: 'I have seen Adam & entirely approve of stirring without doors as soon as possible, and avoiding if we can any more divisions.'[1] Cabinet construction had become the other major hobby of the Whigs during these weeks.[2] On 21 January, Fox sent Portland a full Cabinet list, including complete boards for the Treasury and Admiralty and a close discussion of what should be done for the Burke family.[1] This activity on several fronts gave the superficial impression that, although the Whigs had paid for their Parliamentary indiscretions by having limitations thrust upon their Prince, their confidence of eventual success was unchanged.

In fact, this energy barely concealed the divisions and disillusionment, which ran through all sections of the Whig party. Fox, by his speech of 10 December and his decision to accept a limited Regency, had thrown the party from one policy to another without any co-ordination or management. His attitudes had been entirely determined by an unwillingness to negotiate with the detested Pitt unless absolutely necessary and an initial belief in the incurability of the King. Fox's changes of attitude were logical as the situation developed, but this fact in no way shielded him from openly personal attacks. Once again, Devonshire House was the forum for Whig opinion. On 13 January, Lady Elizabeth Foster observed that 'Lady Dun. [cannon] told us Lady Spencer said she & all the party wish'd they were rid of Charles Fox who was rash & imprudent. This is very unfair.'[3] Burke, in a long and well reasoned letter of complaint to Windham, lamented the vacillation between one policy and the next: 'I observe that though there have been a very few consultations upon particular measures, there have been none at all de summa rerum. It has never been discussed, whether, all things taken together, . . . it would not be the best or the least evil course, for the Publick and the Prince; and possibly in the end for the party that the Prince should surrender himself to his enemies and ours.'[4] The changes in direction in Whig policy had been determined by the statements and speeches of Fox alone. He could not hope to escape entirely from responsibility for the quarrels with Burke and Sheridan and the disappointment in

[1] Add. MS. 47561, f. 95; Fox to Portland, 21 Jan. 1789.

[2] Sir G. Elliot to Lady Elliot, 10 Jan. 1789; Lady Minto, *Life and Letters of Lord Minto*, i. 260.

[3] Journal of Lady Elizabeth Foster, 13 Jan. 1789; Chatsworth MSS.

[4] E. Burke to W. Windham, *c.* 24 Jan. 1789; Copeland, *Burke Corres.* v. 436.

the party as a whole. The burst of activity in early January in no way compensated for these earlier shortcomings.

Fox's departure for Bath, on 27 January 1789, may have been prompted by a desire to escape these criticisms, but paradoxically his absence from politics quickly demonstrated how invaluable he was. His leadership during the crisis had not been of the highest order, but without him the Whigs were completely lost. Those who, like Lord Palmerston, had earlier voiced criticisms, were quickly forced to admit this: 'Charles Fox's Absence throws a damp on the Party. He could not go on in consequence of an immediate Pressure of Illness.'[1] Even leading Pittites like Wilberforce agreed that all interest in the issue had disappeared from Westminster with Fox's departure: 'You cannot imagine how insipid and vapid our debates are without Fox. They serve us up the same tasteless mess day after day, till one loathes the very sight of it.'[2] Under the leadership of Fox, the Whigs ran the risk of disorder, but also enjoyed the prospect of power. Without him, the Whigs were reduced to groups of often highly talented individuals, whose efforts were uncoordinated and who offered no real threat to Pitt. Fox's ideas and policies were not consistent or well thought out, but each in turn was successfully imposed on the party. Neither Sheridan, before Fox's return to England, nor Burke, after his escape to Bath, was able to perform a similar function.

Fox remained at Bath until 21 February. At all times during this period he expressed 'no belief in the K's recovery, but I dare say some of our friends are a good deal alarmed'.[3] In consequence, Portland, Spencer and the Prince of Wales were bombarded with requests and suggestions about patronage. The detail and party spirit behind these instructions makes it clear that, in spite of a number of setbacks, Fox believed that the Whigs would eventually have their own way. An Irish official, who had spoken slightingly of the Whigs three years earlier, was to be instantly dismissed, and Fox threatened to be 'quite vexed if he is not . . .'[4] There was to be a chaplaincy for a brother-in-law and something in Ireland for an indigent cousin.[5] Outstanding vacancies in regimental commands were suitably filled.[6] Fox, still seeing the coming Regency as a triumph for the Whig party, dutifully rewarded the faithful, and, with the aid of a long memory, threatened ruin to his enemies.

1 Palmerston to Lady Palmerston, 31 Jan. 1789; Palmerston MSS.

2 W. Wilberforce to L. Kenyon, 12 Feb. 1789; H.M.C. *Kenyon MSS.* xiv. 4, p. 527

3 Fox to Portland, 12 Feb. 1789; Derry, *The Regency Crisis and the Whigs*, p. 179

4 Add. MS. 47561, f. 100; Fox to Portland, 1 Feb. 1789.

5 Fox to Spencer, 9 and 15 Feb. 1789; Spencer MSS.

6 Fox to Prince of Wales, 4 Feb. 1789; Aspinall, *Corres. of George, Prince of Wales*, i. 484–5.

There was even some attempt on Fox's part to superintend the Whig campaign in London. William Adam received a steady flow of letters offering opinions on the best way of handling a petition passed by the electors of Westminster in the Whig's favour, and on which amendments should be moved to Pitt's regency bills. But, in spite of this concern, there is some reason to suppose that Fox was in no hurry to return to the battle. The bickering with Sheridan and Burke had been very disagreeable and very wearing. Equally, the determining factor in the situation, while Fox was at Bath, was the speed of the King's recovery. Any further initiatives on Fox's part could not have changed this position. Reports therefore soon began to reach London that Fox was making his stay in Bath longer than considerations of health alone strictly required. William Eden had two letters to this effect in consecutive days. One correspondent reported that 'Fox is not yet returned from Bath, & yet I am assured by his particular friends that he is very well.'[1] The other 'did not find that he was much indisposed'.[2] Fox shut his eyes to the possibility of the King recovering, and, with this comfortable thought, toyed with the pleasing details of patronage dispensation, and abstained from further effort.

The excursion to Bath was the first step in Fox's withdrawal from the contest. After each of his Parliamentary campaigns, the effort involved became too great, and, once the central point had been decided, Fox took very little interest in the tidying of details. In his view, all interest in the crisis had ended with the decision to accept a limited Regency, which then depended for its fulfillment on the state of the King's health alone. When he returned to London at the end of February, therefore, he found himself hopelessly out of touch. He continued to talk happily to Portland about the coming Council of Regency only a matter of days before the King's convalescence was announced.[3] Once the point became clear, Fox gave up, because logically he 'did not know how to Advise going on.'[4] The vindication of past action had no appeal for him whatever. Nor was he in any way concerned with the securing of tactical withdrawals. Only the broad outlines of policy, involving party defeat or victory, held Fox's attention. The securing of retreats was for him a scarcely worthwhile operation.

Allied to these temporary withdrawals from politics was a bitter and frustrated self-indulgence. Petulant attacks on Pitt[5] were paralleled by nights of heavy drinking in the London Clubs. At one

[1] Archbishop of Canterbury to W. Eden, 12 Feb. 1789; Derry, *The Regency Crisis and the Whigs*, p. 174.

[2] W. Fraser to W. Eden, 13 Feb. 1789; ibid. p. 175.

[3] Add. MS. 47561, f. 111; Fox to Portland, 21 Feb. 1789.

[4] Add. MS. 47568, f. 258; Fox to W. Adam, 15 Mar. 1789.

[5] Journal of Lady Elizabeth Foster, 10 Mar. 1789; Chatsworth MSS.

of these, Fox was responsible for an outbreak of brawling among the members, which later involved the Prince of Wales and the Duke of York in a duel with an irate Pittite.[1] Released from the sobriety imposed upon them by the immediate prospect of office, the Whigs lost all coherence, and compensated for their disappointment in wilful irresponsibility. Lady Elizabeth Foster's diary is full of such incidents in March and April 1789: 'The crowd was very great but without the least disturbance. They once stopp'd the P. & bid him cry God save the King, & he did, then Pitt for ever—wch he wd not do, but said Fox for ever—he then got in Brooks' open'd the windows & huzza'd.'[2] While Adam and Burke tried to save what credit they could for the Whigs therefore, Fox threw the matter over, and, with much ill grace, was forced to wait for the next issue, which might offer the party a chance of unseating Pitt.

Many years later, in his historical work on the reign of James II, Fox attempted to erect a theory of Whiggery, which would embrace both the Exclusionists of 1679, and their heirs in 1788–9:

In truth, the question between the exclusion and restrictions seems particularly calculated to ascertain the different views in which the different parties in this country have seen, and perhaps ever will see, the prerogatives of the Crown. The Whigs, who consider them as a trust for the people, a doctrine which the Tories themselves, when pushed in argument, will sometimes admit, naturally think it their duty rather to change the manager of the trust, than to impair the subject of it; while others, who consider them as the right or property of the King, will as naturally act as they would do in any other case of property, and consent to the loss or annihilation of any part of it, for the purpose of preserving the remainder to him, whom they style the rightful owner. If the people be the sovereign, and the King the delegate, it is better to change the bailiff than to injure the farm; but if the King be the proprietor, it is better the farm should be impaired, nay, part of it destroyed, than that the whole should pass over to an usurper.[3]

In the Exclusion crisis, the Whigs preferred to interrupt the natural workings of the hereditary principle rather than endanger the constitution. In 1789, their concern for the constitution remained the same, but was, on this occasion, expressed in a defence of the executive against being limited or defined by the legislative Houses. Some degree of coherence was at last imposed on Whig actions.

Those critics, who chose to attack Fox by attempting to show discrepancies between Whig conduct in 1688 and during the Regency crisis, missed the mark.[4] Although Fox's theoretical justification

[1] Journal of Lady Elizabeth Foster, 12 Mar. 1789; Chatsworth MSS.

[2] Journal of Lady Elizabeth Foster, 10 Mar. 1789; Chatsworth MSS.

[3] C. J. Fox, *A History of the Early Part of the Reign of James II*, p. 39.

[4] *Morning Chronicle*, 1 Jan. 1789. W. Combe, *Letter from a Country Gentleman to a Member of Parliament*.

appeared long after the events it was intended to defend, it was proof against this particular argument. Much more damaging was a comparison between Fox's conduct in 1788–9 and his championing of the rights of the legislature four years earlier.[1] Fox could argue that on both occasions he was defending the essential points of the constitution, but, as the pamphleteers pointed out, how were these points to be made known. Majorities in the Commons were first elevated as the final arbiters and then, four years later, ignored. The interpretation of constitutional values came to depend on Fox alone, and such a situation was open to question. As one pamphleteer pointed out,

> There was a moment too, when you thought that majorities in the House of Commons were entitled, not only to respect, but the submission of his Majesty and the House of Peers. What is the language of today Why, that majorities are nothing and are not to be regarded . . . your present doctrine is not only contradictory of that which you formerly possessed, but cannot be reconciled even to itself: for whilst you assert that the Rights of the reigning Monarch are defeasible, and actually null; you maintain that those of the Heir Apparent are indefeasible: which amounts to this, that Possession is vacancy, and that Reversion is true possession.[2]

Fox's only defence against such an indictment was that Pitt was inevitably guilty of the same offence. All Pittite pamphlets, however, were liberally sprinkled with references to faro-tables, racehorses and insolvency, and Fox's private life was always successfully brought in to make his political misdemeanours more heinous than those of his opponent. Consistency was not to be looked for in the Regency crisis, and with regard to Fox, this merely confirmed a widespread belief in his general irresponsibility.

The damage inflicted on the Whig party by the failure of the efforts during these months was restricted to the higher échelons moving between Devonshire and Burlington Houses. The rank and file of the party voted with consistency and determination. The party nature of the crisis, leading on from 1784, guaranteed this, but it could not save the Whigs from the effects of having within their ranks an excess of clever men. The cohesion of the party was destroyed by personality as much as by the issues raised by the French Revolution. The Fitzherbert affair in 1787 and the full impact of the Regency crisis only a year later gave free reign to egocentric ambition and flamboyant self-assertiveness. In 1802, the Duchess of Devonshire, whose favours and sympathy had been generously distributed to all sections of the party, saw the beginning of its disintegration in these years:

[1] Anon, *A Letter to Mr. Fox on the Late Conduct of his Party*, p. 9 seq.
[2] Anon, *A Letter to Mr. Fox on the Late Conduct of his Party*.

I read with concern those seeds of disunion in the opposition party which have since so fatally for itself and for the County operated against it. And here too at the distance of 13 years I can trace that beginning of negligence and want of ensemble which together with the indulgence of imprudent language has destroy'd the importance of the opposition and, . . . seems to shut out the assistance of Men of the first talents and integrity.[1]

Pitt only had to control an administration of clerks. Fox had to impose order on several formidable intellects little accustomed to receiving direction.

Looking forward to the French Revolution, the relations between Burke, Fox and Sheridan demand closer examination. Each represented a different view of the Revolution initially, and each cut out of the body of the Whig party a personal following. The events of 1787–9 must make it very hard to accept that their independent stands on the Revolution were initially prompted by political considerations alone. Sheridan in particular had systematically used the Regency crisis to create in independent interest for himself within the party centred on Carlton House. Fox had checked this separatism, but the breach between the two men was well known. Pittite pamphleteers, with tongue in cheek, pretended to applaud Fox's determination to keep Sheridan out of the Exchequer, which would have been 'a lamentable jest, a tragifarcical burlesque . . .'[2] By May 1789, news of this quarrel had reached North Wales, where it was firmly believed that Fox had fled to Bath, because he feared that the question of Mrs. Fitzherbert was again about to be raised in the Commons.[3] Bickering between Fox and Sheridan had been a constant factor throughout the crisis, and there is no indication that it terminated with this particular issue. As long as Mrs. Fitzherbert hated Fox and owed gratitude to Sheridan, no one could count on he undivided attention of the Prince of Wales.

An even greater menace rested in the degree to which the crisis had pushed Burke and Fox further and further apart. Ever since the death of Rockingham, Burke, the Nestor of the party, had believed himself to have been repeatedly slighted and ignored. In his view, only he and Francis took the impeachment of Warren Hastings seriously, while Fox and Sheridan lost interest as soon as the great set-piece speeches in Westminster Hall gave way to the mundane, daily cross-examination of an endless stream of witnesses. Fox, in January 1789, had also gone over to Sheridan's belief, that a limited Regency should be accepted, without informing Burke of his intentions. Later in 1789, insult was added to this very real injury. When

[1] Diary of Duchess of Devonshire, 1802; Sichel, *Sheridan*, ii. 400.
[2] Anon, *A Letter to Mr. Fox on the Late Conduct of his Party*, p. 29.
[3] Diary of Lady E. Butler, 5 Feb. 1789; Bell, *The Hamwood Papers*, p. 181.

the moment came for the Prince of Wales to justify his conduct to his parents, Burke submitted a memorandum demanding an unequivocal denunciation of the conduct of Pitt, his colleagues, and even of the Queen. This was read out at a meeting at Burlington House, and took two hours to be completed, during which time, as the Prince of Wales later recalled, 'Fox kept digging his fingers into the corner of his eye, a trick he had when anything perplexed him.'[1] Only two people, of whom Fox was not one, supported Burke's views. The memorial which was eventually submitted to the King took a quite different line, protesting the Prince's filial emotions and his concern with safeguarding the rights of his family.[2] Throughout the whole crisis, Burke's views were rarely solicited, and when presented on their author's own responsibility, ran a grave risk of being rejected.

At the conclusion of this same meeting, George IV remembered that, 'Fox told Sheridan what had passed, and described the paper as having, I remember the words as Sheridan repeated them to me, "all Burke's bitterness".'[1] In fact Burke complained angrily that the whole affair had been mismanaged. Power had not been won, nor had an honourable retreat been secured.[3] Burke believed that his age and experience gave him an incontrovertible claim to be consulted, if not to direct, and that, because this point had been neglected, the affair had gone badly. Burke entertained for Sheridan a distaste that was even greater than Fox's. His fellow Irishman had only the gift of intelligence to rely upon, and yet, with the same qualifications as Burke, was proving so much more successful. But this common suspicion of Sheridan did nothing to bring Fox and Burke closer together. Their approaches to both the impeachment of Hastings and the Regency crisis were very different, and Burke convinced himself that he was being systematically isolated. His melodramatic outbursts against the French Revolution, even in its earlier stages, were the weapons of a man who believed that he had nothing further to lose by these acts, and that they might possibly re-establish his badly tarnished reputation as the oracle of the Whigs.

Fox's position in 1789 was incredibly weak. His reputation at Court was even lower, if that were possible, than in 1784. At the levée he was snubbed, and George Selwyn took pleasure in reporting the fact; 'Charles Fox was at Court, but was scarcely spoke to. *Il n'en fut pour cela plus rebuté*.'[4] His position vis à vis the Crown was

[1] Jennings, *The Croker Papers*, i. 289.

[2] Memorial of the Prince of Wales; *Memorials and Correspondence of C. J. Fox*, ii. 309 seq.

[3] E. Burke to Charlemont, 10 July 1789; F. Hardy, *Memoirs of Charlemont*, ii. 218.

[4] G. Selwyn to Lady Carlisle, 6 Nov. 1789; Roscoe and Clergue *George Selwyn: His Life and Letters*, p. 262.

one of uncharacteristically grovelling subservience: 'Your Royal Highness who knows me, knows that not only I am incapable of any personal disrespect to his Majesty, but that my political principles are strong in favour of keeping up the Royal power entire, undivided, and full of vigour.'[1] The disaster of the Regency crisis had therefore reduced Fox to asking for royal favours only four days after the taking of the Bastille. He was further 'uneasy at having been told that his re-election at Westminster wd. be contested'.[2] By far the most threatening development, however, was the disputes with Sheridan and Burke. The one was ambitiously piling up credit at Carlton House. The other was defensively apprehensive for his standing and reputation, and might break out into irresponsibility. Both had the intellectual equipment and tenacity to establish distinct followings, which would threaten the cohesion of the Whig party, so carefully built up since 1784, with destruction.

When the outbreak of the French Revolution threw all other issues in English politics into the shade, the Whig party was already in a precarious position. Its greatest asset was still the resentment and bitterness engendered by the events of 1782–4. Although the leadership was riven by personal feuding, Whig voting in the House of Commons was firm and unwavering. But Fox had been unable to make any capital out of the most promising situation for the Whigs since their ejection from office in 1784. The disillusion and disappointment of the party on the eve of the Revolution reflected this. More sinister still was the fact that the Regency crisis had shown how vulnerable the party was to the interplay of personalities. The Regency crisis raised points of strategy only, and yet the party had come under strain. When the French Revolution involved a reappraisal of politics as a whole, the tension would become unendurable.

[1] C. J. Fox to Prince of Wales, 18 July 1789; Aspinall, *Corres. of George, Prince of Wales*, ii. 20–2.

[2] Journal of Lady Elizabeth Foster, 11 Jan. 1789; Chatsworth MSS.

V

THE FRENCH REVOLUTION AND THE WHIGS, JULY 1789–SEPTEMBER 1792

THE outbreak of the French Revolution came upon the Whigs at a highly inopportune moment. Superficially, the strength of the opposition to Pitt was as strong as ever. William Adam's party machinery was working smoothly, and he had succeeded in setting up a fund designed to finance Whig activities in the coming General Election, in April 1789. Whig voting in the House of Commons had remained steady, in spite of complaints that the Prince's case had not been presented in the Regency debates with all the skill, which might have been expected. Great danger was, however, very near. The Regency crisis had brought to a head the conflicting ambitions and fears of the party's clever men. Burke fought to salvage some of his influence within the party. Sheridan and Grey fought to establish a rival intellectual interest. Fox, the principal neutral between these two groups, had been unable to reconcile their differences or to impose a common policy. If fissures of this kind could be induced by an issue dominated by discussions of tactics rather than principle, Fox would have done well to consider seriously the threats presented by a movement across the Channel which would involve not only questions of strategy, but also a fundamental re-examination of the intellectual basis of English Whiggery.

The Whig leaders could claim, with some justice, that they were experts on French affairs. Fox himself had visited Paris in 1769, 1771, and 1776, and, in return, leading members of French society swarmed across the Channel after the conclusion of the American War in 1783. Lord Spencer kept his mother informed of the details of 'this inundation' of French visitors.[1] In May 1783, the Whigs were entertaining Monsieur de Conflans and the Duc de Chartres, who achieved a certain notoriety by being able to fall asleep while sitting between Lady Jersey and Mrs. Crewe. A year later, the dinner list at Devonshire House included the Duc de Coigny, the Duc de Polignac and Prince Esterhazy.[2] Significantly, French aristocratic visitors naturally gravitated towards Whig society, and, although the

[1] Lord Spencer to Countess Spencer, 10 May 1783; Spencer MSS.
[2] ibid. 20 May 1784; ibid.

range of views represented by these men was extensive, Fox and his immediate friends were more intimately linked to that group of liberal noblemen, who were to play such an important part in the early stages of the Revolution. The Vicomte de Noailles[1] wrote to congratulate Fitzpatrick on the formation of the Whig government in 1783: 'J'ai appris avec un extrême plaisir mon cher Fitzpatrick votre nomination au ministre. heureusement pour la france votre roy n'a reunis les rênes de l'état entre les mains des personnes faites pour le gouverner qu'au moment ou il n'étoit plus tems d'opérer de grandes choses.'[2] This correspondence had been begun before the American War, and Noailles now begged for its resumption.

The link between these men was more than merely social. Fox and Lafayette believed that they belonged to a common intellectual tradition, which would lead them to take similar views of a whole range of political issues. The common factor was, what Lafayette called, 'cette Sympathie de Liberté et de patriotisme qui Unira toujours, j'ose le dire, Certaines Ames'.[3] In practical terms, it found expression in a mutual detestation of the slave trade. Lafayette made a point of writing to Fitzpatrick offering his full support for the Whigs' attempt to effect 'the destruction of a trafick so disgracing to Mankind'.[4] When Fox visited France in 1802, Lafayette was naturally his host, and the guest was entertained with stories of how the Marquis de Condorcet, another leader of Europe's liberal[5] aristocracy, had died the death of a Stoic during the Revolution. These men believed that they were fighting the same enemies and pursuing the same ideals. War had to be made on despotic kings and intolerant priests, in order to defend what was loosely described as liberty. These objectives were universally applicable to the whole of Europe, and differences between the scale and bitterness of the campaign in individual countries were merely matters of degree.

Fox's long association with such men as Noailles and Lafayette must have had a very considerable influence on his attitudes towards the Revolution as a whole. Lafayette, with whom Fox enjoyed a very close friendship, was still prominent in French politics as late as June 1792. Certainly, Fox's initial response to the fall of the Bastille was everything his French friends could have wished: 'How much the greatest event it is that ever happened in the world, & how much the

[1] Vicomte de Noailles, Louis Marie (1756–1804); French liberal politician; elected Vice-Pres. of the Nat. Assembly, 1789; presented the Declaration of the Rights of Man; moved the total abolition of feudal dues, 4 Aug. 1789; fled from France during the Terror.

[2] Add. MS. 47582, f. 168; Noailles to R. Fitzpatrick, Apr. 1783.

[3] Add. MS. 51468, f. 49; Lafayette to Fox, 6 Nivôse 1800.

[4] Add. MS. 47583, f. 11; Lafayette to R. Fitzpatrick, 6 Jan. 1788.

[5] Add. MS. 47590, f. 9; Commonplace Book of Samuel Rogers.

best.'[1] In the same letter, he asked Fitzpatrick to convey his best wishes to the Duc d'Orléans,[2] with whom he had spent many convivial evenings during his convalescence at Bath earlier in the year, and to investigate the possibility of paying a visit to Paris itself. References to Fox's views about France in 1789 are few, but his enthusiasm was already sufficient to engender in certain members of the Fitzwilliam family that mixture of admiration for his abilities and fear of his ideas, which was to become increasingly pronounced during the course of the Revolution: 'Mr. Fox has been speaking again—he is a wonderful Man, his toast of the Majesty of the People I suppose will make another Fuss, he loses himself very much in these sort of things, and yet how can one but bend to his amazing talents.'[3] Toasts of this kind could be made in the political climate of 1789 without seriously disturbing conservative minds, but they hardly suggest that Fox was preparing to exercise that diplomacy and tact, which would be required to deal with the strains imposed on the party by the events in France. In Fox's view, Noailles and Lafayette were Whigs, who deserved unstinted support.

Fox was not, however, able to pursue this policy of sympathetic detachment for very long. Within seven months of the fall of the Bastille, the bitterness, which had grown up between Burke and Sheridan during the Regency crisis, contributed to the fact that each of them quickly set up a personal interpretation of the events in France, which each then attempted to impose on the Whigs as a whole. In early February, news of this feud had reached Lady Elizabeth Foster in Paris: 'They met at Burlington House & there made it up very amicably, Burke extended his hand to them & every thing was over, when unfortunately all at once Mr. Burke began talking it over again, & work'd himself up into such a passion that he ran out of the room, exclaiming that he should not think himself safe with such a set of men as they all are, Sheridan did everything he could to appease him, but nothing would do, he said he could never be reconciled to a Man who maintain'd opinions equally diabolical, ferocious & cruel.'[4] The debate on the Army Estimates, on 5 February 1790, brought the matter into the open. Fox and Sheridan opposed the increased estimates on the ground that England's alliances were firm, and because the French people had ceased to be the mercenaries of despotic kings and had become free citizens, who in no way

[1] Fox to R. Fitzpatrick, 30 July 1789; *Mems. and Corres. of C. J. Fox*, ii. 361.

[2] Duc d'Orléans, Louis Philippe Joseph (1747–93); cousin of Louis XVI, and well-known figure in English Whig society in the 1780s; elected to support the Rev., and acquired the nickname Égalité; guillotined 1793; father of Louis Philippe.

[3] F. Wentworth to Lady Fitzwilliam, 11 Oct. 1789; Milton MSS. Box 40.

[4] Journal of Lady Elizabeth Foster, 4 Feb. 1790; Chatsworth MSS.

challenged the liberties of England.[1] Burke violently dissented from the second of these opinions. This occasioned yet another party peace conference at Burlington House, which was even more acrimonious than the first. From ten at night until three in the morning, the debate was carried on between Sheridan and Burke, and ended in deadlock. Significantly, Burke's principal complaint was not that Sheridan's views on the Revolution were dangerous, but that he had the design 'of gaining the ascendancy over himself and Fox'.[2]

Disputes between such egocentric men could never be confined to private party meetings, and, within a few days, the debate had again been transferred to the open forum of the House of Commons. Fox himself had no wish to take sides between Burke and Sheridan. Indeed he was in an ideal position to offer mediation. Burke knew that Fox's personal reservations about Sheridan were as great as his own, while Sheridan rightly believed that Fox shared his views on the events taking place across the Channel. In answer to Burke's impassioned plea that England should take every step necessary to contain the disease of French ideas, Fox adhered rigidly to a Whig text. He denied all sympathy for an absolute form of government, in the Aristotelian sense, be it tyranny, oligarchy or democracy, and insisted that Frenchmen like Lafayette were only effecting in French politics what the English Whigs had had to do in 1688:

> From that period we had, undoubtedly to date the definition and confirmation of our liberties; and the case was certainly more parallel to the revolution in France than his rt. hon. friend (that is Burke) seemed willing to allow. The reason why France had been so long settling her constitution, and why we had so soon adjusted ours in 1688, was owing to there being so much despotism to destroy in France, and so little which called for destruction when the revolution in our government took place.[3]

Confronted by two clever and plausible men setting up rival standards, Fox stuck firmly to the Whig creed, around which the bulk of the party could rally.

The political climate of February 1790 was not yet so emotionally charged, that most Whigs would be affected by the posturings of Burke and Sheridan, but the debates of this month saw the formulation of two basic attitudes, between which the Whig party would ultimately have to choose. The attempted reconciliation of the principal protagonists was, according to reports reaching the Duchess of Devonshire, 'perfectly irish, for they are now on worse terms than

[1] *Fox Speeches*, iv. 32; 5 Feb. 1790.

[2] J. Watkins, ed. *Memoirs of the Rt. Hon. R. B. Sheridan*, ii. 56; 7 Feb. 1790.

[3] *Fox Speeches*, iv. 51 seq.; 9 Feb. 1790.

ever'.[1] James Hare was keenly appreciative of the difficulties of Fox's position:

I thought myself particularly fortunate in not being in the House of Commons on St. Patrick's day, for I should have died with the Reaction. Burke continues quite implacable, and his Son, Dr. Lawrence,[2] and every Irishman that has access to him, encourages him to persist in his Madness, I despair of a cure. He says, that it is only the Dissolution of a Friendship, not the Creation of an Enmity, which, You know, is just what he would say if he determined to poison Sheridan. Charles is perpetually talking it over, and is still full of Astonishment at such a mixture of superior Sense & Absurdity . . . Charles Fox says, that when Burke had fairly got the start in Absurdity, it proves very superior Parts in Sheridan to have recovered the lost ground, & made it a near Race.[3]

Fox's position of studied neutrality was not, however, easily maintained. As early as July 1790, the credibility of his refusal to commit himself was already being called into question. Burke concluded that, if Fox was not in sympathy with him, then he must be so with Sheridan. He enlisted the support of Fitzwilliam in an attempt to check Fox's drift towards French ideas: 'You know the facility of Fox. You know that he is surrounded & in many ways govern'd by those who have not $\frac{1}{100}$th part of his parts, no share in his judgment; & principles absolutely bad. . . . If Fox engages in it, will you not also be committed? and he is not far from it. Independently of the arts & absurd councils by which he is push'd rather than guided, he has in himself a strong disposition to fall in with the spirit, which Dr. Price, the dissenters & Lord Stanhope & all the french emissaries are endeavouring to raise.'[4] Fitzwilliam agreed that Fox should be admonished, and wrote accordingly.[5] This point of view was not restricted to Burke. Sir Gilbert Elliot, at the end of the year, outlined his fears to a friend, and, in doing so, waxed prophetic: 'I regret this thing extremely also, because it threatens to embark Fox in a set of opinions, & in a course of politics, which will not do him credit, & in which it will be impossible for the truly respectable & weighty part of his support to follow him.'[6] It is significant that the original

[1] Lady Jersey to Duchess of Devonshire, 12 Feb. 1790; Chatsworth MSS.

[2] Dr. F. Lawrence (1757–1809); eminent civil lawyer and firmly Whig in politics; wrote pamphlets for Fox in the Westminster Election 1784; close friend and literary executor of Burke; broke with Fox over the French Revolution; Regius Professor of Civil Law at Oxford, 1796.

[3] J. Hare to Duchess of Devonshire, 23 Feb. 1790; Chatsworth MSS.

[4] E. Burke to Fitzwilliam, 29 July 1790; Milton MSS. Burke A. iv, f. 71(b).

[5] Fitzwilliam to R. Burke, 8 Aug. 1790; Wentworth Woodhouse Muniments, Burke 1.

[6] Sir G. Elliot to W. Elliot, 5 Dec. 1790; Lady Minto, *Life and Letters of 1st Earl Minto*, i. 369.

Fox Club was founded in 1790.[1] Although this was not intended to act as a rival to the Whig Club itself, its name and membership suggested that this group of men believed that they mutually entertained views and ideas which required a separate establishment. Only Fitzwilliam and two elderly Cavendishes, of those who could be expected to share Burke's conservative fears, found their way into the new association. There was no question of the Whigs splitting up in 1790, but real concern for the future was already present, and the first steps in physical separation had been taken.

In November 1790, Burke effectively declared open war by publishing his *Reflections on the Revolution in France*. He did so as a conscious challenge to Sheridan and his friends and to the neutral position adopted by Fox. Whenever the book was mentioned, Burke was 'in very good Spirits'.[2] He had every reason to be pleased. The book demanded that every member of the party should take up some stance on the issue of the Revolution, a crystallizing of opinion which Fox had been at pains to avoid. Lady Elizabeth Foster recorded the list of reactions: 'Everyone is taken up with Burke's book . . . Sheridan means to answer it. . . . Mr. Hare admires it very much more than C. Fox does, and I think he has the same opinion of it as the D. of D.'[3] One aged Cavendish was so worried that the political faith of a lifetime might be shaken that he refused to read the book at all.[4] The political climate of 1790 was not such as would allow the book its maximum wrecking effect, but it made definitions of attitude essential. Sheridan and his friends were exceedingly irritated and might be provoked into overplaying their hands. The timorous became more anxious.

The reaction of Fox himself to Burke's book was mature and restrained. Anyone with any close knowledge and contact with French leaders in 1790, knew that Burke's picture was premature and overdrawn. Benjamin Vaughan, who knew France well as a member of Lansdowne's philosophic circle at Bowood, thought there was 'little or no value' in 'detecting Mr. Burke's inaccuracies', and therefore preferred to remain 'idle for a fortnight'.[5] Fox was therefore less concerned by the matter of the book than the style and intention in which it was written. He considered 'the writing of that work to be in very bad taste'.[6] It seemed that, in order to indulge a fit of personal

[1] Add. MS. 51516, 1790; List of members of the Fox Club.

[2] Palmerston to Lady Palmerston, 1 Dec. 1790; Palmerston MSS.

[3] Journal of Lady Elizabeth Foster, 25 Nov. 1790; Chatsworth MSS.

[4] H. Walpole to Lady Ossory, 9 Dec. 1790; *Letters Addressed to the Countess of Upper Ossory*, ii. 425.

[5] B. Vaughan to Lansdowne, 12 Dec. 1790; Bowood MSS.

[6] Add. MS. 47590, f. 24; Commonplace Book of S. Rogers (undated).

pique, Burke had launched an assault on the nerves of the party. The Pittite press eagerly seized on Fox's embarrassment:

The *Party* know not what to do with Edmund—he is as dangerous as a mine; two of the *squadron* have already been *blown up*, and some of the remainder, apprehensive of the same fate, are eager to *change ground* and *colours*.[1]

The Bishop of Peterborough interpreted the situation in the same way.[2] Fox was unmoved by the intellectual content of the book, but feared the effect of its hyperbole on weak constitutions.

Responsibility for countering the effect of Burke's initiative lay, as the most recent authority on this period has insisted, squarely with Fox.[3] His only possible course of action was to prevent Sheridan from taking up Burke's challenge, in the hope that the clamour would eventually die down. In this he was successful. Between January and April 1791, the diaries and correspondence of leading Whigs fall silent on the topic of Burke's work, suggesting that its immediate impact had been sharp, but short in duration. Only the Pittite *Public Advertiser* attempted to keep the matter before the public eye, and its tactics are of interest. The target chosen is not Fox, but Sheridan. Accorded the title of Joseph Surface, Sheridan is held up to Fox as a dangerous innovator and potential rival. Fox is upbraided for allowing into the once respectable Whig party men, 'who have no mode of subsistence but by adopting the practices of political adventure',[4] All Fox's known prejudices are therefore played on, in an attempt to give substance to the rumour that Fox was about to break with Sheridan, in order to join Burke in coming to terms with the Minister.[5]

Fox refused to be provoked. He was determined that time should be allowed for tempers to cool. On 5 April 1791, at a meeting of the Whig Club, a young member asked the Club to vindicate 'the people's rights' by petitioning against the undertaking of any war against Russia over Oczakov. It was reported in the press next day that, in reply to this suggestion:

Mr. Fox said that he was afraid that any proceeding of this kind by the Club might be liable to misrepresentation, as a mark of attachment to the opinions of particular men. Petitions and Remonstrances would come with more propriety from cities and from counties, because less liable to misconstruction; and such every Member of the Whig Club might, without any fear of invidious interpretation, support.[6]

[1] *Public Advertiser*, 5 Jan. 1791.
[2] Bishop of Peterborough to Grafton, 7 Dec. 1790; Grafton MSS. f. 741.
[3] O'Gorman, *The Whig Party and the French Revolution*, p. 55.
[4] *Public Advertiser*, 21 Mar. 1791.
[5] *Public Advertiser*, 18 Feb. 1791.
[6] *Morning Chronicle*, 6 Apr. 1791.

Fox refused to be drawn into any action, which, in the climate of opinion created by Burke's book, could conceivably exacerbate the situation further, or substantiate Burke's views.

The events of the next two months must be taken as a whole and closely related to each other. It is generally held that Fox's speech in the Commons, on 15 April 1791, regenerated debate within the party, which led directly to the almost theatrically dramatic breach between Fox and Burke on 6 May. This may seem too simple. During the 15 April speech, Fox gave it as his opinion that he 'admired the new constitution of France, considered it altogether as the most stupendous and glorious edifice of liberty, which had been erected on the foundation of human integrity in any time or country'.[1] Such a statement, which would be used against Fox for the next three years, is certainly less restrained than the language adopted at the Whig Club two weeks earlier, but its immediate impact must not be over-estimated. Fox was admittedly excited by the prospect of being able to check Pitt's rearmament proposals, by insisting that war against Russia was unnecessary and wasteful. He told a friend that 'by a strong appearance on Wednesday, we shall actually dissuade the Ministers from entering into this war, from which so much Evil is to be apprehended and no good.'[2] Less dramatically, he confessed to Mrs. Armistead that, 'What hurts him [Pitt] in public opinion must do us some good.'[3] The exhilaration of being able to stop Pitt in anything might well lead Fox to utter incautious remarks, but these were not necessarily responsible for the breach with Burke a month later.

In fact, the reaction to Fox's remarks in this debate was not as dramatic as might have been expected. Pitt won the ensuing division by 254 to 162, a very similar result to that on the first reading of the Armaments Bill (253–173) three days earlier, when French affairs had not been mentioned. If Whigs were shocked by Fox's remarks, they clearly had little effect on their voting behaviour. Thomas Grenville took a similar view, in reporting the debate: 'Burke at this time walking up the house attracted much attention; he rose to speak when Charles concluded but gave way to the impatient cry for the question with so much readiness that I took for granted he felt no great anxiety to enter into any debate. . . . Upon the whole I really do not apprehend that any further notice will be taken of this, in future debate as there was no personal allusion, or any thing that exceeded the fair scope of the subject that Charles was speaking upon.'[4]

[1] *Fox Speeches*, iv. 194; 15 Apr. 1791.

[2] Bodleian MSS. Curzon 6.25, f. 16; Fox to J. Lee, 1 Apr. 1791.

[3] Add. MS. 47570, f. 183; Fox to Mrs. Armistead, 14 Apr. 1791.

[4] T. Grenville to Fitzwilliam, 19 Apr. 1791; Wentworth Woodhouse Muniments, F. 115. d.

A certain amount of damage had been done. Fitzwilliam was uneasy at being increasingly unable to distinguish Fox's views from those of Priestley and Paine. Portland was equally sure that Fox was trying to swing the party behind his own opinions, but significantly made no evaluation of this strategy.[1] Apart from such murmurings, however, there is very little evidence that Fox's speech on 15 April was so shocking to Whig minds, that Burke could use it as an excuse for his much publicized exit from the Whig party on 6 May. Fox's remarks had been intemperate, and had caused doubt, but, without active stimulation from another quarter, it is very likely that the matter would have passed unnoticed. Nothing had so radically changed in France in two years, that Fox could not repeat his opinions of 1789 without fear of giving too much offence. The inspiration for Burke's celebrated renunciation of Fox must therefore be sought elsewhere.

The only section of the political world to take Fox's remarks up seriously and persistently was the Pittite press. Rumours that Burke was about to break with Fox were repeatedly published, as though setting the scene for the debate of 6 May.[2] Pitt had good reason to snatch at any issue which might divert attention from his own temporarily embarrassing position. His relations with Thurlow had degenerated so far that the King would shortly have to choose between them. Further, Pitt had been badly shaken over both the Nootka Sound dispute of 1790 and the Orczakov affair of 1791. Burke later admitted that Pitt's position in April 1791 was unusually weak. Although naturally denying that he was Pitt's catspaw, Burke agreed that the Minister's relations with the King were dangerously strained.[3] For a Minister desperately trying to re-establish his position at Court and in the country, Fox's remarks on 15 April presented too good an opportunity to miss. By encouraging Burke's fears and playing on his prejudices, the opposition could be diverted, if not split.

Prominent Whigs, including Fox himself, were convinced that Pitt was deliberately stirring up trouble. Tom Grenville justly pointed out that Fox's outburst on 15 April had been provoked by Pitt fixing the title of republican upon him.[4] Accordingly, as Portland recorded, Fox saw Burke on 20 April, and accused him of being Pitt's agent: 'F. asked him whether he had not been encouraged to it by Ministers, who finding themselves in a tottering situation in the Closet as well as in publick opinion & knowing that there was now no objection on the part of the K. to take F. into his service, had instigated him

[1] Portland to Fitzwilliam, 21 Apr. 1791; F. O'Gorman, *The Whig Party and the French Revolution*, p. 62.

[2] *Public Advertiser*, 20 Apr. 1791.

[3] E. Burke, *An Appeal from the New to the Old Whigs*, pp. 23–4.

[4] T. Grenville to Fitzwilliam, 22 Apr. 1791; Wentworth Woodhouse Muniments, F. 115. d.

[Burke] to bring on the subject of the French Revolution for the purpose of fixing on him [Fox] a predilection for Republican Principles & Republican Forms of Government.'[1] Grenville and Fox called on Burke the next day but still could not persuade him to keep silence, and Pitt was aware of this.[2] Grenville's suspicions about Pitt's conduct were confirmed in the debate of 22 April: 'A conversation took place in which Burke professed himself ready & Pitt & Dundas urged it as necessary to discuss general principles of government: Charles was in his language as conciliating as possible, denied the necessity of any such discussion, but confessed that as a publick man, the publick had a right to his views.'[2] At this stage, Fox was so uninterested in trading dialectics with Burke, that he had not yet read Paine's recently published book.

On 22 April, Parliament was prorogued on a motion of Sheridan, who was himself doing nothing to antagonize Burke further. A great deal was now demanded of Fox. Both Grenville and Portland asked Earl Fitzwilliam to see Fox and persuade him that, even if Burke took the opportunity of the Quebec Bill readings on 6 May to launch into a diatribe on general constitutional principles, no reply should be made. This Fitzwilliam promised to do. Unfortunately, there is no evidence that either Portland or Fitzwilliam succeeded in seeing Fox before Parliament reassembled. For at least a week of the prorogation, Fox was at Newmarket,[3] and, when he went to dine at Burlington House, he was unaccountably refused admittance by the Duke's porter. Portland was therefore forced to pin his hopes on Fox's good sense to avoid an open confrontation with Burke: 'Nor can I feel those punctilios from which B. has deviated a satisfactory justification of the opinion avowed by F. & yet such is my confidence in the superiority of F—'s Talents & the Rectitude of his Heart & Head that I know not how not to believe that this Crisis (alarming as it is) may be productive of Good.'[4] Such faith involved a risk, which the Whigs could ill afford. There was therefore no inevitable progression from Fox's unguarded words of 15 April to the breach with Burke on 6 May. Rash statements had been seized upon by a Minister in difficulties, whose efforts to throw Fox and Burke at each other's throats had not been successfully countered by the party as a whole. The rather contrived, theatrical aspect of the debate on 6 May stems from these facts.

[1] Portland to Fitzwilliam, 21 Apr. 1791; Wentworth Woodhouse Muniments, F. 115. d.

[2] T. Grenville to Fitzwilliam, 22 Apr. 1791; ibid.

[3] Add. MS. 47568, f. 261; S. Rollaston to Mrs. Armistead, 26 Apr. 1791.

[4] Portland to Fitzwilliam, 26 Apr. 1791; Wentworth Woodhouse Muniments, F. 115. d.

Parliament reassembled on 6 May, and, when the Quebec Bill came up for debate, it is not clear that any further steps had been taken to prise Burke and Fox apart. Richard Burke,[1] writing from a Committee Room of the House of Commons before the debate began, explained to a friend why his father felt obliged to act:

> Fox totally disapproves of my father's book & as far as private sentiments & public declarations can go, expresses his Approbation of the French Revolution. As the partizans of that event out of doors do not even attempt to conceal their design to subvert the present Constitution in all its parts; it seems to be that the Coincidence of Sentiment . . . in a man of such ability & consideration, the avowed head of the greatest party that perhaps ever was in this Kingdom, cannot but be Extremely dangerous.—What it is that Induces Fox to take this line I cannot conceive.[2]

The elder Burke, as the self-appointed interpreter of Whiggery, set out 'to counteract the Impression which must be produced by Fox's last panegyric on the French Revolution'.[2] Pitt was aware of his intended course of action and naturally did nothing to dissuade him.

The debate itself took a predictable course, but is of interest because, in answering Burke's strictures on the Revolution, Fox was obliged to elaborate more fully than hitherto his precise views on these events. Fundamentally, Fox still believed that the rights of man, a loose but convenient term, underpinned any rational or acceptable constitution. The events in France had done nothing to alter this fact:

> The rights of man, which his rt. hon. friend had ridiculed as chimerical or visionary, were in fact the basis & foundation of every rational constitution, & even of the British constitution itself, as our statute book proved; since, if he knew anything of the original compact between the people of England & its government, as stated in that volume, it was a recognition of the original inherent rights of the people as men, which no prescription could supercede, no accident remove or obliterate.[3]

Phrases like 'the rights of man', cloaked in sound Lockean political philosophy, had been the stock in trade of Whig orators for many years. The Whig press printed extracts from speeches made during the American War and the crisis of 1782–4 to prove the point.[4] The difficulty was, however, that events in France and the associated writings of Thomas Paine had imposed considerable restraint on the normal vocabulary of politicians. Fox never admitted this fact. Besides, if the party was to be held together, ambiguity of language was a

[1] Richard Burke (1758–94); only son of Edmund Burke; strongly supported his father's views on every occasion, and particularly on the French Revolution.

[2] R. Burke to L. O'Beirne, 6 May 1791; Wentworth Woodhouse Muniments, Burke 1.

[3] *Fox Speeches*, iv. 212; 6 May 1791.

[4] *Morning Chronicle*, 28 Sept. 1791.

distinct advantage. Troubled Whig minds could never be sure whether Fox was giving to his words the values of 1784 or those of the revolutionaries. Denying Burke's emphasis on prescriptive law and practice, therefore, Fox could logically go on to defend the necessity of change and reform from time to time, in order to adapt institutions to different circumstances. However admirable the English constitution might be, it could still be improved by reform.[1]

Fox clung to these views because he still believed that basically the events taking place in France were directly analogous to what happened in England in 1688:

> With a civil list ten times as large as ours; with a navy almost as large; and army tenfold; a Church more than tenfold, must they not, as we have done, pursue the course of diminishing its power . . . Surely, we do not wish that liberty should be engrossed by ourselves![2]

Faced with a despotic king and an intolerant Church, the revolutionaries of 1791 were merely doing their Whig duty in attacking both. Whiggery was no longer an exclusively English product, but was capable of universal application. With Fox's many contacts in France, his views, in 1791, were entirely plausible, while Burke's appeared unnecessarily melodramatic. In the long term, however, Fox's misinterpretation of French affairs was disastrous. As Burke remarked with regard to Fox's trust in France, 'his attachment has been great and long and like a Cat, he has continued faithful to the house long after the Family has left it.'[3] With every month that passed, Fox's receiving of the revolutionaries into the Whig communion became increasingly embarrassing.

With the benefit of hindsight, the writer of the obituary of Fox in the *Gentleman's Magazine* singled out the debate of 6 May as 'the rock on which he split, and on which the mind of his Country was alienated from him.'[4] In fact, however, it would be a mistake to see this debate as an immediate turning point in Whig politics. Whig pamphleteers generally took the view that Burke had allowed himself to become the agent of Pitt, and, out of unreasoning panic, had attempted to circumscribe political liberty. Fox was seen, on the other hand, to be extending the boundaries of that same liberty in accordance with changing circumstances. Addressing himself to Burke therefore, the pamphleteer concluded that

> While you are libelling freedom, Mr. Fox is extending her dominion—while you are canonizing departed despotism, he is crushing adult oppression—

[1] Russell, *Life and Times of C. J. Fox*, ii. 260 seq.
[2] *Fox Speeches*, iv. 220; 6 May 1791.
[3] Add. MS. 47590, f. 26; Commonplace Book of Samuel Rogers.
[4] *Gentleman's Magazine*, Sept. 1806.

while you are indulging the petty frolics of literary vanity, he is exerting his unequalled powers for the noble purpose of repairing and fortifying the tottering fabric of our freedom.[1]

It seemed that Burke, in order to vindicate his own views, had forced debates on matters of little relevance to English politics, and, in doing so, had deliberately tried to split the ranks of Whiggery. Fox himself was so hurt and annoyed at Burke's performance, that he indulged in an uncharacteristic burst of personal abuse, calling Burke 'a damned wrongheaded fellow . . . always jealous and contradictory'.[2]

Superficially, Fox had scored a great triumph in his encounter with Burke. The Whig press was unanimous in the opinion that a vast majority of English Whigs, presented with a clear choice between these two men, had decided in Fox's favour.[3] Independent observers like Romilly agreed that Burke had been worsted: 'Fox has gained much with the public by his Conduct and Burke has lost as much. It is astonishing how Burke's book is fallen; though the tenth edition is now publishing, its warmest admirers at its first appearance begin to be ashamed of their admiration. Paine's book, on the otherhand, has made converts of a great many persons.'[4] This reaction in no way implied that Fox's views on the Revolution were immediately accepted, but only that the climate of politics, in May 1791, was such that Burke's adoption of the role of Cassandra seemed unduly melodramatic and premature. Burke himself admitted defeat, but characteristically his hostility to Fox became more implacable, and there was no sign of a wish for accommodation. Instead, he believed himself the victim of a concerted campaign to destroy his reputation. Somewhat disingenuously, Burke claimed that the views presented in *Reflections on the Revolution in France* were not relevant to the matter of this debate with Fox, and yet 'Fox took that opportunity, when nothing of my Book was in question, to declare strongly & vehemently against all the doctrines it contained in the whole, & every part. He then brought out, in an elaborate review (which I had reason to believe had been for some time compiling & digesting) every action & every expression almost of my whole life . . . & misrepresenting them, with little Logick & less candour; to make me pass for an apostate from my principles . . .'[5] This apologia hardly meets the facts, however.

[1] Anon. *Parallel Between the Conduct of Mr. Burke and that of Mr. Fox*, p. 37.

[2] Add. MS. 47590, f. 14; Commonplace Book of Samuel Rogers.

[3] *Morning Chronicle*, 12 May 1791.

[4] Sir S. Romilly to ?, 20 May 1791; Romilly, *Memoirs*, i. 426.

[5] E. Burke to Fitzwilliam, 5 June 1791; Wentworth Woodhouse Muniments, Burke 1.

The set-piece encounter with Fox had been entirely prompted by Burke himself, while Fox's response was, as usual, unrehearsed and spontaneous.

Whatever the immediate advantages Fox derived from these debates, their long-term effects were disastrous. Robert Adair,[1] writing four years later, rightly traced the dissolution of the Whigs to this debate. It was an opinion, which many later writers were to follow. The breach between Fox and Burke had intellectually broken the back of the Whigs. Fox and Burke would henceforth lead different schools of political thought, both called Whig, but which inevitably began to compete for Whig loyalties. The events in France gave prominence to men, who could set these disturbing occurrences within some recognizable political framework. Fox and Burke could both fulfill this function, but unfortunately their interpretations were antagonistic instead of complementary. As Adair pointed out: 'That was, indeed, a day of mourning to the Whig cause. Then began to rush in upon us, through the yawning chasm left by this convulsion in our system, the full tide of those waters of bitterness of which we have so largely tasted. . . . Men of their size could not break company without dividing the world between them.'[2]

On the more mundane level of party politics, the encounter between Fox and Burke had not passed off without causing damage. Sheridan, whose rôle throughout this crisis had been unusually conciliatory, reported to Lady Elizabeth Foster that, 'it was the worst day the poor Whigs ever had.'[3] Similarly, it was generally known that, although Burke's views had been rejected by the Whigs as a whole, Fox's warm admiration for the work of the revolutionaries had not gone unnoticed, and had caused considerable embarrassment.[3] Ironically, however, no one regretted the breach with Burke more than Fox himself. If the dispute between these two men undermined the faith of all Whigs, Burke's ideas and the tenacity with which they were held led Fox himself into self-questioning. Burke had been his tutor in the mysteries of Whiggery, and Fox freely acknowledged his personal and intellectual debt. To separate from such a man involved a thorough reappraisal of political values, and it is no coincidence that, shortly after the debate of 6 May, Fox first announced a desire to retire from politics altogether: 'You will easily imagine how much I felt the separation from persons with whom I had so long been in

[1] Robert Adair (1763–1855); very close friend and admirer of Fox as early as 1783; remained attached to Whig principles all his life; undertook diplomatic mission to St. Petersburg on Fox's behalf, 1791; similarly employed by Whig administrations of 1806–7, 1831–4.

[2] R. Adair, *A Whig's Apology for his Consistency*, p. 23.

[3] Journal of Lady Elizabeth Foster, 6 May 1791; Chatsworth MSS.

the habit of agreeing: it seemed some way as if I had the world to begin anew, and, if I could have done it with honour, what I should best have liked would have been to retire from politics.'[1]

The aged Horace Walpole had no difficulty in setting this debate into a recognizable context. As in earlier crises, Fox had intemperately committed himself to a set of extravagant opinions, which then had to be modified a few days later in the face of horrified protestations by political allies.[2] Certainly, five days later, on 11 May 1791, Fox declared his attachment to a constitution based on King, Lords and Commons, and including an aristocracy 'of rank and property', At the same time, however, he was careful to add that he was 'decidedly of the opinion that the constitution of this country was more liable to be ruined by an increase in the power of the Crown, than by an increase in the power of the people.'[3] In general, however, Walpole's criticism is too harsh. The crisis of May 1791 was entirely provoked by Burke. Fox had little choice but to counter an attempt to shift the centre of gravity of the party in a direction which he believed mistaken and, in the long term, disastrous. Further, although authors, writing with the benefit of hindsight, have rightly picked on these debates as turning points in the history of Whiggery, it must be remembered that their effect lay in the future. In May 1791 itself, Burke's departure from the party had been borne with relatively little disturbance.

Between the May debates of 1791 and the beginning of August 1791, when the publication of Burke's *Appeal from the New to the Old Whigs* re-opened the question, the Whigs were continuously involved in a process of reappraising their position. The central point was whether, after the defection of Burke, the term 'Whig' itself could any longer be supposed to carry its old value. The *Morning Chronicle* was at pains throughout these months to insist that Burke's action had not in any way changed the values of the party. Wisely, however, this thesis was defended less by a discussion of political theory, than by an appeal to the absurdity of thinking that wealthy and aristocratic men like Portland and Fox would 'engage in wild and visionary schemes, in which they would have everything to lose, and nothing to gain. Does it follow, in one word, that the enemies of despotism must be the friends of anarchy? It does not though that is Government logic and Ministerial reasoning.'[4] Whatever the comfort offered by such thoughts, the fact remained to be decided whether

[1] Quoted in *Gentleman's Magazine*, Mar. 1855, p. 227.

[2] H. Walpole to Miss M. Berry, 12 May 1791; Toynbee, *The Letters of Horace Walpole*, xiv. 430–1.

[3] *Fox Speeches*, iv. 228; 11 May 1791.

[4] *Morning Chronicle*, 11 July 1791. See also ibid. 2 June 1791.

12

Fox or Burke was the guardian of the authorized version of English Whiggery. At the Whig Club on 7 June, Fox was accorded a more than usually enthusiastic vote of thanks for his work on the Libel Bill, and was specifically hailed as the repository of true constitutional principle.[1] The climate of politics was such, that this reaffirmation of faith, which this measure entailed by easing restrictions on the press, was necessary. Even so, at this same meeting, the Whigs chose not to discuss plans for an English dinner to celebrate the French Revolution, and this ambiguity between praise for Fox, the professed admirer of France, and the refusal to be even remotely associated with French events, was eagerly seized on by the Pittite press.[2]

While the façade of confidence in Whig orthodoxy was kept up therefore, the uncertainty in the party after Burke's defection came to the surface in every crisis. Everything was done to prevent Sheridan from attending a dinner in honour of the Revolution. As Thomas Pelham[3] reported, even accidental meetings could be alarming. At a reception, Sheridan and Pelham 'walked upon the Terrace in the Evening, where very unexpectedly, we met Burke, who . . . was coming to see Mrs. Crewe.[4] the first meeting was rather alarming, but three clever men could have no difficulty in finding entertaining Subjects of Conversation without alluding to the French Revolution, & tho' Mrs. Crewe was in a constant Alarm, we talked . . . for near two hours.'[5] This amity was, however, only guaranteed by Sheridan just having time to remove from his lapel a badge of the French Fédération celebrations, which had been sent to him by a French admirer. The social life of Mrs. Crewe was made more difficult by the knowledge that several leading Whigs had taken the opportunity of the Parliamentary recess in the summer of 1791 to visit Paris itself. There, they ostentatiously dined with leading revolutionaries. Palmerston, for example, dined with Helvétius, Noailles and Lavoisier, and reports in his diary indicate that other Whigs in Paris included Tarleton, Francis, Windham, Crauford, Lord Edward Fitzgerald, Sir Ralph Payne and Lord Thanet.[6] All these men were closely

[1] *Morning Chronicle*, 8 June 1791.

[2] *Public Advertiser*, 18 June 1791.

[3] Thomas Pelham (1756–1826); M.P. (Sussex) 1780–1801; opposed North and American War; refused to resign in July 1782, but generally well disposed towards Fox; joined Coalition as Chief Sec. Ireland, Aug. 1783; broke with Fox over French Revolution; succeeded father as 2nd Earl of Chichester, 1805.

[4] Mrs. Crewe (?–1818); Frances, dau. of Fulke Greville; married John Crewe in 1766; husband cr. Baron Crewe 1806; famous Whig hostess and enthusiastic politician.

[5] Add. MS. 51705, f. 4; T. Pelham to Lady Webster, 13 June 1791.

[6] Diary of Lord Palmerston, 19 July 1791; Palmerston MSS.

acquainted with Fox, Fitzgerald being his cousin, and it is perhaps no coincidence that most of them remained with Fox after his breach with Portland in 1794. The reports they brought back from the dinner tables of Paris must have confirmed him in his opinion that Burke's assessment of the Revolution was altogether too overdrawn. Even so, the presence of so many Whigs in Paris could have done little to reassure Whig minds that the defection of Burke had not materially altered the nature of the party, to which they belonged.

Burke was determined that this *crise de nerfs* within the party should not be allowed to die away. It was important that the Whigs remain uneasy, if Burke's views were to win any general acceptance. By publishing the *Appeal from the New to the Old Whigs*, in August 1791, Burke was hoping artificially to stimulate Whig anxieties. He candidly told his son that 'you know that the whole of those who think with the French Revolution (if in reality they think at all seriously with it) do not exceed half a score in both Houses . . . It may be asked why I represent the whole party as tolerating, & by a toleration countenancing, these proceedings. It is to get the better of their inactivity, & to stimulate them to a publick declaration of, what every one of their acquaintence privately knows, to be as much their Sentiments as they are yours & mine.'[1] Such frankness makes the melodrama of the May debates even more fraudulent, and underlines the point that nothing had really occurred in France, which, without heavy embroidery, could seriously trouble conservative Whig minds. Loughborough himself, whose political nerve was not strong, saw no point in Burke's publishing yet another book, and had asked the Duke of Portland to dissuade him from doing so.[2] In August 1791, the French Revolution was still primarily a matter for a battle of books and treatises between Burke and Mackintosh.[3] Any political result had to be artificially stimulated.

This second literary broadside fired by Burke was more potentially threatening to the Whigs than the first. The first aim of the *Appeal from the New to the Old Whigs* was to emphasize the relationship between English and French affairs, and not to deal with France alone. Burke was at pains to show that the May debates on the Revolution had doctrinally broken the back of Whiggery, at least two interpretations of which were now extant. After characteristically

[1] Edmund Burke to Richard Burke, 5 Aug. 1791; Wentworth Woodhouse Muniments, Burke 1.

[2] Loughborough to Fitzwilliam, 1 Aug. 1791; ibid. F. 115. a.

[3] Sir James Mackintosh (1765–1832); Whig lawyer and historian; author of 'Vindiciae Gallicae', refuting Burke's views on French Revolution; Sec. of the Assoc. of the Friends of the People, 1792; turned against French Revolution, 1800; Recorder of Bombay, 1803; later supported Romilly's law reforms and the Reform Bill of 1832.

complaining at some length of the treatment he had received at the hands of the Whigs,[1] Burke went on to substantiate his thesis by contrasting the doctrines set out in the articles of impeachment against Sacheverell with those presented recently by Fox in the House of Commons. The Whigs of Anne's reign, Burke argues, accepted the elementary point that government was based on a contract between rulers and governed;

> Neither the few nor the many have a right to act merely by their will, in any matter connected with duty, trust, engagement, or obligation. The constitution of a country being once settled upon by some compact, tacit or expressed, there is no power existing of force to alter it, without the breach of the covenant, or the consent of all the parties.[2]

Fox, by contrast, had abandoned the idea of contract, in favour of making the people the sole repository of sovereignty. According to Burke, Fox held 'that the people are essentially their own rule, and their will the measure of their conduct; that the tenure of magistracy is not a proper subject of contract; because magistrates have duties but no rights.'[3] However premature such a clear cut separation of ideas was in August 1791, the long term division of Whiggery on something like these terms makes this one of the most important of Burke's writings.

With the benefit of hindsight, one Whig lady later traced all the tribulations of the Whigs to the publication of this work, suggesting that 'to this book I think most of this controversy owing'.[4] It would be quite wrong, however, to think that this was the immediate reaction. Horace Walpole, who had for many years castigated Fox's impetuosity, now swung round and accused Burke of carrying the debate too far beyond any reasonable limit: 'To Mr. Burke's appeal, I answer, it is well and carefully written; but I think he had better not have wanted it, by accepting Mr. Fox's tender and handsome apology.'[5] The Duke of Portland was deeply insulted at having his pretensions to the title of Whig challenged, and complained that the tone was that of 'Buckingham House'[6] itself: 'I never read any work that ever gave me the pain which that has done, nor could it, had it come from any other hand.'[7] Burke himself had to admit that the reaction

[1] Burke, *An Appeal from the New to the Old Whigs*, p. 7.
[2] ibid., p. 90 seq.
[3] ibid. p. 53 seq.
[4] Lady E. Ponsonby to Lady L. Ponsonby, 2 Mar. 1792; Hickleton MSS. A. 1.2.1, f. 30.
[5] H. Walpole to Lady Ossory, 8 Aug. 1791; *Letters Addressed to the Countess of Upper Ossory*, ii. 442.
[6] Portland to Dr. Lawrence, 30 Aug. 1791; Portland MSS. PWF 6241.
[7] Portland to Dr. Lawrence, 23 Aug. 1791; Portland MSS. PWF 6239.

to his book was not that, for which he had hoped. Whereas the publication of the *Reflections on the Revolution in France* had produced congratulatory letters from several leading Whigs, on this occasion there was 'Not one word from one of our party. They are secretly galled. They agree with me to a tittle—but they dare not speak out for fear of hurting Fox.'[1] It simply was impossible for most of the party to believe that Fox could conceivably be guilty of any of the views imputed to him by Burke. Stormont, according to Burke, 'is of opinion that Fox, so far from countenancing the mischevious doctrines I complain of has given a very unexceptionable Creed. . . . In short he does not really know in what we differ; That Fox is too sensible to wish the destruction of the Constitution etc etc etc for the rest of the party he has not yet seen one person who approves of the doctrines of Payne, or anything like them, & that they seem all (as he himself is) of my mind.'[2] Events in France had not yet reached the point, where they could make real in Whig minds the kind of severe distinctions, which Burke was already beginning to insist upon.

Fox himself showed very little interest in this battle of the books. In May 1791, he told his nephew that he had neither read Burke's *Reflections on the Revolution in France* nor Mackintosh's *Vindiciae Gallicae;* 'I have not read Burke's new pamphlet but hear a very different account of it from yours. It is in general thought to be mere madness, and especially in those parts where he is for a general war for the purpose of destroying the present Government of France.'[3] When he finally made a pronouncement later in the year, it was in favour of Mackintosh, who was thought to represent the middle course between Burke and Paine.[4] Such moderation and surprising unconcern with the theoretical struggles of the summer of 1791 on the part of Fox made no impression on Burke, who refused to admit that there was any material difference between the writings of Mackintosh and Paine: 'There are found amongst (what I still am willing to call) our people, those, who like the principles of Payne, better dressed, or rather more disguised. I have not read, nor even seen Mackintosh;—but Richard tells me, that it is Paine at bottom.'[5] There is no doubt, however, that the bulk of the Whig party agreed with Fox in wishing to take no part in unnecessary theoretical debates, and in eschewing extremes. As Fox was later reported to have said, 'It was lucky that Burke . . . took the side against the French Revolution,

[1] E. Burke to R. Burke, 18 Aug. 1791; Wentworth Woodhouse Muniments, Burke 1.

[2] E. Burke to R. Burke, 10 Aug. 1791; ibid.

[3] Add. MS. 47571, f. 1; Fox to Holland, May 1791.

[4] R. J. Mackintosh, *Memoirs of the Life of Sir J. Mackintosh*, i. 61.

[5] E. Burke to Dr. Lawrence (undated); C. and J. Rivington, *The Epistolary Correspondence of the Rt. Hon. E. Burke and Dr. French Laurence*, p. 240.

as . . . [he] would have got hanged on the other.'[1] Burke seemed to be making statements and charges which had no immediate political relevance, and accordingly Fox's studied moderation allowed his personal stock to rise steadily.

If Fox was to defeat Burke by taking up a stance as leader of the moderate centre of the party, the test of his sincerity came with an invitation to attend the Revolution Dinner on 14 July 1791, in honour of the taking of the Bastille. As early as May, Fox had foreseen the problem, and had adopted a prudent reserve: 'I rather agree . . . that it would be better that Sheridan should not attend the meeting of the 14th of July, if he can be absent without an appearance of being frightened of the conduct he held last year.'[2] In this decision, Fox was quite consciously bowing before the weight of Whig opinion, which believed that the appearance of Whig leaders at such a dinner would inevitably be too compromising. Both Fox and Sheridan were called to Carlton House, where the Prince's marked antipathy to such a dinner was made known.[3] Mrs. Crewe added her voice against the proposed meeting, reporting that Sheridan '. . . was in a great fidgit about the meeting which at last he determined on not going to, & Ch. Fox & he both said they repented, but I cd. not help telling them my little opinion when Ch. Fox called that Evg. which was that people cd. not be wrong that took the advice of all their best friends.'[4] Burke may have lost the battle for a sympathetic hearing, but Fox had still to be restrained from entering into any obligation, which could, however slightly, bring his general, political opinions into question.

Fox practised moderation conscientiously. He not only refused to attend the Revolutionary Dinner, but also abstained from addressing several smaller societies, some of which were not even political in character.[5] Instead, he was persuaded to join the Prince of Wales for the races at Ascot, where he lost a great deal of money, but no doubt saved the Whig party from further embarrassment.[6] The pressures on Fox to take this line of action were great, but there is some evidence that he was not unwilling to fall in with his party's suggestions. At the same time that he was accusing Burke of indulging in melodramatic hyperbole, Fox was also happily comparing Lauderdale,[7]

[1] Ld. J. Russell, *Memoirs, Journals and Correspondence of Thomas Moore*, iv. 265.
[2] Add. MS. 47571, f. 1; Fox to Holland, May 1791.
[3] *Morning Chronicle*, 13 July 1791.
[4] Mrs. Crewe to Duchess of Portland, July 1791; Portland MSS. PWG 130.
[5] J. Cundee, *Life of the Late Charles James Fox*, p. 166.
[6] Add. MS. 51845, f. 3; A. Storer to Lady Webster, 12 July 1791.
[7] Lauderdale, James Maitland, 1st Baron (1759–1839); M.P. (Newport) 1780–4; (Malmesbury) 1784–90; violent partisan of the radical Whigs; manager of Hastings' Impeachment; member of the Assoc. of the Friends of the People; friend of Brissot; cr. Baron Lauderdale, 1806;

one of the most uncritical admirers of the Revolution within the Whig ranks, to Benedict Arnold.[1] The middle ground, which Fox had occupied between Burke and Paine, was not only the best vantage point for holding the Whigs together, but also corresponded very closely to Fox's personal predilections.

Horace Walpole had already guessed that much of Fox's moderation was conditioned by his being 'afraid of alarming the opulent aristocracy'.[2] The fundamental linking mechanism in the Whig party was the understanding between intellect and landed respectability, as represented by Fox, Portland, and, to a lesser extent, by Fitzwilliam. If these three men stayed united, the party would be provided with theoretical justifications, and would remain, under Portland's leadership, free of all charges of fostering dangerous or democratic innovations. The dependence of Fox on Portland's name and rank was taken by certain Whigs as the greatest guarantee of his responsible behaviour. As an Irish Whig pointed out, Fox had need of 'those twenty thousands a year, and the natural connexions commanding the most powerful Interest, which are not to be warped from his Grace's Person, or Interest, or Dignity. . . . Had I no other security for Mr. Fox's adherence to the Duke of Portland but this, [I] should be satisfied with it . . .'[3] Although this dependence was, to a certain extent, mutual, Fox's need of Portland was the greater. The Duke's name and position guaranteed him influence in politics. Fox's standing was, by contrast, entirely dependent on his controlling the politics of the grandees. Without them, his impact on politics would be slight.

The tour of the Whig country houses, which Fox undertook in the summer of 1791, therefore carried the twin advantages of avoiding any more entanglements with the more extreme London societies, and of giving him an opportunity to lecture the Whig dukes on their duty in the present situation. It was a good moment to choose. Fox's success in modifying Pitt's policy in both the Nootka Sound controversy of 1790 and in the Orczakov affair of 1791 had restored his popularity in the country as a whole. He entered Doncaster to the pealing of bells,[4] and at York, he was given the freedom of the city amid the acclamations of the same people who had overturned the Rockingham interest in 1784. Fitzwilliam was very relieved that the speeches made during the ceremony at York were restricted to

[1] Add. MS. 51731, f. 46; Holland to Caroline Fox, 18 July 1791.

[2] H. Walpole to Miss M. Berry, 14 July 1791; W. S. Lewis, *The Correspondence of Horace Walpole*, xii. 313–14.

[3] L. O'Beirne to R. Burke, 25 July 1791; Wentworth Woodhouse Muniments, Burke 1.

[4] *Sheffield Advertiser*, 26 Aug. 1791.

innocuous generalities, but even so, Fox had convincingly demonstrated that much of what had been lost in 1784 had since been regained. As he moved between Milton Abbey, Chatsworth and Wentworth Woodhouse, this point was no doubt made. Burke himself had to admit that Fox had dealt with the situation with unaccustomed skill: 'It is a slap to me. I had thoughts of going to the North; but what has happen'd at York, & more of the same kind which I forsee in other places, makes me think that my presence would rather embarrass our friends.—I could not meet Fox quite at ease.'[1] Fox's careful and prudent moderation had therefore resulted, at the end of the summer of 1791, in his making a triumphal progress through the North, leaving Burke an isolated and embittered figure at Beaconsfield.

This tactical victory over Burke in no way produced that over-confidence in Fox, which had marred his earlier career. In fact, Fox was himself deeply concerned at the development of events in France, particularly after the flight to Varennes. At least two attempts were made by Fox in the summer of 1791 to influence the leaders of the Revolution by counselling moderation. At the instigation of Lady Elizabeth Foster and, oddly enough, of Sheridan, Fox was asked to write to Barnave and Lafayette, requesting their guarantee for the safety of the French Royal Family. Sheridan reported that Fox responded eagerly to the scheme: 'He wants more people to write. He says the more people write & the more that are written to, the greater chance our scheme will have of being successful.'[2] These letters were entrusted to Thomas Pelham, who was about to visit Paris, but it is not clear whether they were ever delivered. Later, Fox thought this campaign 'a silly thing',[3] but this remark was clearly much influenced by the embarrassment occasioned by the bringing up of his name in the French Assembly, as that of an alien trying to put pressure on French leaders.

The second packet of letters was entrusted to Lord Palmerston. These were delivered, and it is to these documents that Lameth[4] and others are referring, when they introduced Fox's name into the debates in the French Assembly. Thomas Pelham himself, the carrier of the first consignment, refers to them in a letter to Palmerston: 'I am very sorry that Fox's name has been used in the Assembly, tho' the Manner in which you describe it to have been mentioned

[1] Edmund Burke to Richard Burke, 1 Sept. 1791; Wentworth Woodhouse Muniments, Burke 1.

[2] Journal of Lady Elizabeth Foster, 2 July 1791; Chatsworth MSS.

[3] ibid. 9 Aug. 1791; Chatsworth MSS.

[4] Lameth, Alexande Théodore Victor, Chevalier de (1760–1829); Constitutional monarchist; founder member of the Feuillant Club; fled from French with Lafayette, June 1792; returned in 1800, and held office under both Napoleon and the Bourbons.

can not I think be construed to his disadvantage. L'Ameth must certainly have alluded to the Letters you brought & I know that Noailles had very imprudently mentioned to Barnave that Letters were expected the tendency of which were recommending Moderation.'[1] Unfortunately, the dearth of evidence makes it impossible to speculate on why Fox chose to send two bundles of letters by two distinct carriers. It seems, however, that their contents were not materially different, and therefore it is just possible that the second despatch of letters was aimed at establishing a personal initiative free of the superintending guidance of Sheridan, of which Fox was always suspicious. Whatever the motives involved, however, this attempt at moderation backfired slightly. Grenville thought this essay by opposition into foreign policy was 'an impeachable misdemeanour',[2] and Fox himself was very anxious to deny that something similar had been in contemplation later in the war.[3] The methods employed were clumsy and open to misrepresentation, but at least they testified to Fox's deep concern for, and appreciation of, the potential threat of the French Revolution to English politics.

In theoretical terms also, Fox refused to make extravagant replies to Burke's charge that he was leading a 'republican, frenchified Whiggism'.[4] Whenever Fox made reference to political theory, he always took his stand on traditional Whig principles. For him Whiggery was the defence of popular liberties against the incursions of kings. The 'King and Church' mobs, which destroyed Priestley's house in Birmingham, allowed Fox to expand on this theme.[5] The historical references for this speech were provided by the historian Francis Hargrave,[6] with whom Fox had struck up a friendship.[7] For Fox, who was later to write a history of the reign of James II, the historical growth of Whiggery, seen as a struggle against an encroaching executive, was of immense importance. Even with the challenge presented by the Revolution, Fox still believed that the greatest danger to English liberty came from the Crown. He told Fitzwilliam that

> You seem to dread the prevalence of Paine's opinions (which in most part I detest as much as you do) while I am much more afraid of the total annihila-

[1] T. Pelham to Palmerston, 22 July 1791; Palmerston MSS. f. 293.

[2] W. Grenville to Auckland, 29 July 1791; H.M.C. Fortescue II *Dropmore MSS*. p. 144.

[3] Add. MS. 51467, f. 58; Fox to D. O'Brien (undated).

[4] E. Burke to W. Weddell, 31 Jan. 1792; Fitzwilliam, *Burke Corres*. iii. 383–409.

[5] *Fox Speeches*, iv. 296; 31 Jan. 1792.

[6] Francis Hargrave (1741–1821); lawyer, antiquarian and bibliophile; correspondent of Fox on historical topics; his library bought by the British Museum for £8,000.

[7] Add. MS. 47568, f. 269; Fox to F. Hargrave, 29 Jan. 1792.

tion of all principles of liberty & resistence, an event which I am sure you would be as sorry to see as I. We both hate the two extremes equally, but we differ in our opinions with respect to the quarter from which the danger is most pressing . . . You will observe that I have not mentioned the french Revolution, I have not because I never can allow that while we agree about what ought to be the constitution of our own country, it can be of any importance how far we do so about what passes in France. I certainly thought the Revolution of France the greatest event that ever happened for the happiness of mankind. The present state of that country alarms me very much, because if confusions there should terminate in the re-establishment of the antient despotism, I shall think it a decisive blow to all liberty in Europe, at least for centuries.[1]

Burke's two assaults on the weak nerves of the Whigs, each prefaced by a book, were therefore foiled by Fox, both because he studied moderation, and also because he was able to set the French Revolution, even in March 1792, in a recognizably Whig context. Burke may have succeeded in demonstrating that two distinct groups now laid claim to the title of Whig, but it was not clear which of them had the better credentials. Fox's point that the revolutionaries were good Whigs reacting against the sort of system which had crushed their English counterparts in 1784, was a strong and plausible one. So too was the argument that confusion was to be feared in France, not because it offered an opportunity for democratic experimentation, but because it made the return of the Bourbons more likely. With this kind of argument, Fox held the party together. The first two Whig Club meetings of 1792 were exceptionally well attended, and the toasts included 'grateful remembrances of Mr. Fox and other persons, distinguished by their exertions in the cause of freedom'.[2] Sir Gilbert Elliot was typical of many Whigs, who, although apprehensive of certain parts of Fox's conduct, believed his general policy to be sound, and who were determined not to allow themselves to be overborne completely by Burke's hyperbole.[3] The middle ground in the Whig party could be held against Burke's attacks from the right. It remained to be seen whether it was equally resistant to assaults from the left.

The Association of the Friends of the People sprang not from a feeling of over-confidence on the part of Sheridan and his friends after Burke's defeat,[4] but from the fear that the party was in fact drifting in the direction of Burke's views. The Association was a quite

[1] Fox to Fitzwilliam, 16 Mar. 1792; Milton MSS. Box 44.

[2] *Morning Chronicle*, 18 Jan. 1792 and 8 Feb. 1792.

[3] Sir G. Elliot to Lady Elliot, 24 Mar. 1792; Countess of Minto, *Life and Letters of Lord Minto*, ii. 1.

[4] O'Gorman, *The Whig Party and the French Revolution*, p. 82.

conscious effort to check this movement. Grey was later reported to have said that 'The fact was that observing an opinion was rising in the country that was likely to lead to danger if means to prevent it were not taken in time, a set of gentlemen, of whom he had the honour to be one, had thought the best means possible of preventing mischief was to look to the constitution, and to suggest the correction of such abuses as might be found to exist in its practice.'[1] Adair agreed that, fearful of Pitt on one side and Paine on the other, the Associators believed themselves to be trying to stabilize the constitution on the basis of moderate reform, prior to its collapse before one of these threats.[2] Unless Burke's tirades were answered, the constitution would fall to either democracy or despotism. A restatement of what they took to be the traditional Whig case seemed to be essential. Inevitably, the whole project was characterized by some contemporaries as simply another vehicle for the promotion of Sheridan's ambition. He had, they claimed, only 'prevailed upon a set of wild, unthinking young men . . . Presbyterian parsons and some desperate people'.[3] In fact, Sheridan had, until March 1792, adopted a consistently conciliatory attitude to Burke, and there seems no reason to doubt the general accuracy of the accounts given by Grey and Adair.

The Association was formed at an impromptu dinner given by Lord Porchester,[4] on 11 April 1792.[5] According to Lord Holland, the Association 'was originally founded, I believe, without the knowledge, certainly without the sanction, of Mr. Fox'.[6] Even so, the list of founder members drawn up by Cartwright is of considerable interest for the future. Twenty-three of the twenty-four parliamentarians listed were to follow Fox after the breach with Portland, in 1794.[7] Here lay the danger for Fox. He could adopt an attitude of studied moderation towards Burke, with whom he felt increasingly little personal and intellectual sympathy. The Associators, by contrast, were his personal friends, voicing, albeit in unnecessarily strong language, views which he generally wished to support. The delicate situation within the Whig party would impose an equal

[1] C. Grey, *The Life and Opinions of the 2nd Earl Grey*, pp. 11–12.

[2] R. Adair, *A Whig's Apology for his Consistency*, p. 35.

[3] J. Burges to Col. Sincoe, 4 May 1782; Hutton, *Letters and Corres. of Sir J. B. Burges*, p. 220.

[4] Porchester, Henry Herbert, 1st Baron (1741–1811); M.P. (Wilton) 1768–July 1772, Dec. 1772–1780; supported American War throughout; voting after 1782 highly erratic; initially associated with Friends of the People; cr. Baron Porchester, 1780 and Earl of Carnarvon, 1793.

[5] Cartwright, *Life and Correspondence of Major Cartwright*, Appendix vii.

[6] Holland, *Memoirs of the Whig Party During My Time*, i. 13.

[7] Cartwright, *Life and Correspondence of Major Cartwright*, Appendix vii.

restraint on Fox against a commitment of this type, but it was by no means clear which of these forces would ultimately prove the stronger.

In April 1792 therefore, concern for what Fox's reaction to this new pressure group might be was uppermost in Whig minds. The *Morning Herald*, which had indignantly refused to publish any details of the Association's meetings, reported at the end of the month, with evident relief, that Fox was standing firm against the siren calls from this circle of young men, who formed so large a part of his drinking and gambling entourage at Brooks's.[1] James Hare, knowing Fox better, was more uneasy: 'Charles Fox upon this as upon most other occasions will probably suffer himself to be led, and perhaps act against his own judgment, this is his nature, and however one may lament it, there is no remedy.'[2] Grey's influence at this time was reported to be particularly strong with Fox.[3] The danger of Fox succumbing to this pressure group and abandoning his control of the party from the centre was made more real by the conduct of the Associators. From the very beginning, they eschewed all contact with the more radical Society for Constitutional Information, and they did so in terms which Burke himself might have suggested.[4] Further, the Scottish wing of the Association was, if anything, still more moderate in outlook.[5] Palmerston's sarcastic belief that all the Associators would succeed in doing would be in driving themselves into the political wilderness, was therefore decidedly premature.[6] But there was a real danger, which his close friends readily admitted, that Fox would abandon his neutrality.

Initially, Fox held to his position as the linking mechanism keeping the Whig party together. He asked Fitzpatrick to come up to Town early, so that the initiative could be kept by himself, still holding the middle ground in the party: 'I wish very much too that we should be numerous at the Whig Club Tuesday for reasons which I have not time to explain. There are several unpleasant things going forward.'[7] Tom Pelham was relieved to find that Fox was as apprehensive about the divisive effects of the Association as he was himself: 'I found Fox in the temper & disposition I could wish & I can express to you how much satisfaction it gave me to find that my Sentiments

1 *Morning Herald*, 30 Apr. 1792.

2 J. Hare to Devonshire, 1 May 1792; Chatsworth MSS. f. 1126.

3 Thomas Green, *Extracts from the Diary of a Lover of Literature*, p. 57.

4 Ld. J. Russell to Maj. Cartwright, 12 May 1792; *Papers Presented to Parliament* 1789–1796.

5 E. Hughes, 'The Scottish Reform Movement and Charles Grey', *S.H.R.* xxxv. 1956.

6 Palmerston to Lady Palmerston, 14 May 1792; Palmerston MSS.

7 Add. MS. 47580, f. 143; Fox to R. Fitzpatrick, 25 Apr. 1792.

so perfectly agreed with his on the Subject; & I trust that we shall be able to put an end to a scheme so very injurious to us as a Party & at this time so peculiarly improper for the Country.'[1] Significantly, however, Fox, while parading his orthodoxy to Pelham, made no attempt to stop the Associators by exercising his very considerable influence. Grey and other Associators later noted this fact with some regret. Fox, when challenged on this point, replied that he 'didn't like to discourage the young ones'.[2] As Hare had earlier intimated, the danger for the Whig party was not that Fox would be carried away by extravagant ideas, but that he would be extremely reluctant to relinquish the leadership of that group of men, who were his friends. If they were determined to take a new course, the claims of friendship, rather than the novelty of their ideas, would prompt Fox to follow.

This became clear as soon as the issues raised by the Associators were put to the vote. Fox then found himself supporting Parliamentary Reform with the Associators, not because he entirely approved of their policy of forcing decisions on the Whig party, but because he had no reason to change opinions, which he had held for almost twenty years, even if this gave the impression of taking sides in Whig party struggles. As a loyal relative, he had already written to his cousin the Duke of Leinster, congratulating him on becoming Chairman of a similar Association in Ireland, even though the aims of this body were couched in highly emotive terms, advocating 'a hereditary monarchy, an assembly of nobles emanating from the Crown, and a body of representatives to be chosen by the people.'[3] Similarly therefore, he supported Grey's motion for a reform of Parliament on 30 April, because he always had taken this view. The difficulty was that, although Fox was at pains to say how much he disapproved of both Burke and Paine,[4] the mere fact of his voting with the Associators was enough to compromise him severely. Much of Fox's strength in dealing with Burke earlier lay in issues like Parliamentary reform being kept out of the political arena. The initiative of the Associators, forcing Fox to demonstrate his consistency in the division lobby, gravely impaired his impartial stand.

Fox does not seem to have been aware of how greatly the political climate had changed. Most people were finding it increasingly difficult to make those distinctions between Fox and the Associators, which alone would allow Fox to retain control of middle ground in the Party.[5]

[1] Add. MS. 51705, f. 117; T. Pelham to Lady Webster, 29 Apr. 1792.
[2] C. Grey, *The Life and Opinions of the Second Earl Grey;* pp. 10–11.
[3] B. Fitzgerald, *Emily, Duchess of Leinster*, pp. 221–2.
[4] *Parl. Hist.* xxix. 1338; 30 Apr. 1792.
[5] Diary of Lord Malmesbury; *Diaries and Corres. of Ld. Malmesbury*, ii. 458–9.

By some Whigs, Fox was accused of misconceiving 'the true character of the democratic philosophers of the day, whom he confounded with the old advocates for reform'.[1] The less discriminating, like George III, were prepared to go further: 'I cannot see any substantial difference in their being joined in debate by Mr. Fox, and his not being a member of that Society.'[2] Even those who, like Sir Gilbert Elliot, could distinguish Fox voting independently for reform from Fox the committed Associator, had to agree that the drawing of politics in blacks and whites left Fox in an increasingly embarrassing position: 'One effect will be, if not certainly to divide & break up our party, at least to expose it to a very great danger of being separated, & drive Fox still further than ever from any hope of reconciling to him the moderate & prudent part of the country.'[3] By adopting an unchanging attitude towards reform in a changing political context, Fox was presented to the Associators as a gift by an undiscriminating public opinion.

Pitt naturally did everything in his power to make Fox's position more uncomfortable. The timing of the Proclamation against Seditious Practices, of which Fox could be expected to disapprove strongly, supports Lord Holland's contention, which became the standard Whig interpretation of these events, that the measure was nothing more than a device to split the Whigs. Pitt, as Lord Spencer observed, had seized the opportunity offered him by the formation of the Association to test the Whigs' strength; the 'Proclamation would probably never have appeared if the late Association of many of the Members of Parliament & others had not made these other publications more talked of & more alarming.'[4] The Duke of Portland was accordingly told of the provisions of the Proclamation, before it was taken to the floor of the House, and he in turn communicated its contents to selected friends at a meeting, to which Fox was not invited.[5] This glaring omission seemed to justify Pitt's high expectations of party advantage. As predicted, Fox felt obliged to oppose the Proclamation in the Commons. Admitting the deep anxiety he felt at seeing his friends divided on the issue, he nevertheless chose to defend himself in uncompromising terms:

The plain intention of this proclamation was, to strive to make a division between that great body of united patriots, known by the name of the Whig interest . . . It was not, in his opinion, a republican spirit that we had to dread

[1] Green, *Diary of a Lover of Literature*, p. 139.

[2] D. G. Barnes, *George III and William Pitt, 1783–1806*, p. 220.

[3] Sir G. Elliot to Lady Elliot, 1 May 1792; Lady Minto, *Life and Letters of Lord Minto*, ii. 16.

[4] Spencer to Dowager Lady Spencer, 22 May 1792; Spencer MSS.

[5] Holland, *Memoirs of the Whig Party*, i. 153 seq.

in this country; there was no tincture of republicanism in the country. If there was a prevailing tendency to riot, it was on the other side. It was the high church spirit, and an indisposition to all reform, which marked, more than anything else, the temper of the times.[1]

According to Tom Pelham, only 'Fox's good humour & good Sense'[2] prevented Pitt from fully achieving his aim. Even so, the Proclamation debate inevitably connected Fox more closely with the Associators, and this in turn made his hold on the vital centre of the party, represented by Portland and Fitzwilliam, more precarious.

The immediate effect of the decisions forced on Fox by the Associators and Pitt was that any influence he may have retained over the actions of Burke and his friends was now forfeited. Burke and his followers no longer took the accommodation of Fox into consideration in the formulation of their policies. They were reported by one Whig lady to 'hate Fox worse than . . . the French Democrats'.[3] This, however, was too sweeping. Windham severed all ties with Fox for very practical considerations: national defence simply demanded such a move; there was no alternative. Lord Spencer's feelings, in taking the same step, were a mixture of profound regret at forfeiting Fox's friendship and uncertainty at foregoing his intellectual guidance.[4] Whatever the motives, however, a recognizable right-wing pressure group was formed within the Whig Party after the experiences of April and May 1792, which rejected Fox's leadership absolutely.

Equally awkward, from Fox's point of view, was the fact that, if Burke was anxious to brand Fox as a democrat, the Associators were eagerly ready to claim him for their own. At a meeting of the Friends of the People on 2 June, formal thanks were voted to Fox, for supporting Grey in his efforts to amend the late Proclamation.[5] Brooks's became the headquarters of the Associators, and Fox's social life brought him continually into contact with them. In July, he acted as a second for Lauderdale in a duel.[6] Two months earlier, the young gentlemen of the same club had been ceremoniously burning copies of Paine's books to demonstrate their orthodoxy and 'from the deference they paid to Mr. Fox's judgment'.[7] The Associators were just as anxious as Burke to draw a line down through the Whig party, which would separate orthodoxy from heresy, and were equally anxious that Fox should fall on the right side of it. Every indication of his moving nearer their position was propagated by the Associators.

[1] *Fox Speeches*, iv. 438 seq.; 25 May 1792.
[2] Add. MS. 51705, f. 131; T. Pelham to Lady Webster, 28 May 1792.
[3] Lady Palmerston to Palmerston, 18 May 1792; Palmerston MSS. f. 166.
[4] Spencer to Dowager Lady Spencer, 3 May and 7 May 1792; Spencer MSS.
[5] Wyvill, *Political Tracts and Papers*, iii. Appendix 159.
[6] Add. MS. 51705, f. 143; T. Pelham to Lady Webster, 1 July 1792.
[7] *Morning Herald*, 8 May 1792.

When Fox was angered by Mackintosh being black-balled at the Whig Club, John Tweddell, one of the Associators, eagerly reported to a friend; 'Mr. Fox told his Grace [i.e. Portland] that, on subjects of reform they held no principle in common.—that he heartily agreed in principle with Lord L. and Mr. Grey—that a thorough reform was wanting, though not so immediate as they wished.'[1] A bout of illness made Fox's position even more difficult, if he was to make any attempt to counter these hopeful reports that he had committed himself to the Associators.[2]

In September 1792, Burke had a momentary spasm of sympathy for the difficulties facing his antagonist: 'Fox was put in great straits—The young & vigorous & enterprising of his party had led in that Business—The weighty, grave, important, the Men of settled Character & influence were strongly against it. In this situation you may believe he found himself embarrased. . . . However when the affair came to the Test, he shewed which division of the Party he thought it the most useful for his purpose or the most agreeable to his inclination to adhere to.'[3] This diagnosis of Fox's position, while true in itself, misses the most important point. The events of April and May 1792 had certainly prompted the creation of pressures to the right and left of Fox. These groups could, however, never hope to be anything more as long as the alliance of wealth and intellect at the centre of the party, represented by Fox, Portland and Fitzwilliam, held. While this lasted, there remained some substance in the claim that the Whig party, as a viable political force, survived.

Fortunately for Fox, Portland and Fitzwilliam had hopes for his redemption. Portland's attitude was conciliatory,[4] and, although prepared to admit that he was no longer politically associated with Grey,[5] he refused to give up Fox. the Duke's intellectual dependence on Fox was long-established, and would not be easily broken. Further, both grandees feared that, if Fox were prematurely ostracized from Whig politics, they would be providing the Associators with a powerful new leader. As Lord Spencer observed, the price, which had to be paid for holding Fox, was high: 'The Duke's . . . Conduct lately respecting Politicks having taken a less decided turn in favour of the Ministers, & appearing still to keep himself attached to Mr. Fox notwithstanding the essential difference which seems to exist in their

[1] J. Tweddell to Dr. Parr, May 1792; J. Johnstone, *The Works of Dr. Parr*, i. 443.

[2] Add. MS. 51731, f. 68; Caroline Fox to Holland, 7 May 1792.

[3] Edmund Burke to William Burke, 3 Sept. 1792; Milton MSS. Burke A. iv., f. 34.

[4] Adair, *A Whig's Apology for his Consistency*, p. 37.

[5] Diary of Lord Malmesbury, 18 June 1792; *Diaries and Corres. of Ld. Malmesbury*, ii. 464.

opinions on the present state of Affairs has certainly contributed very much to lower him in the publick opinion.'[1] Fitzwilliam later dated the disintegration of the Whig party from May 1792,[2] but, at the time, he shared all Portland's hopes and fears about Fox. It was still possible to believe that the problem had been of Burke's making: 'An attack on C. Fox . . . could not prove the means of reclaiming him . . . it was sure to produce the contrary effects. By pinning the words upon him it pinned him to the sentiment, whether he would or not, and by interesting many for the individual, it riveted them to the opinion. . . . Even now, while C. is deprecating generally the Revolution, he holds fast to his original sentiment, which, had it not been so much marked, would have passed bye very little noticed . . .'[3] Fitzwilliam and Portland clung to Fox therefore because, before the storming of the Tuileries in August 1792, Burke could plausibly be called an alarmist, and because they could not bring themselves to cut loose from a man, who had defined their politics since 1782.

The position adopted by these grandees was tenable because Fox himself was very anxious to temporize. The names and wealth of Portland and Fitzwilliam were just as important to him as his intellectual leadership was to them. Fox's moderation owed less perhaps to an instinctive dislike for democratic[4] ideas than to a realistic grasp of the situation, which convinced him that as long as his link with Portland and Fitzwilliam held, the Whig party could be kept together. Before the debate on Pitt's Proclamation therefore, Fox called a meeting of the Whigs at his own house, 'to prevent things going to extremities tomorrow'.[5] Sir Gilbert Elliot, who attended this meeting, appreciated the fact that Fox was trying very hard to be effective in an uncharacteristic rôle: 'He endeavours to trim, which is not natural to him, & he does not do it well.'[6] Even so, this essay in moderation had its effect. Many contemporaries noted the lack of rancour, with which, in the ensuing debate, the Whigs argued about the issue of the Proclamation amongst themselves. Further, Fox was most anxious that the Whigs should concentrate exclusively on such matters as India, on which a large measure of agreement could

[1] Spencer to Dowager Countess Spencer, 8 July 1792; Spencer MSS.

[2] Fitzwilliam to W. Adam, 2 Aug. 1793; Milton MSS. Box 45. Fitzwilliam to Lady Rockingham, 23 Feb. 1793; Wentworth Woodhouse Muniments, R 164.

[3] H. Butterfield, 'Charles James Fox and the Whig Opposition in 1792', *C.H.J.* ix (1949), 295.

[4] Diary of Fanny Burney, 18 June 1792, A. Dobson, *Diary and Letters of Madame D'Arblay*, pp. 92–3. Green, *Extracts from the Diary of a Lover of Literature*, pp. 91–2.

[5] Butterfield, 'Charles James Fox and the Whig Opposition in 1792', *C.H.J.* ix (1949), 310.

[6] Sir G. Elliot to Lady Elliot, 24 May 1792; Lady Minto, *Life and Letters of Ld. Minto*, ii. 30.

normally be found throughout the Whig ranks. At the Whig Club too, Fox studied moderation: 'However warmly he wished for a moderate Reform in the system of our Representation, he did NOT AGREE with a considerable number of his friends, who had revived the subject with such spirit and vigour, that the PRESENT was a PROPER season for AGITATING THE QUESTION.'[1] The Club was becoming invaluable as the one forum, in which all sections of the Whig party continued to meet, and the persons toasted on this occasion represented a fair cross-section of Whig views.

Throughout June and July 1792, Fox was at pains to demonstrate that his connection with the Associators was no more than one independent vote given on the reform issue in the House of Commons. He told Tom Pelham that, 'he had never been consulted about it, & that on the contrary the Associators seemed determined not to have any Advice, & particularly not to have his.'[2] As proof of his good intentions, he went so far as actively to dissuade Pelham from opposing a loyalist address being drawn up in Sussex. The proof was accepted. Fox continued to be numbered among 'the heads of opposition' by the press, which recorded Fox's appearance at party councils.[3] On a social level, which, as far as the Whigs were concerned, ran parallel to the political, Fox's name figured in the same Club lists as Windham and Elliot as late as December 1792. Fox had therefore been just as successful in obviating the dangers to Whig unity presented by the Associators as he had been in checking Burke. This second essay in temporizing was the more commendable, however, because Fox's personal sympathies with the young men of the Association had been kept under control. Whig unity had, however, only held because the understanding between Fox, Fitzwilliam and Portland had not been broken. Wings had been formed on each of the party's extremities. The struggle for the centre of the party, as represented by these three men, was now the principal factor in Whig politics.

Both Pitt and Burke were determined that the Whig party should not be given time to regroup its forces. The Minister's first offer to Portland was made through Auckland on 1 May.[4] The timing of this manoeuvre could not have been better. Portland had been frightened by the Association, and would soon be flattered by the trust placed in him by the Minister on the subject of the Proclamation. Adair believed quite rightly that Pitt was simply trying 'to push these dissensions still further, or at least to find out how far they had

[1] *Morning Herald*, 7 June 1792.

[2] Add. MS. 51705, f. 134; T. Pelham to Lady Webster, 15 June 1792.

[3] *Public Advertiser*, 11 June 1792.

[4] Pitt to Auckland, 1 May 1792; *Journal and Corres. of Ld. Auckland*, ii. 402.

actually carried us',[1] but even so, the response aroused among the Whigs was encouraging. Loughborough was enthusiastic,[2] and, although Portland finally rejected Pitt's offer of a coalition, he took three weeks to do so, and then only demurred on a question of patronage and not, significantly, of principle.[3] Adair had to admit that Pitt's probing offers of a coalition in May had clearly demonstrated the Whig vulnerability to such temptations, and 'had at least effected that which made it as much as we could do to keep together'.[1]

The pressure on Portland's loyalty to Fox was kept up with a single-mindedness on Pitt's part, which confirms his very clear understanding of the relationship, on which the effectiveness of the Whig party depended. He attacked it again in June, this time employing Malmesbury as his agent. Initially, considerable progress was made. Both Loughborough and Malmesbury reported that Portland was very conscious of the desirability of some accommodation with Pitt, and that even Fox was not averse to the idea: 'Duke of Portland said he had seen Fox for two hours. Fox, he said, was a friend to Coalition. That he only wished it to be brought about in such a way as should appear that they had not acceded to Pitt's Ministry, but went to it on fair and even conditions to share equally with him all the power, patronage etc.'[4] In fact, however, neither side in the negotiation took the possibility of a coalition seriously. Pitt had told neither the King nor his colleagues about his activities, and, when the details were discussed, the Minister very quickly began to backpedal, demanding of Fox a full recantation of his views on the issue of reform.[5] Fox similarly had so deep a distrust of Pitt that he could freely inform Malmesbury that, 'it was impossible to suppose Pitt would admit him to an equal share of power, and that whatever might be his own feelings or readiness to give way, he would not, for the sake of the honour and pride of the party, come in on any other terms.[6] His initial caution was therefore prompted by the very real consideration that Portland's hopes for a coalition would have to be deflated slowly, and not embittered by outright intransigence. Pitt had attempted to separate Fox and Portland, by suggesting that Fox himself was the only obstacle standing in the path of the Duke's

[1] Adair, *A Whig's Apology for his Consistency*, p. 39.

[2] P. R. O. Chatham MSS. 30/8. 53, f. 83; Loughborough to Pitt, 4 May 1792.

[3] Portland to Loughborough, 25 May 1792; Portland MSS. PWF 9,220.

[4] Diary of Ld. Malmesbury, 13 June 1792; *Diaries and Corres. of Ld. Malmesbury*, ii. 459. See also Loughborough to Burke, 13 June 1792; Wentworth Woodhouse Muniments, Burke 1.

[5] Elliot of Wells to Sir G. Elliot, 29 June 1792; Lady Minto, *Life and Letters of Ld. Minto*, ii. 41.

[6] Diary of Ld. Malmesbury, 16 June 1792; Earl Malmesbury, *Diaries and Corres. of Ld. Malmesbury*, ii. 461–3.

entry into the Ministry. To give the lie to this claim, Fox once again had to study moderation.

By the end of June, Fox had succeeded. Portland had learnt his lesson, and repeated it by rote to Fitzwilliam; 'I believe D[undas] hurried P[itt] into the negotiation on the hope & perhaps belief of its being a favourable opportunity for breaking the opposition & dividing us & F. & that when they found us insist upon F—'s being not only a member of the Cabinet but of his being placed there in as respectable & efficient a situation as he held in the years –92 & –93 [meaning 82 & 83] they were totally unprepared & found it impracticable. . . .'[1] The essential problem was, as one Whig lady succinctly observed, 'that Mr. Pitt & Mr. Fox should be the same thing'.[2] After their experiences of 1782–4, the personal and political bitterness between these two men precluded their co-operation. Late in the nineteenth century, there was a story still commonly retailed that 'Charles Fox as Chancellor of the Exchequer never understood what Consols were —he knew they were things that went up and down in the City and he was always pleased when they went down, because it so annoyed Pitt.'[3] Such a legendary rivalry was unlikely to give way to necessity, particularly in the charged political atmosphere of 1792. If Portland persisted in his efforts to join Pitt in office, he would have to abandon Fox. The dilemma was acute. To follow his natural political instincts would mean joining a conservative coalition and forsaking the man, who had defined the terms of politics since 1782. In short, Portland would ultimately have to chose between 'Pompey & Caesar, Pitt & Fox'.[4]

Fox's relations with Portland in the summer of 1792 were therefore the determining factor. Fox succeeded in persuading the Duke that the French Revolution, which had prompted Pitt to make the offers of May and June, had not materially altered the principles, upon which the opposition to Pitt had been started in 1784. The context for political decision making remained unchanged: 'You will do me the justice to say that my nature is not inclined to suspicion, but I confess if we can not have a coalition upon proper terms of which I despair, I shall be glad to find the two parties in their old state of declared hostility again.'[5] Most contemporaries were very aware of how firmly the continued friendship between Portland and Fox would effectively block any coalition initiative.[6] Burke himself was conscious

[1] Portland to Fitzwilliam, 27 June 1792; Wentworth Woodhouse Muniments, F. 31. a.

[2] Add. MS. 51845, f. 40; Ann Pelham to Lady Webster, 31 Oct. 1792.

[3] Sir Algernon West, *Recollections* 1832–1886, ii. 295.

[4] Add. MS. 51845, f. 35; Sheffield to Lady Webster, 21 July 1792.

[5] Add. MS. 47561, f. 130; Fox to Portland, 12 Aug. 1792.

[6] G. Rose to Auckland, 13 July 1792; *Journal and Corres. of Ld. Auckland*, ii. 417.

of the link, which he had to break, if he was to succeed in thrusting Fox into the political wilderness: 'You see, that the Duke is more & more in Fox's power, indeed is now delivered over to him bound hand & foot & must be so until he puts his conduct upon some distinct principle on which issue between them may be fairly joined.'[1] In July and August 1792, Burke and Pitt joined forces in an attempt to inject just such a division of principle into the understanding between Portland and Fox.

The atmosphere, in which the Burke family launched its third onslaught on the nerves and consciences of the Whig grandees, was now much more suited to their designs. The discovery of a pair of breeches burning in a cupboard in the House of Commons had been enough to convince some people that it was the prelude to a full-scale Jacobin attack.[2] At party meetings in June, the full Burkean interpretation of events was expounded and developed. The formation of the Association of the Friends of the People effectively marked the end of the old Whig party, and, because Fox had never publicly disavowed the reformers, he had to be considered as one of their principal sympathizers. [3]Just to ensure that the point went home, one of Burke's relations sent Portland a twenty-page letter, setting out this argument more fully:

> It is little worth the enquiry how Mr. Fox himself came by these opinions, which naturally made it impossible for Mr. Burke to continue in a party where Mr. Fox's new Sentiments, or perhaps more correctly speaking Mr. Sheridan's sentiments, were apparently to predominate. I can scarcely think it an affectation of foresight to ensure myself that it will not be long before higher names than Mr. Burke's will be forced away from that School,[4] to which . . . Mr. Fox means to lead his admirers.[5]

In spite of a telling analogy between Fox and Lafayette, Portland could not bring himself to believe that Fox was guilty of holding dangerous views. He told Loughborough that, 'I can't say that the inference I drew from Fox's conversation corresponds with that which has been given You, I don't recollect a word in favor of the French Revolution.'[6] Under the barrage of Burkean invective, however, Portland's faith in Fox came to rest less on reason and argument than on a blind belief in Fox's basic reliability.

The Duke's faith was most severely tested by Pitt's third offer of an arrangement, in July and August 1792. Fox himself was delighted

[1] E. Burke to W. Burke, 2 Sept. 1792; Milton MSS. A. iv, f. 34.

[2] Lady Palmerston to Palmerston, 10 May 1792; Palmerston MSS. f. 166.

[3] Diary of Lord Malmesbury, 2 June and 9 June 1792; *Diaries and Corres. of Ld. Malmesbury*, ii. 453, 466.

[4] *School for Scandal*.

[5] W. Burke to Portland, 8 June 1792; Milton MSS. A. xxi, f. 10.

[6] Portland to Loughborough, 23 Aug. 1792; Portland MSS. PWF 9225.

that a serious proposal had at last emerged. It would allow him to demonstrate just how firm was his control over Portland's thoughts and actions. When Pitt offered the Garter to the Duke as a preliminary, Portland dutifully consulted Fox 'on this as well as every other part of my publick conduct'.[1] Advising against acceptance, Fox took the opportunity to impress certain ideas on Portland. 'I may possibly be too suspicious but I own I cannot bring myself to think that Pitt has ever meaned anything but to make a division among us or, if that could not be done, to give the public the ideas of such a division.'[2] Further, since this negotiation, unlike the two previous initiatives, was to be carried on with the knowledge of the King, Fox could state his full terms openly, which would obviate the risk of Pitt being able to inveigle the Whigs into office on imprecise terms. The fact that George III was aware of these negotiations was Fox's guarantee that Pitt's room for manoeuvre would be severely restricted. It also implied ultimately that the negotiations would founder, because, as Fox told Portland, it was clear that, while the King would not give Pitt up, 'we can never with honour or advantage come in under him . . . and I deceive myself if I do not ground this opinion much more upon party than Personal reasons and feelings'.[2] Convinced that Pitt was insincere,[3] Fox approved of negotiations carried on under the royal eye, because, in restricting the Minister's capacity for dissimulation, they would prove to Portland that the whole attempt was futile.

The initiative for this third negotiation therefore came from the Whigs themselves. On 20 July 1792, Portland asked the Duke of Leeds to act as an intermediary between the Whigs, Pitt and the King.[4] Fox was very much in favour of bringing the whole matter out into the open, because 'it might be the means of establishing whether there is any possibility of our coming in on any other terms than those of submission to Pitt. If such a possibility exists I am as eager for seizing & improving it, as I am and I believe always shall be totally averse from acting under him.'[5] From the very beginning, Leeds was firmly told that the King had to be informed of the undertaking, as a guarantee of Pitt's sincerity.[6] Similarly, Fox immediately made the condition that Pitt would have to leave the Treasury. The Duke of Leeds later noted that, 'Mr. Fox repeatedly dwelt on the

[1] Add. MS. 47561, f. 119; Portland to Fox, 21 July 1792.

[2] Add. MS. 47561, f. 116; Fox to Portland, 21 July 1792.

[3] Fox to Carlisle, 25 July 1792; H.M.C. *Carlisle MSS*. xv. 5.6, 696.

[4] Browning, *Political Memoranda of the 5th Duke of Leeds*, pp. 175 seq.

[5] Add. MS. 47561, f. 122; Fox to Portland, 26 July 1792. Portland to Fitzwilliam, 22 July 1792; Milton MSS. Box 44.

[6] Add. MS. 28067, f. 43; Portland to Leeds, 29 July 1792.

indispensable necessity of an alteration in the Treasury & that without that was admitted, nothing could be done.'[1] To come in on any other terms would be to forgive Pitt the manner in which he had assumed that office nine years earlier, and to throw grave doubt on the opposition's protestations of principle during the 1780s. When Leeds set out on his commission, therefore, Fox had effectively undermined Pitt's capacity to subvert Whig loyalties with vague promises of office. Either the Minister would accept the Whig terms, which, under the eye of the King, would not prove easy; or he could refuse them, and, by so doing, convince Portland of his own unreliability.

Loughborough immediately realized that Fox had succeeded in making the possibility of an arrangement very remote: 'No arrangement would be satisfactory to F. that does not put it in his power to distinguish men as he pleases, and if he had the power he could not avoid using it in favour of those who have professed an exclusive attachment to him.'[2] As Fox had predicted, as soon as the King was informed by Leeds of what was under consideration, George's reaction emphatically showed that no association with Pitt was possible on terms which the Whigs could accept. The King found any suggestion that Pitt should resign ridiculous, and was prepared to allow the Whigs 'Anything Complimentary . . . but no Power.'[3] Fox's strategy had therefore worked well. The Duke of Portland had to admit defeat, because he refused to move without Fox, whose low standing with the King had been convincingly demonstrated.[4] Further, as a result of the Leeds negotiations, Pitt found himself in trouble with the King, whose suspicions had been aroused that he had not been fully informed of all his Minister's manoeuvres.[5] In order to defend his position at Court, Pitt himself had to scotch any further ideas of taking Portland into partnership. He told Leeds that 'There had been no thoughts of any alteration in the Government, that circumstances did not call for it, nor did the people wish it, & that no new arrangement, either by change or coalition, had ever been in contemplation.'[6] When Pitt was at last brought to admit this, Fox's task of holding the loyalty of Portland was made much easier. The Leeds initiative forced Pitt to admit that, in making the two earlier offers of coalition, he had never meant them to be taken seriously.

[1] Add. MS. 27918, f. 261; Memoranda of the Duke of Leeds, 3 Aug. 1792. Diary of Lord Malmesbury, 30 July 1792; *Diaries and Corres. of Ld. Malmesbury*, ii. 472.

[2] Loughborough to Carlisle, 1 Aug. 1792; H.M.C. *Carlisle MSS.* xv. 5.6, 696.

[3] Browning, *Political Memoranda of the 5th Duke of Leeds*, p. 187.

[4] Portland to Loughborough, 17 Aug. 1792; Portland MSS. PWF 9223.

[5] W. Pitt to George III; Aspinall *The Later Corres. of George III*, i. 607

[6] Browning, *Political Memoranda of the 5th Duke of Leeds*, pp. 191–3.

Between April and August 1792 therefore, the unity of the Whig party had been subjected to yet another theoretical broadside from Burke, two tempting offers from Pitt, and the fear engendered by the enthusiasm of a group of young reformers. As Richard Burke had to admit, Fox had held the party together by refusing to do anything which could conceivably impair his relationship with Portland and Fitzwilliam; 'Ld. F.[itzwilliam] did not speak quite so strongly of F[ox] as I expected; he said he would safely & conscientiously trust him with considerable trust in gov^{t} but I think he said it, with a little hesitation. It is clear he is not quite at his ease about him, tho' as far as I can see determin'd not to abandon him.'[1] The grandees were clearly uneasy, but at this stage, Portland was not yet so blinded by fear that he believed that French ideas would necessarily be imported into England. He told Windham that there was 'something that, if it is not good sense, will be as a substitute for it, which will prevent our being overun by French Principles.'[2] For such a statement to be made only a month after the September Massacres emphasizes Fox's success in soothing jaded Whig nerves.

Certain other factors, besides common-sense, were working in Fox's favour. Memories were long, and the traumatic experiences of 1782–4, which had underpinned the Whig opposition of the 1780s, still contributed greatly to the formulation of Portland's ideas. Under Fox's tuition, his distaste for Pitt was kept alive, and this in turn led him to make a spirited defence of party. In speaking of the Ministers, Portland claimed that 'They do not wish for power for the only purpose which makes that wish justifiable. They have no principle. They know not what party is, but for the desire of annihilating it, & suppose favours, emoluments & Patronage a compensation for the loss of Consistency & Character. Whenever their mode of thinking is reformed, I shall be willing to take them by the hand. But until then, I can hold no connection with them.'[3] The titular leader of the Whigs would not therefore join Pitt, because he believed that the circumstances of 1782–4 had divided the political world between the protagonists of party, which was now a wholly acceptable political phenomenon, and those who clung to the old, corrupt methods of patronage and management. To desert to Pitt would therefore be to justify his attacks on party. As his duchess assured a close friend: 'they suffer'd very much by coming in before & that they will never do it but upon such terms as shall please & be honourable to all their

[1] R. Burke to E. Burke, 1 Sept. 1792; Wentworth Woodhouse Muniments, Burke 1.

[2] Add. MS. 37845, f. 5; Portland to W. Windham, 13 Oct. 1792.

[3] Portland to E. Burke, 12 Sept. 1792; Wentworth Woodhouse Muniments, Burke 1.

friends.'[1] Intellectually, Portland and, to a lesser extent, Fitzwilliam were the disciples of Fox.

Reinforcing this theoretical position was the assurance that Fox could not conceivably approve of the events taking place in France, which, Portland believed, militated against all his past political conduct. He told Fitzwilliam that 'It is not to be expected that he [Fox] will retract what he said of his expectations of the effect of the French Revolution in its outset, I mean the opinion that he unfortunately gave respecting the beauty of its Fabrick, but I have little if any doubt but that he will declare that no part of the Building has been carved in conformity to the expectations he had formed, & that in itself, in all its parts, excepting its foundations, & in all the measures used to raise & establish it, He will condemn it most explicitly.'[2] Paradoxically therefore, the attack on the Tuileries and the September Massacres, far from pushing Portland and Fitzwilliam away from Fox, merely confirmed their belief that it was inconceivable that the latter should in any way condone such proceedings.[3] There was even the hope that the violence in France would persuade the Associators, whom Fitzwilliam saw as simply a group of ambitious young men using the issue of reform to oust an ageing Whig leadership, to adopt more cautious policies. Fitzwilliam told Carlisle that the door had to be kept open for the possible return of these 'not unimportant men'.[4] In particular, nothing must be done to drive such a talented man as Fox into the arms of extremists: '. . . is he to be shaken off from his connection with sound constitutional men, & forced into the arms of the Tookes & Paines: we must be sure that the Colossus is theirs before we take a step to make him so . . . an attack upon C. without notice . . . would not prove the means of reclaiming him, nor of reforming publick opinion: it was sure to produce the contrary effects, by pinning the words upon him, it pinned him to the sentiment, whether he would or not, & by interesting many for the Individual, it rivetted them to the opinion.'[5] Fox was still too valuable an ally and would be too dangerous as an opponent. Consequently, in October, the Whigs assembled as usual at Holkham for the shooting, where Fox was 'very active for his size'.[6] Superficially the several threats of the summer of 1792 seemed to have passed away.

[1] Lady E. Ponsonby to Lady L. Ponsonby, 31 Oct. 1792; Hickleton MSS. A. 1.2.1, f. 43.

[2] Portland to Fitzwilliam, 26 Sept. 1792; Milton MSS. Box 44.

[3] R. Burke to E. Burke, 10 Oct. 1792; Wentworth Woodhouse Muniments, Burke 1.

[4] Fitzwilliam to Carlisle, 31 Oct. 1792; Milton MSS. Box 44.

[5] Fitzwilliam to Carlisle, 31 Oct. 1792; Milton MSS. Box 44.

[6] Spencer to Dowager Lady Spencer, 25 Oct. 1792; Spencer MSS.

In fact, during the same period, Fox's views on France had changed substantially, and in a direction which Portland could scarcely approve. In catechizing his nephew in true Whig principles, Fox kept up a regular commentary on French events. The attack on the Tuileries he saw as deeply distressing to all adherents of 'the true cause', because 'There is a want of dignity & propriety in everything they do.'[1] The difficulty was that the choice lay between the French and the armies of Austria and Prussia, which represented, in Fox's eyes, 'the Invasion of the Barbarians'.[1] The French had to be forgiven, if only because the behaviour of the despotic sovereigns of Europe was worse: 'It seems as if the Jacobins had determined to do something as revolting to the feelings of mankind as the Duke of Brunswick's Proclamations; but though it must be owned that they have done their utmost for this purpose, yet with respect to mine they have not succeeded for the Proclamation in my judgment still remains unrivalled.'[2] The September Massacres presented even greater problems to the friends of France in England, but Fox accepted them again as the lesser of two evils: 'Any thing that proves that it is not in the power of Kings and Princes by their great armies to have every thing their own way is of such good example that without any good will to the French one can not help being delighted with it, and you know I have a natural partiality for what some people call rebels.'[3] Fox was quite sure that, if Brunswick had succeeded in taking Paris, the slaughter would have been much more extensive, and despotism would have been restored. Against such possibilities, Fox was forced to allow the revolutionaries great latitude.

Throughout the first four years of the Revolution, Fox was continually led into idosyncratic views on French affairs, because he insisted on translating English ideas and situations across the Channel. Instead of viewing the Revolution from above, thereby becoming apprehensive of its democratic tendencies, Fox, obsessed with his struggle with George III, associated himself with what he took to be a common struggle against kings. His personal knowledge of Lafayette and other early leaders of the Revolution clearly assisted this development. Therefore, he was forced to approve of the overthrow of the Feuillant party in August 1792, because these men had ceased to act on good Whig principles:

If you admit that the Jacobins or any other parties having the Confidence of the Assembly & Country ought to be Ministers what can be said for the Feuillans who encouraged, who supported the King in supporting an administration of an adverse faction & in using his Veto & other prerogatives

[1] Fox to Holland, 3 Sept. 1792; *Mems. and Corres. of C. J. Fox*, iii. 368.

[2] Add. MS. 47570, f. 11; Fox to Holland, 20 Aug. 1972.

[3] Add. MS. 47570, f. 189; Fox to Mrs. Armistead, 7 Oct. 1792.

in opposition to the will of the Assembly & Nation He who defends this ever can *not* be a Whig.[1]

Fox is therefore forced to defend the Jacobins, under which title he is in fact speaking of such Girondins as Roland and Vergniaux, because they seemed to be adopting many of the principles, to which the English whigs themselves subscribed. The very real differences in the political circumstances in the two countries were ignored. The Rolands were now baptized as good Whigs because they seemed 'to show more sense and principle than any other has yet shown in France'.[2]

In European terms, by the late autumn of 1792, the middle ground in politics had been cut away. The choice presented to politicians was the stark one between the Duke of Brunswick and the republicans. Although Fox had made his personal decision on this issue by August, the full impact of this choice had not yet been brought home to the majority of Whigs. The middle ground, represented by Fox, Portland and Fitzwilliam, still held for the reasons set out above. The question was now simply how long this understanding would last. As the opening of the 1792–3 Session of Parliament approached, pressure again began to build up on both flanks. The crude polarization of political loyalties, which had already divided Europe, could not be long delayed in striking England.

[1] Add. MS. 51731, f. 88; Holland to Caroline Fox, 23 Oct. 1792.
[2] Add. MS. 51751, f. 20; Fox to Holland, *c.* Nov. 1792.

VI

THE FRENCH REVOLUTION AND THE WHIGS, OCTOBER 1792–JULY 1794

In the months before the reassembling of Parliament, in December 1792, there was the common impression on both the extreme wings of the Whig party that matters had to be brought to a final issue. Fox's position at the centre of the party was becoming increasingly anomalous. Tierney[1] told Grey that 'In this extravagant ferment of Men's opinions our task becomes every day more difficult. The Leveller and the Reformer, the King and the Tyrant, seem in the new vocabularies of Courtiers and Patriots to be confounded and considered as synonymous. . . .'[2] In spite of Fox's efforts, political titles were being redefined. As early as November 1791, the *Public Advertiser* had set out in parallel columns rival definitions of such words as 'Whig', 'Tory' and 'Patriot', one being that of 'times past' and the other that of 'times present'.[3] While Fox was still at pains, in 1792, to demonstrate that the values of the Whigs had not been substantially altered by the French Revolution, both Burke and some of the Associators were equally determined to prove the opposite. Fox's own nephew, Lord Holland, produced the most startling redefinition of all:

> What then you will say is it that I disapprove of in our present Whig party? It is this the idea that any family or families have any particular influence in this party—the Duke of Por. may be in opposition, may be a sensible man, may call & think himself a Whig & yet be a Tory . . . I mean that it is not any particular families that make a party a Whig party, but it is the Whiggism of the particular men that makes me respect them.[4]

As the mounting violence in France prompted both Burke and the Associators to intensify their efforts, and to define Whiggery according to their own precepts, Fox was brought by necessity nearer to committing himself to one of these two pressure groups. Long before

[1] George Tierney (1761–1830); M.P. for six different boroughs, 1789–90, 1796–1830; initially a Pittite in 1784, moved across to Fox over the French Revolution; Pres. of the Board of Control, 1806–7; leader of the Whigs in the Lower House, 1818–21.

[2] G. Tierney to C. Grey, 29 Oct. 1792; H. K. Olphin, *George Tierney*, pp. 22–3.

[3] *Public Advertiser*, 22 Nov. 1791.

[4] Add. MS. 51731, f. 96; Holland to Caroline Fox, 9 Nov. 1792.

Parliament reassembled in December therefore, both campaigns were already under way. Each was designed to capture control of Fox's political soul.

The events in France in 1792 had made some Associators, like Grey, hesitate,[1] but Sheridan was determined to press forward. Like Burke, he was convinced that Fox's allegiance was crucial, as the lynch-pin of Whig unity. He told a friend that 'Charles Fox must come to the Reformers openly and avowedly; and in a month four-fifths of the Whig Club will do the same.'[2] By November, certain of the more staid members of the party believed that the Associators were about to make another challenge. Lord George Cavendish was looking for 'Wisdom to Steer the old Boat steadily & I am afraid we shall depend on Nothing but Cleverness'.[3] Lord Spencer was expecting 'great Violences' when Parliament met.[4] The party managers were also alarmed. Adair told Adam that the resolutions offered at the first Whig Club meeting of the new Session should be such as could be passed by all sections of the party, without appearing to favour one faction at the expense of the other. Fox fully approved such caution.[5]

The Reformers were determined, however, to bring matters to a head, in the belief that Fox would ultimately join them. The issue of Parliamentary Reform was to be raised at the Whig Club, and a standing Committee of Associators was to meet regularly at the Freemasons Tavern, in order to co-ordinate their campaign before the new Session officially opened.[6] Fox was reported to be willing to support the Reform measure, and his views were specifically invited. Parliamentary Reform had been the issue, earlier in the year, on which Fox had committed himself. There was a very real hope that he would do so again in December. The Associators were very aware that Fox's position was rapidly becoming untenable. Tierney told Grey: 'I am quite satisfied that if Fox does not speedily come forth in his true colours and speak boldly what I am certain he thinks, he will be lost... Let Fox but take the lead and everything may yet go well with him, but if he acts upon a cold system of caution . . . he will forfeit his character with all parties. In one word, my Opinion is, that, disagreeable as I know the alternative to be, matters are now brought to that Pass, that either Fox must ruin that cabal at Burlington House, or that cabal will ruin him.'[7] The Reform campaign mounted by the

[1] Grey to Norwich Society for Parliamentary Reform, 24 Sept. 1792; E. Hughes, 'The Scottish Reform Movement and Charles Grey', *S.H.R.* xxxv (1956), 37.

[2] Sheridan to ?, 1792; Moore, *The Life of R. B. Sheridan*, ii. 184.

[3] Lord G. Cavendish to Lady Ponsonby, 19 Nov. 1792; Grey MSS.

[4] Spencer to Dowager Lady Spencer, 29 Nov. 1792; Spencer MSS.

[5] Add. MS. 47565, f. 159; Fox to R. Adair, 14 Nov. 1792.

[6] G. Tierney to C. Grey, 5 Nov. 1792; Grey MSS.

[7] G. Tierney to C. Grey, 15 Nov. 1792; Grey MSS.

Associators in the autumn of 1792 was designed to provoke just such a positive response. In their eyes, unless Fox openly took over the leadership of the anti-Pittite movement, it would inevitably fall into the dangerous hands of Horne Tooke.

Burke and his friends were equally determined to bring matters to an issue. The events of August and September 1792 in Paris had greatly magnified their fear of what might follow in England. In October, Carlisle told Fitzwilliam that, 'as an opposing party, driving at the old object, viz, the overthrow of the administration, with the fair intention of replacing it with our own forces, I conceive we exist no longer.'[1] Even so, Fox could not be abandoned without a final effort. In spite of Burke's personal animosities, Fox was too dangerous a man to bequeath to the Associators by over hasty action. Thomas Grenville was still wrestling with Fox's conscience as late as November: 'I had a long conversation with Charles & with Windham last week in which both Windham and I agreed in the apprehensions we entertained, but did not I think succeed more than usual in endeavouring to make Charles share those apprehensions with us.'[2] The difficulty was that, since Fox believed that the greatest danger to English liberties still came from the Crown rather than the people, any show of strength by Burke produced the most violent reactions. When Loyalist Associations were formed in the summer of 1792, in order to check all kinds of sedition, Fox claimed, in the House of Commons, that, 'these associations were at present made an instrument of tyranny over men's minds almost as bad as the clubs in France.'[3] If Fox was to be held back from joining Grey and Sheridan, the right wing of the Whig party would have to demonstrate that the course of French politics directly threatened England.

At the same time as Grey and Sheridan were preparing to attack through the Whig Club, Burke and his friends were putting a counter-offensive into effect on two fronts. An agent of the Duke of Leeds was again sent down to St. Anne's Hill in a last, despairing attempt to bring Fox and Pitt into some kind of understanding. Pitt's attitude from the outset was one of condescension, in that he was very aware of the extremely difficult position, in which Fox now found himself. Under pressure from the two pressure groups within the Whig party, Fox could not hope for improved terms. Even so, Leeds was told that, 'F. is for no Deviation whatever from the first plan . . . it's being as difficult to do without him as to arrange any Thing with him.'[4] Among certain Pittites, there was genuine regret that the negotiations

[1] Carlisle to Fitzwilliam, 15 Oct. 1792; Milton MSS. Box 44.
[2] T. Grenville to Fitzwilliam, 15 Nov. 1792; Milton MSS. Box 44.
[3] A. Mitchell, 'The Association Movement, 1792–3'; *H.J.* iv (1961), 67.
[4] Add. MS. 28067, f. 87; R. Woodford to Leeds, 22 Nov. 1792.

had come to nothing, because they realized that this would ultimately mean that Fox would lead the Associators. Lord Grenville was told by his brother that he was 'very sorry to find by your letter that all your hopes from Opposition have vanished, because it is clearly the strongest proof of the influence which Fox retains over their minds, and which he will use to the worst purposes.'[1] After the failure of this initiative, the right wing of the Whig party, with a mixture of regret and apprehension, abandoned Fox forever.

As soon as this decision had been taken, Burke opened up the alternative line of attack with a twenty-page letter to Fitzwilliam, aimed solely at destroying that nobleman's understanding with Fox. After reiterating his view that any real hope of reclaiming Fox had now been dashed forever, Burke asked Fitzwilliam to engineer a formal separation, because Fox was now the only obstacle to an alliance with Pitt, and because the Duke of Portland, still intellectually the prisoner of Fox, very badly needed to be set an example. As Burke reported, Windham

> had, not long since, seen Fox. He found him no way altered. His opinion was, that the danger to this Country chiefly consisted in the growth of Tory principles, and that what happened in France was likely to be useful to us in keeping alive and invigorating the spirit of Liberty. He was disposed to lower and palliate whatever seemed shocking in their procedure. I was informed ... that he has lived, more than with any body, with the Ladies here belonging to Monsr l'Egalité—and was of frequent parties with the Bishop of Autun and Chauvelin . . .[2]

This catalogue of enormities was completed by the report that Fox was prepared to recognize a French republic, wished the Low Countries could be independent of Austria, and believed that the answer to any danger facing England was to relieve Catholics and Dissenters of their disabilities. This epistolary campaign was quickly followed up by more direct action. 'Hunting in couples',[3] Burke, Windham, Loughborough and others had interviews with Ministers, at which their personal support was pledged. The Duke of Portland was kept informed of these visits, and 'seemed not at all displeased'.[4] In fact, under pressure from events in France, Burke's ideas were at last making an impression on Portland. The Duke told Burke in November that, in his opinion, 'this Country can not see with indifference

[1] Buckingham to Grenville, 27 Nov. 1792; H.M.C. Fortescue II *Dropmore MSS*. p. 344.

[2] E. Burke to Fitzwilliam, 29 Nov. 1792; Wentworth Woodhouse Muniments, Burke 1.

[3] E. Burke to R. Burke, 18 Nov. 1792; ibid.

[4] E. Burke to R. Burke, 18 Nov. 1792; ibid.

the strides which France is making to universal domination & disorder . . .'[1] Well before Parliament reassembled in December therefore, the campaigns of both wings of the Whigs were already well advanced, encroaching from both directions on that middle ground from which Fox had hitherto contrived to hold the party together.

As the opening of the new Parliamentary session drew nearer, many were aware that the pressure building up on Fox from both sides was becoming insupportable. An intermediary in the latest round of negotiations told Leeds that he looked forward with 'a kind of dread to the approaching Collision of Parties, in both Houses of Parliament. Although I have never heard Mr. F. intimate any thing of the kind, yet I am not without my apprehensions, that after the very fair, moderate & conciliatory Disposition which he manifested last Summer, he may feel the Conduct of P[itt] towards him . . . as mounting to a Declaration of War against him.'[2] There can be no doubt that Fox's studied neutrality had been gravely undermined by these campaigns, and that his sympathies had been engaged by the Associators, rather than by Burke. He told Adair that the Associators were more honest and more amenable; 'I am sure that Lauderdale Grey and Sheridan are all manageable men, and the rascals of the Democratic party (for there are such on all sides), have not set their wits to pervert them, in the way that those on the Aristocratic side have to pervert the Duke of Portland, Fitzwilliam, Windham etc.'[3] Very conscious that the centre of the Whig party was rapidly fragmenting, Fox himself was forced to revalue his own line of action. If division was inevitable, Fox had to chose his future political allies.

In making this choice, certain points were of supreme importance. Above all, he was determined to resist any suggestion that the formal opposition to Pitt should be abandoned: 'This with me is the most real cause of separation of any that was started. . . .'[4] According to Fox, the context, in which political decisions were to be made, remained the same. His concept of political divisions was wholly static. Refusing the admit that the French Revolution had overlaid the disputes of 1782–4 with new and more pressing questions, Fox complained bitterly to Adair about being charged with sympathizing with the Associators: 'It were no wonder if I did make continually these larger strides that are complained of, tho' I am not conscious of having made any.'[5] As he went on to explain, he had supported the Associators on such issues as Parliamentary Reform, because he always had done so. In

[1] Portland to Loughborough, 16 Nov. 1792; Portland MSS. PWF 9229.
[2] Add. MS. 27918, f. 300; S. Rolleston to Leeds, 11 Dec. 1792.
[3] Fox to R. Adair, 26 Nov. 1792; Trevelyan, *Grey of the Reform Bill*, pp. 61–2.
[4] Add. MS. 47565, f. 163; Fox to R. Adair, 29 Nov. 1792.
[5] Add. MS. 47565, f. 163; Fox to R. Adair, 29 Nov. 1792.

this view, the context of politics had not changed so violently, that he should be forced into inconsistency. What Fox failed to realize, however, was that, if he himself continued to fight old battles, most of the political nation had already decamped, in order to engage in new struggles. Burke could therefore misrepresent Fox's actions effectively, because the two men were no longer operating on the same political level. Tom Grenville ruefully admitted that Fox, lingering at Holkham and St. Anne's Hill, was not aware of the new slant, which the Revolution had given to English politics: 'I, who think constant communication & discussion with him still more important upon points where we disagree than upon those where we agree, see much advantage in his being here and very much wish that I saw [him] oftener than I do.'[1]

Before the new session opened therefore, Fox had again to go to Town 'to counteract some of Ld. L[oughbourough]'s mischief'.[2] He and Portland met on 24 November. The Duke's reaction to this meeting underlines how firmly two political systems, that taking shape in reaction to the Revolution and that prompted by the events of 1782–4, were now in existence, confusing political terms and making loyalities difficult to determine. Publicly, the Duke reported that he was entirely happy with Fox's views. Burke once again had to report defeat: 'I find that they have had an Interview with Mr. Fox. I don't know whether you were at it—By what I hear, if Monsr L'Egalité were himself to dictate a plan of politics, it would not differ materially from that of Mr. Fox . . . Every Interview with Fox disables all their faculties at once.'[3] In Whitehall, the Duke declared, according to a report reaching Leeds, that 'he never could be satisfied till Mr. Fox was seated in the Cabinet, & that he would never enter it while he lived unless accompanied by Mr. Fox.'[4] Privately, however, Portland had been deeply disturbed by Fox's views. He decided to go to St. Anne's Hill on 1 December, only three days before Fox's famous speech at the Whig Club, in the hope that Fox could be persuaded to soften his views. As Portland reported to Fitzwilliam before this second meeting,

> The disposition & temper of his mind seemed to me so much more warped than it was in the beginning of the year when we conversed with Him upon the subjects of the French Revolution . . . He appeared so little affected by the horrors . . . produced in the course of the summer. He is so hostile to what he calls the cause of Kings, & consequently so satisfied & pleased with the failure

[1] T. Grenville to Fitzwilliam, 24 Nov. 1792; Milton MSS. Box 44.

[2] Add. MS. 47571, f. 22; Fox to Holland, 23 Nov. 1792.

[3] E. Burke to Loughborough, 28 Nov. 1792; Wentworth Woodhouse Muniments, Burke 1. Loughborough to E. Burke, 30 Nov. 1792; ibid.

[4] Add. MS. 27918, f. 297; Memoranda of Fifth Duke of Leeds, Nov. 1792.

of the Prussian & Austrian powers, that He is in a manner insensible to the effects of the increasing power of France & to that lust of Dominion which is to me as evident in their present Republican Government as in the Zenith of their Monarchical Glory.[1]

The dilemma of whether Whig politics should still turn on the issues raised in 1782–4, or on those prompted by the Revolution, here becomes explicit. Because Fox had adhered to the first, while a majority of the political nation had moved on to the second, Portland could plausibly accuse him of closing his eyes to the dangers facing England. The charge would not be easily answered.

In the fortnight before Parliament reassembled, therefore, Fox was brought to realize that the twin campaigns mounted in the autumn of 1792 by the two pressure groups within the party, allied to the violence of events in France, had obliterated that middle ground in Whig politics, on which he had hitherto stood.[2] If the unity of the Whig party was to be saved now, Fox had no choice but to try to impress a personal policy upon Portland and Fitzwilliam, which would probably drive Burke into association with Pitt, but which might hold the remainder of the party together. Such a decision was greatly assisted by the announcement that Pitt intended to call out the militia as the first of a series of precautionary measures to avert the threat of insurrection. Unless Portland were to be allowed to drift into supporting such groundless incursions into English liberties, Fox believed that an open challenge had to be presented. When news of the Militia Bill reached him, he told Adam that 'I am too mad to trust my self to write but if they have assigned Insurrection (or rather Rebellion for that is the legal word as their cause) I will move an Impeachment let me be supported by ten or one or none.'[3] His language to Portland was even more positive: 'I fairly own that if they have done this I shall grow savage, and not think a french Lanterne too bad for them. Surely it is impossible, if anything were impossible for such Monsters who, for the purpose of weakening or dismaying the honourable connection of the Whigs would not scruple to run the risque of a civil war.'[4] In December 1792, Fox therefore decided that a policy of quiescence no longer guaranteed Whig unity, and, in the face of what he took to be Pitt's onslaught on English liberties, was in any case insupportable.

Before the first meeting of the Whig Club, an attempt was made at a gathering at Burlington House, to find a policy, which all the

[1] Portland to Fitzwilliam, 30 Nov. 1792; Wentworth Woodhouse Muniments F.31.a.

[2] Moore, *Memoirs of R. B. Sheridan*, ii. 201 seq.

[3] Add. MS. 47568, f. 272; Fox to W. Adam, 1 Dec. 1792.

[4] Add. MS. 47561, f. 133; Fox to Portland, 1 Dec. 1792.

Whigs could follow. Fox refused to make any concessions at this meeting, and reiterated his belief that France represented no danger to England whatever. This dramatic change in Fox's tone was reported to Lord Charlemont: '. . . he and Sheridan and Erskine and Grey will be on these points a phalanx by themselves, & Fox will be at the head of that republican party which is now beginning to lift up its head and to utter publicly sentiments which they would not have dared to mutter two months ago.'[1] At the famous Whig Club meeting of 4 December 1792, Fox made his effort to hold the Whig party on his own terms. After toasts which included such pointed phrases as 'the Friends of Liberty all over the World', Fox, prefacing his speech with a few commonplaces on the magnificence of the English constitution, concluded that

> It follows, therefore, that I am, and I declare myself to be an advocate for 'The Rights of the People', upon whose Rights alone can, in my opinion, be founded any real, sound, and legitimate Government, since the very end and object of all just Governments is the SECURITY, FREEDOM, AND HAPPINESS OF THE PEOPLE.[2]

Such an explicit confession of political faith, contrasting so clearly with the moderate policies pursued earlier in the year, must be taken as a deliberate initiative by Fox, in the forum of the Whig Club, to hold his party together on what to him seemed acceptable terms. In effect he presented the grandees with an ultimatum, banking heavily upon their intellectual dependence.

The results of such a speech could only be explosive, and in the event, Fox's reliance upon the dukes' pliability was not entirely well founded. Fitzwilliam lost all patience: 'last night I saw C. F. at Burlington House: I by no means like him: . . . at the Whig Club on Tuesday, he explain'd the grounds of his constitutional creed by comments upon the ordinary toasts of the Club, the wording of which, when taken abstractedly we all might, & all do cordially subscribe to, but I must say, when coupled with the times, & with the constructions & uses, these sentiments & sentences have continually put upon them by others, his commenting on them at all does not meet with my approbation.'[3] Portland, whose name had been included among those who had applauded Fox's speech at the Club, was even more outraged. In fact, he had only attended the Club fleetingly, and had heard neither the offending speech nor the toasts. Dr. Lawrence was

[1] E. Malone to Charlemont, 3 Dec. 1792; H.M.C. *Charlemont*, ii. 202–3.

[2] *The Speech of the Rt. Hon. C. J. Fox Containing the Declaration of his Principles, Respecting the Present Crisis of Public Affairs . . . Spoken at the Whig Club Dec. 4 1792*, p. 2.

[3] Fitzwilliam to Lady Fitzwilliam, 6 Dec. 1792; Milton MSS. Box 45.

commissioned to insert a paragraph in the major newspapers, disassociating the Duke from any such remarks.[1] Pitt not unreasonably took advantage of this situation to offer Portland a preview of the King's Speech for the new session.[2] This displeasure was not, however, communicated to Fox. On 11 December, he dined with Portland and Fitzwilliam, and continued to treat domestic alarms as entirely imaginary.[3] On the same day, he wrote to Mrs. Armistead to report that 'there is little doubt but we shall at least set out together. I am not very sanguine about the continuance of our Union because I see so many Persons on both sides so maliciously set upon breaking it, but one must hope for the best.'[4] In view of the opinions of Portland and Fitzwilliam quoted earlier, even so restrained an assessment was unduly optimistic.

Sir Gilbert Elliot, among others, later complained that, since there had been no meeting of the Whigs before Parliament opened to decide whether the Address, containing Pitt's Militia proposals, should be opposed or not, the Whig split owed more to a lack of organization than to incompatible political theories.[5] A pamphleteer agreed that Fox's decision to oppose the Address was only mentioned 'to some gentlemen at the gaming table the night before; but this was not known at the time beyond the walls of Brooks's.'[6] In fact, however, there was a meeting of Whig Lords on 12 December 1792, the day before Parliament was due to meet, when it was decided to allow the Address to pass without opposition. Difficulties only arose when Fox arrived at 12.30 a.m, when most of the grandees had already gone home, and announced that he intended to move amendments. When informed of the decision of the meeting, he told Lord Malmesbury that 'He disapproved it highly, and on our telling him our determination, he said he should certainly advise another line of conduct in the House of Commons, and on my remonstrating, he with an oath declared that there was no address at this moment Pitt could frame, he would not propose an amendment to, and divide the House upon.'[7] Unknown to most of its members therefore, the Whig party approached the opening of the new Session with two totally uncoordinated policies.

[1] Dr. Lawrence to E. Burke, 8 Dec. 1792; Wentworth Woodhouse Muniments, Burke 1.

[2] P. R. O. Chatham MSS. 30/8. 153, f. 87; Loughborough to Pitt, 9 Dec. 1792.

[3] Diary of Lord Malmesbury, 11 Dec. 1792; *Diaries and Corres. of Ld. Malmesbury*, ii. 473.

[4] Add. MS. 47570, f. 191; Fox to Mrs. Armistead, 11 Dec. 1792.

[5] Sir G. Elliot to Lady Elliot, 13 Dec. 1792; Lady Minto, *Life and Letters of Ld. Minto*, ii. 79.

[6] Anon. *Observations on the Conduct of Mr. Fox by a Suffolk Freeholder*, p. 12.

[7] Diary of Lord Malmesbury, 12 Dec. 1792; *Diaries and Corres. of Ld. Malmesbury*, ii. 475.

Fox's speech, on 13 December 1792, was therefore directly related to his statement of faith given at the Whig Club nine days earlier. Together they represented an attempt to impress upon the Whig party as a whole a restatement of what Fox took to be their traditional creed. In moving an amendment to the Address, Fox tried again to set Pitt's actions within a recognizable context. The insurrection thesis, on which Pitt had based his proposals, was merely the pretext, according to Fox, for allowing him to achieve his long cherished design of surrendering the authority of the Commons into the hands of the executive: 'Now this, Sir, is the crisis, which I think so truly alarming. We are come to the moment, when the question is, whether we shall give to the king, that is, to the executive government, complete power over our thoughts.'[1] The Minister was deliberately driving politics into extremes, in order that 'the middle order' of men among whom Fox included himself, should be reduced to powerlessness. Once this was done, the Crown could then override popular liberties by posing as the only safeguard against supposedly democratic insurrections. Such a tactic, according to Fox, should not cause any true Whig surprise. Ever since 1783, Pitt's sole aim had been to denigrate the authority of the Commons:

> It was not merely at the outset of their career, when they stood up against the declared voice of the House of Commons, that this spirit was manifested, but uniformly and progressively throughout their whole ministry the same disposition has been shewn. . . . Is it not wonderful, Sir, that all the true constitutional watchfulness of England should be dead to the only real danger that the present day exhibits, and that they should be alone roused by the idiotic clamour of republican phrenzy & of popular insurrection, which do not exist [2]

According to Fox therefore, the crusade undertaken by the Whigs in 1783 was still entirely relevant. The French Revolution had simply given Pitt a more plausible excuse to effect what he had always hoped to do. Fox took his stand on the attitudes adopted in 1784, and refused to accept that anything, which had occurred since that time, made any revaluation of political principles necessary. The fact that his amendment was lost by 290–50 suggests, however, that this kind of appeal to the battles of 1782–4 was at last forced to yield before the fear of revolution.

Before this debate, Fox had been quite hopeful of holding the party together by parading familiar slogans.[3] The actual division came as a considerable shock, suggesting to him for the first time how far the discussion of politics had moved onto new issues. He told Mrs.

[1] *Fox Speeches*, iv. 444; 13 Dec. 1792.
[2] ibid. iv. 462; 13 Dec. 1792.
[3] Add. MS. 47570, f. 193; Fox to Mrs. Armistead, 13 Dec. 1792.

Armistead that 'Our division as you will have seen in the papers was miserable, I expected it bad, but not quite *so* bad. It is good thing and a great comfort to me that the danger of separation from those I regard is much lessened, but when I have said this, I have no more good to say. War I think inevitable, and the rage against the French & what they call Republicans is such that the King is at this moment quite master of the country . . . but it does not signify as long as one is satisfied that one is doing right, and I am quite so.'[1] Confidence in the correctness of his own views could, however, hardly compensate Fox for the acknowledged fact that he had lost the intellectual control of the party. The speeches at the Whig Club and in Parliament had laid before the party a reading of the constitution, based on the experiences of 1782–4, which had been decisively rejected. All contact with such people as Fitzwilliam had not been lost,[2] but Fox could no longer dictate theory. Whig politics now turned on how far Fox was prepared to compromise, in order to retain some kind of authority over the party as a whole.

Initially, there was no question of Fox moderating his tone. He was determined to continue with his personal initiative, which was aimed at impressing upon the party the need for keeping up opposition. On 15 December, he moved a motion in the Commons, which asked that an ambassador be sent to France, in order to try to avert the threat of war by the processes of negotiation. Fox argued reasonably that, if war was to be avoided, the Minister would have to negotiate with the *de facto* government of France, and that it was absurd to refuse such a meeting simply because the French lived under a régime with the title of republic.[3] This speech invited the Whigs to take a further step away from Pitt's position. Hitherto, Fox had only challenged Pitt on his analysis of domestic affairs. Now he was proposing to treat with a régime, which, in a month, would execute a king. This motion was negatived without being brought to a division. The Whig party, led step by step by Fox in his three public speeches in the first two weeks of December, could go no further.

The defence of Fox's actions was written by Robert Adair in two pamphlets, one of which was published in 1795 and the other in 1802. According to the orthodox version, Fox believed that, unless he personally intervened in politics in December 1792, the Whig party would inevitably slide into association with Pitt. The speeches of this month represented a last opportunity of saving the integrity of the Whig party. Pitt, Fox believed, was deliberately fomenting popular hysteria, by describing dangers which he knew to be entirely

[1] Add. MS. 47570, f. 195; Fox to Mrs. Armistead, 15 Dec. 1792.
[2] Fitzwilliam to Lady Fitzwilliam, *c.* 15 Dec. 1792; Milton MSS. Box 44.
[3] *Fox's Speeches*, iv. 473; 15 Dec. 1792.

imaginary, solely in order to confirm his own position in government. Popular liberties were to be the principal victims of this campaign. As Adair pointed out, in 1802, 'Popular liberty was discredited as a resource, and disavowed as a principle of our constitution.'[1] As part of his strategy, the Minister was prepared to countenance a wholly unnecessary war. Fox was from the start anxious to establish the motives prompting the proposed intervention in French affairs.[2] If Pitt was moved solely by the apprehension that the French threatened the Low Countries, his refusal to negotiate was curious. Rejecting this idea therefore, Fox concluded that the Ministers had decided to intervene in French affairs with the sole purpose of restoring the Bourbons, and this he conceived to be indefensible. This conviction was strengthened by the Minister's declared refusal to negotiate with a republican régime. When this proved unavoidable in 1802, Adair could not forego the pleasure of pointing out to his readers that, 'It will be seen that by whatever title the peace of Amiens may claim to be distinguished, Ministers to obtain it, have been obliged to walk in the very steps Mr. Fox recommended to their predecessors.'[3] Fox's abandoning of a policy of moderation, in December 1792, was therefore directly prompted by the belief that, unless he acted quickly, Pitt would use popular hysteria to undermine the basis of English liberty, and to persuade English armies to assist in the restoration of a despotic dynasty.

It was this speech of 15 December, which most seriously compromised Fox in the eyes of the political world. By appealing for negotiations with a *de facto* régime, it could be too easily asserted that Fox was also countenancing the principles, on which that régime stood. As a Pittite pamphleteer shrieked; 'Negotiate! with whom?—The unhappy King was immured—and had neither will, nor power—to negotiate with his jailors was beneath the dignity of the wearer of the British diadem. Where then—or with whom should or could we negotiate? . . . If anarchic principles agitate, we should not only despise, but punish.'[4] Several leading Whigs dated their political separation from Fox from the delivery of this speech. Malmesbury reported that, 'The cry against him out of doors was excessive, and his friends were hurt beyond measure.'[5] Lord Spencer took the same view, in writing to his mother two days later: 'Our party which has

[1] R. Adair, *Fox's Letter to the Electors of Westminster and its Application to Subsequent Events*, p. 9.

[2] Adair, *A Whig's Apology for his Consistency*, p. 41.

[3] *Fox's Letter . . . Events*, p. 83 seq.

[4] Anon, *The Letter of the Rt. Hon. C. J. Fox to the Electors of Westminster Anatomized*, p. 8.

[5] Diary of Lord Malmesbury, 16 Dec. 1792; *Diaries and Corres. of Ld. Malmesbury*, ii. 475–6.

acted together for so long in so many trying and difficult occasions is broken up in a very extraordinary manner all on a sudden.'[1] A special dinner party was called together at Burlington House on the day after Fox's speech, specifically to consider its implications for the Whig party as a whole. According to Malmesbury, Gilbert Elliot, among others, took the view that Fox's action had effectively severed him from the main body of English Whigs, and the Duke of Portland was so 'benumbed and paralysed', that he could not answer this assertion.[2] Hitherto, the Duke had always been able to fall back on the argument that in fact the only disruptive element within the party was Burke, and that Fox's conduct could in no way justify suspicion of his general principles. After 15 December, this comforting reflection was denied him.

Even so sanguine a politician as Fox was left in very little doubt that the attempt to impress his personal authority on the Whig party had failed. Lord Charlemont was told by a correspondent that 'You probably have been much surprized at some of the movements here during these last ten days. C. Fox, as I told you he would, set off at a very smart pace towards republicanism; but, finding the whole people of England against him, has become somewhat more moderate.'[3] Acting on a promise given to Portland, Fox had no choice but to back down, if he was to salvage anything of his standing within the Whig party. On 17 December, he clarified his terms of reference for the benefit of the Commons: 'As those who had read Italian operas might recollect to have seen prefixed an advertizement by the author, that when he introduced the names of heathen gods and goddesses he meant nothing against the holy catholic religion; so he must advertize the House, that when he made use of the words liberty, equality, impartiality, he used them only in the true sense of the British Constitution, and not as understood . . . in any other country whatsoever.'[4] Three days later, he went out of his way to call the trial of Louis XVI unjust and pusillanimous.[5] As a further demonstration of his reliability, Fox went so far as to join the Loyalist Association of St. George's parish, Westminster, although, according to Fanny Burney, he did so with a very ill grace.[6] In order to balance his position, he joined the Society of the Friends of the Liberty of the Press at the

[1] Spencer to Dowager Countess Spencer, 17 Dec. 1792; Althorp MSS. See also Brit. Mus. Egerton MS. 3262, f. 173; Hertford to Beauchamp, 18 Dec. 1792.

[2] Diary of Lord Malmesbury, 16 Dec. 1792; *Diaries and Corres. of Ld Malmesbury*, ii. 476–8.

[3] E. Malone to Charlemont, 22 Dec. 1792; H.M.C. *Charlemont*, ii. 209.

[4] *Fox Speeches*, iv. 478; 17 Dec. 1792.

[5] ibid. iv. 481; 20 Dec. 1792.

[6] Miss F. Burney to Mrs. Lock, 20 Dec. 1792; Dobson, *Diary and Letters of Madam D'Arblay*, v. 160.

same time.[1] By such selfconscious attempts to allay conservative Whig fears, Fox still hoped to keep the Whigs together. He told Mrs. Armistead that '. . . the Cry was very great against me & so I fear continues. . . . But the Cry be it as loud as it will does not make me feel a tenth part of the uneasiness that I suffer and have suffered from the apprehension of separating from the D. of P. & Ld. Fitz., which I hope will not happen: indeed I think it will not.'[2]

Again, Fox was being too sanguine. His conduct in the first three weeks of December had not succeeded in re-establishing his position among the Whigs. His tortuous changes of front had not inspired confidence so much as bewilderment. On 24 December, Fox protested in the House of Commons about the dismissal of two army officers for subscribing to a fund designed to help the French.[3] On the next day, he was reported to be addressing a Loyalist meeting in Westminster.[4] Lord Auckland was told that, by these tergiversations, Fox 'has brought a contempt on himself that he will not soon get rid of'.[4] A leading member of Whig society in Hertfordshire had to write to Adam to point out that the Foxite case was going by default in his county, because no one could be quite sure what Fox's exact views were. In fact, Fox was now in an extremely precarious position. The attempt to bring the Whig party round by the exercise of personal authority had failed. A return to the moderate and neutral position of the summer was now equally hollow and suspect. As Lauderdale told Fox's nephew, Fox now had to commit himself:

> If . . . Mr. Fox thinks in such a half way, if he is neither for the broad idea of public government, nor for the Court, if he really thinks it the People's interest to have the Court opposed by a union of moderate Men—he can never expect to find that union as he [is] now almost single in his opinions & he can hardly hope to convert even with his abilities a sufficient number to make the vigorous exertions he hopes for. In this situation then, says Ld. L—, there is one of these measures to be taken—to retire to St. Anne's Hill—or to join what he thinks the best of two bad parties.[5]

The indecisive behaviour of December suggests that Fox was still unhappy about making such an irrevocable decision.

Fox hesitated, because he was not yet sure that he had lost control of the Duke of Portland's political thinking. If this influence remained, it could be plausibly argued that the Whig party was still one. Malmesbury, Windham and Elliot, very aware that this link was the crucial

[1] E. Burke, *Observations on the Conduct of the Minority*, p. 307; 18 Dec. 1792.

[2] Add. MS. 47570, f. 197; Fox to Mrs. Armistead, 18 Dec. 1792.

[3] *Parl. Hist.* xxx. 170; 24 Dec. 1792.

[4] Archbishop of Canterbury to Auckland, 25 Dec. 1792; *Journal and Corres. of Ld. Auckland*, ii. 475.

[5] Add. MS. 51731, f. 100; Holland to Caroline Fox, 25 Dec. 1792.

one, called on Portland, on 24 December, as an accredited delegation representing a considerable proportion of Whig M.P.s. Arguing that Fox's actions since the beginning of the month had to be publicly disavowed, they extracted from Portland the firm promise that he would come forward openly, during the debate on the Aliens Bill on 26 December.[1] A day later, he had to write to Loughborough, in order to explain why he had found it impossible to do this: 'It is a direct renunciation & denunciation of Mr. Fox, to which I can not in conscience accede; it binds to an unqualified & unconditional support of the present Administration, against which I enter my most decided protest.'[2] Malmesbury was undeceived about Portland's vacillation. He had not spoken out because 'Fox is his vampire—he fascinates him, benumbs the operation of his reason & judgment & even of his conscience—nothing has been left untryed—lenient medicines have been hitherto given, but he must now come to Hard physick.'[3] While such a situation obtained, Fox was naturally reluctant to take Lauderdale's suggestion of final commitment to the Associators seriously. If Portland himself could be held, the union of the representatives of wealth and intellect would indisputably allow them to claim that they were in fact the true guardians of the Whig creed, from which Burke and his friends were simply apostates.

In order to break out of this dilemma, Sir Gilbert Elliot took the initiative into his own hands, and declared in the House of Commons, on 28 December, that he had the Duke's express commission to announce Portland's disassociation from the policies of Fox. Fox himself refused to believe this possible.[4] He told Mrs. Armistead that 'The D. of P. has been quoted I hope and believe incorrectly by Sir G. Elliot, and in a way so hostile to me that I can not bear it . . . I can not help loving the D. of P., and if with him the D. of D. & Ld. Fi are to go I never can have any comfort in Politics again.'[5] Both Elliot and Fox hurried to Burlington House that same evening to lobby the Duke personally. Portland, whose agitation was extreme, attempted to square the political circle by saying that, although he had never promised to break with Fox, he was not at all unwilling to support the Minister's present measures.[6] The only result of this equivocation was that both Fox and Elliot went away believing that

[1] Diary of Lord Malmesbury, 24 Dec. 1792; *Diaries and Corres. of Ld. Malmesbury*, ii. 482–7. See also Sir G. Elliot to Lady Elliot, 23 Dec. 1792; Lady Minto, *Life and Letters of Ld. Minto*, ii. 92.

[2] Portland to Loughborough, 27 Dec. 1792; Portland MSS. PWF 9231.

[3] Add. MS. 28067, f. 98; Malmesbury to Leeds, 29 Dec. 1792.

[4] *Fox Speeches*, v. 1 seq.; 28 Dec. 1792.

[5] Add. MS. 47570, f. 199; Fox to Mrs. Armistead, 28 Dec. 1792.

[6] Diary of Lord Malmesbury, 28 Dec. 1792; *Diaries and Corres. of Ld. Malmesbury*, ii. 491–4.

the Duke had decided in their favour.[1] The Elliot initiative, so far from bringing Portland to a decision, had simply made the situation even more muddled. But when the Duke had had time to collect his thoughts, it was clear that the influence of Fox upon his thinking was still strong. He told Fitzwilliam that he had 'expressed great averseness from doing any thing that could be considered hostile to Fox, whose difference, though I most sincerely lamented, I could not attribute to any bad motive or intention injurious to the welfare of the country.'[2]

The final act in this rather confused tragedy took place in the House of Commons three days later. Elliot read out a statement, which had previously been agreed to by Portland, announcing the Duke's intention to allow the Ministers his full support. Immediately after, Lord Titchfield, Portland's son, rose to make such a blistering attack on Pitt, that the effect of Elliot's speech was entirely lost.[3] Elliot, unaware that Fox had visited Burlington House again after his own statement had been agreed upon, was predictably infuriated by this change of front. Titchfield's speech was the direct result of Fox's second visit, but unfortunately the Duke had omitted to countermand Elliot's assertions. The result was that both were presented to the Commons, and, since the Foxite version of the Duke's attitudes were expressed through the mouthpiece of his son, it was duly taken to be the more authoritative. To achieve this success with Portland, Fox had had to call on all the old themes. Elliot's initiative was represented as a totally unwarranted attempt to compel Portland to commit himself against Fox, and to force a breach between the two men. As a counter-measure, Fox had to demand an explicit denial of the trend of Elliot's arguments. Giving support to individual measures had always been allowed, but Fox insisted that Lord Titchfield's speech should make it clear that, in general terms, a consistent opposition would be kept up. Fox told the Duke that he had no choice but 'to press you by every consideration both of friendship to me, and regard to yourself as well ... as ... for the preservation of the Whig party, to think justly of the importance of this day, to see the necessity of being completely explicit.'[4] Titchfield's performance on 31 December duly came up to Fox's expectations.

Superficially therefore, it seemed that the power of Fox's personality had once again been able to support that relationship with Portland,

[1] Sir G. Elliot to Lady Elliot, 29 Dec. 1792; Lady Minto, *Life and Letters of Ld. Minto*, i. 96.

[2] Portland to Fitzwilliam, 29 Dec. 1792; Wentworth Woodhouse Muniments, F.31.a.

[3] Diary of Lord Malmesbury, 31 Dec. 1792; *Diaries and Corres. of Ld. Malmesbury*, ii. 494–5.

[4] Add. MS. 47561, f. 136; Fox to Portland, 31 Dec. 1792.

upon which the unity of the Whig party depended. Country Whigs, inquiring after the true state of politics in London, were confidently referred to Titchfield's speech. At a meeting at Lord Loughborough's on 3 January, Elliot and his friends had to concede that nothing further could be done to influence Portland's attitudes before Parliament adjourned on 9 January.[1] Fox himself was reasonably satisfied that all immediate danger of disunity had disappeared. He told Mrs. Armistead; 'Lord Titchfield spoke out very distinctly and as favourably to me as I could wish & I have no doubt but that Burke and Pitt are as much discontented as what he said as you could wish them. Thus the evil of the separation is at least put off & the chapter of accidents may prevent it entirely . . . I am as well pleased as the circumstances of the present time will allow me to be.'[2] His nephew agreed wholeheartedly: 'As to the party The Duke of Po. etc etc seem more inclined to my Unc. than they were & He is still in hopes in a reunion thorough & satisfactory.'[3] The choice of the word 'reunion' is not without significance, in that it implies that some breach had already taken place, but the overall air of confidence is well in keeping with Fox's own attitude.

This optimism was entirely misplaced. The events of December 1792 had shaken the Whigs badly. Loughborough's acceptance of the Great Seal, in January 1793, confirmed the fear that Ministerial offers to individual Whigs would continue,[4] and the atmosphere within the Whig ranks was such, that there was every chance that they would be taken up. Similarly, Fox's views on France might be tolerated by Portland, but they were still very far from winning acceptance. After the publication by the French Assembly of the Decree of 19 November, promising assistance to revolutionary movements in other countries, Fox's insistence that England was in no danger sounded a little hollow.[5] The French ambassador's sophistries on this point in no way made Fox's position easier.[6] Although the official Whig leadership had remained firm therefore, George III was delighted to notice that, in terms of votes at least, the Whig party had already fragmented into three parts.[7] Further, the blame for the creation of party divisions had shifted from Burke to Fox. As one Whig lady observed: 'I

[1] Diary of Lord Malmesbury, 3 Jan. 1793; *Diaries and Corres. of Ld. Malmesbury*, ii. 497–8.

[2] Add. MS. 47570, f. 201; Fox to Mrs. Armistead, 31 Dec. 1792.

[3] Add. MS. 51731, f. 104; Holland to Caroline Fox, 5 Jan. 1793.

[4] ? to F. Ponsonby, Jan 1793; Hickleton MSS. A.1.3, f. 161.

[5] *Fox Speeches*, v. 6; 4 Jan. 1793.

[6] Chauvelin to Grenville, 27 Dec. 1792; *Papers Presented to Parliament 1789–1792*, p. 16.

[7] George III to W. Pitt, 22 Jan. 1793; Aspinall, *The Later Corres. of George III*, ii. 148.

think the world is gone mad. I know that Mr. Fox is often indiscreet but I never thought he could have gone such lengths how a person of his Abilities can have such ideas in such times is inconceivable . . .'[1] More bluntly, Lord Carlisle believed that, having failed to control the Associators, he was now in the process of losing his right wing, and that 'between the two stools he had an unlucky tumble'.[2] Against this kind of criticism, Fox had to consider whether even his close co-operation with Portland would be enough to prevent the Whig party from flying apart.

This consideration became even more pressing, when the pamphlet war of interpretations about the events of December demonstrated just how embittered the political atmosphere had become. As the audience for his vindication, Fox again chose the electors of Westminster. His opposition to the Address was grounded entirely on the opinion that, before large areas of English liberty were surrendered by Parliament, the Ministers should show good reasons why this should be necessary. Similarly, before Pitt was allowed to plunge England into war with France, it was essential to explore every possibility of settling the matter by negotiation, if only because such a course would at least clarify the issues, and make explicit what the purpose of the war actually was.[3] Basically, Fox was calling for more evidence that an offensive against Jacobinism both at home and abroad was in fact necessary. A rational discussion of such topics was, however, hardly in fashion.

By way of reply, one pamphleteer gave a graphic description of the revolution which had been prepared by French agents in London, and which had been planned for 1 December.[4] Another insisted that Fox was himself implicated in the projected uprising, which he had planned in daily conversations with the French Ambassador, Chauvelin.[5] Even the most rational of Fox's opponents had to conclude that, although the Jacobin threat had been gravely overstated, the political situation in England was so open to manipulation by a handful of determined men, that Pitt's measures had to be accepted.[6] As

[1] Lady E. Ponsonby to Lady L. Ponsonby, 2 Jan. 1793; Hickleton MSS. A.1.2.1, f. 50.

[2] Testament of Lord Carlisle; H.M.C. *Carlisle MSS.* xv. 5.6, p. 702.

[3] C. J. Fox, *A Letter from the Rt. Hon. C. J. Fox to the Worthy and Independent Electors of Westminster.*

[4] Anon. *Remarks on a Pamphlet . . . on the Nature and Causes of the Present War.*

[5] Anon. *A Letter from an Independent Elector of Westminster to the Rt. Hon. Charles James Fox.*

[6] Anon. *A Letter to the Rt. Hon. C. J. Fox in which is Proved the Absolute Necessity of an Immediate Declaration of War Against France.*

this last pamphleteer observed, politics had moved irrevocably into extremes:

On one side are displayed the banners of democracy, under which are arranged the pertinacious sectaries of the new philosophy, the deluded visionaries of equality, the enemies of all constituted authorities: on the other side is erected the standard of loyalty and of honour, around which are rallied the lovers of order and peace . . . Who can hesitate on what side to place himself?[1]

Unfortunately, Fox could not bring himself to believe that this was the essential choice. He continued to qualify and rationalize at a time when fear was reducing politics to a simple exchange of slogans.

In effect, Fox's reliance on the prestige of Portland's name as a unifying force was misplaced. The events of December had taken the initiative out of the hands of the party leadership. By the end of the month, as one Scottish Whig told Windham, 'that which was a Party seems to be typified by the Legs of an Isle of Man halfpenny all standing different ways.'[2] All official leadership had in fact disintegrated. After his tergiversations in Parliament, Portland had fled to Bulstrode for the express purpose of avoiding the necessity of making any more decisions between his friends.[3] Individuals and groups of Whigs were left to take their own decisions without interference. At a meeting at Windham's, on 10 February 1793, twenty-one Whig members of Parliament decided to offer the Ministry their unequivocal support, and such spontaneity was unavoidable in a situation, in which, as Windham himself put it, '. . . We all find ourselves now acting without a leader and with no other concert than that which we have been able to make out amongst ourselves. The only meetings therefore of the party that have taken place on our side have been at my house. Much against my will I have been obliged to act as a sort of head of a party.'[4] Throughout January and February, individual Whigs like Malmesbury and the Prince of Wales sought interviews with Pitt, in order to assure him of their support.[5] Portland had neither the desire nor the ability to act any longer as the linking mechanism between Fox and the Whig right wing. Events had removed them beyond his control. There was less a sudden breakdown in Whig unity, than a slow disintegration by unchecked attrition.

[1] *A Letter . . . War Against France*, p. 39.

[2] Add. MS. 37873, f. 203; ? to W. Windham, 20 Feb. 1793.

[3] Loughborough to E. Burke, 19 Jan. 1793; Wentworth Woodhouse Muniments, Burke 1.

[4] Butterfield, 'Charles James Fox and the Whig Opposition in 1792', *C.H.J.* ix (1949), 329–30.

[5] Grenville to Buckingham, 19 Jan. 1793; Duke of Buckingham & Chandos, ii. 236.

In separating from Fox, the right wing entertained a variety of feelings. For Malmesbury, it was a matter which provoked deep regret: 'It grieves me to separate from him; it grieves me still more to see how completely he has set the whole country against him, and how far he has driven himself from a probability of holding a high office in it.'[1] By contrast Sir Gilbert Elliot, believing the disintegration of the party to be Fox's fault, took a more hard-headed line. Fox's conduct was daily becoming more unbridled and dangerous, requiring all the upholders of order to disavow his principles immediately.[2] Certain Whig ladies took a similar view: 'Fox has entirely ruined his party & at a time when there might have been a better prospect than ever I have always thought that there is not in the world so disgusting an employment as that of a politician to an Honest man.'[3] According to Foxite orthodoxy, the apostasy of the Whig right wing was entirely motivated by malice,[4] but such as interpretation cannot really be substantiated, apart from one delighted exclamation from Windham, that Fox had now put himself so far outside the accepted political pale, that only a revolution could make him minister.[5] In general, apostasy was undertaken with regret, and only considered because the pressure of events was now so great, that Fox's idiosyncratic behaviour could no longer be supported. The right wing deserted, not as an affronted bloc, but in a trickle of harassed and nervous individuals.

At the centre of the party was a large body of neutral opinion, which, although unable to approve of Fox's conduct, could not yet bring itself to follow this argument through to its logical conclusion by joining Pitt. This paralysing reluctance to abandon Fox finally was rationalized in a number of ways. Lord John Cavendish determined to believe that Fox's principles were sound, and that he had simply fallen temporarily under malign influences; 'C. Fox has suffered himself to be led too far one way by some hotheaded people, whom I believe He thought he could lead, & has suffered himself to be led by them.'[6] Lord Spencer took a similar view in a letter to his mother, which was full of convinced uncertainty: 'I continue to have

[1] Malmesbury to Portland, 16 Jan. 1793; *Diaries and Corres. of Ld. Malmesbury*, ii. 499–501. See also Malmesbury to Lady Palmerston, 3 May 1793; Malmesbury MSS. Box 3.

[2] Sir G. Elliot to Malmesbury, 27 Jan. 1793; *Diaries and Corres. of Ld. Malmesbury*, ii. 504–6.

[3] Lady E. Ponsonby to Lady L. Ponsonby, 1 Mar. 1793; Hickleton MSS. A. 1.2, f. 1.

[4] Adair, *A Whig's Apology for his Consistency*, p. 110.

[5] W. Windham to J. Hippisley, Mar. 1793; Benjamin, *The Windham Papers*, i. 115.

[6] Lord J. Cavendish to Miss Ponsonby, 26 Jan. 1793; Grey MSS.

the greatest opinion of Mr. Fox's integrity & well-meaning, & his Letter to the Electors of Westminster . . . is a very good justification (in my Opinion) of his Conduct, but I lament to see him so much united to a set of violent People who hold opinions & I am afraid have intentions which they would not like to avow, & which I think I am sure he could not support.'[1] Alternatively, if Fox's conduct was thought to be too outrageous, there was refuge in the idea that Pitt was worse. As a Whig lord told Portland, 'Oh what a moment for Mr. Fox, yet I fear the voice of the Kingdom is against him. If the words put into his mouth be true, I know not what to think. Push me against the wall and ask me whether I am a republican or a Royalist, I say a republican. Whether I prefer Thomas Paine or Pitt, I say Thomas Paine.'[2] Any suggestion that they should actually accept office under Pitt, as Loughborough had done, was always rebutted with horror by members of this middle, neutral group.[3]

By far the most popular argument employed, however, to justify inactivity, was that the issue of the war was the only point of difference, and that this would soon be resolved. It was merely a question therefore of waiting, with studied neutrality, until the resolution of the war problem should make the prospect of a reunion possible.[4] Meanwhile, a distinction could be made between Fox as a man, and Fox as a statesman holding views which were temporarily unacceptable. Mrs. Crewe, whose social arrangements were being gravely disrupted by political divisions, was particularly anxious to establish this point: 'I asked Ldy P. last night how Ch. F. stood with the Corps diplomatique & if they would feel awkward with him in Company . . . I feel sure, however, from all she said, that there can be *no danger* in their meeting Ch. F. as *an Individual*.'[5] As the Whig party simply drifted and fragmented after December 1792, intellectual surrogates were understandably produced by a large group of people, who found themselves uncomfortably caught between a fear of Fox's views on the Revolution and a profound and ingrained distaste for in any way appearing to countenance Pittite politics.

The position of this group, under the titular leadership of Portland and Fitzwilliam, became increasingly incongruous. Against all existing precedent, they were being driven away from Fox and towards

[1] Spencer to Dowager Lady Spencer, 31 Jan. 1793; Spencer MSS.

[2] Bute to Portland, 20 Jan. 1793; Portland MSS. PWF 8619.

[3] Add. Ms. 42058 (Grenville Papers), f. 117; T. Grenville to W. Windham, 10 Feb. 1793. See also Spencer to Dowager Lady Spencer, 18 June 1793; Spencer MSS.

[4] Memoranda of Lord Upper Ossory; *Letters Addressed to the Countess of Upper Ossory*, ii. 97. See also Lady E. Ponsonby to Lady L. Ponsonby, 19 June 1793; Hickleton MSS. A.1.2.1, f. 36.

[5] Mrs. Crewe to Portland, 19 May 1793; Portland MSS. PWF 3174.

a man, whom they abhored. In this respect, the resilience of the experiences of 1782–4 in moulding opinions is astonishing. Under their influences, highly conservative and unimaginative men, enormously disturbed by the events in France, still held back from openly joining Pitt even though his party was rapidly taking on the mantle of the accredited guarantors of order. As Fitzwilliam observed, full-co-operation was impossible, 'when they cannot approve either the mode by which such a system has been introduc'd, or the principles of the persons, who so introduced them; but still thinking the measure right will support the naked measure, engaging for nothing further.'[1] Robert Adair and other prominent Foxites kept up the pressure on these two leading grandees. The problem was traced 'to the unconstitutional advice given his Majesty in the year 1784 . . . We can give no confidence to Men who entered into Office in direct Violation of the constitution, and in the Spirit of Violation, rendered peculiarly dangerous by its co-incidence & affinity with those wide doctrines which threaten the subversion of all regular Government in the World.'[2] Another prominent neutral, Lord John Cavendish, explained that, 'with the temper & disposition of Pitt & the Systems & Schemes of the K. & his friends, it is not possible for any man who has the feelings of a Gentleman to continue for any time to act with them.'[3] Individual ministerial measures could be supported, but there was no question of any formal arrangement. Even after the execution of Louis XVI, the attitudes formed in 1782 had not been entirely overlaid by fear of revolution.

This vacillation between Fox and Pitt largely resulted in an unwillingness to take any decisions and a mere waiting upon events. Fitzwilliam believed that there was nothing to be done, except to allow the party to drift and 'to hope for better times.'[4] There was no question any longer of trying to keep all sections of the Whig party together. By way of explanation for this inactivity, Portland was reduced to arguing that no real change could be observed in Fox's basic attitudes:

In the very many conversations I have had with the principal person to whom I imagine Your Royal Highness to allude, I have not observed any such difference as should seem to me to preclude a rejunction, or to render it not desirable. I certainly very much lament his conduct at the opening of the Session and the time he chose for recommending a negotiation to be entered into with France, and yet I am sure that that conduct could only be dictated by the purest motives and that in a cooler moment the expediency of the

[1] Fitzwilliam to Lady Rockingham, 28 Feb. 1793; Wentworth Woodhouse Muniments, R.164.

[2] R. Adair to Portland, 7 Feb. 1793; Portland MSS. PWF 33a.

[3] Lord J. Cavendish to Lady Ponsonby, 4 Apr. 1793; Grey MSS.

[4] Fitzwilliam to Lady Rockingham, 28 Feb. 1793; Wentworth Woodhouse Muniments, R.164.

Measure which in particular gave so much offence, may not only be admitted but approved.[1]

The confusion created by this ambivalent position was enormous. After the resignation of many of the Duke's friends from the Whig Club, in February, no one quite knew whether Portland himself remained a member or not.[2] Similarly, after calling a special meeting to concert opposition to the Traitorous Correspondence Bill, Portland then proceeded to vote for the measure in the Lords.[3] Torn between distaste of Pitt and distrust of Fox, the official leadership was paralysed. As the party disintegrated, in a piecemeal manner, the initiative from Portland, which might possibly have checked this development, was not forthcoming.

Unfortunately for Portland and Fitzwilliam, decisions could not be avoided. The Whig Club was an early victim of Portland's indecision. In January, Portland first sanctioned a vote of thanks to Fox for the speech of 4 December,[4] and then opposed the whole idea three days later.[5] Similarly, for the meeting in February 1793, Portland was reduced to asking for what, in political terms, had become almost an impossibility: 'It w^{d} be much more agreeable to me could such a Resolution be formed as w^{d} express the good opinion & attachment of the Club to Fox without intimating or insinuating any disapprobation or even doubt of the propriety of the conduct wch other of our Friends & myself have thought it necessary to pursue for the safety of the Constitution & the Kingdom in gen'.[6] When, at the meeting of 20 February, a large number of Portland's friends resigned from the Club, it was not clear what the Duke's standing was, and he was unwilling to clarify the situation. Such clarifications always implied that another body of Whig opinion would be affronted. When, after February 1793, the Whig Club became an exclusively Foxite organ, the Duke was unable either to applaud or condemn. Until fear could overcome their distaste for Pitt, neutrals like Portland could only temporize in the hope that matters would gradually improve.

After the failure of his personal initiative in December, Fox was as free as any other member of the Whig party to define his own line of action. In essentials, his thinking on French affairs had not changed a great deal. The execution of Louis XVI led him to exclaim, 'How

[1] Portland to Prince of Wales, 31 Jan. 1793; Barnes, *George III and William Pitt*, p. 260.

[2] Sergeant Adair to Portland, 3 Mar. 1793; Portland MSS. PWF 18.

[3] Spencer to Dowager Lady Spencer, 23 Apr. 1793; Spencer MSS.

[4] W. Adam to Portland, 14 Jan. 1793; Portland MSS. PWF 45.

[5] Portland to Fitzwilliam, 17 Jan. 1793; Wentworth Woodhouse Muniments, F.31.a.

[6] Portland to Sergeant Adair, 17 Feb. 1793; Portland MSS. PWF 15.

miserably have those Frenchmen by their wild extravagance & unfeeling cruelty stained the noblest cause that ever was in the hands of Men',[1] but he immediately comforted himself with the thought that the behaviour of the Austrian and Prussian armies had been worse. As he observed to his nephew 'I do not know whether there is not some comfort in seeing, that while the French are doing all in their power to make the name of liberty odious to the world, the despots are conducting themselves so as to show that tyrrany is worse.'[2] There had therefore been no advance on the position he had taken up after the September Massacres. The social and political cost of holding such views, however, had risen considerably. At the Literary Club, Fox was systematically snubbed by bishops and politicians alike.[3] The weight of this isolation led Fox to think seriously of abandoning politics completely, and, according to his nephew, the first steps in this direction had been taken.[4] Unfortunately, such a retirement was not yet really feasible. The question of a French war was now imminent, and Fox was inevitably faced with the task of leading the opposition to Pitt's proposals.

In February 1793, Fox could not believe that a war with France was either necessary or inevitable. For him, the war was the final stage in a campaign to found an extension of executive power on mounting hysteria. To the historian Francis Hargrave, Fox compared the war scare to the Popish Plot.[5] Both were designed to provide an excuse for an assault on the constitution. Pitt was cast as the willing ally of the King in this undertaking: 'Do I think Mr. Pitt a Fool? no—but I think he has for the sake of office surrendered himself up entirely into the hands of the Court than which there can be in no part of Europe any thing more weak in every respect, and what is worse it is a weakness accompanied by the most sure and at the same time the most fatal symptom of Weakness—Rashness.'[6] According to his nephew, Fox again refused to consider an offer of coalition from Pitt at this time.[7] The war therefore, like all continental developments since 1789, was considered entirely from an English standpoint. English political ideas are freely transported onto the Continent, and European affairs are only observed in so far as they could affect domestic politics. Fox's insular assessment of French affairs had led him into misunderstandings before, and it now prompted him

[1] Add. MSS. 51467, f. 29; Fox to D. O'Brien, 23 Jan. (1793?).

[2] Fox to Holland, 14 June 1793; Holland, *Memoirs of the Whig Party*, i. 66–7.

[3] Dr. Burney to Miss Burney, 31 Jan. 1793; Dobson, *Diary and Letters of Madame D'Arblay*, v. 168.

[4] Holland, i. 85.

[5] Add. MS. 47568, f. 268; Fox to F. Hargrave, n.d.

[6] Bodleian. North MSS. C.12, f.8; Fox to T. Coutts, 1 Jan. 1806.

[7] Holland, i. 30–1.

to offer an interpretation of the war, which was wildly at odds with the mood of the political nation in general.

His public attitude about the war was announced to the House of Commons in two speeches on 1 and 18 February 1793. Fox refused to admit that the European powers had any right to intervene in the affairs of a sovereign state. Even if the French decided to execute their king, this act, admittedly disagreeable, was still a nationally self-regarding decision: 'He thought the present state of government in France anything rather than an object of imitation; but he maintained as a principle inviolable, that the government of every independent state was to be settled by those who were to live under it, and not by foreign force.'[1] Pitt himself, at this stage, denied that he wished to impose a government on France, but Fox plausibly countered with the argument that, if Pitt refused to negotiate with the republican régime about the Low Countries and other outstanding differences, it implied that ultimately he expected, and was determined to work for, some change of system. The war of 1793 was, therefore, for Fox a deliberately contrived operation, designed to advance the cause of monarchy in England and to stamp out ideas, which were offensive to the absolute rulers of Europe. The forces of monarchy, English and European, were now turned against France. Fox, by opposing George III, believed himself caught up in this much broader conflict. This conviction was confirmed by the fact that, while French incursions into the Low Countries were met with protests and threats, there was not even an expression of regret from Pitt that Poland had just fallen victim to the territorial ambitions of three autocratic rulers.[2] The revolutionaries were, in many respects, not ideal allies, but Fox could not escape the point that, by calling the war a crusade of kings, he had come near to making the cause of the Revolution his own. In private, his language was such as would not have appeared unduly out of place in Paris itself. He told Lord Sheffield[3] that, 'the sovereignty was absolutely in the people; that the monarchy was elective, otherwise the dynasty of Brunswick had no right, & that when a majority of the people [thought] that another kind of government [was] preferable, they undoubtedly had a right to cashier the king.'[4] As the First Coalition generalized the cause of kings in Fox's eyes, so he was forced to associate with strange allies, in order to offer effective resistance.

[1] *Fox Speeches*, v. 14; 1 Feb. 1793.

[2] *Fox Speeches*, v. 38; 18 Feb. 1793.

[3] Sheffield, John Holroyd, 1st Baron (1735–1821); political economist; supported North throughout the period of the American War and the Coalition; broke with Fox over the French Revolution; widely known in English literary circles.

[4] Sheffield to Auckland, 5 Feb. 1793; *Journal of Corres. of Ld. Auckland*, ii. 495.

Between February and June 1793 therefore, as Pitt prepared the legislative base for fighting a major war, Fox, on issue after issue, found himself forced to stand out, with very few supporters, against what he took to be an attempt to subvert English liberties. In doing so, he inevitably had to clarify his position with regard to France, and even more to affront conservative Whig opinion. His attack on Pitt was mounted on both the domestic and foreign fronts. First, he consistently tried to discover what the exact purpose of the war was, and, if possible, to make Pitt admit that it had been undertaken for the sole purpose of imposing a settlement on France.[1] This point was a powerful one by June, when the French defeat at Neerwinden and the defection of Dumouriez effectively removed any immediate threat to Holland. Fox moved a resolution, asking for peace negotiations to be opened as soon as possible, with a rhetorical question: 'Was a dislike of the doctrines of the rights of man to be pushed so far, that the people were to be denied the right of knowing why they were to suffer the expenses and distresses of war?'[2] The only answer Pitt could offer was once again to stress the dangers facing the old order of society. In the climate of apprehension and fear, in which politics were being played out in the summer of 1793, no more explicit explanation of the war was necessary.

In domestic terms, Fox found himself defending traditional liberties against men, who were prepared to surrender them to their fear. Fox, on such issues as the decision to build barracks in large cities, the denial of Muir's and Palmer's rights to appeal against the sentence of transportation to the House of Commons, and the Traitorous Correspondence Bill, tried two lines of approach. He attempted to convince the political nation that they were surrendering fundamental liberties out of unreasoning fear, and, in doing so, were betraying the achievements of their century. Fox 'hoped that the mildness, philanthropy, and liberality for which the eighteenth century had been distinguished, would still remain its characteristics.'[3] By playing on people's fear, Pitt was in danger of leading England back into a new dark age. Secondly, the destruction of so many constitutional safeguards allowed him to appeal to tradition, which, he hoped, might yet have some influence on former Whig minds. He presented petitions for Parliamentary reform on the grounds that this had always been a perfectly acceptable Whig function.[4] Similarly, the creation, in May 1793, of a new class of revenue appointments, all of which were in the gift of the Crown, allowed him to complain

[1] *Fox Speeches*, v. 84; 25 Apr. 1793.
[2] ibid. v. 136; 17 June 1793.
[3] ibid. v. 83; 9 Apr. 1793.
[4] *Parl. Hist.* xxx. 461; 21 Feb. 1793.

'not only of Mr. Burke, but of other gentlemen who had joined him in the vote upon the influence of the crown in the year 1780. It appeared to him to be their duty to attend the discussion of this bill, and to assign their reasons, if they had any for thinking that the influence of the crown ought to be now increased in the manner which it would be if this bill should pass into law.'[1] Such speeches made no impression on Pitt's position. Neither a reasoned discussion of the aims of war, nor an appeal either to the achievements of the eighteenth century or the pure, Whig tradition could overcome the fear of Jacobinism. The difficulty lay in the simple fact that few, besides Fox, saw the danger of the war of 1793 as lying in a union of kings rather than an army of revolutionaries. In the summer of 1793, Fox's attitudes, as enunciated in debate, were decidedly eccentric, and therefore ignored.

These speeches between February and June 1793 established Fox as the leader of English Whiggery. The terms Foxite and Whig had been interchangeable for some time. Now Fox's interpretation of the Whig creed was paramount, not because he had successfully convinced large numbers of people of its value, but because Portland and his friends were on the point of losing their identity in the broad, Pittite Establishment. It was almost impossible to oppose Pitt now without subscribing to Fox's ideas. In these months, Fox won the allegiance of a small but devoted band of adherents, to whom he expounded his political ideas, now unrestrained by considerations of holding the allegiance of the more conservative Whigs. In return, his friends moved a resolution at the Whig Club on 4 June 1793, declaring, 'that it deeply concerns and may effectually promote the Service as well as the Honour of the Nation that the example of disinterestedness held out to the future by Mr. F—'s publick conduct, should not descend to posterity unaccompanied by some evidence of the general impression it has made and the sense which His Country entertains of it.'[2] Gratitude was to be expressed in monetary form, and, on the next day, a committee was formed at a meeting in the Crown and Anchor Tavern, who were to collect funds, in order to relieve Fox of his debts.[3] Within six months, the very considerable sum of £61,402 6*s.* 0*d.*[4] had been collected, with which all Fox's outstanding debts were defrayed, and a life annuity of £2,000 per annum guaranteed.

The collection of this money is of interest, because it gives some indication of Fox's standing in the country. The actual size of the

[1] *Parl. Hist.* xxx. 940; 24 May 1793.
[2] Sergeant Adair to Portland, 4 June 1793; Portland MSS. PWF 20.
[3] *Papers Presented to Parliament* 1789–1796.
[4] Add. MS. 47569, f. 63; Statement of Receipts.

sums collected is astonishing, but so too are some of the contributors. Fitzwilliam,[1] Spencer and Bessborough, men who had ceased to act with Fox politically, contributed generously, for, as Lord Sheffield put it, 'Although I detest his principles I cannot help liking him. I feel a kind of satisfaction at his being relieved yet I am hurt by the kind of degradation which I think he suffers.'[2] Money came either from devoted admirers of Fox like Dr. Parr,[3] or from old friends like Lord Bessborough, who saw the subscription in personal rather than political terms.[4] With one or two outstanding exceptions, however, the subscription was the response of the aristocratic, Whig world only. There is little evidence that Fox enjoyed much popularity at a lower level. One Whig M.P. had to decline a contribution on the grounds that he would stand no chance of being re-elected, if he did subscribe. Fitzwilliam reported a similar state of affairs in Yorkshire.[5] Even so stalwart a Whig as Mrs. Crewe had doubts about the manner in which the subscription was handled: 'Mr. Adam & a few more of Ch. Fox's friends have often pushed things on imprudently & I only hope this may be the last instance we shall have of their intemperance on matters of such *real consequence* to the former supporters of Ch. Fox!'[6] This enormous sum was therefore raised by the enthusiasm of Fox's young supporters, anxious to demonstrate the authority of their oracle, and by the effective appeal to nostalgia, which made Whig Lords pay homage to the past. For some, it was a pledge of future loyalty, for others a severance payment. Even so, so large a sum was not an unreasonable estimate of Fox's past and future value to the Whig party as a whole.

As the new session of Parliament approached, in December 1793, it was very clear that the whole balance of politics had shifted markedly. According to Thomas Grenville, the question now facing the Whigs was no longer which brand of Whiggery was to be regarded as official policy, but rather when some kind of formal alliance with Pitt could reasonably be undertaken. Loughborough had already come to terms. Burke and Windham were keen to follow suit.[7] Even Spencer

[1] Bedford to Fitzwilliam, 13 Dec. 1793; Milton MSS. Box 45.

[2] Add. MS. 51845, f. 54; Sheffield to Lady Webster, 14 June 1793.

[3] Dr. Samuel Parr (1747–1825); theologian and pedagogue; referred to as 'the Whig Dr. Johnson'; headmaster of Hatton; fervent admirer of Fox; collected money for Fox's annuity, 1793; disavowed both Burke and Paine; remained a Whig throughout his life. W. Adam to Dr. Parr, 27 June 1793; Johnsone, *The Works of Dr. Samuel Parr*, i. 223.

[4] Bessborough to Lady Bessborough, 11 June 1793; *Lady Bessborough and her Family Circle*, p. 90.

[5] Fitzwilliam to W. Adam, 21 July 1793; O'Gorman, *The Whig Party and the French Revolution*, p. 143.

[6] Mrs. Crewe to Duchess of Portland, July 1793; Portland MSS. PWG 131.

[7] Add. MS. 42058, f. 128; Memorandum by Thomas Grenville, 18 Nov. 1793.

and Thomas Pelham were having regular interviews with Pitt, in order to discover how their support could be most effectively deployed.[1] Their actions were now determined less by nervous apprehension than by open hysteria. Windham opposed the Associators because 'Here is a full exemplification of the state to which they wished, and endeavoured, and are endeavouring to bring the world—robbery, murder, atheism, universal proflicacy of manners, contempt of every law divine and human.'[2] There was to be no longer any question of trying to reconstitute the old party. Indeed Spencer wanted to be 'Openly hostile to the Views of the violent Party, because we shall thereby cut off all Idea of Any lingering after the old Opposition as it used to be formed . . .'[3] In more explicit terms, this attitude implied that the right wing had come to deny all possibility of dealing with Fox. Indeed, his actions and statements over the previous twelve months had done much to overcome their scruples about joining Pitt. Spencer agreed with Windham that he 'could not go the least out of my way upon a hope of Reunion with the other Gentleman [Fox], whose opinions, if they really are such as his late Conduct would lead one to infer, are such as I should be extremely sorry to give any countenance to.'[4] In the eyes of these men, Fox had placed himself so far outside a meaningful political context, that his views had lost all relevance.

If the right wing could now ignore Fox with impunity, the decisions of Portland and Fitzwilliam were still important to them. To join Pitt without these men would provoke charges of opportunistic apostasy from the great body of Whigs. To persuade Portland and Fitzwilliam to take a similar step would be to leave Fox in a position of impotent and discredited isolation. In the summer of 1793 therefore, a further campaign was launched. Windham told Portland that Fox's views were now such, 'that the world in my time is not likely to be in a state, in which . . . I could wish to see him Minister of the Country.'[5] Richard Burke, recently refused Fitzwilliam's nomination for the borough of Higham Ferrers, attacked the Earl's decision in a fifteen page letter of bewilderment and complaint. After pointing out, not unreasonably, that it was very hard of Fitzwilliam to insist that his representative in the Commons should vote with Fox, when the Earl himself found it impossible to do so in the Lords, Burke insisted that Fox had been tolerated for too long, and now needed to be taught a sharp lesson: 'By bearing that treatment &

[1] Add. MS. 37848, f. 122; Spencer to W. Windham, 3 Nov. 1793. See also Add. MS. 42058, f. 96; Spencer to T. Grenville, 10 Dec. 1793.

[2] W. Windham to Mrs. Crewe, 26 Dec. 1793; *The Crewe Papers*, Section 1, Philobiblon Society, Vol. 9.

[3] Add. MS. 37848, f. 124; Spencer to W. Windham, 8 Dec. 1793.

[4] Add. MS. 37848, f. 112; Spencer to W. Windham, 14 Sept. 1793.

[5] Add. MS. 37845, f. 13; W. Windham to Portland, 3 Sept. 1793.

shewing him, that tho' your anger might threaten, your tenderness would not strike, You have lost all the salutary authority your situation & weight in the country gave you over him. Instead of his making his option between your Lordship & Sheridan—He has forced your Lordship to make *your* option between himself & my father. And you have made it.'[1] By way of defence, Fitzwilliam insisted that, to bring any but an avowed Foxite into Parliament, would be an open affront to Portland, to whom his first duty lay.[2] The vital nexus of common sympathy between Portland, Fitzwilliam and Fox was still in being. The frustration of Richard Burke's electoral ambitions was only one of the disappointments meted out to the right wing of the Whigs as a result.

In spite of Fitzwilliam's non-committal reply, Richard Burke's arguments had had their effect. The Earl told Adam that Fox was now a prisoner of the extreme democrats, and that therefore he could no longer support him. Portland was informed of the Earl's views in similar language.[3] Unfortunately, however, Portland remained unconvinced. He was prepared to support individual ministerial measures,[4] but found any suggestion of formal co-operation with Pitt anathema. Even with Robespierre in power in France, Portland could still not forget the trauma of 1784. He objected to joining Pitt, because he was still 'holding his own situation in such a way as to make it inconsistent with the principles we have constantly professed for us to have anything to do with him'.[5] Unless the right wing could convince Portland to break with both Fox and the memories of 1784, their entry into government would hardly have the effect they desired.

Where the son failed, the father hoped to succeed. Edmund Burke who, according to one authority, was busily engaged in drawing up articles of impeachment against Fox,[6] published the *Observations on the Conduct of the Minority*, in September 1793, as a last attempt to ruin Fox's reputation. Fox himself saw the book as designed 'to destroy me in the opinion of those whom I so much valued'.[7] Fifty-four charges against Fox were set out in this book, and the conclusion left Fitzwilliam and Portland little room for manoeuvre: 'There is no trifling in this subject . . . to pursue the political exaltation of those whose political measures we disapprove, and whose principles we

[1] R. Burke to Fitzwilliam, 16 Aug. 1793; Milton MSS. Burke A. iv, f. 19.

[2] Fitzwilliam to R. Burke, 27 Aug. 1793; ibid. Burke A. iv, f. 18.

[3] Fitzwilliam to Portland, ? Sept. 1793; Wentworth Woodhouse Muniments, F.31.a.

[4] Add. MS. 37845, f. 11; Portland to W. Windham, 26 Aug. 1793.

[5] Portland to Fitzwilliam, 23 Sept. 1793; Milton MSS. Box 45.

[6] Moore, *Memoirs of R. B. Sheridan*, ii. 133.

[7] Fox to Dr. Parr, 24 Feb. 1802; Johnstone, *The Works of Dr. Samuel Parr*, i. 287.

dissent from, is a species of modern politics not easily comprehensible, and which must end in the ruin of the country, if it should continue and spread. Mr. Pitt may be the worst of men, and Mr. Fox may be the best; but, at present, the former is in the interest of the country, and of the order of things long established in Europe: Mr. Fox is not.'[1] Such a painstaking and thorough indictment could not fail to have its effect. Portland, in passing on an advance copy of the book to Fitzwilliam, agreed that 'it is a direct arraignment of Fox's conduct, shewing the certain impractibility of our acting with him in office, and the difficulty of our siding with Him out of it for purposes too obvious to mention.'[2] After this double broadside from the Burke family, Fox's standing with Portland and Fitzwilliam rested solely in their belief, that, if Fox was wrong, his conduct was determined by misplaced sincerity rather than outright malevolence.[3]

Part of the effectiveness of this last Burkean campaign was due to the fact that there was no answer offered by Fox, who seems to have resigned himself to following his chosen course of action whatever the cost. Only William Adam, whose managerial functions allowed him to keep in touch with all sections of the old party, attempted to counter Burke's arguments. He had, however, very little room to manoeuvre. He could play on Fitzwilliams' recognition that some of the Associators were indisputably aristocratic, and that their views could not reasonably be those imputed to them by Burke.[4] He could suggest that it was not illogical for Fitzwilliam, while approving the aims of the war, to join Fox in condemning its mismanagement.[5] Fundamentally, however, he was reduced to the old expedient of arguing that Fox's views had been misrepresented:

> . . . What I am anxious about now is to remove a mistake which Your Lordship appears to me to lye under. I mean the supposition that Charles has made his Election between two parties & that He had preferr'd The friends of the people to the Old Whigs. . . .
>
> I am quite sure, from all I have ever heard him say, that he would satisfy you that this is not the case. His support of the Motion for Parliamentary reform steered quite clear of anything that could be construed into a support of principles which desert the ancient and only practicable foundation of civil liberty.[6]

Unfortunately for the Foxites, this kind of approach was no longer realistic. Fitzwilliam refused to believe it practicable to attack the

[1] Burke, *Observations on the Conduct of the Minority*, pp. 342–3.
[2] Portland to Fitzwilliam, 6 Oct. 1793; Milton MSS. Box 45.
[3] Portland to E. Burke, 10 Oct. 1793; Fitzwilliam, *Burke Corres.* iv. 161.
[4] Add. MS. 42058, f. 120; Fitzwilliam to T. Grenville, 7 Nov. 1793.
[5] W. Adam to Fitzwilliam, 31 Oct. 1793; Milton MSS. Box 45.
[6] ibid.

conduct of the war without impugning the motives, for which it was undertaken, and both he and Portland could not bring themselves to agree that further conversations with Fox could prove useful.[1] Fox's consistent opposition to measures made necessary by the outbreak of war, between February and June 1793, had convincingly demonstrated to these men how great the differences between Fox and themselves actually were. After these debates, Burke's formal indictment of Fox at last fell on receptive ears.

By December 1793, Thomas Grenville was confidently reporting that Portland was preparing to commit himself to a wholehearted acceptance of the war.[2] Indeed Portland was intending to deliver the ultimatum himself. On 25 December, he told Fitzwilliam that he intended to go to St. Anne's Hill to state 'my determination to support the War with all the effort & energy in my power, that for that purpose it must be clearly understood & manifest that no connection exists between the friends of the People & me, & that it will be my endeavour to collect in the best manner I can all the force which the Old Whig Party can supply . . .'[3] It is in fact doubtful if this formal leave-taking ever took place, in that Fox was staying with the Duke of Grafton at Euston until 31 December, but the change of attitude here expressed is important. The declaration of war and the debates on the measures made necessary by such a situation had at last convinced Portland that politics were now turning on different issues. The anger generated in 1784 had to give place to the fear inspired by the French Revolution. Once this change in attitude was effected, all Fox's influence on Portland vanished.

While the loyalty of Portland and Fitzwilliam was being subverted, Fox was disinclined to take any countermeasures. Towards the end of 1793, he realized that a separation from these two men was probably inevitable. In letters to his nephew, he lapsed into a kind of fatalism: 'Regrets are vain, but one cannot help thinking, if Burke had died four years ago, if Lauderdale had not made his Association . . . if our friends would have been right headed upon the subject of that association, or even after all if last winter they would have kept aloof upon the Question of the War, and contented themselves with talking Nonsense about domestic alarms—I really believe any one of these ifs would have ruined Pitt.'[4] In fact, while the opinions of most Whigs were undergoing considerable changes, Fox's attitudes remained remarkably static. Even the prospect of Marie Antoinette being

[1] Portland to Fitzwilliam, 11 Nov. 1793; Milton MSS. Box 45.

[2] T. Grenville to Spencer, 26 Dec. 1793; Spencer MSS.

[3] Portland to Fitzwilliam, 25 Dec. 1793; Wentworth Woodhouse Muniments, F.31.a.

[4] Add. MS. 47569, f. 14; Fox to W. Adam, 18 Sept. 1793.

executed could not shake his long held belief that the actions of the First Coalition were worse. He told his nephew that: 'Everything in the world seems to be taking a wrong turn; and, strange as it sounds, I think the success of the wretches who now govern Paris is like to be the least evil of any that can happen.'[1] This choice between two relative evils, the Jacobins and the First Coalition, came increasingly to be that, on which the Whig party divided.[2]

Fox's decision was determined by the opinion that the French Revolution was less likely to produce a European-wide threat of democracy, than an excuse for monarchs to launch a concerted campaign against popular liberties. The initiation of a number of state trials, in the autumn of 1793, convinced Fox that England too was to be involved in this campaign. He observed that 'Prosecutions unbelievable both here & in Scotland are going on every day & nobody seems to mind them. The very name of Liberty is scarce popular.'[3] Further, in Fox's mind, the methods employed by royal judges were not too far removed from those of the revolutionary tribunals: 'If you have any curiosity to see a close imitation of the late french judicial proceedings, pray read Muir's trial.'[4] Inevitably therefore, Fox was drawn into the defence of the men being prosecuted under Pitt's emergency legislation. Palmer[5] engaged Fox's sympathy and assistance by personal appeal.[6] Dr. Parr brought Fox's attention to the case of one of his old pupils, who had been arrested in Scotland.[7] Erskine was entrusted with the task of preparing the case for the defence. By the end of 1793, therefore, the Foxites were actively leading the opposition to what they took to be a calculated attempt to undermine the fundamental safeguards of political and civil liberty. As a gesture of defiance, Fox, Lauderdale, and Sheridan dined with Muir[8] and Palmer in the convict ship, which was waiting for the order to take them to Botany Bay.[9] Muir and Palmer were taken to be the first English victims of the First Coalition, the threat from

[1] Fox to Holland, 22 Aug. 1793; *Mems. and Corres. of C. J. Fox*, iii. 47.

[2] Journal of Lady Elizabeth Foster, 20 Oct. 1793; Chatsworth MSS.

[3] Add. MS. 47571, f. 58; Fox to Holland, 17 Sept. 1793.

[4] Add. MS. 50829 (Adair MSS.), f. 5; Fox to Sergeant Adair, 26 Dec. 1793.

[5] Thomas Palmer (1747–1802); unitarian minister and follower of Dr. Priestley; member of the 'Friends of Liberty' in Edinburgh; convicted of sedition, 1794; transported to Australia for 6 years.

[6] Add. MS. 47569, f. 18; T. Palmer to Fox, 22 Oct. 1793.

[7] Johnstone, *The Works of Dr. Samuel Parr*, ii. 285.

[8] Thomas Muir (1765–98); trained as a lawyer; member of the Edinburgh club called 'The Friends of the People'; strongly supported the French Revolution and visited Paris, in 1793; convicted of sedition, 1794, and sentenced to 14 years transportation; rescued by the Americans.

[9] F. Bickley, *The Diaries of Sylvester Douglas, Lord Glenbervie*, i. 21.

which was infinitely more tangible and apparent than any speculative theorizing by Parisian politicians.

Taking up the cases of these men not only allowed Fox to substantiate his views on where the threats to the English constitution lay, but also offered a rallying point for all former Whigs. Fox could not believe that Portland or Fitzwilliam could condone these proceedings: 'I grow quite nervous sometimes when I consider these things in one point of view, I mean with respect to our old friends. Can they, if they approve of what has passed (at home I mean) this year have the least spark of Whiggism left in them?'[1] Dundas was accordingly lobbied on Palmer's behalf, and his petition to the House of Commons itself was drawn up by Adam and Erskine. In the debates on the Scottish trials, Fox was at pains both to point out the dangers of such precedents, and to define the crime of sedition more precisely. The Commons, Fox claimed, fearing the destruction of political liberty in France, reacted strangely by emasculating liberty in England: 'If every action is to be examined, if evidences from different quarters are to be collected to prove different charges, without any specific act being stated in the indictment, I appeal to every man who hears me, whether there can be any liberty in the country where such practices are allowed.'[2] The voting down of Fox's proposals by 171–32 emphasizes just how badly Fox had lost touch with the political nation as a whole. Far from acting as a rallying point for the Whigs, the trials merely emphasized their differences. The only consolation, which this situation afforded, was that Fox was released from the constraints of moderating his views, and could freely travel down to Maidstone to give evidence on behalf of another prisoner, without any fear of causing further offence.[3] Fox's involvement in these trials underlined his political ideas, but, in doing so, emphasized also how far those ideas were removed beyond the accepted political boundaries.

By the beginning of 1794 therefore, all hope of reconciliation had to be abandoned. The debates on Pitt's war measures had shown how deep the divisions within the Whig Party had gone. Burke still cherished a despairing hope that Fox might be reclaimed at the last moment, because 'he sees that the Body of his party is melting away very fast, & that in a little time, nothing will remain to him but an handful of Violent people.'[4] Even so devoted a Foxite as Robert Adair agreed that, ultimately, Fox would break with Grey and his friends. In fact, however, there was, at this date, no possibility of this.

[1] Add. MS. 47568, f. 28; Fox to Adam, 17 Dec. 1793.

[2] *Fox Speeches*, v. 218; 24 Mar. 1794.

[3] R. Fulford, *Samuel Whitbread*, p. 63.

[4] E. Burke to R. Burke, 10 Jan. 1794; Wentworth Woodhouse Muniments, Burke 1.

The issue of the War had so neatly divided up politics, that few politicians would have the agility to leap from one side to the other.[1] The debates of 1793 had determined loyalties as sharply as those of 1784 had done. The attitudes generated in response to these two crises were not necessarily incompatible. The Foxites believed that Pitt had acted criminally in 1784, and that he had compounded his felony by declaring war nine years later. The major theme of their opposition was therefore unbroken. By contrast, the alarmist Whigs took the view that so menacing and so powerful was the threat from France, that all political controversies before 1789 were no longer of any importance. The Foxite creed stretched consistently back to 1784, while that of the Portland Whigs represented a quite definite change of direction, giving politics new priorities and new preoccupations.

Before the new session of Parliament opened therefore, in January 1794, the right wing of the Whig party prepared to deliver the coup de grâce. All the signs were hopeful. Fitzwilliam was actively subverting Fox's remaining influence in Yorkshire. Pitt was ready to give the Whigs a preview of intended government legislation,[2] and even Portland was thought ready to commit himself. By 21 January, Spencer could report that, 'I hope so much of my object has been attained as to secure the co-operation of most of those whose co-operation I very much desire . . .'[3] Four days earlier, Portland had called a special meeting at Burlington House for the specific purpose of announcing his determination to support the War in every way he could.[4] He communicated this decision to Fox personally, and this important encounter was recorded by Lady Elizabeth Foster: '. . . the D. of P. in the meantime saw C. Fox & told him that he intended supporting the war. C. Fox, W. Hare told us, had with his candour & openess, said, "Then I suppose you will not censure any part of the conduct of it"; to which the D. of P. said no & they each stand on their own ground, but without any acrimony or coolness.'[5] Burke, Windham and Spencer had good reason to be pleased.

Even at this eleventh hour, however, the trauma of 1784 was still influencing politics. It was one thing to wean Portland away from Fox, but it was quite another to persuade him to join Pitt in government. After giving Windham a definition of the term 'Whig', which was very different from that put forward earlier by Holland,[6] basing

[1] Lady E. Ponsonby to Lady L. Ponsonby, 6 Feb. 1794; Hickleton MSS. A.1.2.1, f. 88.

[2] Add. MS. 37844, f. 17; Pitt to W. Windham, 16 Jan. 1794.

[3] Spencer to Dowager Lady Spencer, 21 Jan. 1794; Althorp MSS.

[4] W. Windham to E. Burke, 18 Jan. 1794; Wentworth Woodhouse Muniments, Burke 1.

[5] Journal of Lady Elizabeth Foster, 23 Jan. 1794; Chatsworth MSS.

[6] Above, p. 1.

itself exclusively on 'the principles upon which the Revolution of 1688 was founded & pursued', and on loyalty 'to all its establishments & Order Religious & Civil',[1] Portland went on to explain his hesitation. He could not formally join Pitt because

It will not be denied to me that the Characteristick feature of the present Reign has been its uniform & almost unremitting attention & study to debase & vilify the natural aristocracy of the Country, & under the popular pretence of abolishing all party distinctions, to annihilate, if possible, the Whig Party. For these express purposes the present Ministry was formed, & that they have most religiously adhered to & most exemplarily fulfilled the purposes of their creation every Year of their existence would furnish us with abundant instances.[1]

Significantly, Portland saw the events of 1784 as an attempt to debase aristocracy, while Fox interpreted the same events as an assault on the privileges of the Commons. The effect of these two views was, however, the same. In the Duke's eyes, Pitt's policies might be supported from outside the Cabinet only. Formal co-operation would only give substance to the belief that the events of 1784 had been forgiven. Any hope of Fox re-establishing his reputation, admittedly unlikely, lay in this deeply-ingrained conviction.

It is, however, doubtful, by January 1794, whether Fox was any longer interested in keeping his connections with Portland and Fitzwilliam artificially alive. The restraint and moderation imposed upon his actions over the previous two years had placed great strain on his naturally volatile personality. Once Portland had declared himself, however, Fox was equally free to develop his ideas without constraint. When Thomas Grenville wrote to sever his connection with Fox formally,[2] the reply was frank, even brutal; 'Whatever pain it may give me to express myself in this manner, I feel that I ought to tell you that I think you all, by which I mean the D. of P, Fitz & yourself, very very wrong not only in your opinions but in your conduct even upon a supposition of those opinions being just.'[3] The apostates were roundly accused of abandoning the principles of Whiggery, 'particularly that of keeping up a regular & systematic opposition to a Tory & unconstitutional Ministry',[3] without attempting to find a way of supporting individual Pittite measures, while yet remaining in the general body of opposition. In the conditions of 1794, such a demand could never be met, but Fox had at last the opportunity and freedom to express views, which before had of necessity to be concealed.

[1] Add. MS. 37845, f. 18; Portland to W. Windham, 11 Jan. 1794.
[2] T. Grenville to Fox, 29 Dec. 1793; *Mems. and Corres. of C. J. Fox*, iii. 62.
[3] Add. MS. 42058, f. 135; Fox to T. Grenville, 6 Jan. 1794.

With a sense of relief, Fox threw away all checks on his Parliamentary language. As soon as the new session opened, Fox went on to the offensive on the issue of the war. Seizing on the words of an incautious Pittite, who suggested that peace was out of the question while a Jacobin government survived in France, Fox set out to demonstrate that the sole purpose of the war was in fact to impose a régime on France, a point which Pitt had always denied: 'In the presumption of certain theories of our own, we were to stake the wealth, the commerce and the Constitution of Great Britain, on the probability of compelling the French to renounce opinions for which we had already seen that they were ready to sacrifice their lives.'[1] Rejecting this premise, Fox called for the immediate opening of negotiations. The First Coalition was a hypocritical crusade of kings, who wept salt tears over the fate of Holland without one word of reference to their own dismemberment of Poland. Pitt had led England into war on false pretences, and, even on his own premises, the war was a failure because the only consequence of military action was that 'the French were now inspired with such an enthusiasm for what they miscalled Liberty, that nothing but absolute conquest could induce them to listen to any plan of internal government proposed by a foreign power.'[2] Only fifty-eight other Whigs supported Fox's motion, and contemporaries of all shades of opinion saw it as the final watershed. George III noted with pleasure that the minority consisted only 'of the followers of Mr. Fox'.[3] Lord Spencer was equally sure that Fox and his disciples had been entirely cut adrift: 'This has in general been understood (& I confess it is what I meant by it) to be charging Mr. Fox with entertaining something of Republican or even Jacobinical Principles, & accordingly has given both him & his particular friends some uneasiness.'[4] From a Foxite point of view, restraint no longer served any tactical or strategic purpose.

No longer inhibited by considerations of party unity, the Foxites began to express their views in a more self-confident manner. The Whig Club was now exclusively their forum. In January, Fox's conduct in the previous Parliament was toasted among cheers and acclamations.[5] A month later, the Members laid claim to an unbroken stewardship of Whig principles. They congratulated themselves that 'This Club which has for the last ten years maintained its steady and patriotic course without becoming Alarmists on one side or

[1] *The Speech of the Rt. Hon. C. J. Fox in Reply to the Address to his Majesty*, p. 1.

[2] ibid, pp. 6 seq.

[3] George III to W. Pitt, 22 Jan. 1794; Aspinall, *The Later Corres. of George III*, ii. 148.

[4] Spencer to Dowager Lady Spencer, 28 Jan. 1794; Althorp MSS.

[5] *Morning Chronicle*, 15 Jan. 1794.

Innovators on the other, displayed last night the same zeal for the true cause of liberty which has ever distinguished their conduct.'[1] This theme of continuity became a major characteristic of the Foxite faith. They believed themselves the guardians of true Whig principles, from which Burke and Portland had deviated. Convinced of this central dogma, the Foxites began to mobilize support. At Norwich, Coke successfully impeded the raising of a public subscription in support of the war, and the weapons he used were, significantly, references to Pitt's conduct in the Norfolk election of 1784.[2] There was even, for a short time, the rumour that the Foxites were going to challenge the Portland interest in Nottinghamshire itself. In February, the Town Clerk offered the Recordership of Nottingham to Fox, without consulting the Duke,[3] and two months later, it was suggested that Fox should stand against the Duke's brother in the election for the county.[4] Fox very sensibly placed a veto on such unreasoning optimism, but such projects suggest a spirit in the Foxite group, which had earlier been absent or muted.

Further, once the battle lines were drawn up at the beginning of 1794, Fox set about consolidating his forces. New recruits on the war issue, like the Duke of Grafton[5] received a warm welcome. Waverers like the Duke of Devonshire[6] were sedulously lobbied.[7] The most difficult negotiation of all, however, had to be undertaken with Shelburne himself, now Marquess of Lansdowne. The same events which drove Fox further and further away from Portland inevitably brought him nearer to Lansdowne, whose many French connections led him to take a less jaundiced view of French affairs than most of his English contemporaries. As early as 1792, Fox had leapt to the defence of Lansdowne's son in the House of Commons, when he was attacked for expressing views similar to his own. This community of sentiment could not, however, immediately overcome the long-established personal antipathy between the two men. After the events of 1782–4, Holland could reasonably conclude that 'I perceived there was not much reliance on either side of the other's professions and intentions, and I let both see that I thought so.'[8] Even so, by 1794, the necessity of mustering as strong an opposing force to Pitt

[1] *Morning Chronicle*, 4 Feb. 1794.

[2] W. Windham to Portland, 13 Apr. 1794; Portland MSS. PWF 9536.

[3] T. Hawksley to C. Grey, 27 Feb. 1794; Grey MSS.

[4] Add. MS. 50829, f. 2; Portland to Sergeant Adair, 16 Apr. 1794.

[5] Fox to Grafton, 19 Jan. 1794; Grafton MSS. f. 159.

[6] Duke of Devonshire, William Cavendish, 5th Duke (1748–1811); head of one of the most important Whig families; firmly connected with Rockingham and then Fox; broke with Fox temporarily over the French Revolution.

[7] Journal of Lady Elizabeth Foster, 19 Jan. 1794; Chatsworth MSS.

[8] Holland, *Memoirs of the Whig Party*, i. 44 seq.

as possible led Fox to put out feelers to Lansdowne through mutual friends.[1] In February of that year, Lansdowne was becoming a regular guest in Whig houses,[2] but the hostility engendered by the events of 1782–4 had not been overcome by July, when Portland joined Pitt's ministry. Such an understanding between Lansdowne and Fox had been prepared, but had not yet come to fruition. Spencer admirably summed up their difficulties by referring to 'Ld. Lansdowne, who now stands as clearly at the head of the opposition in one House as Mr. Fox does at the Head of that in the Ho. of Commons; how far the latter Gentleman may like the Idea of being in a Coalition with the Ms. of Lansdowne I do not know; but I shall think that if that circumstance should become notorious to the Publick . . . it will not add much credit or popularity to Mr. Fox among the thinking & *remembering* Part of the Country.'[3] Some kind of understanding was not, however, impossible. Foxite hostility since 1784 had come increasingly to be directed against Pitt alone. Lansdowne was seen as a rather inept politician, who was used by the King for a specific purpose, and then discarded. Reconciliation would not be easy, but the French Revolution had already prompted stranger alliances.

Finally, Portland's outright commitment to the war released Fox from all remaining obligations. Although still on terms of personal friendship with some of the Portland Whigs,[4] Fox was absolutely resigned to the loss of the Duke, and could therefore act freely. He told his nephew that 'It seemed some way as if I had the world to begin anew, and if I could have done it with honour, what I should best have liked would have been to retire from politics altogether, but this could not be done, and therefore there remains nothing but to get together the remains of our party, and begin, like Sisyphus, to roll up the stone again, which long before it reaches the summit may probably roll down again.'[5] Portland's defection, however distressing, had at least clarified the principles, on which the small Foxite party now stood. Their primary objection was directed against the build-up and misuse of large amounts of power in the hands of an executive body. In Foxite eyes, it was of little relevance whether this power was wielded by George III or Robespierre. Fox had always been anxious to compare the situations in France and England, and, in June 1794, he congratulated his nephew on 'that parallel you drew between the Jacobins of France and the Crown party here'.[6] An

[1] Lansdowne to Lady Ossory, 1794; Fitzmaurice, *Life of William, Earl of Shelburne*, ii. 397–8.

[2] Add. MS. 51731, f. 199; Caroline Fox to Holland, 22 Feb. 1794.

[3] Spencer to Dowager Lady Spencer, 18 Feb. 1794; Spencer MSS.

[4] Add. MS. 51706, f. 109; T. Pelham to Lady Webster, 21 Jan. 1794.

[5] Fox to Holland, 9 Mar. 1794; *Mems. and Corres. of C. J. Fox*, iii. 66.

[6] Fox to Holland, 23 June 1794; ibid. iii. 74.

unbridled executive executed people unfairly in Paris and punished people unfairly in Edinburgh. The root cause of these injustices was the same. The Foxites therefore believed themselves to stand on the old Whig principle of checking the unrestrained exercise of executive power. Fox believed that 'We live in times of violence and extremes, and all those who are for creating or even for retaining checks upon power are considered as enemies to order.'[1] Fox had learnt his lessons in Whiggery well. The doctrines taught by Burke about the dangers involved in the existence of a strong executive were still being applied by the disciple, even when the master no longer believed them relevant.

Although, in Foxite eyes, Jacobinical and royal excesses might be equally deplorable, even Fox had to admit that his followers might have to choose ultimately between these two evils. Faced with this decision, Fox, significantly for the future, opted for French principles. He told his nephew that he could hardly hope for an English victory, because it would so enhance the power of the Crown.[1] At the Whig Club, he was reported by the press to be even more explicit:

> It was said by Mr. Fox and other Members of the two Houses who were present, that the Friends of Liberty felt that there was at this time danger to be apprehended to the Constitution, but not on the side of the persons who were now the objects of Ministerial prosecution—That the danger came from persons much more considerable in the country, and therefore came with more alarm to every true and faithful Whig. The opinion was received as a truth to which the judgment of every Member of the Club bore witness.[2]

In spite of indiscriminate attacks on the abusive exercise of executive power in both England and France, therefore, Fox was in practice committing himself to the cause of the Revolutionaries. Royal atrocities were less defensible than those committed by a nation in arms. Fox himself had to admit that a middling policy between these two extremes, which he had for so long tried to pursue, was no longer feasible. Portland's defection gave Fox the freedom to speak openly.

This decision was, however, made at a price. The loss of close, political friends and growing isolation led Fox to wish for an early retirement. His niece reported that he was 'quite sick of politics',[3] while he himself informed his nephew that only a sense of duty kept him in politics at all: 'They go on according to the Irish translation of *semper eadem*, worse and worse. I am heartily tired of them but one must do one's duty.'[4] Pitt's assaults on fundamental English liberties had to be resisted, but Fox's assessment of politics in 1794 was

[1] Fox to Holland, 28 Dec. 1793; *Mems. and Corres. of C. J. Fox*, iii. 61.
[2] *Morning Chronicle*, 4 June 1794.
[3] Add. MS. 51732, f. 10; Caroline Fox to Holland, 19 May 1794.
[4] Add. MS. 47571, f. 120; Fox to Holland, 25 Apr. 1794.

uniformly gloomy. His former colleagues, who had joined Pitt, were outdoing their new friends by expressing a violent and unforgiving Toryism, which entirely matched the mood of the country. Even to speak of liberty 'is not popular'.[1] Further, politics had degenerated into a simple exchange of slogans. Instead of a rational discussion about the best methods of safeguarding English liberties, Fox, 'furnished with the common cant of my party', thought himself 'very lucky to be opposed only by the common cant of the other.'[2] The opposition to Pitt's measures in 1794 was therefore undertaken in a spirit of weary resignation. The disillusionment with politics, which was to lead to Fox's withdrawing from Parliament in 1797, was already apparent. Duty demanded that as an effective opposition as possible should be mounted, but the task was assumed without enthusiasm.

Fox's consistent opposition to Pitt's foreign and domestic policies between March and July 1794 was therefore less an attempt to overthrow a Ministry, than a determination to have his dissenting voice placed on record. Free of party restraints, Fox could elaborate the basic themes of his policy, many of which had been outlined in the previous year. In foreign affairs, the attack was directed not only against the management of the war, brought into question by the failure of the Toulon expedition,[3] but also against the premises on which it had been entered into. The aim of the war, according to Fox, was increasingly seen to be nothing less than a restoration of monarchy in France. The decision to employ French émigrés in the English army[4] and the refusal to intercede with the Austrians on behalf of Lafayette[5] confirmed the belief that the war was in fact a despotic crusade. The outcome of this policy was that Pitt had involved England in a costly and expensive war, requiring enormous subsidies for Prussian and Austrian autocrats, fresh from the spoliation of Poland, who, by threatening to withdraw from the struggle, could effectively hold England up to blackmail.[6] On 30 May 1794, Fox incorporated all these arguments into fourteen resolutions, with which to substantiate a call for the immediate opening of negotiations with France.[7] This motion was defeated by 208 votes to 55. It was not enough to demonstrate that Pitt had led the country into war on false pretences in 1793. Fox had to convince the Commons that a monarchical crusade, in the context of politics in 1794, was an undesirable

[1] Fox to Holland, 18 Mar. 1794; *Mems. and Corres. of C. J. Fox*, iii. 69.
[2] Add. MS. 51732, f. 24; Caroline Fox to Holland, 19 June 1794.
[3] *Parl. Hist.* xxxi. 256; 11 Apr. 1794.
[4] *Fox Speeches*, v. 245 seq.; 17 Apr. 1794.
[5] ibid. v. 212 seq.; 17 Mar. 1794.
[6] ibid. v. 260 seq. and 195 seq.; 6 Mar. and 30 Apr. 1794.
[7] ibid. v. 293 seq.; 30 May 1794.

thing, and this he could not do. A poor showing in votes, however, was not now important. Fox had succeeded in establishing an interpretation of the war to which his small band of followers could subscribe, and which, in some measure, they believed was vindicated in 1802, when negotiations had to be opened with a France still free of kings. In the political situation of 1794, this simple recording of views was all that Fox could hope for.

Home affairs were seen only as part of Fox's general thesis about the advance of executive power. On a large number of issues debated in Parliament early in 1794, the point is again and again reiterated that the war was being used as an excuse for Pitt to launch a concentrated assault on English liberties. Popular hysteria was being deliberately whipped up, in order to effect this. Pitt could at last realize aims, which he had cherished since 1784. Fox told the Commons in June 1794 that 'He believed the old faction he had mentioned in a former debate, which, by whatever name, had uniformly pursued the same plan of throwing all power into the hands of the crown, to be spreading a false alarm of danger from one quarter to cover a real danger from another.'[1] Using this contrived emergency as a pretext, Pitt was able to ban societies without appeal, land foreign troops in England, and even suspend Habeas Corpus. In spite of an illness, Fox went down to Westminster to oppose this last measure, which was being indecently hurried through the House in two days. In a speech of great vigour and authority, Fox declared unremitting opposition to Pitt's ideas, because he 'saw the complete extinction of liberty; and he dreaded to think what must be the shocking alternative which he, and others who loved the true principles of the constitution, must be reduced to in the impending struggle.'[2]

Once again, the immediate motive for Fox's Parliamentary campaign was simply to establish his thesis of advancing executive power in England and on the Continent, and to have these views recorded. There was, however, just a slim chance that Fox's former colleagues could be shocked into returning to this former allegiance. Scattered among general denunciations of the war, therefore, were several arguments and motions more familiar to Whig ears. In April, Fox introduced a measure to tax office and pension holders for the duration of the war.[3] A month earlier, Fox had made great play with the Pittite suggestion that a voluntary subscription should be opened, with which to furnish the king with direct financial assistance.[4] On this occasion, the appeal to Whig tradition had some effect. Even Portland was moved to protest against the idea 'that any aid of any

[1] *Fox Speeches*, v. 316 seq.; 16 June 1794.
[2] *Fox Speeches*, v. 280 seq.; 17 May 1794.
[3] ibid. v. 239; 18 Apr. 1794. [4] ibid. v. 228; 28 Mar. 1794.

sort in any shape whatever can or ought to be given to the Crown but through the medium of Parliament.'[1]

A Whig lady's irritation at Fox 'every day moving questions that they know they can hardly divide 50 upon in the present state of things',[2] was therefore a little misplaced. At best, Fox, by emphasizing the links between his present opposition and that undertaken in the 1780s, might hope to act successfully on the conscience of Portland and his friends. At worst, Fox was elaborating the new creed, to which his small band of fifty or sixty followers could adhere. By continually bringing issues to the vote, the Foxites acquired a sense of common purpose. Therefore, in July 1794, the Foxite opposition was naturally carried on within a much circumscribed compass, but it was as intellectually cogent and spirited as that of the 1780s. The Parliamentary campaign of 1794 provided the scriptural basis, on which opposition was in future to be based.

As the Foxite group began to define its position, Portland's friends were placed under a similar necessity. At a meeting at Burlington House on 27 January, attended by thirty-two Whig M.Ps, the Duke formally assumed Fox's former office as 'spokesman of the meeting'.[3] Although unequivocal support of the war effort was pledged, the final step of joining Pitt's ministry had to be taken, and this could not be done without overcoming certain obstacles. The Cavendish family, for example, was totally divided on the issue.[4] Significantly, the Duke of Devonshire, while supporting the war, left James Hare, a staunch Foxite, in undisturbed possession of the borough of Knaresborough, and consistently advised against any formal arrangement with Pitt.[5] The difficulties surrounding such a commitment still sprang from the experiences of 1784. As Robert Adair observed, respect for the old party of Lord Rockingham was still strong enough for it to be impossible not to 'contemplate without sorrow . . . its chiefs in hopeless bondage to the power they had combined to limit, and that haughty instrument of its will from whose hands they would have torn its symbols.'[6] When the details of Portland's entry into the Ministry were at last discussed, all the old hostility and suspicion of Pitt once again made itself apparent.[7] As late as April 1794, Portland was very

[1] Add. MS. 37845, f. 37; Portland to W. Windham, 23 Mar. 1794.

[2] Lady E. Ponsonby to Lady L. Ponsonby, 31 Mar. 1794; Hickleton MSS. A.1.2.1, f. 96.

[3] J. Greig, ed. *The Farington Diaries*, i. 37.

[4] Lady E. Ponsonby to Lady L. Ponsonby, July 1794; Hickleton MSS. A.1.2.1, f. 89.

[5] R. Adair, *A Sketch of the Character of the Late Duke of Devonshire*, p. 14. See also Devonshire to Portland, 9 Apr. 1794; Portland MSS. PWF 2706.

[6] Adair, *A Whig's Apology for his Consistency*, p. 16.

[7] Add. MS. 50829 (unfoliated); Sergeant Adair to Portland, *c*. July 1784.

unwilling to make any commitment to Pitt personally.[1] At every step of Portland's halting progress towards full co-operation with Pitt, the memories of 1784 delayed and impeded his course.

Portland's final commitment to Pitt was therefore in the manner of a steady slide into submission. In February, the Duke began to attend the levée on a regular basis.[2] In April, all contentious measures due to come up in the Commons were presented to the Duke for his prior inspection.[3] These consultations allowed Portland to absorb the full range of Pittite ideas in small, but regular, doses. By May, the Duke was calling for 'the Restoration of the French Monarchy & Restitution of Property or at least a Government of which Property forms the Basis.'[4] The preliminary agreement was made in June,[5] and the formal alliance was announced a month later, on 11 July. Beyond asking Fitzwilliam for an explanation of his behaviour, Fox made no attempt to check his friends' drift into the Ministry.[6] His capacity to exercise such influence had long since ceased to exist. Even so, this final break was deeply felt: 'The truth is I never had so great a dislike to writing or talking about any event that ever happened as about those that took place in the beginning of last month. I have nothing to say for my old friends nor indeed as Politicians have they any right to any tenderness from me, but I can not forget how long I have lived in friendship with them nor can I avoid feeling the most severe mortification when I recollect the certainty I used to entertain that they never would disgrace themseves as I think they have done.'[7] Until the very end, Fox held to the belief that Portland would not give in completely to the agent and purveyor of royal influence in 1784.

Portland's entry into Pitt's Ministry transferred political debate onto new axes. Burke's distinctions between 'old' and 'new' Whigs no longer had any relevance. As the *Morning Chronicle* observed; '... thus coalition is founded between the Whigs and Tories of England, by which, for the future, all the old distinctions are to be lost, and all men are to be divided into two classes, Royalists and Republicans.'[8] In July 1794, the Pittite Ministry had become the representative of all forms of English property, reacting solely against French events. For

[1] Add. MS. 50829 (unfoliated); Sergeant Adair to Portland, 3 Apr. 1794.
[2] *Morning Chronicle*, 12 Feb. 1794.
[3] Pitt to Portland, 8 Apr. 1794; Portland MSS. PWF 7701.
[4] Portland to Fitzwilliam, 25 May 1794; Wentworth Woodhouse Muniments, F.31.b.
[5] Add. MS. 51706, f. 180; T. Pelham to Lady Webster, 19 June 1794.
[6] Fox to Fitzwilliam, *c.* 11 July 1794; Wentworth Woodhouse Muniments, F.115.b.
[7] Add. MS. 47571, f. 143; Fox to Holland, 10 Aug. 1794.
[8] *Morning Chronicle*, 27 June 1794.

the Pittite of 1794, politics began in 1789. By contrast, the Foxite party would claim a longer history for itself. For them, political decisions were dominated by a long-standing struggle with executive power, as exercised by George III. Because Fox was the principal interpreter of this creed, it largely took shape after his experience in 1782–4. Many of the men who remained with Fox in 1794 were young politicians, whose earliest political experiences would be of these same events. The French Revolution had grafted onto these fundamental assumptions other causes and other allies, some of which were not always welcome, but, in essence, Fox's views on that Revolution sprang directly from his experiences of English politics. Fox toyed increasingly with the French ideas and slogans, because, in the context of 1794, these were the fashionable and the most effective weapons to use against kings. The Foxite creed was not born in 1789, however. It sprang directly from the double-dishing of the Whigs between 1782 and 1784.

VII

ROCKINGHAMS AND FOXITES

IN the period 1782–94, it is impossible to speak of the Whig party as one homogeneous unit, representing throughout these years the same political prejudices and aiming at the same constitutional ends. As Burke repeatedly asserted, the impact of the French Revolution had been so violent, that all political debates which took some topic other than the Revolution as a starting point, were no longer of importance. The issues giving life to the party of Lord Rockingham were now irrelevant. Two Whig parties must therefore be studied. First, the party of 1784, which drew from the disasters of 1762, 1765–6, and the more recent trauma of 1782–4, a common creed on which to act. Secondly, there is the Whig opposition of 1794, which, while associating themselves still with all the proscriptions experienced during the reign of George III, were characterized essentially by the attitudes adopted towards the events in France. In both Whig parties, Fox was of the first importance. In the 1780s, Fox made Whiggery articulate, and worked up its political experiences into constitutional theory. By being the only major Whig leader to refuse to join Pitt a decade later, Fox so imprinted his character and ideas on the diminished numbers still in opposition, that his control of the Whig cause was almost proprietory. The word Foxite was taken by contemporaries to be a term of great value in defining political allegiances effectively. By 1794, Fox was so conspicuously isolated in opposition, that the direction taken by Whiggery became his personal responsibility. As the son of Henry Fox therefore accommodated himself more and more into the rôle of Whig champion, political circumstance allowed him an unrestricted stage, on which to perform. By 1794, Fox was without a rival, and could, if he so wished, substantially modify the character of English Whiggery.

The number of division lists which have survived from the period 1782–4 make it possible to establish with some confidence those Members of Parliament, who were to a lesser or greater degree associated with the Whigs. Five division lists have survived from the last two months of Lord North's administration (20 February–15 March 1782).[1] Since the survival of North's administration very clearly depended on the outcome of these divisions, they must represent

[1] I. R. Christie, *The End of North's Ministry*, pp. 390–405.

a very good indication of party allegiances. Voting patterns during Shelburne's administration must be taken from the division lists on the peace proposals, which Shelburne presented to the Commons on 18 February 1783.[1] Again, however, the fate of a Ministry was known to hinge on the result of this vote, which would keep capricious voting down to a minimum. The division list on the crucial issue of the East India Bill similarly offers a reliable indication of political allegiances during the Coalition Ministry.[2] Unfortunately, no division list survives for the period December 1783 to March 1784, when Pitt successfully established his position in defiance of Fox's control of the Commons. Allegiances here must be taken from a list drawn up by John Stockdale, shortly before the dissolution in March 1784, arranging members of the House of Commons according to their attitudes towards Pitt's embryonic administration.[3] For each of the four administrations of the period 1782–4 therefore, some kind of reliable indication of voting patterns survives.

Division lists can be supplemented by other pieces of evidence of varying quality. The record of members attending Lord Rockingham's first levée as Chief Minister, in April 1782, is of some interest, but it clearly includes a large number of Shelburne's followers, and also a number of people, whose adherence to the new administration stemmed from convenience rather than conviction.[4] Shelburne's attempt to define the allegiances of the members of the House of Commons, in November 1782, is of even more doubtful value, since he parsimoniously allowed the Whig opposition only thirty-nine firm supporters.[5] Of more interest are John Robinson's essays into the same field. His long experience of political management gives authority to his opinions about voting probabilities. In March 1783, he drew up a list of eight-nine names, all of which he believed to be committed to the Whigs.[6] Ten months later, he attempted to define the allegiance of all M.P.s, in order to weigh the chances of Pitt surviving in the existing House of Commons.[7] Both lists merit serious attention. The most interesting list drawn up by an individual, however, is that attempted by Burke in February or March 1784.[8] This document is important for a number of reasons. It is the only specifically Whig assessment of Whig numbers and loyalties, and it not only lists those who were for and against Pitt's ministry in 1784, but also attempts to

[1] *Morning Post*, 27 Feb. 1783.

[2] *Parl. Hist.*, xxiii. 309; 27 Nov. 1783.

[3] J. Stockdale, *Debates 1784–90*, Appendix. i.

[4] Rockingham MSS. Apr. 1782; Wentworth Woodhouse Muniments.

[5] Lansdowne MSS. Nov. 1782.

[6] Christie, *The End of North's Ministry*, p. 212.

[7] W. T. Laprade, ed. *The Parliamentary Papers of John Robinson*, p. 66.

[8] Milton MSS. Burke A. xxxviii, f. 19; *c.* Feb. 1784.

relate those loyalties to voting habits in the period 1782–4 as a whole. Although Burke's political judgement was rarely unclouded by prejudice, his evidence on this particular occasion must be accorded considerable weight.

Few members have left complete voting records. Abstentions or absences account for the gaps, and it is impossible to know whether the failure to vote was due to a considered judgement or simply to a lack of interest. Emphasis has therefore been laid on two groups of lists in particular; those relating to the fall of North, which establishes opposition votes very clearly; and those dividing the political world between Fox and Pitt in 1784, which in turn separates out Foxite Rockingham votes from the other groups, who, two years earlier, had joined them in opposing the American War. The lists drawn up by individuals, particularly Burke's, can therefore be kept in reserve for the purposes of comparison. For the reasons stated above, very little account is taken of Shelburne's list or that recording the attendance at Rockingham's first levée.

Applying the above test, some ninety-four members of the House of Commons in March 1784 had never cast an anti-Foxite vote. The regularity of their attendance naturally varies considerably, but these men may be taken to form the hard core of the Whig party.[1] This is marginally higher than the estimates of both John Robinson, who quoted eighty-nine names in March 1783, and I. R. Christie,[2] who put the core of the Whig party at seventy-seven. As the latter authority points out, some of these men chose to act with the Rockinghams for ends unrelated immediately to events in the House of Commons, but the fact remains that, in terms of practical politics, their votes could be relied upon. These figures would suggest, that since February/March 1782, the date to which Christie's figures

[1] E. Anderson, W. A'Court, W. Baker, Sir C. Bampfylde, R. Beckford, Ld. Ed. Bentinck, R. Benyon, W. Braddyll, Sir H. Bridgman, J. Bullock, Sir T. Bunbury, J. Burgoyne, E. Burke, G. Byng, Ld. G. Cavendish, Ld. G. A. Cavendish, Ld. J. Cavendish, Sir R. Clayton, T. Coke, E. Coke, H. S. Conway, H. Dawkins, Duncannon, C. Dundas, Sir T. Dundas, T. Erskine, Sir H. Fetherstonehaugh, R. Fitzpatrick, G. Fitzwilliam, Sir H. Fletcher, A. Foley, E. Foley, G. Forester, C. Fox, Sir T. Gascoigne, R. Gregory, T. Grenville, B. Grey, J. Hare, J. Harrison, D. Hartley, W. H. Hartley, P. Honeywood, Sir R. Hotham, J. C. Jervoise, J. Lee, T. Lister, D. Long, Lucan, J. Luther, Maitland, Sir H. Mann, C. Medows, H. Minchin, E. Monckton, F. Montague, N. Newnham, W. Nedham, J. Nesbitt, W. Owen, C. Pelham, H. Pigot, W. Plummer, Sir J. Ramsden, Sir M. Ridley, C. Ross, Sir J. Rushout, G. St. John, A. St. John, S. Salt, J. Sawbridge, J. Scudamore, R. Sheridan, W. Sloper, J. Smith, R. Smith, R. Spencer, H. Stanhope, T. Stanley, T. Staunton, H. Sturt, Sir J. Thorold, W. Tollemache, J. Townsend, Upper Ossory, Verney, R. Walpole, H. Walpole, W. Weddell, T. Whitmore, J. Wilkinson, Sir E. Winnington, P. Wyndham, Sir W. Wynn.

[2] Christie, *The End of North's Ministry*, p. 212.

related, the Whig party had, by March 1784, picked up some twenty additional votes. The figure goes even higher when there are added the names of ten members,[1] entering Parliament between 1782 and 1784, and who seem to have sided with the Whigs. The evidence available for these members is more exiguous, but nevertheless the bitterness of politics between December 1783 and March 1784 makes any assessment of allegiances at that time significant. The core of the Whig party must therefore be taken to consist of some 104 members in 1784. Happily, all of these names appear in Burke's list as 'members of the old opposition [i.e. to Lord North] voting with Mr. Fox'.

Around this core, there was a penumbra of a further thirty-five M.P.s, who appear in Burke's list as Whigs without qualification, but who in fact showed some independence of mind. Twenty-five voted against Fox once,[2] and ten did so twice,[3] but on the crucial issues of bringing down North's administration in 1782 and attacking Pitt's two years later, they were all to be found in the Whig lobby. These were votes, which normally inclined to the Whigs, but which could not be absolutely commanded, and which might from time to time stray. As perhaps might be expected, as many as twenty-six out of these thirty-five either sat for countries or for boroughs in their own interest. Marsham and Honeywood of Kent, Powys of Northamptonshire and Anson of Litchfield are typical of this group. Their votes could not be dictated by a borough proprietor or patron, and, although generally sympathetic to the Whigs, could not be absolutely relied upon. Some, like the Earl of Surrey, even took a leading part in the efforts of the St. Alban's Tavern group to effect a union between Pitt and Fox in February 1784. These men must therefore be regarded as Whig independents. Burke's attempt to include them in a general list of absolutely committed Whigs is an example of political sleight of hand.

Finally, there are a further six M.P.s, about whose allegiance there is a certain amount of doubt. Although not included by Burke in his list of Whigs, the actual voting record of John Elwes, R. P. Carew and General H. S. Conway would certainly qualify them for membership. The latter admittedly had strayed from the straight Foxite path by joining Shelburne's administration, in July 1782, but he returned safely to the Whig fold in time to vote for the India Bill in November

[1] J. F. Cawthorne, W. S. Conway, J. Cotes, S. Davies, G. Elphinstone, Sir Jas. Erskine, F. Foljambe, S. Lushington, J. Nicholls, Sir J. St. Aubyn.

[2] G. Anson, C. Barrow, J. Crewe, Sir W. Codrington, Sir G. Cornewall, Sir C. Davers, G. Dempster, Sir G. Elliot, T. Halsey, G. Hunt, W. Hussey, R. Knight, J. Lambton, T. Lucas, Ludlow, R. Ladbroke, Middleton, E. Morant, A. Rawlinson, T. Rouse, Surrey, C. Taylor, B. Thompson, Sir G. Vanneck, J. Webb.

[3] W. Bouverie, F. Honeywood, Sir R. Lawley, C. Marsham, Sir R. Mostyn, Sir T. Powys, Sir T. Skipwith, J. Tempest, R. Thistlethwaite, T. Trevanion.

1783. Conversely, Burke includes three names in his list of Whigs, Sir P. J. Clerke, James Crauford and Sir J. Harris, whose credentials must appear suspect when tested against their actual voting record. All came from impeccable Northite backgrounds, and there is no *a priori* reason for not thinking that they still, in 1784, belonged to that wing of the Coalition. However, allowing Burke these three names, the Whig party in March 1784 could muster a potential force of 145 votes, made up of 104 hard core members, a penumbra of thirty-five Whig independents, and six others whose claims to that title are a little more doubtful.

Of these, only twenty-seven[1] of the hard core of the party and four[2] of those in its penumbra received office, promotion or some other kind of material advantage from the two administrations, of which Fox was a member. This unusually low figure was due less to a foregoing of party obligations than to the King's known unwillingness to grant any favours to the supporters of Fox, and to the fact that both these administrations were coalitions, in which offices were notoriously hard to come by. The followers of Shelburne and later North had to be accommodated, and on both occasions, the distribution of offices and places between the groups in the coalition administration produced difficulties and tensions. The fact that offices were reserved for Fox's immediate friends like Spencer and Fitzpatrick must therefore be ascribed almost entirely to this pressure. Even so, this lack of places could be embarrassing, and in no way promoted the interests of the Whig party as a whole. Even Lady Sarah Napier, one of Fox's doting aunts, when complaining that her husband had not received the expected promotion in the army, was almost led to believe 'that Charles cuts his old friends'.[3] Clearly, this shortage of patronage was a very real problem for both Rockingham and the Coalition.

Equally interesting is an analysis of the seats for which the Whigs sat.[4] Eighty-three members were returned by some forty-one patrons. Only four of these interests accounted for more than four members, however. The Cavendish interest brought seven members into Parliament, the Fitzwilliam seven, the Portland five and the Eliot five. The remainder were returned singly or in pairs by a large number of smaller proprietors. The Lister control of Clitheroe, which guaranteed

[1] Government Office: Burgoyne, Burke, Ld. J. Cavendish, Duncannon, Fitzpatrick, Fox, Lee, Minchin, Montague, Pigot, St. John, Sheridan, Spencer, Townshend. Promotion: H. S. Conway, Sir J. Erskine, P. Honeywood, H. F. Stanhope. Other: Anderson, Sir T. Dundas, T. Erskine, R. Gregory, T. Grenville, S. Lushington, N. Newnham, H. Walpole, J. Wilkinson.

[2] C. Barrow, J. Lambton, Ludlow, Surrey.

[3] Lady S. Napier to Lady S. O'Brien, 10 Nov. 1783; Ldy. Ilchester and Ld. Stavordale, *Life and Letters of Lady S. Lennox*, ii. 40.

[4] See Appendix III.

the electoral safety of Thomas Lister and John Lee, is typical. The remaining sixty-two members were returned individually for boroughs or counties, in which their respective families could normally be accorded political respect, or where they themselves provided the money to carry on a contest. William A'Court represented his family interest at Heytesbury and Robert Ladbroke bought his way into the representation of Warwick. Since this latter group was not subjected to the control or influence of a patron, it is not surprising to find more of the 'penumbra' than the hard core of the party among its numbers. As has been already observed twenty-six out of the thirty-five members of the penumbra of the Whig party were free of patrons.[1] As might have been anticipated therefore, the degree of commitment to the Whig cause is reflected in the strength and nature of the pressure upon each individual member. This control was not necessarily tyrannical. James Hare, one of Fox's oldest friends, although sitting for the Cavendish borough of Knaresborough, needed no prompting from the Duke of Devonshire to take the straight Whig line on any issue, and he was in fact left undisturbed in his seat even when the Duke began to be uneasy about his views on the French Revolution. Even so, this proprietory control of the hard core of the party must have been ultimately reassuring.

Another test of interest made possible by the publication of electoral results in *The House of Commons 1754–1790* is to compare the fortunes of these 145 members in the election of 1784 with the myth surrounding the concept of 'Fox's Martyrs'.[2] According to this evidence, eighteen Whigs were defeated outright in large boroughs or counties.[3] A further seventeen were displaced because of a change of front on the part of their patrons.[4] Four of these members managed to find alternative seats,[5] however, and therefore the party only suffered a net loss of thirteen. A further nine either refused to stand again or withdrew during the course of the campaign having met with strong opposition, and none of these found alternative seats.[6] Approximately

[1] Anson, Bouverie, Barrow, Crewe, Codrington, Cornewall, Davers, Dempster, Halsey, Honeywood, Hunt, Hussey, Knight, Ladbroke, Lambton, Lawley, Marsham, Morant, Mostyn, Powys, Rous, Taylor, Tempest, Thistlethwaite, Vanneck, Webb.

[2] See Chapter III.

[3] Anderson, Baker, Bunbury, Byng, Cavendish Ld. Jo., W. Conway, Foljambe, Halsey, Hartley D., Hartley W., Hotham, Lucan, Pigot, Rous, Smith J., Smith R., Townshend, Verney.

[4] Crauford, Eliot, Gascoigne, Grenville, Grey, Long, Lucas, Maitland, Nedham, Ramsden, Salt, Skipwith, Stanhope, Thompson, Tollemache, Trevanion, Wyndham.

[5] Long, Maitland, Nedham, Salt.

[6] Braddyll, Clayton, Coke, Conway Gen. H. S., Elwes, Erskine T., Gregory, Lushington, Sturt.

forty members of the Whig party were therefore totally displaced at the election. This evidence accords reasonably well with the figures derived earlier using the classifications of Burke and Robinson.[1] Contemporary estimates, which made the Whig defeat even more crushing, were almost certainly influenced by the retirement of a further nineteen M.P.s.[2] The withdrawal of these men from politics was not, however, immediately demanded by political pressure, and, in all cases, they were succeeded by men, whose views were identical to their own. Equally, although Robert Knight and John Bullock found it expedient to change seats, they quickly found alternatives, and their votes were not lost to the Whig party. Even so, the loss of forty votes in this election was a heavy blow, although perhaps not quite the irredeemable disaster that some contemporaries believed.

The sense of common purpose and organizational capacity shown by the Whig party in the 1780s has already been dealt with.[3] There remains the important task of discovering the nature of the Foxite party after the break with Portland in 1794, and of trying to decide how much this group owed to the past and how far their politics were remodelled by Fox, under extreme pressure in opposition. Further, if something approaching a distinct Foxite party can be distinguished after 1794, some assessment, however tentative, must be made of the influence of this group on the Whig party of the early nineteenth century. Although strictly outside the terms of reference of this study, such a foray into the nineteenth century might help to demonstrate the lingering effects of the experiences of 1782–4 and 1789–94 upon Fox himself and upon the young men he taught.

Any claims advanced on behalf of Fox's influence will be contested. A reviewer of a biography of Fox, in 1874, refused to allow him any part in the intellectual expansion of Whiggery in the early nineteenth century: 'The growth of modern Liberalism will be historically explained as a reaction against the system of the successors of Pitt, and as the catastrophe of their mistakes, which have thrown a false halo round the name of Mr. Fox, and redeemed the discredit of his life.'[4] Half a century earlier, however, opinions were quite different. When, in 1812, the Prince of Wales attempted to set up a coalition ministry of Whigs and Tories, his efforts were negatived by the ghosts of Pitt and Fox, who were 'quoted at every step'.[5] Of even greater interest is the testimony of Grey's son. Writing a biography of his

[1] See Chapter III, pp. 92–6.

[2] Beckford, Carew, H. S. Conway, Davies, Dawkins, C. Dundas, Sir J. Erskine, Fitzwilliam, Forester, P. Honeywood, Hunt, Luther, Mann, Ross, St. Aubyn, G. St. John, Staunton, Walpole, Wilkinson.

[3] See Chapter III, pp. 102–4.

[4] *Blackwood's Magazine*, cxvi. 514; Oct. 1874.

[5] M. Roberts, *The Whig Party* 1807–12, p. 374.

father in 1861, the younger Grey believed that the meaningfulness of party had come to an end in 1832, and that the terms Whig and Tory, hitherto of value, had since become of no significance whatever:

I make use of the appellations 'Whig' and 'Tory' as they applied to the parties as they stood opposed to each other at the time of which I write; by no means as they are now assumed by parties and individuals who have no earthly claim to be characterized as either one or the other. In fact since the settlement of all the great questions formerly dividing men on somewhat higher grounds than those of mere personal pretentions and individual rivalry, these names have lost all significance. From the time that the Reform Act was accepted by the Conservative Party . . . there has indeed been no difference between public men as to the principles on which the Government of the country should be conducted.[1]

Grey goes on to claim that the Whig ministry of 1830 was the vindication of nearly half a century spent in opposition.[2] If such an expert witness can therefore see the years 1782–1830 as a political whole, and as a period in which party divisions were meaningful, some examination of Fox's contribution to the opposition of these years becomes crucial.

Throughout the 1780s, the terms 'Foxite' and 'Whig' had been interchangeable. Burke, for example, in drawing up his list of the House of Commons, in March 1784, referred to members of his own party as 'friends of Mr. Fox' and not as friends of the Duke of Portland or as Whigs. Since Fox was the interpreter of the events of 1782–4, this close, personal identification with Whiggery is not perhaps too surprising. After 1792, however, the two terms become quite distinct. The Whigs, who followed Portland into an alliance with Pitt, turned their backs on the dogmas of 1784. Many later returned to them, but this is not immediately to the point. The Foxites, by contrast, although in most cases taking their politics from the events of 1784, had grafted on to these received truths new loyalties concerning France. It is these, which were distinctively Foxite after 1794, and which gave them their title. In order to evaluate Fox's contribution to the intellectual advancement of Whiggery, a closer study of these men is essential.

The happy survival of eighteen opposition division lists from the period of February 1793 to May 1794 makes it reasonably easy to establish the identities of the Foxites, once certain problems have been overcome. During these months, no less than 106 members of the House of Commons voted with Fox at least once, but, since all of these were clearly not committed Foxites, some more exacting criteria will have to be brought in. The division of these members into Foxite

[1] Grey, *The Life . . . Earl Grey*, Preface V.
[2] ibid. p. 29.

and non-Foxite must of necessity be a little arbitrary, and the test imposed in the following calculations was the recording of at least five Foxite votes out of a possible eighteen in these months. Since, by this reckoning, such a close friend of Fox as Thomas Coke has to be omitted from the list of Foxites, the method cannot be taken as foolproof, but there are good reasons for its adoption. For example, even if Coke was generally sympathetic to Fox's views, the recording of only four votes out of a possible eighteen in this period would not suggest that the member for Norfolk was particularly anxious to declare his loyalties publicly. Similarly 49 per cent of the votes of the fifty-one M.P.s who voted with Fox between one and four times, were accounted for in four divisions only.[1] The fact that Lord George Cavendish and Lord Sheffield felt obliged to support a motion requesting assistance for Lafayette, who was their personal friend, in no way committed them to a wider support of Foxite measures. Equally, Sir Henry Fetherstonehaugh's vote in favour of Parliamentary reform again cannot be taken as approval of the whole range of Foxite ideas. These fifty-one M.P.s, voting with Fox between one and four times, were therefore disengaged members, who, while generally accepting Pitt's policies, might be persuaded to cast the odd vote against the Ministry. This was particularly true on issues calculated to appeal to the independent country gentleman. A proposal to divert court pensions towards defraying the cost of the war brought even Bastard of Devon into the Foxite camp. In general terms, however, these men cannot be included safely in any list of committed Foxites. Once these fifty-one names have been excluded therefore the Foxite party is reduced to those fifty-five[2] M.P.s who voted with Fox between five and eighteen times over the same period.

[1] Grey's motion for reform 7 May 1793. Motion to end war 2 Jan. 1794. Motion asking for Pitt to intercede for Lafayette 17 May 1794. Motion to end war 30 May 1794.

[2] W. Adam (Ross), W. Anthonie (Gt. Marlow), J. Aubrey (Clitheroe), W. Baker (Herts.), Sir F. Baring (Chipping Wycombe), E. Bouverie (Northampton), J. Burch (Thetford), G. Byng (Middlesex), J. Church (Wendover), J. Courtney (Tamworth), T. Crespigny (Sudbury), J. Crewe (Cheshire), J. Curwen (Carlisle), T. Erskine (Portsmouth), R. Fitzpatrick (Tavistock), C. Fox (Westminster), P. Francis (Bletchingley), C. Grey (Northumberland), J. Harcourt (Ilchester), J. Hare (Knaresborough), J. Harrison (Grimsby), H. Howerd (Arundel), D. Howell (Mitchell), W. Hussey (Salisbury), J. Jekyll (Calne), J. Jervoise (Yarmouth), W. Lambton (Durham), Ludlow (Hunts.), N. MacLeod (Inverness), T. Maitland (Haddington), J. Martin (Tewkesbury), Sir W. Milner (York), D. North (Grimsby), J. Philips (Carmarthen), W. Plummer (Herts.), J. Rawdon (Appleby), Ld. W. Russell (Surrey), St. A. St. John (Beds.), R. Sheridan (Stafford), W. Smith (Camelford), H. Speed (Huntingdon), Ld. R. Spencer (Wareham), C. Sturt (Bridport), B. Tarleton (Liverpool), M. Taylor (Heytesbury), T. Thompson (Evesham), Ld. J. Townshend (Knaresborough), B. Vaughan (Calne), R. Vyner (Thirsk),

Inevitably, the amount of evidence available on each of these people varies considerably, but one preliminary point can be made with some confidence. The Foxite group in 1793–4 was in no sense more directly representative of opinion than its Whig parent a decade earlier. There were only four county members to be found in their ranks (Baker, Byng, Crewe and Plumer), and only six others, who represented boroughs with significantly large electorates (Fox, Hussey, Martin, Milner, Tarleton and Walwyn). Together, these two groups make up only 18 per cent of the whole. The largest single group, 31 per cent of the whole, still owed their seats to aristocratic patrons. The Marquess of Lansdowne returned four members for Calne and Chipping Wycombe (Baring, Jekyll, Vaughan and Wycombe), and the Duke of Bedford similarly guaranteed Fox four votes from the scattered Russell estates (Fitzpatrick, Russell, St John and Whitbread). At a lower level, Lord Sandwich brought in two members for Huntingdon (Ludlow and Speed), and the Duke of Devonshire, in spite of personal reservations about Fox's politics, allowed his members, James Hare and Lord John Townshend to follow them without disturbance. Finally, a further five noblemen could offer Fox one vote each: Grafton (Burch), Norfolk (Howerd), Lauderdale (Maitland), Townshend (Courtney) and Thanet (Rawdon). To these must be added a further 16 per cent who owed their seats to non-aristocratic patrons.[1] The remainder either represented their own electoral interests (20 per cent)[2] or bought their way into notoriously venal boroughs (15 per cent).[3] In total, 55 per cent of the Foxite group in 1794 represented constituencies with less than 200 voters. In times of adversity therefore, the Foxites took refuge, not in those areas of the eighteenth-century system, where public opinion was most vocal, but in those parts, where proprietory control was most firm.[4] Clearly, the linking mechanism holding this group together was not pressure from large electorates protesting against the repressive nature of the Pittite system.

In fact, the nucleus of the Foxite party was in evidence at least as early as 1782. I. R. Christie, in his analysis of the Whig party at the

J. Walwyn (Hereford), C. Western (Malden), S. Whitbread (Bedford), R. Wilbraham (Bodmin), Sir E. Winnington (Droitwich), Wycombe, (Chipping Wycombe).

[1] Aubrey (Lister Interest), Francis (Clayton Interest), Howell (Basset Interest), North and Harrison (Pelham Interest), Smith (Philips Interest), Spencer (Calcraft Interest), Vyner (Frankland Interest), Wilbraham (Morshead Interest).

[2] Adam, Bouverie, Curwen, Grey, Jervoise, Lambton, MacLeod, Philipps, Sturt, Western, Winnington.

[3] Anthonie, Church, Crespigny, Erskine, Harcourt, Taylor, Thompson, Sheridan.

[4]

Electorate	0–100	101–200	201–500	501–1,000	1,001–3,000	3,000+
M.P.s	21	9	7	7	6	6

time of North's fall from office, divides its members into groups looking to Fitzwilliam, Devonshire and the other grandees, but also adds a caucus of thirteen M.P.s who took their lead specifically from Fox himself.[1] There was no question of this group challenging Portland's leadership. Nor was there any attempt to use its compact and talented membership, in order to try to impose a given set of ideas or policies on the Whig dukes. From time to time, contemporaries tried to persuade these men formally to adopt a party programme, in order to avoid the charge of factionalism, but such advice misses the point.[2] The Foxites in the 1780s were simply the personal friends of Fox, and, although talented and ambitious, they had no cause to differ substantially from the official Whig leadership. If they were more enthusiastic about Parliamentary Reform and relief for the Catholics than Portland or Fitzwilliam, these differences could easily be tolerated within the broad framework of the party. The cohesion of this group lay in social, and not political, activities. Their world was essentially that of Brooks's and not Westminster. These two centres only overlapped because a friendship with Fox almost always led to political commitment.

Fox himself was ideally suited to lead a party on these terms. A story circulated long after his death retailed the opinion that Fox's greatest happiness lay in being 'much'd by his friends'.[3] Even Burke, in the late 1790s, would admit that Fox's personality was instantly compelling.[4] By 1782, Fox's friends were, socially at least, already a self-conscious group. When Fitzpatrick went into exile as secretary to the Lord Lieutenant of Ireland, Burgoyne, another of the fraternity, kept him in touch with affairs in England, and added as a footnote that, 'a large party of your friends dined at Charles's at three this morning where you were cordially remembered.'[5] Inevitably, however, this friendship for Fox was carried over into politics. Emily, Duchess of Leinster, was another of Fox's adoring aunts, who carried their admiration for him to the point of believing he could hardly ever be wrong.[6] At times, friendship with Fox seems to have been the only reason for political decisions, taken without reference to any other considerations. The obituary of Edward Bouverie, one of those remaining loyal to Fox in 1794, records the astonishing fact that, quite simply, 'Mr. Bouverie invariably voted in favour of almost every motion proposed by the late Charles James Fox, who was one

[1] Christie, *The End of North's Ministry*, p. 216.
[2] Nicholls, *Recollections . . . Reign of George III*, i. 206 seq.
[3] *Gentleman's Magazine*, Apr. 1835, p. 352.
[4] R. J. Mackintosh, ed. *Memoirs of the Life of Sir James Mackintosh*, i. 325.
[5] Add. MS. 47582, f. 77; J. Burgoyne to R. Fitzpatrick, 8 May 1782.
[6] Fitzgerald, *Emily, Duchess of Leinster*, p. 173.

of his dearest and most intimate friends.'[1] Fox's enormous capacity for friendship, which even his most bitter political enemies had to admit, therefore came to be a political weapon of some considerable value. In the 1780s, it attracted talented young men onto the Whig benches, and, during the two years of tension prior to Portland's association with Pitt, helped to restrain men like Spencer and Thomas Grenville from severing all political ties, until the sheer pressure of events left them no other choice.

Although the simple call on long-established friendships might hold the allegiance of a small band of disciples, it was ill-adapted to meet the problems of holding a larger party together. Many of the defects in Fox's general leadership, which are constantly rehearsed by his critics, are due entirely to the fact that he was surrounded by a Praetorian guard of devoted protégés, who insulated him to a certain extent from more general contacts. Windham, who in 1793 was still trying to bring Fox into some kind of association with Pitt, was told by a friend that 'The Misfortune of Fox (one misfortune) has been, that he avoids or, at least does not invite the knowledge of what is said out of his own circle.'[2] The warm circle of adulation at Brooks's could appear dangerously self-sufficing.

In more practical matters, Fox was equally at a disadvantage. The uncritical approbation of his friends must have helped him to neglect many of the political weapons open to any prominent eighteenth-century politician. According to one early nineteenth-century diarist, Fox refused to have any contacts with the writers and journalists normally employed by the government. On coming into office in 1782, 'Mr. Fox, in an interview with these writers, told them that they must never expect either money, or encouragement from him, and desired that they should all be paid up to that day. He then discharged them.'[3] Such conduct, while not critical, was certainly impolitic. Even in the most elementary matters of patronage dispensation, Fox, from indolence or neglect, failed to mobilize such forces as were at his disposal. As late as November 1783, his aunt's husband was still waiting for his regiment.[4] Although prepared to act on these matters on direct commission,[5] there is no evidence that Fox was seriously concerned with this aspect of leadership. By 1793, Fox himself was beginning to have pangs of conscience: 'I have ever thought it a strong instance of my ill fortune, that though I have been

[1] J. Wilson, *A Biographical Index to the Present House of Commons*, p. 442.

[2] Add. MS. 37873, f. 226; S. Douglas to W. Windham, 22 Oct. 1793.

[3] R. Edgcumbe, *The Diary of Lady Frances Shelley, 1787–1817*, i. 72.

[4] Ldy. Ilchester and Ld. Stavordale, *Life and Letters of Lady S. Lennox*, ii. 39 seq.

[5] C. Fox to Spencer, 22 Dec. 1786; Althorp MSS.

twice a Minister, with the single exception of the Bishop of Downe (an exception in which I am sure you rejoice) not one of my friends is the better for my power.'[1] Fox's authority and standing was not therefore dependent on the usual eighteenth-century techniques. The quality of his leadership was certainly poorer for this fact, but, in trying to discover the bonds holding the Foxites together, these factors must be discounted.

The first point to be established is that the Foxites were, in spite of their views on the French Revolution, a remarkably aristocratic group of men. Of the fifty-five individuals under examination, ten[2] were the younger sons of peers, one was the grandson of a peer[3] and three were to inherit peerages.[4] To this list could plausibly be added an émigré French count and a descendant of Caractacus.[5] Further, thirteen members of this group married legitimate, and one the illegitimate, daughters of peers.[6] At least twenty-five Foxites therefore had a direct connection with the peerage, either through birth or marriage. Against this background, Portland's long refusal to believe that Fox and his friends could seriously countenance events in France becomes readily comprehensible. Most of the leading Foxites came from impeccable Whig families, and, in at least nine cases, substantiated their claims to political respectability by marrying into other Whig dynasties.[7] The early years of the French Revolution had demonstrated that aristocratic connections were no guarantee against revolutionary politics, but even so, Burke's campaign to brand the Foxites as Jacobins predictably met with incredulity for a very long time.

The habits of friendship and co-operation between the Foxites had in many cases been acquired long before the 1790s. School and university registers are uncertain pieces of evidence, because the educational background of some Foxites cannot be traced at all, and because the sharing of the same school or university is no guarantee in itself of long-standing friendships. In the narrow social world of the eighteenth century, however, the chances of such friendships forming would be considerable. Fox's firm association with Carlisle,

[1] Add. MS. 51467, f. 28; Fox to D. O'Brien, 23 Jan. 1793.

[2] Bouverie, Erskine, Fitzpatrick, Fox, Howerd, Maitland, Rawdon, Russell, Spencer, Townshend.

[3] Courtney.

[4] Grey, St. John, Wycombe.

[5] Henry Speed (Comte de Viry) and J. Philipps.

[6] Adam, Byng, Crespigny, Crewe, Grey, Lambton, Ludlow, North, Russell, Speed, Sturt, Tarleton, Whitbread, Winnington.

[7] Adam–Elphinstone, Byng–Townshend, Grey–Ponsonby, Lambton–Jersey, Milner–Sturt, Russell–Jersey, Spencer–Bouverie, Whitbread–Grey, Winnington–Foley.

Fitzwilliam and Hare began at Eton in the 1760s. Even earlier, the Duke of Newcastle had asked a favour on behalf of Carteret's son on the pretext that he was 'persuaded that, as well on my Lord Carteret's account, as from the consideration that Mr. Carteret issues from a place where you, and I, had our Education, you will show him all the Civilities in your Power.'[1] No absolute conclusions can be drawn from the following tables therefore, but the coincidence of names is not uninteresting:

SCHOOLS

(a) ETON

Baker (1753–6)	Fox (1758–64)	Crespigny (1773–81)
Bouverie (1753–6)	Hare (1760–5)	Grey (1773–81)
Harrison (1753–6)	Winnington (1763–5)	Lambton (1778–82)
		Western (1776–84)
		Whitbread (1775–80)

(b) WESTMINSTER

Jekyll (1766–70)	Byng (1773–80)
Taylor (1766–73)	Philipps (1773–9)
	Anthonie (1774–?)

UNIVERSITIES (*From Matriculation dates*)

(a) OXFORD

Christ Church		*University*
Winnington (1767)	Wycombe (1783)	MacLeod (1770)
Adam (1769)	Russell (1784)	Tarleton (1771)
Jekyll (1771)		

(b) CAMBRIDGE

Trinity

Crespigny (1779)
Grey (1781)
Lambton (1782)

INNS OF COURT

(a) LINCOLN'S INN

Jekyll (1767)	St. John (1773)
Hare (1768)	Townshend (1774)
North (1769)	Erskine (1775)
Adam (1769)	

[1] B. Williams, *Carteret and Newcastle*, p. 85.

Friendship between the Foxites, in both social and political terms, was made easier by the fact that many of them shared a common feeling of irritation against their parents' generation. Indeed, there is some evidence to suggest that the young were the most responsive to the French Revolution. A Scottish Whig later recalled that

> Grown-up people talked at this time of nothing but the French Revolution and its supposed consequences; younger men of good education were immersed in chemistry and political economy . . . But this food of the liberal young was by no means relished by the stomachs of their seniors. It all tended towards awakening the intellect and exciting speculation, which were the very things that most of the minds that had been formed a little earlier thought dangerous.[1]

Fox was ideally suited to lead young men. With some deliberation, promising young politicians were sought out and invited to join the Foxite circle. Fox's meeting with Robert Adair is typical.[2] In return for the almost fawning admiration of his protégés, Fox took their views seriously. As has been noted, even over so important an issue as the formation of The Friends of the People in 1792, Fox refused to restrain Grey and his associates, because, as he confided to a friend, 'he did not like to discourage the young ones.'[3] The degree of familiarity arrived at within Fox's circle is astonishing.[4] There was quite often a mutual exchange of carriages, mistresses, and even houses. Similarly, the pleasure of a weekend spent with Fox at St. Anne's Hill was such, that Erskine coined a new verb, 'to Charley it', in order to describe it.

In some cases, Fox was explicitly accused of leading the younger generation against the political system of their fathers. In 1792, the elder Samuel Whitbread suffered the embarrassment of organizing a petition in Bedfordshire in favour of Pitt's emergency measures, while his son canvassed opinion against them. With some regret, the old man had to admit that, 'My son is very very very much with Fox & Co.'[5] The family disagreements between General Grey and his son Charles followed a similar pattern. In the 1790s, the Foxites prided themselves on the newness of their ideas, and castigated their opponents as unimaginative and oldfashioned. In *The Rights of Man*, Tom Paine specifically made this point: 'But who are those to whom Mr. Burke has made his appeal? A set of childish thinkers, and halfway politicians born in the last century, men who went no further with

[1] H. Cockburn, ed. *Memorials of His Time*, pp. 40–1.

[2] Earl of Albemarle, *Fifty Years of my Life*, i. 226.

[3] Grey, *Life . . . Earl Grey*, p. 11.

[4] R. Sheridan to C. Sheridan, 2 Apr. 1782; Price, *The Letters of R. B. Sheridan*, i. 139.

[5] S. Whitbread (snr.) to ? (undated); Fulford, *Samuel Whitbread*, p. 67.

any principle than as it suited their purpose as a party.'[1] One of Burke's more well-founded complaints was that he, as the Nestor of the Whig party, was no longer accorded that respect and attention, which his position merited. A new generation of Whig politicians had transferred their allegiance to Fox. As late as 1804, Creevey, then aged 36, answered a Pittite suggestion that he should come into office as follows; 'I returned their fire by telling them I should save them much time and trouble by stating to them at once that my political creed was very simple and within a very narrow compass—that it was "Devotion to Fox".'[2] An analysis of the fifty-five members of the Foxite party by age group gives the following figures for 31 December 1792, when Fox himself was 43:

Foxites	20–29	22 per cent	1784 *Parliament*	18 per cent
	30–39	26 per cent	*as a whole*	27 per cent
	40–49	28 per cent		22 per cent

According to these figures therefore, 48 per cent of the Foxites were under 40, and 76 per cent were under 50. By comparing these figures with those for most eighteenth-century Parliaments, the Foxites were, as a group, slightly younger than the House of Commons as a whole.[3] Too much cannot be made of the differences (4 per cent in those under 30, 3 per cent in those under 40 and 9 per cent in those under 50), but the point is significant in view of the stress laid by Foxites themselves on the importance of their age.

Of perhaps even greater interest is the fact that only seventeen out of the fifty-five had come into Parliament before 1780. Six (11 per cent) came in during that year, fourteen (25 per cent) in 1784 and eighteen (33 per cent) in 1790. In practical terms therefore, 69 per cent of those remaining with Fox in 1794 had had their politics substantially moulded by the crises of 1782–4, in which Fox had taken such a prominent part. It is among the 1790 intake of eighteen Foxites that the most enthusiasm is to be found. Fourteen of them (78 per cent) voted with Fox on at least ten, out of a possible eighteen, occasions between February 1793 and May 1794. No other group showed such keenness. The smallness of the sample makes it impossible to claim too much significance for the above figures, but there can be no doubt that the Foxites themselves laid great emphasis on the question of age, and that they were marginally younger than the House of Commons as a whole.

[1] T. Paine, *The Rights of Man*, p. 144.

[2] T. Creevey to Dr. Currie, 21 Jan. 1804; H. Maxwell, ed. *The Creevey Papers*, i. 22.

[3] Sir L. Namier and J. Brooke, *The History of Parliament; The Commons 1754–1790*, i. 97.

No doubt as an immediate corollary of the above set of facts, Fox's active social life, for which he was constantly castigated by the Pittite press, was a not unimportant guarantee of his position within the party. His nephew, Lord Holland, later recalled 'how greatly the strength and union of parties depended on private dinners, tavern suppers, convivial meetings and perhaps intemperance itself.'[1] It was a tradition, which Holland House was to take up and develop. In the 1780s, before the influence of Mrs. Armistead allowed him the tranquillity of St. Anne's Hill, Fox was indisputably master of the revels. Young men coming into Parliament at this time not only found in Fox a political speaker with exciting and colourful views, but also discovered one of the most amusing dinner companions of the whole eighteenth century. Characteristically, however, Fox's reign was based on an easy exchange between social sovereign and subject. Burgoyne's absence in Ireland, in May 1783, allowed Fox to overcome a temporary embarrassment: 'Understanding that your house is unoccupied and wanting one for the moment, I mean to go into it until I can get one to my own mind. If you come over (as I hope you will) you may live in mine.'[2] Such a request was considered perfectly normal, and in no way put friendships under strain. Burgoyne in fact chose to die at St. Anne's Hill.[3]

Fox's court was centred in Brooks's Club. The metaphor is George Selwyn's,[4] who described Fox, in 1782, as holding court in the Club, and distributing favours to his disciples. At least thirty-nine of the members still voting with Fox in 1792 were members of Brooks's, and fifteen[5] of these had been put up for election either by Fox himself or by his two closest friends, Fitzpatrick and 'Fish' Crauford.[6] After the formation of the Coalition, unsuspecting Northites were drawn into the Club's orbit, and had to admit that they found it diverting. Lord Palmerston confessed to his wife that, 'I have kept some bad hours since I have been here, having found Brooks' remarkably pleasant, & supped there sometimes with Fox & Hare, Fitzpatrick Sheridan & Ld. North who are all in Town.'[7] Equally, there is little doubt that Fox was the centre of attraction. As late as

[1] Fulford, *Samuel Whitbread*, p. 149.

[2] Fox to J. Burgoyne, *c.* May 1783; de Fonblanque, *Life and Corres.* of *J. Burgoyne*, p. 429.

[3] P. R. O. Pitt Papers, 30/8. 157, f. 131; Dundas to Pitt, 5 Aug. 1792.

[4] G. Selwyn to Carlisle, 19 Mar. 1782; H.M.C. *Carlisle MSS.* xv. 5.6, p. 599.

[5] J. Carswell, *The Old Cause*, pp. 332–3.

[6] John Crauford (?1742–1814); M.P. (Old Sarum) 1768–74, (Renfrew) 1774–80, (Glasgow) 1780–4, Feb.–June 1790; very close friend of Fox from Eton onwards; voting erratic, but committed himself to Fox, Mar. 1782, and remained with him until the outbreak of the French Revolution.

[7] Palmerston to Lady Palmerston, 17 Dec. 1786; Palmerston MSS.

February 1792, when a dinner engagement with Fox might be politically compromising, Palmerston regretted an appointment with Sir Philip Francis, because he was 'asked to meet Charles Fox at the Paynes which would be a better thing'.[1]

At times, the social importance of Fox seemed to overlay the political. In May 1782, James Hare, although delighted that the Rockinghams had returned to office, complained to Fitzpatrick that 'It is shocking to lose Charles and You together, and to see all one's Friends become Men of Business, whilse I remain the sole incorrigible Rogue of the Gang . . .' and that Fox, 'seldom goes there [Brooks's] except for half an hour, if he wants to speak to any body, and never dines there after the H of Commons, so that some of these Northern Gentry [Scots] who have paid up Arrears of four or five years Subscription will not perhaps have laid out their money so wisely as they apprehended.'[2] In fact, Fox's stay in office was brief, but even so there is little evidence that he unduly neglected his social obligations while a minister. His horses figure prominently in the racing at Newmarket throughout his terms in office, and even the Faro table at Brooks's was not entirely abandoned.[3] In view of Fox's dominance of the social organs of the Whig party, it is perhaps not too surprising that he was able to retain control of both Brooks's and the Whig Club after his break with Portland. Both were forums of considerable importance.

The social links of London had their parallels in the countryside. The Oakley Hunt in Bedfordshire was presided over by the Duke of Bedford, Whitbread and Anthonie, and its members included Fitzpatrick and St. John.[4] Similarly, the Whig addiction to horse-racing was not without political significance. A large turn-out of Whig notables at Doncaster or York was designed to promote the Fitzwilliam and Cavendish influence in those areas. At Stafford, as the press reported, Sheridan's electoral standing received a fillip by such a gathering: 'Among the distinguished persons of rank in that and the neighbouring counties, lodgings have been taken for the Duchesses of Devonshire and Portland, the Right. Hon. Mr Fox, Lord Surrey, Col Fitzpatrick and many others, by whom Mr & Mrs Sheridan and their friends are to have the honour of being accompanied.'[5] For a local M.P. to be able to command the patronage of such people for his own borough was not without electoral significance. Again, the Northite assimilation into the Whig party after 1783 seems to have

[1] Palmerston to Lady Palmerston, 3 Feb. 1792; Palmerston MSS.
[2] Add. MS. 47582, f. 81; Hare to Fitzpatrick, 16 May 1782.
[3] *Morning Herald*, 12 Apr. 1782:
[4] Fulford, *Samuel Whitbread*, pp. 83–4.
[5] *Morning Chronicle*, 26 Oct. 1784.

gone smoothly in this respect. Palmerston inevitably found himself at Newmarket for the autumn meeting in 1784, and described the scene for the benefit of his wife: 'We had plenty of racing, it began at 12 and lasted till four. The Prince was there and afterwards dined at the Club (which is a kind of Brooks's) and play'd deep at whist in the Evening to the great Mortification of his Partner.'[1]

From a Pittite point of view, Fox's social activities were a scandal. A pamphleteer in 1789 insisted that 'The gaming table is a place where I should never look for a single virtue; and how much of his [Fox's] time, his fortune and his honour, have been wasted there, I do not wish to enquire.'[2] Fox was, on this interpretation, 'one of the most notable examples of intellectual perversion we have ever known.'[2] The truth and justice of this remark would have been readily admitted by many contemporaries, but this is to present only one side of the case. In a very real sense, Fox's leadership of Whig social life materially assisted his political standing within the party. The obituaries of many of the fifty-five members of the Foxite party in 1794 underline the fact that political and social activities were, for the Whigs, barely differentiated. Sir Edward Winnington was above all else 'an amiable, entertaining and instructive companion',[3] while Michaelangelo Taylor's house was 'for many years . . . a rendezvous for the Whig party; and his liberal and elegant, but unostentatious, hospitality will long be remembered.'[4] Within the context of English Whiggery, Fox's dominance of the party's social life was a very substantial aid to his overall control. It was an area, in which Burke, his only intellectual rival, could not compete.

Allied to the qualities of youthfulness and social exuberance was that of intellect. Fox and Sheridan had numbered among the first thirty-five members of the Literary Club,[5] and, although Dr. Johnson frequently complained that Fox was too retiring in these assemblies his attendance seems to have been quite regular.[6] The precociousness of the young Fox had been established very early. According to the Eton College Register, Fox had left the school while still very young, 'as too witty to live there—and a little too wicked'.[7] Throughout his life, Fox kept up his interests in the classics, history and modern languages. His correspondence with the scholar Gilbert Wakefield underlines his knowledge and interest in these matters.

[1] Palmerston to Lady Palmerston, 10 Nov. 1784; Palmerston MSS.

[2] Combe, *Letter from a Country Gentleman to a Member of Parliament, on the Present State of Public Affairs*, pp. 23–4.

[3] *Gentleman's Magazine*, Jan. 1805, p. 91.

[4] *Gentleman's Magazine*, Oct. 1834, pp. 430–1.

[5] *Gentleman's Magazine*, Feb. 1785, p. 98.

[6] Boswell, *Life of Johnson*, p. 1196.

[7] R. A. Austen-Leigh, *The Eton College Register* 1753–1790, p. 204.

Indeed, the dating of the Greek poet Lycophron still owes something to the interchange of ideas between these two men.[1] Intellectually, Fox could hold his own with the leading scholars and literary men of his day, and was known and recognized by them.

Such accomplishments would undoubtedly form part of many an eighteenth-century gentleman's education and upbringing, but, although it is not possible to point to these features as definitively Foxite, the recurrence of references to these matters by the writers of obituaries remains impressive. Of the fifty-five members of the Foxite group, at least fifteen are mentioned as having outstanding literary or artistic qualifications. A further seven were marked down as wits or conversationalists. Sir John Aubrey 'was a good classical scholar, and a highly finished and polished gentleman';[2] J. C. Jervoise was 'a great supporter of the Literary Fund';[3] Lord William Russell 'was fond of the arts of design, and his home was full of pictures';[4] and Thomas Thompson was a man whose 'taste in the arts was refined'.[5] To these could be added the playwright Sheridan, the minor poet Townshend, and William Smith and Charles Western, whose collections of books and Greek statuary were outstanding even for the eighteenth century. Too much cannot of course be made of this evidence. The eulogies of obituarists are inevitably to be treated with suspicion, and particularly when they rehearse qualities, which were widely diffused throughout the aristocracy and gentry, but clearly a trend emerges. The Foxites of 1794 were likely to respond to Fox personally as an intellectual leader as much as a political and social one.

By contrast, in these same obituaries, only three Foxites are listed as having an interest in agricultural developments, and only one in field sports. Equally, there were only five in trade and six in banking, although, as the cases of William Smith and Sir Francis Baring demonstrate, these occupations too in no way precluded an interest in the arts or classical scholarship. In general, however, the members of this group, largely country gentlemen, formed a distinct group, who looked more to their counties than to Brooks's. From the often scanty information available, it seems that many of them were what Burke would call Old Whigs, who refused to accept the argument that the French Revolution had materially altered the basic questions in English politics. They held to this view, even if, like John Curwen

[1] A. W. Mair, ed. *Callimachus and Lycophron*, p. 482.

[2] *Gentleman's Magazine*, Mar. 1826, pp. 272–3.

[3] Wilson, *A Biographical Index to the Present House of Commons*, p. 674.

[4] *Gentleman's Magazine*, Aug. 1840, pp. 204–5.

[5] W. R. Williams, *The Parliamentary History of the County of Gloucester 1213–1845*, p. 154.

of Carlisle, individual Foxites were occasionally embarrassed by 'the fickleness of that many-headed monster, whose humour it had ever been his pride and pleasure to serve.'[1] John Harrison, who represented Grimsby from 1780 to 1796 was equally unmoved by the events in France. As his obituary recorded, 'As long as he bore a public character, he was invariably the friend of popular rights, and was celebrated for his inflexible opposition to the administration of his day.'[2] Similarly, John Harcourt's Whiggism was of so stolid a kind, that he promised his constituents at Ilchester to bury them in 'true blue coffins'[3] if they so desired. Such views were equally those of William Plumer of Hertfordshire and C. C. Western of Essex. Although not necessarily connected with the socio-political world of Brooks's, they voted happily with Fox in the belief that French upheavals had little relevance to the issues confronting English politicians. A decision taken against Pitt in 1784 was still valid a decade later.

Even the often embarrassing effects of Fox's vices could be mitigated by application to one of his close friends. In 1785, while the bailiffs were taking his books and paintings away as sureties for his outstanding debts, Fox's struggle over the Westminster Scrutiny was entirely financed by Fitzwilliam and Portland.[4] Four years later, when political differences with the Dukes made that source of relief difficult to tap, Fox found an alternative in J. B. Church, a figure about whom little is known except that he had made a great deal of money in trading with the Americas. Inevitably, Church remained with Fox after his break with Portland, if less for friendship's sake than to protect a political investment. Even so, the relationship between the two must have been close, in that Fox's requests for quite considerable sums of money are couched in far from servile terms. In 1789, he told Church that he 'was under very considerable difficulties in respect to money... The difficulties are since increased and the truth is that I am in a very awkward situation at this moment: Two thousand Guineas would extricate me in great measure, but would not supercede the necessity of my applying to some other friend for money to begin the Newmarket Campaign. Four thousand would put me quite at my ease...'[5] Two years later, a request is made for a further £2,500.[6] From extant obituaries it is clear that at least nine[7] Foxites suffered similar financial embarrassments, and that at least eighteen[8] were in a position to offer some

[1] *Gentleman's Magazine*, Feb. 1829, p. 178. [2] ibid., Feb. 1811, p. 196.

[3] Wilson, *A Biographical Index to the Present House of Commons*, p. 87 note.

[4] Wheatley, *Memoirs of Sir N. Wraxall*, iv. 71; 25 Jan. 1785.

[5] Add. MS. 51466, f. 34; Fox to J. B. Church, 26 Mar. 1789.

[6] Add. MS. 51466, f. 43; Fox to J. B. Church, *c*. Aug. 1791.

[7] Adam, Courtney, Erskine, Fitzpatrick, Fox, Hare, Sheridan, Spencer, Tarleton.

[8] Anthonie, Baker, Baring, Crewe, Curwen, Francis, Harrison, Hussey, Jervoise, Martin, North, Plumer, Smith, Sturt, Taylor, Thompson, Walwyn, Western.

assistance. A pattern emerges of the talented and indigent being assisted by their more inarticulate, but wealthy friends. William Smith, Dudley North and Michaelangelo Taylor were specifically remembered for their lavish dinners, at which the intellect of Sheridan and Erskine would earn them a meal.

If debts could prove politically distressing, marital complications in such a tight knit group as the leading Whigs were, both before and after the split between Portland and Fox, could be even more debilitating. In the middle of preparations for the introduction of the India Bill itself, Fox ran the risk of losing the electoral support of the Duke of Devonshire by starting an affair with his wife, Georgiana.[1] Grey chose the period of the Regency Crisis to begin a flirtation with the same lady, while Sheridan was simultaneously responsible for almost provoking Duncannon to divorce his wife.[2] Such falls from grace would have been less serious politically in the Pittite ranks, in that they enjoyed the unifying advantages of office. By contrast, the elaborate social cycle developed by the Whigs in opposition was a politically cohesive force of some importance, but one which could be easily damaged by indiscretions of this kind. Even so, such failings underline the close relationship between the political and social aspects of English Whiggery, both before and after the loss of Portland. For the beleaguered opposition after 1792, however, these links were probably even more important. For the generally clever young men who adhered to Fox after 1792, social life became more important and more intimate. To remain a Foxite in 1794 was therefore to accept fully the dogmas surrounding the events of 1782–4 with the caveats made necessary by the French Revolution; to shoulder increasingly the full burden of the reforming programmes of the 1770s and 1780s, on which most of their contemporaries had turned their backs; and to synthesize both these statements of faith in the personality of Fox himself, whether at Brooks's or on the floor of the House of Commons.

Finally, the problem must be faced of how far the Foxites in opposition to Pitt after 1792 established a political tradition, and what debt, if any, is owed them by the Whig party of the early nineteenth century. Within the accepted scope of this study, this question can only be lightly touched upon, but certain trends can be established. The most important is the cult surrounding Fox personally. At Woburn, a Pantheon was built with a bust of Fox in the centre, encircled by other Whig worthies. As late as 1831, this adulation of Fox was undiminished. Macaulay told his sister that 'Yet, even now, after the

[1] Duchess of Devonshire to Lady E. Foster, 18 Oct. 1783; Ld. Bessborough, *Georgiana, Duchess of Devonshire*, p. 68.

[2] R. Sheridan to Lady Duncannon, *c.* 1788–9; Price, *The Letters of R. B. Sheridan*, i. 207.

lapse of five and twenty years, there are those who cannot speak for a quarter of an hour about Charles Fox without tears.'[1] Every Whig house had a bust or painting of this particular, political hero. Mrs. Siddons hung the statesman's portrait in her parlour.[2] Similarly a large number of male children received the Christian name Fox in the early years of the nineteenth century,[3] the precedent being set by Lord Edward Fitzgerald and Pamela de Genlis, who asked Fox to stand as godfather to their son.[4]

Such actions had more than sentimental value. In the climate of politics of the early nineteenth century, any of these practices was tantamount to an explicit declaration of political loyalties. In *Vanity Fair*, Thackeray, attempting to build up the character of Miss Crawley into that of a 'bel esprit and a dreadful Radical for those days',[5] makes his point by noting that 'She had pictures of Mr. Fox in every room in the house.'[5] Samuel Whitbread the younger was even more explicit. In giving away a portrait of Pitt, he explained to a friend that '. . . having lived in his day, having fought in the ranks of opposition to him under Mr. Fox, of whom, and of whose maxims of policy and wisdom my heart and mind are full; and having my house full of memorials of him I can have no satisfaction in the contemplation of the picture of Mr. Pitt, from whose acts Mr. Fox prophesied the consequences we now deplore.'[6] Statements of this kind, made after both Pitt and Fox were dead, underline the point that the constant appeal back to these men and their utterances was not simply nostalgia, but the reaffirmation of two rival sets of policies, on which these two politicians had stamped their names.

A more practical demonstration of loyalty to the Foxite faith was attendance at a Foxite Dinner, held to celebrate the birthday of the Whig hero. According to the most recent historian of the Whig party in the early nineteenth century, these clubs were actually becoming more numerous after 1820.[7] There were at least two principal advantages to be won from such assemblies. In the early 1800s, when opposition was often accompanied by social ostracism or even the threat of legal prosecution, such dinners represented a rallying place for the faithful. In Scotland, as one Foxite later recorded, 'Fox's birthday was generally celebrated by a dinner every year. But only a

[1] T. Macauley to H. Macaulay, 7 June 1831; G. O. Trevelyan, ed. *The Life and Letters of Lord Macaulay*, p. 158.

[2] Fitzgerald, *Emily, Duchess of Leinster*, p. 178.

[3] At least 3 of the 55 Foxite families adopted this expedient: Crespigny, Townshend and Winnington.

[4] Fitzgerald, p. 211.

[5] W. M. Thackeray, *Vanity Fair*, p. 88.

[6] S. Whitbread to R. Ward, n.d.; Fulford, *Samuel Whitbread*, p. 116.

[7] Mitchell, *The Whigs in Opposition 1815–30*, pp. 54–7.

few of the best Whigs could be got to attend, or were wished for. It was not safe to have many; especially as great prudence was necessary in speaking and toasting. Yet even the select, though rarely exceeding a dozen or two, were seldom allowed to assemble without sheriff's officers being sent to take down the names of those who entered.'[1] The dinners were continued in Edinburgh until 1825.

In the less tense atmosphere of England, the dinners were made occasions for the enunciation of Whig principles for the benefit of the faithful. At one such function in Suffolk, Lord Albemarle 'declared . . . Mr. Fox's name to be the rallying point of the constitution: he rejoiced in the utility of these meetings: in them, he said, there was an union of minds to discuss political subjects: they elicit liberal notions, and smooth the rough edges of our nature, so that men of different ranks, and with different degrees of information unite in the support of constitutional principles.'[2] A Scottish witness agreed that these assemblies 'animated, and instructed, and consolidated the Whig party'.[3] The nature of the Whig creed intoned at these dinners is of interest in that it is vital to discover if this Foxite cult was simply a statement of unremitting opposition to the Pittite system or whether it contained specific points of policy. In 1819, the Norfolk dinner was restricted to the objective of raising 'feeling against the unconstitutional conduct of the Tory administration'.[4] Of more interest is a London dinner attended by Creevey, consisting of 'Grandees and Tiers-etat united', at which they were all 'getting very much into the Reform line',[5] thereby suggesting that Fox's name was linked with that particular cause.

This point is made explicit by a close examination of the Fox Dinner held at Bury St. Edmunds in 1822. The Chairman opened the proceedings by saying how gratified he had been that advertisements for the dinner had been accompanied by a plea for Parliamentary Reform, because he considered 'that they were performing a duty by showing their attachment to those principles of civil and religious liberty which Mr. Fox had so boldly and so eloquently asserted.[6] The case for both Parliamentary Reform and religious toleration was then rehearsed, supported by a liberal use of quotation from Fox's speeches and utterances. Finally, new issues, in this case the question of recognizing the South American republics, on which Fox had never pronounced, were added to the standard tenets of the faith,

[1] Cockburn, *Memorials of my Own Time*, p. 83.
[2] Mitchell, *The Whigs in Opposition*, p. 56.
[3] Cockburn, *Memorials of my Own Time*, p. 398.
[4] Lord Albermarle, *Fifty Years of my Life*, pp. 104–10; 23 Jan. 1819.
[5] T. Creevey to Miss Ord, 29 Jan. 1821; Maxwell, *The Creevey Papers*, ii. 6.
[6] *The Times*, 23 Aug. 1822.

and endowed with the aura of Fox's sanction. The three toasts given on this occasion made the connection between the Foxite cult, and the reaffirmation of loyalty to old causes and the adherence to new ones quite clear. After 'The immortal memory of Charles James Fox', the Chairman gave 'The cause of civil and religious liberty throughout the world' and 'The patriots of Spain, Portugal and Columbia.'[1] These dinners not only provided a rallying point for the Whigs in times of extreme adversity, but also provided a forum for the exposition of the Whig creed. In this, the name and personality of Fox were crucial.

Some more detailed examination must now be made of the actual content of the Whig faith. That such a faith existed is beyond dispute. The historian of the Whig party of the early nineteenth century has referred openly to 'the new crop of issues planted and harvested in the reign of farmer George III . . . which created the basis of the division between Whig and tory in the nineteenth century.'[2] Contemporaries were equally aware of such a creed, and had no hesitation in associating it with Fox directly. In 1808, Robert Adair was congratulated upon his 'steady and unvarying attachment to those principles upon which we have uniformly acted together through life, and which ought now to be more than ever dear to us, from the irreparable loss we have sustained by the death of him, who was the invigorating soul of those principles.'[3] In speaking of this creed, the historian again and again is forced back upon the use of religious metaphor to convey its impact and character, and this is not coincidence. The Foxite opposition of the 1790s was seen as a martyrology. Under the Pittite persecution, certain beliefs were jealously guarded, by personal and public sacrifice, which made them all the more valuable to the succeeding generation.

Like a religion, the Foxite faith had many uses not immediately related to politics. In the early nineteenth century, it was employed as a code of instruction for Whig children. The Prince of Wales, as late as 1812, insisted that he made it his 'care to instil into the mind and heart of my daughter the knowledge and love of the true principles of the British Constitution; and I have pointed out to her young understanding, as a model for study, the political conduct of my most revered and lamented friend, Mr. Fox, who has asserted and maintained with such transcendent force the just principles upon which the government under this excellent constitution ought to be administered.'[4] Princess Charlotte learnt her lesson well. Even when

[1] *The Times*, 23 Aug. 1822.

[2] Mitchell, *The Whigs in Opposition*, p. 12.

[3] Duke of Bedford to R. Adair, 5 June 1808; Ld. Albemarle, *Fifty Years of my Life*, i. 233.

[4] ibid. p. 329.

her father had apostasized, she continued to distribute busts of Fox on the anniversary of his birthday, and maintained that 'Happy, thrice happy, will the moment be when the plans Mr. Fox pursued and planned are put into full force.'[1] Significantly, she singled out the abolition of slavery, legislative independence for Ireland, and full religious toleration as the principle planks in the Foxite programme. Such a list squares reasonably well with the rather more general aspirations of the Suffolk Foxite diners already mentioned.

The Foxite faith was also a fixed code, by which conduct could be regulated. Whenever questions of orthodoxy were brought up, appeals to the name of Fox was the surest way of justifying any action. When Samuel Whitbread was taken to task by William Grenville for addressing too many public assemblies, the answer was given that 'In such meetings you cannot meet the current of public opinion "bluff"—according to the expression of poor Fox—but you may guide, moderate and with proper management divert it.'[2] On this kind of evidence, it is not wholly surprising that Sylvester Douglas,[3] as late as 1819, thought it a sufficient description of a friend's politics to say that he was 'of the set of Charles Fox'.[4] In the general election of the previous year, Douglas thought it valuable to make a distinction between the moderate Whigs under Lansdowne and 'the more numerous Foxites, whose unascertained and undeclared leaders are Lord Holland and Lord Grey'.[5] References of this nature establish the point that the term 'Foxite' was of real political currency, involving a set of principles, which could be taught in Whig households and which could be appealed to by way of justifying courses of action. The terms of reference of a biographer of Fox make it difficult to examine this development in great detail, but some attempt must be made to evaluate the influence of the fifty-five Foxites of 1792 upon this situation.

In terms of physical survival, the Foxites enjoyed a reasonable record. Since so many of them were young men, it was to be expected that their stay in politics would be protracted. According to the most recent historian of the Whigs, twenty-one of the fifty-two M.P.s, who had supported Fox's anti-war Address in December 1792, were still in Parliament in 1812.[6] Of the fifty-five M.P.s who have come under scrutiny as firm Foxites in this chapter, eighteen were still in

[1] Princess Charlotte to Albermarle, 17 Jan. 1812; ibid. p. 331.

[2] S. Whitbread to W. Grenville, Apr. 1809; Fulford, *Samuel Whitbread*, p. 252.

[3] *Sylvester Douglas* (1743–1823); Whig barrister and diarist; broke with Fox over French Revolution and occupied a number of minor offices under Pitt; cr. Baron Glenbervie in the peerage of Ireland, 1800.

[4] F. Bickley, ed. *The Diaries of Sylvester Douglas, Lord Glenvervie*, ii. 349.

[5] ibid. ii. 309.

[6] Mitchell, *The Whigs in Opposition*, p. 9.

the House of Commons at this date.[1] This latter figure ignores those, like Wycombe and St. John, who had been called to the House of Lords and those, like Baring, who had been succeeded in their seats and politics by another member of their family. Also by limiting the scope of Foxite principles to the House of Commons in this way, no account is taken of such alternative centres as Holland House, where the Foxite faith was also propagated and given substance. Foxite principles are tested by their open avowal on the floor of the House of Commons.

The most obvious issue, on which the Foxites spoke as a group concerned the war. It was the struggle with Napoleon and European revolutionary movements up to 1822, which set the context for both Foxite and Pittite beliefs. The continuity of theme was made possible by the unchanging questions facing European statesmen. Whitbread, in moving a motion for the immediate opening of peace negotiations, on 29 February 1808, felt no hesitation in naming Fox as his authority: 'Having mentioned the name of Mr. Fox, I willingly acknowledge myself his true and genuine disciple. I am only feebly urging the sentiments which he would have forcibly uttered, if he had not been unhappily taken from us. I trust I am treading in his footsteps; would to God that his countenance were now upon me!'[2] Differences might exist between Grey and Whitbread as to what terms might be acceptable, but the Foxite insistence on peace was accepted by both. On this motion, ten[3] of the twenty-one surviving Foxites at this time supported Whitbread. On Ponsonby's motion against the proposal to send an expedition to Copenhagen on 3 February 1808, fourteen[4] of the twenty-one were to be found in the Opposition lobby. To these might well be added Grey, St. John and Erskine, who supported a similar motion in the Lords. As long as the issue of the war remained current, attitudes adopted towards this problem in the 1790s remained valid a decade or even two decades later.

As has been suggested earlier, this freezing of political attitudes applied equally to questions of reform. To abhor the events in France was to turn against reforms of all kinds. Because the Foxites chose to take a lenient view of the Revolution therefore, they became associated, often against their own inclinations, with the whole range of

[1] Adam, Anthonie, Aubrey, Byng, Curwen, Francis, Howerd, Hussey, Jekyll, Milner, North, Russell, Sheridan, Smith, Tarleton, Taylor, Townshend, Western, Whitbread.

[2] Roberts, *The Whig Party 1807–12*, p. 112.

[3] Adam, Anthonie, Aubrey, Bouverie, Byng, Jekyll, Russell, Sheridan, Smith, Whitbread.

[4] Adam, Anthonie, Byng, Fitzpatrick, Howerd, Jekyll, North, Russell, Sheridan, Smith, Taylor, Thompson, Western, Whitbread.

reforming causes. For Princess Charlotte to pick out Ireland, slavery and religious toleration as specifically Foxite was not at all unreasonable therefore, and she might plausibly have added Parliamentary Reform as well. The toast of the Suffolk Foxites lauding all civil and religious liberties was perhaps nearer the mark. It is doubtful whether Fox himself was ever emotionally attached to some of the causes taken up by his disciples, but, in the early nineteenth century, they were inextricably associated with his name.

The leading sponsors of Catholic Emancipation had long since come to pin their hopes on Fox and his disciples. When he died in 1806, Grattan admitted that, 'Ireland now feels the loss she has sustained by his separation from the cares of the world, and weeps in anguish over his tomb.'[1] In May 1808, a motion was presented in the Commons to relieve Catholics of their disabilities, and ten[2] of the twenty surviving Foxites voted for its acceptance. Crewe, Grey, St. John and Erskine followed the same course in the Lords. Twenty years later, in the divisions which were to place Catholic Emancipation finally on the statute book, four members of the old opposition of the 1790s, Byng, Smith, Taylor and Western, contributed to its success. In these same divisions, however, other names recur, which are just as familiar.[3] At Holland House, there was no doubt about the real victor on this occasion. Lady Holland told her son that 'The world are very just, & ascribe the merit entirely to Fox & Grattan & these worthies who first agitated the matter. Those at the eleventh hour, & Canning even, have not the glory. The old Whigs have acted admirably, & are much respected for their high, disinterested & zealous conduct.'[4] To pass such a measure was therefore to vindicate the past. In particular, Fox's determined stand against Pitt, expecially, but not exclusively, after 1789, was justified in the eyes of the succeeding generation by the ultimate success of measures of this kind.

The area of disagreement between Foxites on the nature and extent of Parliamentary Reform was always broader than on any other issue. The tension between Grey and Whitbread on this issue was real and marked. The important point is, however, that both felt committed to the measure in some form. According to lists put out by Cartwright himself, twenty of the fifty-five Foxites had been founder-members of

[1] *Parl. Hist.* xi. 567.

[2] Byng, Fitzpatrick, Howerd, Milner, North, Russell, Sheridan, Smith, Western, Whitbread.

[3] 3 Barings, Bouverie, Howerd, Grey (Visc. Howick), 2 Maitlands, Martin, North, Philipps, Russell, Townshend, 2 Whitbreads, Wilbraham, Winnington.

[4] Lady Holland to Henry Fox, 10 Apr. 1829; Earl of Ilchester, ed. *Elizabeth, Lady Holland to Her Son* 1821–1845, p. 101.

the Society of the Friends of the People in April 1792.[1] The later reactions of this group were varied. Some consciously and enthusiastically promoted reforming programmes following an avowedly Foxite tradition.[2] Others, like Grey, found their connection with reformers increasingly irksome, particularly after the coming to prominence of Burdett and his friends. The important point is, however, that, in spite of this aversion, Grey could not disentangle himself from his past history.[3] To have stood out against Pitt in the 1780s and1790s had been a glorious thing. As a corollary of that opposition, all kinds of reforming programmes had become a specifically Foxite concern. To withdraw from the campaign for Parliamentary Reform would therefore be to bring into question the whole purpose of their earlier martyrdom. Whether supported enthusiastically or merely condoned, the movement for Parliamentary reform had become a Whig responsibility.

Parliamentary divisions confirm this impression. On Brand's Motion for a Reform of Parliament, on 21 May 1810, thirteen of the surviving eighteen Foxite M.P.s turned out to support the proposal.[4] An even more interesting list is that on the Second Reading of the Reform Bill on 17 December 1831. Three members[5] of the old Foxite opposition survived to cast a vote in its favour, nearly forty years after Grey's motion of 1792. Besides these, members with the following familiar names appear in the same lobby: Adam, Baring, Bouverie, Fox, Grey, McCleod, Russell, Townshend, Whitbread, Wilbraham and Winnington. The same list also includes the names of families, which had apostasized in 1794, and which had since rejoined the Whigs. Inevitably, however, they rejoined on Foxite terms. Acceptance of most of the reform programme was now considered almost essential. The triumph of the Catholics, the anti-Slavers, and the Parliamentary reformers in the space of five years was therefore no accident. These issues were Fox's legacy. The Whig Ministry of 1830 dealt with them as a debt to the past, and in some cases, as the vindication of a whole career.

This debt to Fox was readily admitted in both personal and general terms. Grey concluded a speech in favour of a temperate reform bill, in 1810, by saying, 'If my Lords, any consideration more than another could confirm me in the validity of this doctrine, it would be the concurrent opinion of that great statesman, by whom it is the pride

[1] Cartwright, *The Life and Correspondence of Major Cartwright*, Appendix vii.

[2] Roberts, *The Whig Party 1807–1812*, p. 240.

[3] ibid. p. 173.

[4] Anthonie, Byng, Fitzpatrick, Howerd, Jekyll, Milner, North, Sheridan, Smith, Tarleton, Townshend, Western, Whitbread.

[5] Byng, Howerd, Western.

of my life to have been instructed and informed in the early part of my political career; I mean Mr. Fox . . .'[1] Lord John Russell, writing many years later, realized how much the Foxite legacy of reform, often in advance of what Fox himself would personally have sanctioned, shaped the development of the Whig party of the early nineteenth century. In 1875, he noted that 'Fox, on his side, induced Grey to bring forward reform in 1797, not with a hope of carrying any measure, but as a protest against the whole foreign and domestic policy of the government. Thus, reform became in men's minds closely associated with revolutionary change.'[2] To adhere to this policy in the 1790s was to invite proscription, but many Foxite sons were able to watch the policies of their fathers adopted between 1828 and 1833. The rewards were commensurate with the sacrifice. At least five Foxites had been ennobled by 1847,[3] and at least ten were to establish prosperous Whig/Liberal dynasties.[4]

A reasonable distinction can therefore be drawn between the Whig party before 1792 and the Foxite opposition of 1792–4. The first was still very much the party of Rockingham, dependent, in spite of a penumbra of independent Whig votes, upon the electoral empires of the dukes and borough-mongers. Under the impact of the crisis of 1782–4, Fox, in ideological terms, and Adam, in organizational matters, were able to impose an unprecedented cohesion upon the Whig opposition. Inevitably, however, the success of both men depended on how far they could influence the dukes. The Foxite opposition, after 1792, was of a very different character. In numerical terms, it had obviously to give up all pretensions to office, and since this was the case, it was an opposition whose only concern was to establish certain points at all costs. There was no point in staying with Fox for any other reason. Prudence and careers were clearly best served by joining Pitt. The purpose of opposition had therefore changed. From being a possible alternative administration in the 1780s, the Whig party had shrunk to being a pressure group, determined to voice protests of a moral and political nature.

With no dukes to manage, and no prospect of office to restrain his ideas, Fox was free to develop his thoughts. Fox in the party of the 1780s had always been a figure of weight and influence. As the leader of a rump of fifty-five M.P.s, he was dominant. The use of the term 'Foxite' underlines the extent to which these men were Fox's creatures. In political, social and intellectual life, Fox was a

[1] Lord John Russell, *An Essay on the History of the English Government and Constitution*, p. 271.

[2] Lord John Russell, *Recollections and Suggestions 1813–1873*, p. 37.

[3] Crewe (1806), Erskine (1806), Ludlow (1831), Western (1833), Byng (1847).

[4] Adam, Baring, Byng, Crewe, Fox, Grey, Milner, Smith, Whitbread.

master of long standing, who trained and entertained his disciples at the same time. Often reluctantly, they accepted the full reforming burden as a corollary of their political situation, and, when some of their old friends rejoined them in the years leading up to 1832, they did so on Foxite terms. Using these men as a bridge therefore, Fox bequeathed to the nineteenth century a markedly different party than that left behind by Rockingham in 1782. The Foxites were therefore important, not for their numbers, but for the tenacity with which they clung to the Foxite faith. Again, Lord John Russell was quick to catch the essential point about the Foxites when he recalled that in Fox's 'worst days an observer said of his party, "There are only forty of them, but every one of them is ready to be hanged for Fox"'.[1]

[1] Lord John Russell, *Recollections and Suggestions*, p. 268.

APPENDIX I

Record of Voting in the House of Commons, February 1782–March 1784

KEY

(i) Vote on Fox's motion of censure on Lord Sandwich's administration of the Navy. 20 February 1782.

(ii) Vote on Conway's motion condemning North's American policies. 22 February 1782.

(iii) Vote on Conway's motion demanding an immediate end of the American War. 27 February 1782.

(iv) Vote on Lord John Cavendish's motion of no confidence in North's Administration. 8 March 1782.

(v) Vote on Sir John Rous's motion of no confidence in North's Administration. 15 March 1782.

(vi) M.P.s attending Rockingham's first levée as chief minister. 11 April 1782.

(vii) List of the House of Commons drawn up by Lord Shelburne. November 1782.

(viii) Voting on Shelburne's peace proposals. 18 February 1783.

(ix) Robinson's list of members of the Foxite Party. March 1783.

(x) M.P.s voting for the 'East India Bill on the First Division'.

(xi) Vote on the second reading of the East India Bill. 27 November 1783.

(xii) List of the House of Commons drawn up by John Robinson. January 1784.

(xiii) List of the House of Commons drawn up by Edmund Burke. February 1784.

(xiv) List of the House of Commons drawn up by John Stockdale. March 1784.

*	Voting with Fox.
X	Voting against Fox.
H	Hopeful.
D	Doubtful.

1	'Supporters of Lord North's Administration Voting with Mr. Pitt.'
1A	Former supporters of Lord North's Administration deserting to Pitt after the India Bill.
1B	Former supporters of Lord North's Administration who 'joined Lord Shelburne'.
2	'Members of the old opposition with Mr. Pitt.'
3N	'The Friends of Lord North voting with Lord North.'
4F	'Old opposition voting with Mr. Fox.'
5	'New Members voting with Mr. Pitt.'
6	'New Members voting with Mr. Fox.'
7	'Doubtful.'
8	'Old Doubtfuls voting with Mr. Pitt.'
9	'Old Doubtfuls voting with coalition.'
10	'Not voted.'
P	Paired.
||	Point of entry to, or departure from, the House of Commons.

Member		ii	iii	iv	v	vi	vii	viii	ix	x	xi	xii	xiii	xiv
ACLAND, Jo.							H					H	1B	X
A'COURT, W. P.	*	*	*	*	*	*	D	*	*			*	4F	*
ADAM, W.	X	X	X	X	X		X	*		*	*	*	3N	*
ADEANE, J. W.	*	*	*	*	*		X	X			X	X	2	X
AFFLECK, Ed.			||				H					*		
ALTHORP	*	*	*	*	*	*	*	*	*||					
AMBLER, Chas.							H			*		H	1A	X
AMCOTTS, Wm.	X	X	X	X	X		H			*	*	D	3N	*
ANDERSON, Ev.	*	*	*	*	*	*	D	*		*	*	*	4F	*
ANNESLEY, Fr.	*	*	*	*	*		X	X				X	2	X
ANSON, Geo.	*	*	*	*	*	*	D	X		*	*	*	4F	*
ANSTRUTHER, Sir J.	X	X	X		X		X			*	*	*	3N	*
APSLEY									||			X		X
ARCEDECKNE, Ch.		*	*	*	*		X	X			X	X	2	X
ARDEN, P.							||					X		X
ASHBY, S.											||	D		X
ASTLEY, Sir E.	*	*	*		*		H	X				H	2	X
ATKINSON, C.	X		X	X	X		D	*			||			
AUBREY, Jo.	*	*	*	*	*	*	X	X			X	X	2	X
BACON, A.	X	X	X	X	X		H	*			*	H	3N	*
BACON, E.							H						10	
BAKER, P.	*	*	*	*	P		H		*			*	8	X
BAKER, W.	*	*	*	*	*	*	*	*	*	*	*	*	4F	*
BAMPFYLDE, Sir Ch.	*	*		*	*		X	*	*	*	*	*	4F	*
BANKES, H.	*	*	*	*	*	*	X	X			X	X	2	X
BARING, Jo.		*	*	*	*		X	X			X	X	2	X
BARNE, B.	X	X	X	X	X		X	X			X	X	1B	X
BARRE, Is.	*	*	*	*	*	*	X					X	10	
BARRINGTON, Jo.					*		X				X	X	2	X
BARROW, Ch.	*	*	*	*	*		X	X		*	*	*	4F	*

BARWELL, Ri.			X	X	X		H	*				X	1	X
BASSET, Sir. Fr.	X		X	X	X		X	*		*	*	*	3N	*
BASSET, Fr.	X	X	X	X	X		X	*		*	*	X	3N	*
BATEMAN	X	X	X	X	X		H					X	1	X
BAYNTUN, An.	X	X		X	X		X	*				H	1A	X
BEAUCHAMP	X	X	X	X	X		D	*		*	*	*	3N	*
BEAUFOY, H.									‖			X		X
BECKFORD, R.	*	*	*	*	*	*	D	*	*	*	*	*	4F	*
BENFIELD, P.							H					D	10	
BENTINCK, Ld. Ed.				*	*	*	*	*	*	*	*	*	4F	*
BENYON, R.	*	*	*	*	*		D	*	*	*	*	*	4F	X
BERKELEY, Geo.									‖			D		
BERTIE, P.	*	P	*	*	*		X	X				X	2	X
BISSHOPP, Sir C.	X	X	X	X	X		H					H	1A	X
BLACKWELL, S.	X	X	X	X	X		X	X				H	3N	*
BLAIR, J. H.	X	*	*	X	X	*	X	X				D	1B	X
BLAKE, Sir P.	*	*					H					D	1	X
BOND, J.	X	X	X	X	X		H	*			X	H	1B	X
BOONE, Ch.	X	X	X	X	X		H	X			X	H	1B	X
BOOTLE, R. W.	*	*	*	*	P		H	*	*		X	X	2	X
BOSCAWEN, H.					X		H	X				X	1A	X
BOUVERIE, W. H.			*	*	*		X				X	X	4F	*
BOWES, A. R.	*			*	*		X					H	3N	*
BOWLBY, T.	X	X	X	X	X		X‖							
BOYD, Jo.	X		X	X	X		D	X			X	X	1B	X
BRADDYLL, W.	*	*	*	*	*		X	*	*	*	*	*	4F	*
BRAMSTON, T.	X	X	X	X	X		H	X				H	1	X
BRETT, Ch.					‖	*		X			X	D	2	X
BRICKDALE, Ma.	X	X	X	X	X		X	X				H	3N	*
BRIDGEMAN, Sir H.						‖	H	*	*	*	*	*	4F	*
BRIDGEMAN, H. S.						‖								
BROWN, L.	X	X	X	X	X	*	H			*	*	D	3N	*

Member	i	ii	iii	iv	v	vi	vii	viii	ix	x	xi	xii	xiii	xiv
BRUDENELL, G. B.	*	*	*	*	*		X				X	X	1B	X
BULKELEY	*	*	*	*	*	*	X	X			X	X	2	X
BULL, Fr.	*	*	*	*	*		X				‖			
BULLER, J. (Snr.)	X	X	X	X	X		H	*				X	1B	X
BULLER, J. (Jnr.)	X		‖								‖		1B	
BULLOCK, J.	*		P	*			*		*			*		*
BUNBURY, Sir T.	*	*	*	*	*		D	*	*	*	*	*	4F	*
BURGOYNE, J.	*	*	*	*	*		D			*	*	*	4F	*
BURKE, E.	*	*	*	*	*	*	*	*	*	*	*	*	4F	*
BURRALD, H.							D			*	*	*	3N	*
BURRELL, Sir M.							H					D	10	
BURRELL, Sir P.					‖		H	*		*	*	H	3N	*
BURTON, Fr.	*	*	X				X	X			X	X	10	
BYNG, Geo.	*	*	*	*	*	*	*	*	*	*	*	*	4F	*
CALVERT, Jo. (Snr.)	X	X	X	X	X		X	X				X	1	X
CALVERT, Jo. (Jnr.)	X	X	X	X	X		X	X		*	*	*	1A	X
CAMPBELL, Ld. Fred.	X	X	X	X	X		H	X		*	*	*	1A	X
CAMPBELL, Jas.	X	X	X	X	X		X	X		*	*	*		X
CAMPBELL, Jo.			X	X	X		H	*				H	10	
CAREW, R. P.								‖				*		*
CASWELL, T.	X	X	X	X	X		X	*		*	*	*	1A	X
CAVENDISH, Ld. Geo.	*	*	*	*	*	*	*	*	*	*	*	*	4F	*
CAVENDISH, Ld. G. A. H.	*	*	P	*	*		*	*	*	*	*	*	4F	*
CAVENDISH, Ld. Jo.	*	*	*	*	*	*	*	*	*	*	*	*	4F	*
CAWTHORNE, J. F.								‖				H		*
CECIL, H.	X		X		X		H					H	10	
CHARTERIS, Fr.	X		X	X	X		H	*				*	3N	*
CHAYTOR, W.	X	X	X	X	P		H			*	*	X	1A	X
CHILD, R.				*	*‖									
CLARGES, Sir T.	*	*	*	*	*	*	H	‖						

CLAVERING, Sir T.	X	X	X	P	X		H					H	10	
CLAYTON, W.	X						X				X	D	5	X
CLAYTON, Sir R.	*	*	*	*	*	*	*	*	*	*	*	*	4F	*
CLERKE, Sir P.	X	P	P	P	P	*	X	X		*	*	*	4F	*
CLEVELAND, J.	X	X	X	X	X	*	X	*				X	1A	X
CLINTON, Sir H.							D	*		*	*	H	10	
CLIVE	X	X	X	X	X		H			*	*	*	3N	*
CLIVE, W.	X	X	X	X	X		H	*		*	*	X	3N	*
COCKBURN, Sir J.	X	X	X	X	X		X	*		*	*	*	1A	X
COCKS, Sir C.							X					H	1	X
COCKS, J. S.	‖											H		X
CODRINGTON, Sir W.	*	*	*	*	*		H	X	*			*	4F	*
COGHILL, Sir J.	X			X	X		X			*		D	1	X
COKE, D. P.	*		X				H	*		*	*	H	9D	*
COKE, E.	*	*	*	*	*		H	*	*	*	*	*	4F	*
COKE, T. W.	*	*	*	*	*	*	H	*	*	*	*	*	4F	*
CONWAY, H. S. Gen.	*	*	*	*	*		X	X		*	*	*	4F	*
CONWAY, H. S.	X	X	X	X	X		X	*		*	*	*	3N	*
CONWAY, R. S.	X	X	X	X	X		D	*		*	*	*	3N	*
CONWAY, W. S.												*		*
COOPER, Sir G.	X	X	X	X	X		H	*		*		*	3N	*
CORNEWALL, Sir G.	*	*	*	*	*	*	H	X				D	4F	*
CORNWALL, C. W. (Speaker of the House)														
CORNWALL, Fr.	X	X	X	X	X		X	‖						
CORNWALLIS					‖		X	X				X	1	X
COTES, J.						‖	*	*	*	*	*	*	6	*
COTTON, Sir R.			*	*	*		X	X				X	2	X
COURTNEY, J.		X	X	X	X		D	*	*	*	*	*	3N	*
COURTOWN	X	P	X	X	X		X	X				X	1	X
COX, L.	X	X	X	X	X		H	X		*	*	*	1	X
COXE, R. H.						*	D		*			*	10	

Member	i	ii	iii	iv	v	vi	vii	viii	ix	x	xi	xii	xiii	xiv
CRAUFORD, Jas.													6	
CRAWFORD, Jo.	X	X	X	X	X	*	H	*	*	*	*	*	3N	*
CRESPIGNY, P. C.	X	X	X	X	X		H			*	*	*	3N	*
CREWE, J.			*	*	*	*	X	X		*	*	*	4F	*
CUNYNGHAME, Sir W.	X	X	X	X	X		H	*		*	*	*	3N	*
CURTIS, J.						‖						X		X
CURZON, N.	X	X	X	X	X	*	X	*		*	*	D	1A	X
CUST, F.	X	X	X	X	X		H			*	*	H	10	*
CUST, P.	X			X	X		H			*	*	D	3N	
DALRYMPLE, H.	X	X	X	X	X		X	X			X	X	1B	X
DAMER, G.							H	*		*	*	*	3N	*
DARBY, G.	X	X	X	X	X		H	*		*	*	*	3N	*
DARKER, J.		*					H	*				‖		
DAUBENY, G.	X		X	X	X		X	X		*	*	H	3N	*
DAVENPORT, T.	X	X	X				X	*		*	*	*	3N	*
DAVERS, Sir C.	*	*	*	*	*	*	H	X		*	*	*	4F	*
DAVIES, S.									‖			X		*
DAWES, J.			X	X			H				X	X	1B	X
DAWKINS, H.	*	*	*	*	*	*	X		*			*	4F	*
DELAVAL, Sir J.	X	X	X	X	X		X	*				*	3N	*
DELME, P.	X		X	X	X		D	*		*	*	*	3N	*
DEMPSTER, G.							H	X				*	4F	*
DERING, Sir E.	X		X	X	X		X	X		*	*	H	1A	X
DICKINSON, W.	X	X	X	X	X		H	*		*	*	*	3N	*
DIMSDALE, B.	*	*	*	X	*		X	X			X	X	8D	X
DOLBEN, Sir W.	X	*	X	X	X		H	*		*	*	H	1A	X
DOUGLAS, A.								X				X	1B	*
DOUGLAS, J.	X	X	X	X	X		X	X	‖					
D'OYLEY, Ch.						*	X	*				*	3N	
DRAKE, W. (Snr.)	*	*	*	*	*		H	X			X	H	1B	X

DRAKE, W. (Jnr.)	*	*	*	*			H	X			X	H	2	X
DRUMMOND, A.	X	X	X	X	X	*	H	*		*	*	X	1A	X
DRUMMOND, H.	X	X	X	X	X		H	*				H	1	X
DUNCANNON	*	*	*	*	*	*	*	*	*	*	*	*	4F	*
DUNCOMBE, H.	*	*	*	*	*		H	X			X	X	2	X
DUNDAS, C.			P	P	P	*	*	*	*	*	*	*	4F	*
DUNDAS, H.	X	X	X	X	X		X	X			X	X	1B	X
DUNDAS, Sir T.	X	*	*	*	*	*	*	*	*	*	*	*	4F	*
DUNNING, Jo.	*	*	*	*	*‖									
DUNTZE, Sir J.					X		H					X	10	
DURAND, J.	X	X	X		X		H	*				*	10	
DUTTON, J.				X	X		X			*	*	*	1B	X
EDEN, Sir J.			P	P	P		D	*				*	3N	*
EDEN, W.							D	*		*	*	*	3N	*
EDMONSTONE, Sir A.	X	X	X	X	X		X	X		*	*	*	1A	X
EDWIN, C.	*	*	*				H					D	8	X
EGERTON, J.	X	X	X	X	P		H	*				D	1A	X
EGERTON, Sir T.	X	X	X	X	X		H	*				H	1	X
ELIOT, E.	*	*	*	*	*	*	X	X			‖			
ELIOT, E. J.	*	*	*	*	*	*	X	X				X	2	X
ELLIOT, Sir G.	X	*	*	X	*		D			*	*	*	4F	*
ELLIS, W.	X	X	X	X	X		H	*		*	*	*	3N	*
ELPHINSTONE, G. K.							H	*				*	6	*
ELWES, Jo.	*	*	*	*	*		D	*		*		H		*
ERSKINE, Sir Jas.						‖						*		*
ERSKINE, Th.									‖			*		*
ESTWICK, S.	*	*	*	*	*	*	X	X			X	X	2	X
EUSTON					‖	*		X	*			*	5	X
EVELYN, W.	X	P	P	P	P		H	*				*	3N	*
EWER, W.	X	X	X	X	X		H	X		*	*	D	3N	*
EYRE, A.							H	*		*		H	10	

Member	i	ii	iii	iv	v	vi	vii	viii	ix	x	xi	xii	xiii	xiv
EYRE, F.	X	X	X	X	X		H	*		*	*	*	3N	*
FAIRFORD	X	X	X	X	X		H					X	1	X
FANE, H.	X	X	X	X	X		X	*		*	*	H		*
FARNABY, Sir C.	X	X	X	X	X		H	*				*	1A	X
FARRER, Th.	*	*		X	*	*	D	*				*	2	X
FETHERSTONEHAUGH, Sir H.						‖	H	*	*			*	4F	*
FERGUSON, Sir A.	X		X	X	X		X				X	X	1B	X
FIELDING	X	X	X	X	X		X	X				*	1	X
FIFE	*	X	*	*	*		H	X				D	10	
FITZHERBERT, Thos.	X	P	X	X	X		H	*				D	10	
FITZPATRICK, R.	*	*	*	*	*		*	*	*	*	*	*	4F	*
FITZWILLIAM, G.	*	*	*	*	*	*	*	*	*	*	*	*	4F	*
LE FLEMING, Sir M.				*	*		X	X			X	X	2	X
FLETCHER, H.	*	*	*	*	*		D		*	*	*	*	4F	*
FLOOD, H.									‖			X		X
FLUDYER, G.								‖				H		X
FLUDYER, Sir S.	X	X			*		H		*			D	8	X
FOLEY, A.	*	*	*	*	*		D	*	*			*	4F	*
FOLEY, E.	*	*	*	*	*		D	*	*	*	*	*	4F	*
FOLJAMBE, F.									‖			*		*
FONNEREAU, M.	X	X	X	X	X		H	*		*	*	H	3N	*
FORESTER, G.	*	*	P	P	P		D	*	*	*	*	*	4F	*
FOX, C. J.	*	*	*	*	*		*	*	*	*	*	*	4F	*
FRASER, A.					‖		X	*		*	*		5	
FREDERICK, Sir Ch.				X	X	*	X	*		*	*	*	3N	*
FREDERICK, Jo.	X	X		X	X		X	*		*	*	D	3N	*
FULLER, J.	X	X	*	X	X	*	X	X				H	1B	X
GALWAY	X	X		X	X	*	H				X	X	1B	X
GARDEN, A.	X	*					X	X				X	1	X

GARDINER, J. W.	*	*	*	*	*		X	X			X	X	2	X
GARFORTH, J.	*	*	*	*	*		X	X			X	X	2	X
GASCOIGNE, Sir T.	*	*	*	*	*	*	D	*	*		*	*	4F	*
GASCOYNE, B. (Snr.)	X		X		X		D	*			X	X	1B	X
GASCOYNE, B. (Jnr.)	X	X	X	X	X		D	*			X	X	1B	X
GIBBON, E.	X	X	X	X	X		H	*				H	10	
GIDEON, Sir S.	X	X	X	X	X		X	X		*	*	*	1A	X
GILBERT, T.	X	*	*		X		X	X			X	X	1B	X
GIPPS, G.	*	*	*		*		H	X			X	X	2	X
GODDARD, A.	P	P	P	P	*		X	X		*	*	H	2	X
GORDON, Ld. A.	X		X		X		X	*				H	1A	X
GORDON, Sir W.	X	X	X				H	*	||					
GORDON, Ld. W.	X		X				X					*	1A	X
GOUGH, Sir H.			*				H					D		X
GOULD, Sir C.	X	X	X	X	X	*	X			*	*	*	1A	X
GRAHAM	X	*	*	X	X		X	X			X	X	1B	X
GRAHAM, Geo.	X		X	X	X		H			*	*	D	3N	*
GRAVES, W.		X	X		X		H	*	||					
GREGORY, Ro.	*	*	*	*	*		H					*		*
GRENVILLE, Jas.	*	*	*	*	*	*	X	X			X	X	2	X
GRENVILLE, Thos.	*	*	*	*	*		D	*	*	*	*	*	4F	*
GRENVILLE, Wm.	*	*	*	*	*		X	X			X	X	2	X
GREVILLE, C.	X	X	X		X		H	*		*	*	X	3N	*
GREY, B.	*	*	*	*			*		*	*	*	*	4F	*
GRIFFIN, Sir J.	*	*	*	*	*		H	X		*	X	H	2	X
GRIMSTONE											||	*		X
GROSVENOR, Thos.	*	X	X	X			H	X			X	X	1B	X
GUISE, Sir W.	*	*	*	*	*		H	X	||					
GULSTON, J.	X	X	X	X	X		H					X	3N	*
HALE, F.	X	X	X	X	X		X	X		*	*	*	3N	*
HALLIDAY, J.	X	X			X		X	*		*	*	D	1A	X

Member		ii	iii	iv	v	vi	vii	viii	ix	x	xi	xii	xiii	xiv
HALSEY, T.		*	*	*	*	*	H	X				D		*
HAMILTON, J.											||	H		X
HAMILTON, W.	*		P	*	P		X		*			X	2	X
HAMMET, B.					||		X	X			X	D	5	X
HANBURY, J.	*	*	*	*	*	*	D	X	*			D	10	
HANGER, W.	X	X	P	X	X		D	*		*	*	*	3N	*
HARBORD, Sir H.	*	*	*	*	*	*	D	X				H	10	
HARDINGE, G.											||	X		X
HARE, J.	*	*	*	*	*		*	*	*	*	*	*	4F	*
HARLEY, Th.	X	X	X		X		H					X		X
HARRIS, Sir J.							X					H	6	*
HARRISON, J.	*			*	*		D	*	*			*	4F	*
HARTLEY, D.						||	*	*	*			*	4F	*
HARTLEY, W.	*	*	*	*	*		*	*	*	*	*	*	4F	*
HARVEY, E.							H	X				X	1	X
HATTON, G.	X	X	X	X	X		H	*		*	*	H	3N	*
HENDERSON, Sir J.				X	X		X	*				X	1	X
HENNIKER, J.	X	X	X	X	X		H	*		*	*	*	3N	*
HERBERT	*	*	*	*	*	*	X	X				X	10	
HERBERT, H.	X	X	X	X	X		X	*			X	*	1A	X
HERRIES, Sir R.	X	X	X	X	X		X	*		*	*	D	3N	*
HILL, N.	*	*	*				H	X			X	H	1B	X
HILL, R.	*	*	*	*	*		H				X	H	2	X
HINCHINGBROOKE	X	X	X	X	X		D	*		*	*	X	1A	X
HOGHTON, Sir H.	X	X	X	X	X		H	X		*	*	H	1A	X
HOLDSWORTH, A.	*	*	*	*	*		X	X				*	2	X
HONEYWOOD, F.	*	*	*	*	*	*	X	X			X	X	4F	*
HONEYWOOD, P.	*	P	*	P	*		H					*	4F	*
HOPKINS, R.	*		*	*	*	*	X	X			X	*	2	*

HOTHAM, Sir R.	*	*	*	*	*		H	*	*	*	*	X	4F	*
HOWARD, Sir G.	X		X	X	X		X	*			X	X	1B	X
HOWE	*		*	*	*	*‖								
HUDSON, G.	X				X		H	‖						
HUNGERFORD, J.	X	X	X	*	*		H	*				H	1A	X
HUNT, Geo.	*	*	*	*	*	*	H	X		*	*	D	4F	*
HUSSEY, W.	*	*	*	*	*	*	X	X		*	*	H	4F	*
HYDE			X		X		H	*			X	X	1A	X
IRWIN, Sir J.	X	X	X	X	X		H		‖					
JACKSON, R.	X			X			X	X			X	X	1B	X
JAMES, Sir W.	X	X	X	X	X		*			‖				
JENKINSON, C.	X	X	X	X	X		X	X			X	X	1B	X
JERVIS, Sir J.								‖				D		X
JERVOISE, J. C.	*	*	*	*	*		H			*	*	*	4F	*
JOHNES, Th.	X	X	X	P	P		X	X		*	*	*	1A	X
JOHNSTON, P.	X	X	X	X	X		H	X			X	D	1B	X
JOHNSTONE, Geo.				X	X		H	*			X	X	1B	X
JOLLIFFE, T.	X	X	X	X	X		D	*		*	*	*	3N	*
JOLLIFFE, W.	X	X	X		X		D	*		*	*	H	3N	*
JONES, H.	X		X	X	X		H					H	1A	X
KEENE, B.	*	*	*	*	*		H	X				D	2	
KEENE, W.	X	X	X	X	X		H	*		*	*	*	3N	*
KEMP, T.	*	*	*	*	*	*	X	X			X	D	2	X
KENRICK, J.	X	X	X	X	X	*	D	*		*	*	H	3N	*
KENSINGTON	X		X	X	X		X	X		*	*	*	1A	X
KENYON, L.	*	*	*	*			X	X			X	X	2	X
KEPPEL, A.	*	*	*	*	*‖									
KNIGHT, R.	*	*	*	*	*		X	X		*	*	X	4F	*
KNIGHTLEY, L.	*		*	*	*		H	X			X	X	8D	X

Member		ii	iii	iv	v	vi	vii	viii	ix	x	xi	xii	xiii	xiv
LADBROKE, R.	*	*	*	*	*	*	H	X		*	*	D	4F	*
LAMBTON, J.	*	*	*	*	*		D	X				*	4F	*
LASCELLES, E.	X	X	X		X		H	X				H	1	X
LAURIE, Sir R.	X	X	X	X	X		H	X				D	1A	X
LAWLEY, Sir R.	*	*	*	*	*		H				X	*	4F	*
LAWRENCE, W.	*	*	*	*	*		H	*				H	10	
LEE, J.					||	*	*	*	*	*	*	*	4F	*
LEGH, T. P.							H					*	3N	*
LEIGHTON, Sir C.	*	*	*	*	*		H	X			X	H	2	X
LEMON, Sir W.	*	*	*	*	*		X	X				H	2	X
LENNOX, Ld. Geo.	*	*	*	*	*		X				X	X	2	X
LETHIEULLIER, B.			*	X	X		H	X				*	3N	*
LEWES, Sir W.	*		*	*	*	*	X	X			X	X	2	X
LEWIS, E.	X	X	X	X	X		H	*		*	*	*	3N	*
LEWISHAM	X	X	X	X	X		H	*		*	*	*	3N	*
LINCOLN	X	X										H	1A	X
LISBURNE	X	X	P	X	X		H	*				H	3N	*
LISTER, T.	*		*	*	*	*	H	*	*	*	*	*	4F	*
LLOYD, M.						||	H			*	*	D	3N	*
LONG, D.	*	*	*	*	*	*	*	*	*	*	*	*	4F	*
LONG, Sir J.		X	X	X	X		H	*				H	1	X
LOVEDEN, E. L.									||			H		X
LOWTHER, Jas.	*		*	*	*		X	X			X	X	2	X
LOWTHER, Sir Jas.							X	X			X	X	2	X
LOWTHER, Jo.	*	*	*	*	*		X	X			X	X	2	X
LOWTHER, W.	*	*	*	*	*		X	X			X	X	2	X
LUCAN						||		*	*	*	*	*	4F	*
LUCAS, T.	*	*	*	*	*	*	X	X				*	4F	*
LUDLOW	*		*	*	*	*	X	X		*	*	*	4F	*
LUSHINGTON, S.											||	*		*
LUTHER, J.	*	*	*	*	*		H					*	4F	*

LUTTRELL, F. F.	X		*	X	X		X	X‖						
LUTTRELL, H. L.							H			*	*	D	3N	*
LUTTRELL, Jas.						*	D					*	10	
LUTTRELL, Jo.	X	X	X	X			D	*		*	*	*	3N	*
LUTTRELL, Jo. F.							X	X				H	10	
LYGON, W.			*	*	P		D					D	2	X
MACDONALD, A.	X	X	X	X	X		X	*			X	X	1B	X
MACDOWEL, W.									‖			H		X
MACKRETH, R.	X	X	X	X	X		X	X			X	D	1B	X
MACKWORTH, Sir H.							X	X		*	*	H	3N	*
MACLEOD							X					D	5	X
MACPHERSON, Jas.	X	X	X	X	X		H	*			X	X	1B	X
MAHON	*	*	*	*	*		X	X			X	H	2	X
MAITLAND	*	*	*	*	*	*	H	*		*	*	*	4F	*
MALDEN	X	X	X	X	X		X			*	*	*	3N	*
MANN, Sir H.	*	*	*	*	*		H	*				D	4F	*
MANNERS, Ld. R. (Snr.)						‖								
MANNERS, Ld. R. (Jnr.)					‖									
MANSFIELD, J.	X	X	X	X	X		D	*	*	*	*	*	3N	*
MARRIOTT, Sir J.	X		X	X	X		H	X			*	*	3N	*
MARSHAM, Chas.	*	*	*	*	*	*	H	X			X	X	4F	*
MARTIN, J.	*	*	*	*	*	*	D	X			X	X	2	X
MASTERMAN, W.	X	X	X		X		X	X		*	*	X	1A	X
MAWBY, Sir J.	*	*	*	*	*	*	X	X			X	X	2	X
MAYNE, R.	X	X	X	X	X	‖								
MAYOR, J.	X	X	X	X	X		X	‖						
MEDLEY, G.									‖			*		X
MEDOWS, C.	*	*	*	*	*		H					*	4F	*
MELBOURNE	X	X		X			H	*		*	*	*	3N	*
MELLISH, C.	X	X	X	X	X		H	*		*	*	*		
METHUEN, P.					X		X						1	

Member	i	ii	iii	iv	v	vi	vii	viii	ix	x	xi	xii	xiii	xiv
MICHELL, D.	X	X	X	X	X		H	*				H	3N	*
MIDDLETON	*	*	*	*	*		X	X	*	*	*	X	4F	*
MIDDLETON, Sir W.	*	*	*	*	*	*	X	X				D	10	
MINCHIN, H.	*	P	*	*	*		H	*	*	*	*	*	4F	*
MOLESWORTH, Sir W.											‖	X		X
MOLINEUX, C.			*	*	*	*	X					X	10	
MONCKTON, E.	*	*	*	*	*	*	H	*	*	*	*	*	4F	*
MONKTON, R.						‖					‖			
MONTAGU, F.	*	*	*	*	*	*	*	*	*	*	*	*	4F	*
MONTAGU, J.		*	*	*	*		X	X				D	2	X
MORANT, E.	*	*	*	*	*		X	X	*		*	D	4F	*
MORGAN, C.	X		*	X	X		H	X				D	3N	*
MORGAN, J.	X		*	X	X		H	X				*	3N	*
MORRIS, S. L.	X		X	X	X	*	X	X				*	1A	X
MORSHEAD, J.	X	X	X	X	X		H	*				*	3N	*
MORTIMER, H.			*	*	*	*	X	*	*	*	*	D	2	X
MOSTYN, Sir R.		*	*	*	*	*	X	X				*	4F	*
MOYSEY, A.	*	*	X	X	X		H	*		*	*	H	3N	*
MULGRAVE	X	X	X	X	X		H	*				*	1B	X
MUNRO, Sir H.							H							
MURRAY					X	*	X					D	10	X
MURRAY, J.	X	X	X	X	X		X	X		*	*	*	1A	X
MYDDLETON, R.			*				H					H	10	
NEDHAM, W.	*	*	*	*	*	*	X	*	*			*	4F	*
NESBITT, J.			*		*	*	D	*	*			*	4F	*
NEVILLE, R.		‖	*				H	X			X	*	2	X
NEWHAVEN	X		X	X	X		H	*				H	1A	X
NEWNHAM, N.	*	P	*	*	*	*	H			*	*	*	4F	*
NICHOLLS, J.											‖			*
NOEL, T.							D					D	10	

NORTH	X	X	X	X	X		H	*		*	*	*	3N	
NORTH, G.	X	X	X	X	X		H	*		*	*	*	3N	*
NORTON, E.	*	*	*	*	*		X	X			X	X	2	X
NORTON, F.	*		*	*	*‖									
NORTON, W.						‖	X					X	2	X
NUGENT	X	P	P	P	P		X					H	1B	X
ONSLOW, G.	X	P	X	X	X	*	X	*		*	*	*	3N	*
ONSLOW, T.	X	X	X	X	X		H			*	*	*	3N	*
ORD, J.	X	X	X	X	X		X	X		*	*	H	3N	*
ORDE, T.	X	X	X	X	X		X	X			X	X	1B	X
OSBORN, Sir Geo.	X	X	X	X	X		H	*		*	*	*	1A	X
OWEN, Sir H.							X			*	*	*	10a	
OWEN, H.	X	X	X	X	X		X	*		*	*	*	3N	*
OWEN, W. M.	*		*	*	*		D			*	*	*	4F	*
PAGE, F.	X	X	X	X	X		H	*				H	3N	*
PALK, R.		*	*	*	*	*	X	X			X	H	2	X
PALLISER, Sir H.	X	X	X	X	X		H			*	*	*	1A	
PALMERSTON	X	X	X	X	X		H	*		*	*	*	3N	*
PARDOE, J.	X		X	X	X		H	*		*	X	H	1B	X
PARKER	X	X	X	X	X		X	X				*	10	
PARKER, J. (Devon)	*	*	*	*	*		X	X				X	2	X
PARKER, J. (Clitheroe)	*	*	*	*	*	‖								
PARRY, J.	*	*	*	*	*	*	X	X				X	2	X
PAYNE, Sir R.	X	X	X	X	X		H			*	*	*	3N	*
PEACHEY, J.	X	*	*	X	X		H	X				H	1A	X
PEIRSE, H.	*	*	*	*	*		D		*		X	*	2	X
PELHAM, C.	*	*	*	*	*	*	H	*	*			*	4F	*
PELHAM, H.	X	X		X	X	*	D	X		*	*	*	3N	*
PELHAM, T.		*	*	X	X		X	X				D	9D	*
PENNINGTON, J.			*	*	*		X					H		X
PENNYMAN, Sir J.	*	*	*	*	*		H	X			X	*	2	X

Member	i	ii	iii	iv	v	vi	vii	viii	ix	x	xi	xii	xiii	xiv
PENRUDDOCK, C.	*	*	*	*	*		X	*		*	*	H	3N	*
PENTON, H.	X	X	X	X	X		H	*				H	3N	*
PERCEVAL, C.	X	X	X	X	X		H	*			X	X	1B	X
PERCY, Ld. A.							X					H	1A	X
PEYTON, Sir H.						‖						X		X
PHILIPPS, Geo.				X	X		H	X				D	10	
PHILIPSON, R.	X	X	X	X	X		X	X			X	X	1B	X
PHIPPS, C.	X	X	X	X	X		H				X	X		X
PHIPPS, J.	*	*	*	*	*		X	X			X	X	2	X
PIGOT, H.	*	*	*	*	*	*	X	*			*	*	4F	*
PITT, G.				X	X		X	X				X	1A	X
PITT, T.	*	*	*	*	*	*	X	X			X	X	5	
PITT, W.	*	*	*	*	*		X	X			X	X	2	X
PITT, W. M.	*	*	*	*	*	*	X	X				X	10	
PLUMER, W.	*	*	*	*	*			*	*	*	*	*	4F	*
POCHIN, W.	*	*	*	*	*		D	X			X	H	2	X
POLHILL, N.	*	*	*	*	*	‖								
POULETT, A.	X	X	X	X	X		X	X		*	*	H	3N	*
POWNEY, P.	X	X	X	X	X		H	*			X	X	1B	X
POWYS, T.	*	*	*	*	*	*	H	X			X	H	4F	*
PRAED, W.	X	X	X	X	X		H				X	X	1B	X
PRATT, J.	*	*	*	*	*	*	X	X			X	X	2	X
PRINGLE, J.				X	X		H	X				H	1B	X
PULTENEY, W.		X	X	*	*		H	*			X	H	2	X
PURLING, J.	X	X			P		X	*				*	3N	*
RADCLIFFE, J.	*	*	*	*	*		D	*	*		‖			
RAMSDEN, Sir Jo.	*	*	*	*	*	*	*	*	*			*	4F	*
RASHLEIGH, P.	*	*	X				X	*				D	1	X
RAWLINSON, A.	*		X	*	*	*	X	X		*	*	H	4F	*
RAWLINSON, H.	*		X	X	X		X	X		*	*	H	9D	*

RAWLINSON, Sir W.	X		X	X	X		H	X		*	*	*	3N	*
RIDLEY, Sir M.	*	*	*	P	*		X	*				D	4F	*
RIGBY, R.	X	X	X	X	X		X	X		*	*	*	3N	*
ROBINSON, C.	*	*	*	*	*		X	X			X	X	2	X
ROBINSON, F.	X	X	X	X	X		H	X			X	X	1B	X
ROBINSON, J.	X	X	X	X	X		X	*		*	*	X	1A	X
RODNEY, Sir G.					‖									
RODNEY, G.	X	X	X	X	X		H	X		*	*	X	1A	X
ROGERS, Sir F.	X	X	*	X	X		H	*				D	3N	*
ROGERS, J.	X	X	X	X	X		H	‖						
ROLLE, J.	*	X	*	*	*		X	X			X	H	8D	X
ROSEWARNE, H.	X	X	X	X	X		X	*	‖					
ROSS, C.		*		*	*		X							*
ROSS, G.	X		X		X		X	*		*	*	H	3N	*
ROUS, Sir J.	*	*	*	*	*	*	X	X			X	H	2	X
ROUSE, C.	*	*	*	*	*		D	X		*	*	H	2	X
ROUSE, T.	*	*	*	*	*	*	H	X		*	*	H	4F	*
RUMBOLD, Sir T.	X	X	X	X	X		D					D	3N	*
RUMBOLD, W.	X	X	X	X	X		D					D	3N	*
RUSHOUT, Sir J.	*	*	*	*	*	*	X			*	*	D	4F	*
SALT, S.	*	*	*	*	*	*	X	*		*	*	*	4F	*
SAVILE, Sir G.			*		*		*				‖			
SAWBRIDGE, J.	*	*	*	*	*	*	H	*	*	*	*	D	4F	*
SCOTT, H.	X	X	X	X	X		X	*		*	*	X	3N	*
SCOTT, J.									‖			H		X
SCOTT, T.	*	*	*	*	*	*	X	X	*		X	X	7	
SCUDAMORE, C.					‖									
SCUDAMORE, J.	*	*	*	*	*	*	D		*	*	*	*	4F	*
SELWYN, G.	X	X	X	X	X		X				X	X	1B	X
SELWYN, W.									‖			X		X
SHAFTOE, R.	X	X	X	X	X		H	X		*	*	*	3N	*

Member	i	ii	iii	iv	v	vi	vii	viii	ix	x	xi	xii	xiii	xiv
SHEFFIELD	X	X	X	X	X		X	*	*	*	*	*	3N	*
SHERIDAN, R.	*	*	*	*	*		*	*	*	*	*	*	4F	*
SHUCKBURGH, Sir G.	*	*	*	*	*		D		*		X	D	2	X
SHULDHAM	X	X	X	X	X	*	X					*	3N	*
SIBTHORPE, H.	X	X	X	X	X		H	*				*	3N	*
SINCLAIR, J.	X	X		X			X	X				*	1A	X
SKEENE, R.	X	X	X	X	X		X			*	*	*	10	
SKELTON, A.	X	X	X	X	X ‖									
SKIPWITH, Sir T.	*	*	*	*	*		H	X				*	4F	*
SLOANE, H.	X	X	X	X	X		X	*		*	*	H	3N	*
SLOPER, W.	*	*	*	*	*	*	D	*	*			*	4F	*
SMITH, Ab.	X	X	X	X	X		H				X	H	1A	X
SMITH, J. M.	*	*	*	*	*	*	*	*	*	*	*	*	4F	*
SMITH, Rich.	*	*	*	*	*	*	*	*	*	*	*	*	4F	*
SMITH, Robt.	*	*	*	*	*		H	X			X	X	2	X
SMITH, S.	X	X	X	X	X		H	*			X	X	1B	X
SMYTH, J.									‖					X
SMYTH, Sir R.	*	*	*	*	*		X				X	X		X
SPENCER, Ld. C.		X	X	X	X	*	X	X		*	*	*	3N	*
SPENCER, Ld. R.	*	*	*	*	*	*	*	*	*	*	*	*	4F	*
St. AUBYN, Sir J.											‖	*		*
ST. JOHN, G.						‖						*		*
ST. JOHN, H.	X	X	X	X	X		X		*	*	*	*	3N	*
ST. JOHN, J.	X	X	X	X	X		D		*	*	*	*	3N	*
ST. JOHN, St. A.	*	*	*	*	*		X	*	*	*	*	*	4F	*
STANHOPE, L.	X	X	X	X	X	*	H	*	‖					
STANHOPE, H. F.	*	*	*	*	*		*	*	*	*	*	*	4F	*
STANHOPE, W. S.	*	*	*	*	*	*	X	X				X	2	X
STANLEY, Th.	*	*	*	*	*	*	*	*	*	*	*	*	4F	*
STAUNTON, Th.	*	*	*	*	*	*	H	*				D	4F	*
STEELE, Th.	*	*	*	*	*	*	X	X			X	X	2	X

STEPHENS, P.	X	X	X	X	X	*	X	X		*	*	*	1A	X
STEPHENSON, J.	X	X	X	X	X		H	*		*	*	H	1A	X
STEPNEY, Sir J.	X	X	X	X	X		X					X	10	
STEWARD, G.	X		X	X	X		X	X		*	*	D	8D	X
STEWART, J.		*	*	*	*		D	*	*‖					
STEWART, K.	X	X	X	X	X		X	X				D	1B	X
STORER, A.	X	X	X	X	X		X	*		*	*	*	3N	*
STRACHEY, H.	X	X	X	X	X	*	X	X		*	*	X	3N	*
STRAHAN, W.	X	X	X	X	X		H	*				*	3N	*
STRATTON, G.	X	X	X	X	X		H	*				*	10	
STRUTT, J.	X	X	P	X	X		X	*				X		X
STUART, A.	X	X	X	X	X		X	X				H	3N	*
STUART, Ch.				X	X		X					H	10	
STUART, Jas.	X	X	X	X	X		X			*	*	*	3N	*
SURREY	*		*	*	*		X	X		*	*	*	4F	*
SUTTON, Ld. G.			*	*	*		X	‖						
SUTTON, G.	*	*	*	*	*	*	X	X			X	X	2	X
SUTTON, J.												X		X
SUTTON, Sir R.	X	X	X	X	X		H	*		*	*	*	10	*
SYKES, Sir F.	X	X	X	X	X		H	*			X	X	3N	X
SYMONS, Sir F.	X	X	X	X	X		H	*			X	X	1B	X
TALBOT, J. C.	X	X	X	P	X	‖								
TAYLOR, C.	*	*	*	*	*		X	X		*	*	X	4F	*
TEMPEST, J.	*	*	*	*	*	*	H	X			X	X	4F	*
THISTLETHWAITE, R.	*	*	*	*	*	*	H	X			X	X	4F	*
THOMPSON, B.	*	*	*	P	P		D	X		*	*	*	4F	*
THORNTON, H.						‖					X	X		X
THOROLD, Sir J.	*	*	*	*	*	*	H			*	*	*	4F	*
TOLLEMACHE, W.	*	*	*	*	*		X	*	*			X	4F	*
TOWNSEND, J.						‖		X			X	X		X
TOWNSHEND, C.	X	X	X	X	X		H	*		*	*	*	3N	

Member		ii	iii	iv	v	vi	vii	viii	ix	x	xi	xii	xiii	xiv
TOWNSHEND, J.	*	*	*	*	*		*	*	*	*	*	*	4F	*
TOWNSHEND, T.	*	*	*	*	*		X	X	‖					
TOWNSON, J.	X	X	X	X	X		H	*			X	X	1B	X
TRENTHAM	X						X	*				X	1	X
TREVANION, J.	*	*	*	*	*	*	X	X				*	4F	*
TREVELYAN, Sir J.	*	*	*	*	*	*	H					X	8	X
TUDWAY, C.	*	*	*	*	*		X				X	H	2	X
TURNER, C.	*	*	*	*	*		D	‖						
TYRCONNEL	*	*	*	*	*		D	X				*	2	X
UPPER OSSORY	*	*	*	*	*		X			*	*	*	4F	*
VANNECK, Sir G. W.	*	*	*	*	*	*	H	X				*	4F	*
VAUGHAN, E. L.	*	*	*	*	*	*	H	X				*	10	
VAUGHAN, J. (Cardigan)	*	*	*	*	*		D	X				D	10	
VAUGHAN, J.	X	X	X	X	X		H	*		*	*	*	3N	*
VERNEY	*	*	*	*	*		*	*		*	*	*	4F	*
VERNON, R.	P	P	P	P	P		X	X				H	1	X
VILLIERS, J.												‖		X
VYNER, R.	X	X	X	X	X		H	*		*	*	*	3N	*
WAKE, Sir W.			*	P	*		X				X	X	2	X
WALLACE, J.	X	X	X	X	X		H	*		‖				
WALLER, R.	X	X	X	X	X	*	H	X				X	1	X
WALPOLE, H.	*	*	*	*	*		*	*	*		*	*	4F	*
WALPOLE, R.	*	*	*	*	*	*	D	*	*	*	*	*	4F	*
WALPOLE, T.							D					*	10	
WARD, W.	X	X	X		X		H	*				X	1A	X
WARREN, Sir G.	*	*	*	*	*	*	D	*	*			X	10	
WARREN, Sir J. B.	X	X	X	X			X					X	1	X
WATSON, B.											‖	X		X

WEBB, J.	*	*	*	*	*	*	*	X		*	*	*	4F	*
WEDDELL, W.	*	*	*	*	*	*	*	*	*			*	4F	*
WEMYSS, J.	X	X	X	X	X		H	*				*	3N	*
WENMAN							X	X				D	2	X
WESTCOTE	X	X	X	X	X		H					*	3N	*
WHITBREAD, S.	*	X	X	X	*		X	*			X	D	8D	X
WHITMORE, T.	*	*	*	*	*	*	X					*	4F	*
WHITSHED, J.	X	X	X	X	X		H	*‖						
WILBERFORCE, W.	*	*	*	*	*	*	X	X			X	X	2	X
WILKES, J.	*	*	*		*		X	X			X	D	2	X
WILKINSON, J.	*	*	*	*	*		*	*	*	*	*	*	4F	*
WILKINSON, P.	*			*	*		X					‖		
WILLIAMS, W.	*	*	*	*	*	*	X	X				X	2	X
WILMOT, J.		*					X	X				*	8D	X
WINNINGTON, Sir E.	*	*	*	*	*		D	*	*	*	*	*	4F	*
WOLLASTON, W.							H					D	10	
WOODLEY, W.							X	X				H	5	X
WORSLEY, E. M.	X	X	X	X	X	‖								
WORSLEY, Sir R.	X		X	X	X		X	*				X	1B	
WRAXALL, N.	X	X	X	X	X		H	*			X	D	1A	X
WRAY, Sir C.						‖	*	*			X	D	2	X
WROTTESLEY, Sir J.		*	*		*		X	X				X	8D	X
WYNDHAM, P. C.				‖	*	*	*	*	*	*	*	*	4F	*
WYNN, G.	X	X	X	X	X		X					*	1	X
WYNN, Sir W.	*	*	*	*	*	*	X	X				X	2	X
YEO, E.	X	X	X	X	X		‖							
YONGE, Sir G.	*	*	*	*	*	*	X	X			X	X	2	X
YORKE, J.	X		X		X		X					H	3N	*
YORKE, Ph.		*	*	X		*	X	X			X	D	1B	X

APPENDIX II

Record of Opposition Division Lists, February 1793–May 1794

KEY

(i) Division on Fox's motion condemning the war against France. 18 February 1793.

(ii) Division on Grey's motion for parliamentary reform. 7 May 1793.

(iii) Division on Fox's amendment to the address. 21 January 1794.

(iv) Division on Grey's motion protesting against the landing of Hessian troops. 10 February 1794.

(v) Division on motion to delay the transportation of T. F. Palmer. 24 February 1794.

(vi) Division on Whitbread's motion for peace with France. 6 March 1794.

(vii) Division on Adam's motion respecting the cases of Muir and Palmer. 10 March 1794.

(viii) Division on Grey's motion calling for a bill of indemnity on the landing of Hessian troops. 15 March 1794.

(ix) Division on Fitzpatrick's motion calling for diplomatic assistance for Lafayette. 17 March 1794.

(x) Division on Sheridan's motion against the levying of voluntary aids without the consent of Parliament. 28 March 1794.

(xi) Division on Harrison's motion to divert certain pensions as a means of helping to defray the cost of the war. 8 April 1794.

(xii) Division on Maitland's motion for an enquiry into the conduct of the war. 10 April 1794.

(xiii) Division on bill to allow French émigrés to serve in the British Army.

(xiv) Division on Sheridan's motion to make the provision allowing aliens to serve in the British Army renewable annually. 16 April 1794.

(xv) Division on bill authorizing subsidies for Prussia. 2 May 1794.

(xvi) Division on bill to suspend habeas corpus (second reading). 16 May 1794.

(xvii) Division on bill to suspend habeas corpus (third reading). 17 May 1794.

(xviii) Division on Fox's motion calling for an immediate peace with France. 30 May 1794.

Member	i	ii	iii	iv	v	vi	vii	viii	ix	x	xi	xii	xiii	xiv	xv	xvi	xvii	xviii	*No. of Foxite votes recorded*	*Constituency*
ADAIR, J.								*											1	Highham Ferrars, post 1790. *New Member*
ADAM, Wm.	*		*	*	*		*	*						||					6	Ross
ANSON, Thos.											*							*	2	Litchfield
ANTHONIE, L.	*	*	*						*							*	*	*	7	Great Marlow, elect. 1790. *New Member*
AUBREY, J.			*						*	*	*		*		*	*	*	*	9	Clitheroe
BAKER, Wm.	*	*			*	*		*	*	*	*			*	*				10	Herts.
BARHAM, J. F.					*														1	Stockbridge, post 1790. *New Member*
BARING, Sir Fr.			||									*		*	*	*	*	*	6	Chipping Wycombe
BARLOW, Hugh (Owen)								*											1	Pembroke
BASSETT, Sir Fr.					*														1	Penrhyn
BASTARD, J. P.											*								1	Devon
BOUVERIE, E.	*	*	*	*	*	*	*		*	*	*	*				*	*	*	14	New Sarum
BOUVERIE, W. H.							*												1	Salisbury
BURCH, J. R.	*	*	*	*	*	*	*	*	*	*	*	*	*	*	*	*	*	*	18	Thetford. *New Member*
BURHAN, (Visc. Bayhem)													*						1	Bath
BYNG, Geo.		*	*				*	*	*	*	*	*		*		*	*	*	12	Middlesex
CAVENDISH, Ld. Geo.					*											*			2	Derbyshire
CHURCH, J. B.	*	*	*					*	*							*	*	*	8	Wendover. *New Member*
CLAYTON, Sir R.						*												*	2	Bletchingly
COKE, E.	*		*																2	Derby
COKE, T. W.	*		*	*							*								4	Norfolk
COLHOUN, W.	*	*	*								*								4	Bedford

CORNEWALL, Sir G.					*														1	Herefordshire
COURTENAY, Jo.	*	*	*	*		*	*	*	*	*	*	*	*	*		*	*	*	16	Tamworth
CRESPIGNY, J. C.	*		*			*	*	*	*	*	*		*		*				10	Sudbury. *New Member*
CREWE, Jo.			*	*		*			*									*	5	Cheshire
CURWEN, J. (Christian)		*									*	*		*	*	*	*	*	8	Carlisle, post 1790
DUNCOMBE, H.									*										1	Yorkshire
DUNDAS, Sir Thos.																*			1	Stirling
ERSKINE, Thos.	*	*	*		*		*		*								*	*	8	Portsmouth
FETHERSTONE-HAUGH, Sir H.		*	*															*	3	Portsmouth
FITZPATRICK, R.	*	*	*	*	*		*	*	*	*		*	*		*		*	*	14	Tavistock
FLETCHER, Sir H.			*											*			*	*	4	Cumberland
FOLEY, E.			*								*								2	Worcestershire
FOX, C. J.	*	*	*	*	*	*	*	*	*	*	*	*	*	*	*	*	*	*	18	Westminster
FRANCIS, Ph.	*	*	*	*	*	*	*	*	*	*	*	*		*	*		*	*	16	Bletchingly
GREY, Chas.	*	*	*	*	*	*	*	*	*	*	*	*	*	*	*	*	*	*	18	Northumberland
HARCOURT, Jo.			*			*				*	*							*	5	Ilchester. *New Member*
HARE, Jas.	*		*	*	*		*	*	*								*		8	Knaresborough
HARRISON, Jo.	*	*			*		*	*		*	*	*	*	*	*	*	*	*	14	Grimsby
HIPPISLEY, J. C.					*			*										*	2	Sudbury. *New Member*
HONEYWOOD, F.		*	*													*		*	3	Kent
HOWEL, Dav.	*		*						*		*					*			5	Mitchell
HOWERD, H.	*		*	*	*	*	*	*	*	*	*	*	*	*	*	*	*	*	17	Steyning. *New Member*
HUSSEY, W.	*		*	*	*	*			*		*	*	*	*	*	*	*	*	14	New Sarum
JEKYLL, Jos.	*	*	*	*								*		*	*	*	*	*	10	Calne
JERVIS, Sir Jo.		*																	1	Chipping Wycombe
JERVOISE, J. C.									*	*	*	*					*	*	6	Yarmouth I.o.W.
KEENE, Whit.									*										1	Montgomery Town
KNIGHT, R. P.							*		*										2	Ludlow

20

Member	i	ii	iii	iv	v	vi	vii	viii	ix	x	xi	xii	xiii	xiv	xv	xvi	xvii	xviii	*No. of Foxite votes recorded*	*Constituency*
LAMBTON, W. H.	*	*									*	*	*	*	*	*	*	*	10	Durham City
LANGSTON, J.											*								1	Bridgewater
LAW, E.										*									1	Westbury
LECHMERE, E.								*											1	Worcester
LEMON, Sir Wm.			*					*	*										4	Cornwall
LONG, S.				*														*	2	Ilchester. *New Member*
LUDLOW,				*	*			*		*	*	*						*	7	Huntingdonshire
MACLEOD, Col. N.	*	*	*	*	*		*	*	*	*	*	*	*		*				13	Inverness
MAINWARING, W.											*								1	Middlesex
MAITLAND, Maj. Thos.	*		*	*	*	*	*		*		*	*	*		*	*	*	*	14	Haddington Burghs
MARTIN, Jas.		*	*		*	*			*		*		*	*	*	*			10	Tewkesbury
MILBANKE, Ra.		*	*														*	*	4	Durham
MILNER, Sir Wm.			*	*				*	*		*		*	*	*	*		*	10	York
MILNES, R. S.			*														*	*	3	York
NORTH, D. Long	*	*	*	*	*	*	*	*	*	*	*	*	*	*	*	*	*	*	18	Grimsby
PELHAM, C. A.											*					*			2	Lincolnshire
PHILIPS, J. C.		*						*		*	*		*			*			6	Carmarthen Town
PIERCE, Hen.																		*	1	Northallerton
PLUMMER, Wm.	*	*	*	*		*	*	*		*	*	*	*	*		*		*	14	Hertfordshire
POULETT, W. P.	*		*															*	3	Totnes. *New Member*
RAWDON, Jo.										*	*	*				*	*	*	6	Launceston, post 1790. *New Member*
RIDLEY, Sir W. M.			*										*						2	Newcastle-on-Tyne
ROBINSON, M.										*				*					3	Boroughbridge
RUSSELL, Ld. Jo.	*	*																	2	Tavistock, post 1790. *New Member*

RUSSELL, Ld. Wm.	*		*	*	*	*	*	*	*	*	*	*	*	*	*		*	*	16	Surrey
ST. JOHN, St. A.	*	*	*	*	*	*	*	*	*						*	*	*	*	13	Bedfordshire
SHAWE, W. C.		*	*														*		3	Preston, post 1790. *New Member*
SHEFFIELD,									*										1	Bristol
SHERIDAN, R. B.	*	*	*		*	*	*	*		*	*	*	*	*	*	*	*	*	16	Stafford
SMITH, Wm.	*	*	*	*	*	*	*	*	*	*	*	*	*	*	*	*		*	17	Sudbury, post 1790. *New Member*
SPEED, Henry			*					*	*	*	*	*	*						7	Huntingdon, post 1790. *New Member*
SPENCER, Ld. Robt.	*	*	*	*	*	*	*	*	*	*	*	*	*	*	*	*	*	*	18	Wareham
STANLEY, Jo.					*				*										2	Hastings
STURT, Chas.	*	*	*	*	*						*			*	*	*	*	*	11	Bridport
TARLETON, Col.			*	*	*	*	*	*	*	*	*	*	*	*	*	*	*	*	16	Liverpool
TAYLOR, C. L.	*	*							*			*							4	Maidstone
TAYLOR, M. A.	*	*	*	*	*	*	*	*	*	*	*	*	*	*	*	*	*	*	18	Heytesbury, post 1790
THOMPSON, T.	*	*	*	*	*		*				*	*				*	*	*	11	Evesham. *New Member*
THORNTON, R.									*										1	Colchester
TITCHFIELD					*														1	Buckinghamshire, post 1790. *New Member*
TOWNSHEND, Ld. Jo.	||		*	*		*	*	*	*	*								*	8	Knaresborough, post 1790
UPPER OSSORY									*										1	Bedfordshire
VANE, Sir Fr.			*																1	Carlisle, post 1790. *New Member*
VAUGHAN, B.	*	*	*	*	*	*	*	*	*	*	*	*		*	*	*			15	Calne, post 1790
VYNER, Robt.			*	*		*		*			*		*				*	*	8	Thirsk
WALWYN, J.			*	*			*					*						*	6	Hereford
WESTERN, C.	*	*	*	*				*	*	*	*	*		*	*	*	*	*	14	Malden
WHARTON, J.		*	*													*		*	4	Beverley. *New Member*
WHITBREAD, S. (Jnr.)	*	*	*	*	*	*	*	*	*	*	*	*	*	*	*	*		*	17	Bedford. *New Member*

Member	i	ii	iii	iv	v	vi	vii	viii	ix	x	xi	xii	xiii	xiv	xv	xvi	xvii	xviii	*No. of Foxite votes recorded*	*Constituency*
WHITMORE, Thos.	*	*	*															*	4	Bridgenorth
WILBRAHAM, R.	*		*	*				*		*	*							*	7	Bodmin
WINNINGTON, Sir E.	*		*				*	*	*	*	*	*	*	*	*	*	*	*	14	Droitwich
WYCOMBE,	*	*	*				*	*	*		*	*			*	*	*		11	Chipping Wycombe
WYNDHAM, P. C.	*														*				2	Midhurst. *New Member*
WYNNE, R. W.								*											1	Denbighshire
YORKE, Chas.								*											1	Cambridgeshire. *New Member*

APPENDIX III

The Whig Party, 1782–1784

(a) PARLIAMENTARY INTERESTS (83 members)

(i) FITZWILLIAM	R. Benyon	(Peterborough)
	E. Burke	(Malton)
	Ld. J. Cavendish	(York)
	F. Foljambe	(Yorkshire)
	D. Hartley	(Hull)
	F. Montague	(Higham Ferrers)
	W. Weddel	(Malton)
(ii) CAVENDISH	W. Braddyll	(Lancaster)
	Ld. G. Cavendish	(Derbyshire)
	Ld. G. A. H. Cavendish	(Derby)
	E. Coke	(Derby)
	Duncannon	(Knaresborough)
	J. Hare	(Knaresborough)
	A. Rawlinson	(Lancaster)
(iii) PORTLAND	Ld. E. Bentinck	(Notts.)
	J. Cotes	(Wigan)
	H. Fletcher	(Cumberland)
	C. Meadows	(Notts.)
	H. Walpole	(Wigan)
(iv) ELIOT	D. Long	(St. Germans)
	T. Lucas	(Grampound)
	Sir J. Ramsden	(Grampound)
	S. Salt	(Liskeard)
	W. Tollemache	(Liskeard)
(v) GOVERNMENT	T. Erskine	(Portsmouth)
Apr.–June 1782	H. Fetherstonehaugh	(Portsmouth)
Mar.–Dec. 1783	J. Nesbitt	(Winchilsea)
	J. Trevanion	(Dover)

(vi) BEDFORD	R. Fitzpatrick	(Tavistock)
	St. A. St. John	(Beds.)
	Upper Ossory	(Beds.)
(vii) SPENCER	Lucan	(Northampton)
	H. Minchin	(Okehampton)
	W. Sloper	(St. Albans)
(viii) DUNDAS	C. Dundas	(Orkney)
	Sir T. Dundas	(Stirlingshire)
	G. Fitzwilliam	(Richmond)
(ix) FOLEY	A. Foley	(Droitwich)
	E. Foley	(Worcs.)
	Sir E. Winnington	(Droitwich)
(x) FORESTER	Sir H. Bridgeman	(Wenlock)
	G. Forester	(Wenlock)
(xi) HONEYWOOD	J. Bullock	(Steyning)
	Sir T. Skipwith	(Steyning)
(xii) DERBY	J. Burgoyne	(Preston)
	T. Stanley	(Lancashire)
(xiii) CLAYTON	Sir R. Clayton	(Surrey)
	J. Nicholls	(Bletchingley)
(xiv) FRANKLAND	Sir T. Gascoigne	(Thirsk)
	B. Thompson	(Thirsk)
(xv) PELHAM	J. Harrison	(Grimsby)
	C. Pelham	(Lincolnshire)
(xvi) LISTER	J. Lee	(Clitheroe)
	T. Lister	(Clitheroe)
(xvii) MANNERS	B. Grey	(Leicester)
	H. F. Stanhope	(Bramber)
(xviii) WHITMORE	H. Pigot	(Bridgnorth)
	T. Whitmore	(Bridgnorth)
(xix) SMITH	J. Smith	(Wendover)
	R. Smith	(Wendover)
(xx) BASSET	Sir J. St. Aubyn	(Truro)
	R. P. Carew	(Penrhyn)
(xxi) STURT	R. Beckford	(Bridport)

(xxii)	SHAFTOE	H. S. Conway	(Downton)
(xxiii)	CRAVEN	W. H. Hartley	(Berkshire)
(xxiv)	THANET	P. Honeywood	(Appleby)
(xxv)	GRENVILLE	T. Grenville	(Bucks.)
(xxvi)	NORTHUMBERLAND	Maitland	(Newport)
(xxvii)	GALWAY	W. Nedham	(Pontefract)
(xxviii)	ANKERVILLE	C. Ross	(Tain)
(xxix)	MARLBOROUGH	Ld. R. Spencer	(Oxford)
(xxx)	RICHMOND	P. C. Wyndham	(Chichester)
(xxxi)	DELAVAL	J. F. Cawthorne	(Lincoln)
(xxxii)	CLIVE	S. Davies	(Ludlow)
(xxxiii)	ELPHINSTONE	G. K. Elphinstone	(Dunbarton)
(xxxiv)	SUFFOLK	Sir J. Erskine	(Castle Rising)
(xxxv)	BUCCLEUCH	Sir G. Eliot	(Roxburghshire)
(xxxvi)	MANCHESTER	Ludlow	(Hunts.)
(xxxvii)	SYDNEY	Middleton	(Whitchurch)
(xxxviii)	HOWARD	Surrey	(Carlisle)
(xxxix)	GRAFTON	Gen. H. S. Conway	(Bury St. Edmunds)
(xl)	BOLTON	Sir P. J. Clerke	(Totnes)
(xli)	IRWIN	J. Crawford	(Horsham)

(b) MEMBERS FREE OF PATRONS (62 members)

E. ANDERSON (Beverley)
W. A'COURT (Heytesbury)
G. ANSON (Litchfield)
W. BAKER (Hertford)
SIR C. BAMFYLDE (Exeter)
C. BARROW (Gloucester)
W. BOUVERIE (Salisbury)
SIR T. BUNBURY (Suffolk)
G. BYNG (Middlesex)
SIR W. CODRINGTON (Tewkesbury)
W. S. CONWAY (Coventry)
T. W. COKE (Norfolk)
SIR G. CORNEWALL (Herts.)
J. CREWE (Cheshire)
SIR C. DAVERS (Bury St. Edmunds)
H. DAWKINS (Chippenham)
G. DEMPSTER (Perth)
J. ELWES (Berkshire)
C. J. FOX (Westminster)
R. GREGORY (Rochester)
T. HALSEY (Herts.)
SIR J. HARRIS (Christ Church)

F. HONEYWOOD (Kent)
SIR R. HOTHAM (Southwark)
G. HUNT (Bodmin)
W. HUSSEY (Salisbury)
J. JERVOISE (Hampshire)
R. KNIGHT (Leominster)
R. LADBROKE (Warwick)
J. LAMBTON (Durham)
SIR R. LAWLEY (Warwickshire)
S. LUSHINGTON (Hedon)
J. LUTHER (Essex)
SIR H. MANN (Maidstone)
C. MARSHAM (Kent)
E. MONKTON (Stafford)
E. MORANT (Yarmouth I.o.W.)
SIR R. MOSTYN (Flintshire)
N. NEWNHAM (London)
W. OWEN (Montgomeryshire)
W. PLUMER (Herts.)
SIR T. POWYS (Northants.)
SIR M. RIDLEY (Newcastle)
T. ROUS (Worcester)
SIR J. RUSHOUT (Evesham)
G. ST. JOHN (Cricklade)
J. SAWBRIDGE (London)
J. SCUDAMORE (Hereford)
R. SHERIDAN (Stafford)
T. STAUNTON (Ipswich)
H. STURT (Dorset)
C. TAYLOR (Maidstone)
J. TEMPEST (Durham)
R. THISTLETHWAITE (Hampshire)
SIR J. THOROLD (Lincs.)
LD. J. TOWNSHEND (Cambridge)
SIR G. VANNECK (Dunwich)
VERNEY (Bucks.)
R. WALPOLE (Yarmouth)
J. WEBB (Gloucester)
J. WILKINSON (Honiton)
SIR W. WYNN (Denbighshire)

BIBLIOGRAPHY

A. MANUSCRIPT SOURCES

Althorp, Northants.

SPENCER MSS.: Papers and Correspondence of George John, Second Earl Spencer, 1758–1839.

Blair–Adam, Fife

BLAIR ADAM MSS.: Memoranda, Papers and Correspondence of William Adam, M.P., 1751–1839.

Blenheim, Oxon.

BLENHEIM MSS.: Papers and Correspondence of George Spencer, Fourth Duke of Marlborough, 1739–1817.

Bodleian Library, Oxford.

(i) NORTH MSS.: Papers and Correspondence of Frederick North, Second Earl of Guilford, 1732–92.

(ii) A. GILBERT, 'The Political Correspondence of the Third Duke of Richmond, 1765–1784', Oxford D.Phil. 1956.

(iii) P. J. MARSHALL, 'The Impeachment of Warren Hastings', Oxford D.Phil. 1963.

Bowood, Wiltshire

BOWOOD MSS.: Papers and Correspondence of William Fitzmaurice-Petty, First Marquess of Lansdowne, 1737–1805.

British Museum

ABERGAVENNY MSS.: facs. 340: Papers and Memoranda of John Robinson, M.P., 1727–1802.

ADAIR MSS. Add. MS. 50829: Papers and Correspondence of James Adair, 1743–98.

AUCKLAND MSS. Add. MSS. 34418–19: Correspondence and Papers, Political and Private, of William Eden, First Baron Auckland, 1744–1814.

FOSTER MSS. Add. MS. 41579: The Journal of Lady Elizabeth Foster, 1759–1824.

FOX MSS. Add. MSS. 47559–62, 47565, 47567–71, 47579–80, 47582–3, 47585, 47589–91: Correspondence and Papers of Charles James Fox, 1749–1806

GRENVILLE MSS. Add. MS. 42058: Correspondence and Papers of Thomas Grenville, M.P., 1755–1846.

HARDWICKE MSS. Add. MS. 35641: General Correspondence of Philip Yorke, Third Earl of Hardwicke, 1757–1834.

HASTINGS MSS. Add. MS. 29196: Papers and Correspondence of Warren Hastings, 1732–1818. Add. MS. 24266: Minutes of the Meetings of the Managers of the Impeachment of Warren Hastings.

HOLLAND HOUSE MSS. Add. MSS. 51466–8, 51516, 51705–6, 51731–2, 51751, 51845. Papers and Correspondence of the Fox Family; Particularly Henry Fox, Third Baron Holland, 1773–1840, His Wife Elizabeth, 1771–1845 and Sister Caroline, 1767–1845.

LEEDS MSS. Add. MSS. 27918, 28061, 28067: Memoranda and Correspondence of Francis Osborne, Fifth Duke of Leeds, 1751–99.

NORTHINGTON MSS. Add. MS. 38716: Letter Book of Robert Henley, Second Earl of Northington, 1747–86.

PELHAM MSS. Add. MSS. 33100–1: General and Official Correspondence of Thomas Pelham, Second Earl of Chichester, 1756–1826.

ROBINSON MSS. Add. MS. 37835: Correspondence of George III with John Robinson, 1783–5.

WESTMINSTER ASSOCIATION MSS. Add. MSS. 38594–5: Minutes of the Westminster Committee of Association, 1780–5.

WINDHAM MSS. Add. MSS. 37843–5, 37848, 37873: Correspondence and Papers of William Windham, M.P., 1750–1810.

Chatsworth, Derbyshire

CHATSWORTH MSS: (i) Correspondence of Georgiana, Duchess of Devonshire, 1757–1806. (ii) Journal of Lady Elizabeth Foster, 1759–1824.

Durham Public Record Office, Durham

LEE MSS.: Correspondence and Papers of John Lee, M.P., 1733–93.

Durham University Library, Durham

GREY MSS.: Correspondence and Papers of Charles, Second Earl Grey, 1764–1845.

Hampshire Public Record Office, Winchester

PALMERSTON MSS.: Correspondence and Papers of Henry Temple, Second Viscount Palmerston, 1739–1802.

Hickleton Castle, Yorkshire

HICKLETON MSS.: Correspondence and Papers of Mary Ponsonby, 1774–1861, wife of Charles Grey; and other Members of the Ponsonby Family.

Northamptonshire Public Record Office, Northampton

MILTON MSS.: (i) Correspondence and Papers of Edmund Burke,

1729–97. (ii) Correspondence and Papers of William Wentworth, Second Earl Fitzwilliam, 1748–1833.

Nottingham University Library, Nottingham

PORTLAND MSS.: Papers and Correspondence of William Cavendish-Bentinck, Third Duke of Portland, 1738–1809.

Public Record Office

(i) CHATHAM MSS.: Correspondence and Papers of William Pitt, 1759–1806.

(ii) FOREIGN OFFICE MSS.

Sheffield Public Library, Sheffield

WENTWORTH WOODHOUSE MUNIMENTS: (i) Correspondence and Papers of Edmund Burke, 1729–97. (ii) Correspondence and Papers of Charles Watson-Wentworth, Second Marquis of Rockingham, 1730–82.

West Suffolk Public Record Office: Bury St. Edmunds

(i) BUNBURY MSS.: Correspondence and Papers of Sir Charles Bunbury, 1740–1821.

(ii) GRAFTON MSS.: Correspondence and Papers of Augustus Fitzroy, Third Duke of Grafton, 1735–1811.

B. PRINTED SOURCES

1. *Primary Sources*

R. ADAIR, *A Sketch of the Character of the Late Duke of Devonshire*; London, 1811.

EARL OF ALBEMARLE, *Fifty Years of My Life*; London, 1876.

Diary and Letters of Madame D'Arblay, ed. A. Dobson, vols. 3–5; London, 1905.

Journal and Correspondence of William Eden, 1st Lord Auckland; London, 1861.

W. BELSHAM, *Memoirs of the Reign of George III*; London, 1795.

Correspondence of the Rt. Hon. John Beresford, ed. W. Beresford; London, 1854.

EARL OF BESSBOROUGH, *Lady Bessborough and her Family Circle*; London, 1940.

SIR W. BLACKSTONE, *Commentaries on the Laws of England*; London, 1765–9.

J. BOSWELL, *The Life of Dr. Samuel Johnson*; Oxford, 1965.

Memoirs of the Court and Cabinets of George III, ed. Duke of Buckingham and Chandos; London, 1853–5.

Letters and Correspondence of Sir James Bland Burges, Bt., ed. J. Hutton; London, 1885.

Life and Correspondence of the Rt. Hon. John Burgoyne, ed. E. B. de Fonblanque; London, 1876.

E. BURKE, *Reflexions on the Revolution in France;* London, 1964.

— *An Appeal from the New to the Old Whigs;* London, 1964.

— *Observations on the Conduct of the Minority;* London, 1793.

The Correspondence of Edmund Burke, ed. Earl Fitzwilliam, vols. iii–iv; London, 1844.

The Correspondence of Edmund Burke, ed. T. Copeland; Cambridge, 1965.

(For Burke and Laurence corres. see under Laurence.)

LORD CAMPBELL, *Lives of the Lord Chancellors and Keepers of the Great Seal of England*, vols. 6–10; London, 1856.

F. D. CARTWRIGHT, *The Life and Correspondence of Major Cartwright;* London, 1826.

LORD COCKBURN, *Memorials of His Time*, ed. H. Cockburn; Edinburgh, 1909.

B. CONNELL, *Portrait of a Whig Peer;* London, 1957.

Correspondence of the First Marquis Cornwallis; vols. i–ii, ed. C. Ross; London, 1859.

The Creevey Papers, ed. H. Maxwell, vols. i–ii; London, 1903.

The Crewe Papers, Philobiblon Society, vol. 9; London, 1865–6.

The Croker Papers, ed. L. J. Jennings, vol. I; London, 1884.

J. CUNDEE, *Life of the Late Charles James Fox;* London, 1807.

Georgiana, Duchess of Devonshire, ed. Earl of Bessborough; London, 1955.

The Farington Diary, ed. J. Greig, vol. I; London, 1922.

LORD E. FITZMAURICE, *Life of William, Earl of Shelburne*, vol. 2; London, 1912.

C. J. FOX, *A History of the Early Part of the Reign of James II;* London, 1808.

The Speeches of the Rt. Hon. C. J. Fox in the House of Commons, ed. J. Wright; London, 1815.

Memorials and Correspondence of C. J. Fox, ed. Lord John Russell; London; 1853–7.

Memoirs of Sir Philip Francis, ed. J. Parkes and H. Merivale, vol. ii; London, 1867.

The Francis Papers, ed. B. Francis and E. Keary, vol. 2; London, 1901.

Correspondence of George, Prince of Wales, ed. A. Aspinall, vols. 1–2; London, 1964.

The Correspondence of George III, 1760–1783, ed. Sir J. Fortescue, vol. VI; London, 1928.

The Later Correspondence of George III, ed. A. Aspinall, vols. i–ii; Cambridge, 1963.

The Diaries of Sylvester Douglas, Lord Glenbervie, ed. F. Bickley; London, 1928.

Memoirs of Augustus Henry, Third Duke of Grafton, ed. W. Anson; London, 1898.

T. Green, *Extracts from the Diary of a Lover of Literature;* Ipswich, 1810.

The Hamwood Papers, ed. Mrs. G. H. Bell; London, 1930.

F. Hardy, *Memoirs of Charlemont;* London, 1812.

Elizabeth, Lady Holland to her Son, 1821–1845, ed. Earl of Ilchester; London, 1946.

Lord Holland, *Memoirs of the Whig Party During my Time*, vol. 1; London, 1852.

The Works of John Jebb, ed. J. Disney; London, 1787.

Dr. F. Laurence, *History of the Political Life and Public Services of the Rt. Hon. C. J. Fox;* London, 1783.

The Epistolary Correspondence of the Rt. Hon. Edmund Burke and Dr. French Laurence, ed. C. and J. Rivington; London, 1827.

Political Memoranda of the Fifth Duke of Leeds, ed. O. Browning; London, 1884.

Emily, Duchess of Leinster, ed. B. Fitzgerald; London, 1949.

Life and Letters of Lady Sarah Lennox, ed. Lady Ilchester and Lord Stavordale, vol. i; London, 1901.

Life and Letters of Lord Macaulay, ed. G. O. Trevelyan; London, 1959.

Memoirs of the Life of Sir James Mackintosh, ed. R. J. Mackintosh; London, 1835.

Diaries and Correspondence of Lord Malmesbury, ed. Earl of Malmesbury, vols. i–ii; London, 1844.

G. Martelli, *Life of John Montagu, Fourth Earl of Sandwich;* London, 1962.

Life and Letters of Sir Gilbert Elliot, First Earl of Minto, ed. Countess of Minto; London, 1874.

Memoirs, Journal and Correspondence of Thomas Moore, ed. Lord John Russell; London, 1853.

J. Nicholls, *Recollections and Reflexions of Public Affairs During the Reign of George III*; London, 1820.

T. Paine, *The Rights of Man*; London, 1966.

Papers Presented to Parliament 1789–1796.

The Parliamentary History, vols. 23–31; London, 1818.

Dr. S. Parr, *Characters of Charles James Fox*; London, 1809.

The Works of Dr. Samuel Parr, ed. J. Johnstone; London, 1828.

L. Reid, *Charles James Fox*; London, 1969.

The Parliamentary Papers of John Robinson, 1774–1784, ed. W. T. Laprade; London, 1922.

Reminiscences and Table-Talk of Samuel Rogers, Banker, Poet, and Patron of the Arts, ed. Rev. A. Dyce; Edinburgh, 1903.

Memoirs of Sir Samuel Romilly; London, 1840.

Diaries and Correspondence of the Rt. Hon. George Rose, ed. L. V. Harcourt; London, 1860.

Lord John Russell, *The Life and Times of Charles James Fox*; London, 1859–66.

— *An Essay on the History of the English Government and Constitution*; London, 1821.

— *Recollections and Suggestions, 1813–1873*; London, 1875.

George Selwyn, His Life and Letters, ed. E. S. Roscoe and H. Clergue; London, 1899.

The Diary of Lady Frances Shelley, 1787–1817, ed. R. Edgcumbe, vol. 1; London, 1913.

Memoirs of the Rt. Hon. R. B. Sheridan, ed. J. Watkins; London, 1817.

Memoirs of R. B. Sheridan, ed. T. Moore; London, 1825.

Betsy Sheridan's Journal, ed. W. Lefanu; London, 1960.

The Letters of R. B. Sheridan, ed. C. Price; Oxford, 1966.

The Correspondence of Sir John Sinclair; London, 1831.

A. M. W. Stirling, *Coke of Norfolk and His Friends*; London, 1912.

G. Tomline, *Memoirs of the Life of the Rt. Hon. William Pitt*; London, 1821.

J. B. Trotter, *Memoirs of the Later Years of the Rt. Hon. C. J. Fox*; London, 1811.

Letters Addressed to the Countess of Upper Ossory by Horace Walpole; London, 1848.

The Letters of Horace Walpole, ed. Mrs. P. Toynbee, vols. 12–15; Oxford, 1905.

The Correspondence of Horace Walpole, ed. W. S. Lewis; London, 1952.

The Last Journals of Horace Walpole, ed. A. Stewart, vol. ii; London, 1910.

REV. R. WARNER, *Literary Recollections;* London, 1830.

SIR ALGERNON WEST, *Recollections*, 1832–1866; London, 1899.

The Whig Club Rule Book; London, 1784.

The Windham Papers, ed. L. S. Benjamin; London, 1913.

The Historical and Posthumous Memoirs of Sir Nathaniel Wraxall, ed. H. B. Wheatley, vols. ii–v; London, 1884.

C. WYVILL, *Political Tracts and Papers;* York, 1779–1804.

PAMPHLETS

Speech of the Rt. Hon. C. J. Fox at a Meeting of the Electors of Westminster; London, 1782.

A Letter from a Liveryman on Mr. Fox's Introduction of a Bill for Depriving the East India Company of Their Charter; London, 1783.

Fox's Martyrs or a New Book of the Sufferings of the Faithful; London, 1784.

The Beauties and Deformities of Fox, North and Burke, Selected from Their Speeches from the Year 1770 Down to the Present Time; London, 1784.

The Last Dying Words of Reynard the Fox; London, 1784.

The Fox and the Badger Dismissed. A New Song; London, 1784.

SIR N. WRAXALL, *A Short Review of the Political State of Great Britain at the Commencement of the Year 1787*; London, 1787.

A Reply to 'A Short Review of the Political State of Great Britain'; London, 1787.

The People's Answer to the Court Pamphlet Entitled 'A Short Review of the State of Great Britain'; London, 1787.

Fox Against Fox: Or Political Blossoms of the Rt. Hon. C. J. Fox; London 1788.

A Letter to the Rt. Hon. C. J. Fox on the Late Conduct of his Party; London, 1789.

W. COMBE, *A Letter from a Country Gentleman to a Member of Parliament, on the Present State of Public Affairs;* London, 1789.

Parallel Between the Conduct of Mr. Burke and that of Mr. Fox, in their Late Parliamentary Contest; London, 1791.

Speech of the Rt. Hon. C. J. Fox Containing the Declaration of his Principles Respecting the Present Crisis of Public Affairs, and on

Reforming the Representation of the People. Spoken at the Whig Club; London, 4 December 1792.

A Letter from the Rt. Hon. C. J. Fox to the Worthy and Independent Electors of Westminster; London, 1793.

The Letter of the Rt. Hon. C. J. Fox to the Electors of Westminster Anatomized; London, 1793.

A Letter to the Rt. Hon. C. J. Fox in Which is Proved the Absolute Necessity of an Immediate Declaration of War Against France; London, 1793.

A Letter to the Rt. Hon. C. J. Fox Upon the Dangerous and Inflammatory Tendency of His late Conduct in Parliament; London, 1793.

Remarks on a Pamphlet Published as Mr. Fox's Speech at the Opening of Parliament, Including some Observations on the Nature and Causes of the Present War; London, 1793.

The Speech of the Rt. Hon. C. J. Fox in Reply to the Address to His Majesty; London, 1794.

Observations on the Conduct of Mr. Fox by a Suffolk Freeholder; Bury St. Edmunds, 1794.

J. Owen, *Letter to Mr. Fox on the Duration of the Trial of Mr. Hastings*; London, 1794.

R. Adair, *A Whig's Apology for His Consistency, in a Letter from a Member of Parliament, London*, 1795.

R. Adair, *The Letter of the Rt. Hon. C. J. Fox to the Electors of Westminster, With an Application of its Principles to Subsequent Events*; London, 1802.

NEWSPAPERS AND PERIODICALS

London Chronicle
Morning Chronicle
Morning Herald
Morning Post
Public Advertiser
Sheffield Advertiser
The Times
York Chronicle
Almon's Remembrancer
Blackwood's Magazine
Edinburgh Review
Gentleman's Magazine

HISTORICAL MANUSCRIPTS COMMISSION

Fifth Report
Manuscripts of the Duke of Sutherland. A. J. Horwood. London, 1876.

Eighth Report
Manuscripts of the Duke of Manchester. L. O. Pike. London, 1881.

Ninth Report
Manuscripts of Alfred Morrison Esq. of Fonthill House, Wiltshire. J. A. Bennett. London, 1884.

Tenth Report
Manuscripts of the Marquess of Abergavenny. H. C. Maxwell Lyte. London, 1887.

Twelfth Report
Manuscripts of P. V. Smith, Esq. of Lincoln's Inn. F. H. B. Daniel. London, 1891.

Manuscripts and Correspondence of James, First Earl of Charlemont, 1745–1783. J. T. Gilbert. London, 1891.

Thirteenth Report
Manuscripts and Correspondence of James, First Earl of Charlemont, 1784–1789. J. T. Gilbert. London, 1892.

Manuscripts of J. B. Fortescue, Esq. Preserved at Dropmore. W. Fitzpatrick. London, 1892–9.

Manuscripts of the Earl of Lonsdale. J. J. Cartwright. London, 1893.

Fourteenth Report
Manuscripts of Lord Kenyon. W. J. Hardy. London, 1894.

Manuscripts of the Duke of Rutland. H. C. Maxwell Lyte. London, 1894.

Manuscripts of the Lord Emly of Tervoe. J. T. Gilbert. London, 1895.

Fifteenth Report
Manuscripts of the Earl of Carlisle. R. E. Kirk. London, 1897.

Manuscripts of Mrs. Stopford-Sackville. W. O. Hewlett. London, 1904.

Correspondence of William Knox, Chiefly in Relation to American Affairs, 1757–1808. S. C. Lomas. London, 1909.

2. *Secondary Sources*

D. Barnes, *George III and William Pitt*, 1783–1803; London, 1939.

J. Carswell, *The Old Cause;* London, 1954.

A. Chardon, *Fox et la Revolution Francaise;* Paris, 1918.

I. R. Christie, *The End of North's Ministry, 1780–1782;* London, 1958.

I. R. Christie, *Wilkes, Wyvill and Reform;* London, 1962.

E. Coleridge, *The Life of Thomas Coutts;* London, 1920.

J. W. Derry, *The Regency Crisis and the Whigs, 1788–1789;* Cambridge, 1963.

E. Eyck, *Pitt versus Fox, Father and Son, 1735–1806;* London, 1950.

A. Foord, *His Majesty's Opposition 1714–1832*; Oxford, 1964.

R. Fulford, *Samuel Whitbread, 1764–1815;* London, 1967.

F. O'Gorman, *The Whig Party and the French Revolution;* London, 1967.

I. Leveson-Gower, *The Face without a Frown;* London, 1944.

C. Grey, *The Life and Opinions of the Second Earl Grey;* London, 1861.

R. Lucas, *Lord North, Second Earl of Guilford;* London, 1913.

P. J. Marshall, *The Impeachment of Warren Hastings;* Oxford, 1965.

A. Mitchell, *The Whigs in Opposition, 1815–1830;* Oxford, 1967.

J. Norris, *Shelburne and Reform;* London, 1963.

H. K. Olphin, *George Tierney;* London, 1934.

R. Pares, *King George III and the Politicians;* London, 1953.

N. C. Philips, *Yorkshire and National Politics, 1783–1784;* Christchurch, 1961.

W. F. Rae, *Wilkes, Sheridan and Fox;* London, 1874.

M. Roberts, *The Whig Party, 1807–1812;* London, 1939.

W. Sichel, *Sheridan;* London, 1909.

L. S. Sutherland, *The East India Company in Eighteenth Century Politics;* Oxford, 1952.

G. M. Trevelyan, *Lord Grey of the Reform Bill;* London, 1929.

B. Williams, *Carteret and Newcastle;* Cambridge, 1943.

REFERENCE BOOKS

Sir L. Namier and J. Brooke, *History of Parliament: The Commons, 1754–1790;* London, 1964.

Burke's Peerage

Burke's Landed Gentry

Dictionary of National Biography

Victoria County History

R. A. Austen-Leigh, *The Eton College Register, 1753–1790;* London, 1921.

W. W. Bean, *The Parliamentary Representation of the Six Northern Counties of England;* London, 1890.

W. P. Courtney, *The Parliamentary Representation of Cornwall to 1832;* London, 1889.

W. R. Williams, *The Parliamentary History of the County of Gloucester, 1213–1845;* Hereford, 1898.

— *The Parliamentary History of the County of Hereford, 1213–1896;* Brecknock, 1896.

— *The Parliamentary History of Wales from the Earliest Times to the Present Day, 1541–1895;* Brecknock, 1895.

— *The Parliamentary History of the County of Worcester, 1213–1897;* Hereford, 1897.

J. Wilson, *A Biographical Index of the Present House of Commons;* London, 1806.

ARTICLES

J. C. Beckett, 'Anglo-Irish Constitutional Relations in the Late Eighteenth Century', *I.H.S.* xiv, 1964.

H. Butterfield, 'Charles James Fox and the Whig Opposition in 1792', *C.H.J.*, ix, 1949.

I. R. Christie, 'The Marquis of Rockingham and Lord North's Offer of a Coalition, June/July 1780', *E.H.R.*, lxiv, 1954.

C. E. Fryer, 'The General Election of 1784', *History*, xi, 1925.

Mrs. E. George, 'Fox's Martyres: The General Election of 1784', *T.R.H.S.* xxi, 1937.

D. Ginter, 'The Financing of the Whig Party Organization, 1783–1793', *A.H.R.*, lxxi, 1966.

E. Hughes, 'The Scottish Reform Movement and Charles Grey, 1792–1794', *S.H.R.*, xxxv, 1956.

D. L. Keir, 'Economical Reform, 1779–1787', *L.Q.R.*, l, 1934.

W. T. Laprade, 'William Pitt and the Westminster Election', *A.H.R.* xxiii, 1912.

— 'Public Opinion and the General Election of 1784', *E.H.R.* xxxi, 1916.

A. Mitchell, 'The Association Movement, 1792–1793', *H.J.*, iv, 1961.

C. H. Philips, 'The East India Company Interest and English Government', *T.R.H.S.*, xx, 1937.

INDEX